From Coal to Biotech

Jean-Pierre Jeannet · Hein Schreuder

From Coal to Biotech

The Transformation of DSM with Business School Support

Springer

Jean-Pierre Jeannet
Belmont-sur-Lausanne
Switzerland

Hein Schreuder
Maastricht
The Netherlands

ISBN 978-3-662-46298-0 ISBN 978-3-662-46299-7 (eBook)
DOI 10.1007/978-3-662-46299-7

Library of Congress Control Number: 2015935483

Springer Heidelberg New York Dordrecht London

Printed on acid-free paper

Springer-Verlag GmbH Berlin Heidelberg is part of Springer Science+Business Media (www.springer.com)

Foreword

The composition of world's leading company lists or stock market indexes, such as the Fortune 500, the Forbes Global 2000, the Euro-Next 100, or the Dutch AEX are changing frequently since regularly companies disappear. In order to become a long-lasting successful company, you need to be able to continuously adapt and focus on creating value for all stakeholders.

Royal DSM is one of these companies, established in 1902 as a state-owned coal mining company. It transformed itself first to a (commodity) chemicals company and then to the Life Sciences and Materials Sciences company, the firm it is today, with a strong basis in biotechnology. This book, *From Coal to Biotech*, documents this remarkable achievement of a company that reinvented itself at least twice.

As a biologist I often refer to Darwin: "it is not the biggest, nor the strongest, nor the fastest, but the fittest who will survive." Darwinian fitness refers to the capacity to adapt to ever-changing circumstances and environments. While in nature this is largely a chance process based on frequent mutations, in corporate life we have to aim to adapt purposefully.

At DSM we believe in using our strategy processes to regularly initiate a dialogue on how to do so proactively and then stick to it with the necessary consistency. This book gives an inside view on the major "strategic learning cycles" that have driven DSM's recent transformation.

We at DSM know from experience how necessary but also how complex the renewal of a company can be. It requires so many contributions by so many people during a lengthy period of time. It requires their courage to embark on such a journey, perseverance to overcome difficulties along the way, and consistent communication with all stakeholders to maintain alignment. Many such journeys fail due to opportunism.

I am pleased that Hein Schreuder, who was responsible for DSM's corporate strategy during the second transformation, and Jean-Pierre Jeannet, who provided insights and support from the business school world, have combined their unique vantage points to document a journey that has succeeded.

We at DSM hope and trust that *From Coal to Biotech* will serve as a source of inspiration and reflection on company transformation for many leaders in both the business and the academic world.

Heerlen, The Netherlands Feike Sijbesma

Foreword

Executive education is a huge industry, often hidden by the large and highly publicized MBA programs run by business schools around the world, be they Harvard, Wharton, or IMD. Many books have described how corporations work with large consulting companies, but there are few known instances of how major corporations interact with business schools over an extended period of time. Business schools are generally reluctant to describe their "commercial activities" in which their professors engage with corporations. Many business schools see their mission as purely academic, and it is also true that not every professor has the competence and interest to deal with real-world issues and engage with senior executives on the challenges they face.

This new book, by Jean-Pierre Jeannet and Hein Schreuder, offers a unique contribution to the field of management education and corporate practice as it describes how IMD and other leading business schools supported DSM with its transformation into a global science-based company active in health, nutrition, and materials. The book describes this remarkable transformation and how DSM enrolled some of the best schools and brains over a 25-year-long period. The book also demonstrates how business school ideas can challenge corporate thinking and practice. Similarly, based upon the DSM example, the business community can learn in how many ways an interplay of academic and practical ideas can build stronger companies. In turn, this book exposes business schools to new approaches for practice-oriented research and teaching.

Lausanne, Switzerland

Dominique Turpin

Foreword

From Coal to Biotech is an important story for many reasons, but at its core, its value will be in enabling the reader to recognize and understand the degree of commitment, passion, and proactive behavior that is necessary for a company to not only survive but thrive despite significant changes in markets, environments, leadership, and strategy. Too often, we are presented case studies of companies that are at crossroads where the opportunities that would guarantee survival may be beyond reach or too late in the death spiral to be possible. Yet rarely is the reader provided an in-depth perspective and understanding at what is necessary—over the full life span of the company—to seize those opportunities and reinvent oneself. This book allows the reader to gain such an understanding as well as an appreciation of the multifaceted nature of company transformation.

As Dean of Babson Executive Education at Babson College, the full-time home of author Jean-Pierre Jeannet, I am proud to note the second accomplishment of this book—highlighting the criticality of the contributions of IMD and Babson faculty in serving as expert teachers and advisors in DSM's ongoing self-reflection, reinvention, and transformation. Too often, business school-based educational programs are seen as superficial "ivory tower" training that lacks an understanding of the real-world challenges that organizations face. This book dispels all doubt of the value that comes from well-informed and pragmatic faculty collaborating with managers and executives to take them out of their comfort zone and to challenge the worlds in which they live and compete in order to enable them to identify and implement their own paths for vitality and competitive advantage.

The insights of this book in identifying ways for organizations and business schools to work together are a tribute to the willingness of DSM and the authors to make 25 years of hard work and extraordinary collaboration accessible and transparent in order to provide the reader with new ways to enable the growth of their own companies.

Boston, USA Elaine J. Eisenman

Preface

When DSM, a Dutch company, turned up in 1988 at the doors of IMD, a business school in Lausanne, Switzerland, few of the seven participants in the Dean's meeting room at the time would have thought that they were about to embark on a 25-year-long collaboration that would involve academic institutions and impact hundreds, if not thousands, of managers. Twenty-five years later, with some of the major players retiring, the coauthors of this book believed strongly that the story of this unique collaboration deserved to be reported, illustrated, and explained, all the more so, because during those years DSM executed its second radical transformation. Having started out as a mining company in 1902, it had become a Commodity Chemicals company in the 1980s. By the early 1990s, company management started a journey to migrate out of Commodity Chemicals into "higher value-added products," over time becoming a Life Sciences and Material Sciences company with a strong focus on Biotech. This journey—from Coal to Biotech—is documented in this book, as are the company's interactions with business schools along the way.

This book can be read as a remarkable case study of a company's transformation and the support it enlisted from business schools to achieve its objectives. The authors hope, however, that it also serves a wider purpose, namely to inspire other companies to collaborate with business school academics, as well as to help business schools find ways to build long-lasting collaborations to the benefit of their institutions and their faculty. If business schools aspire to develop young managers, they need to learn about the business environment close-up. This book may help in the creation of ideas about how to turn business connections into learning laboratories, for the benefit of all. Equally, the business community may find encouragement to explore their own ways of linking up with business schools and how to nurture such relationships.

As we were thinking about this book, we were encouraged by members of the academic community to undertake the project. Business leaders, who often lamented the lack of close cooperation, also offered their support and encouragement.

As we began to prepare initial drafts, we soon realized how different our writing styles were. Jean-Pierre is trained in the storytelling technique of case writing. Hein prefers to provide a strategic perspective as a "reflective practitioner." After considerable thought and several discussions, and with the nudging of an experienced text editor, we finally came to the conclusion that amalgamating these two styles into a single style would not do justice to either. Therefore, we took the risky decision to complete a book in, essentially, two different styles, alternating our contributions chapter by chapter with the exception of Chap. 14 which represents the joint conclusions of the authors with respect to the "lessons learned for academia and business."

The book is organized into 15 chapters, of varying lengths, and including many exhibits. The odd-numbered chapters, written by Hein, document the transformation of DSM from Coal Mining to Commodity Chemicals and, ultimately, to a Life Sciences and Material Sciences company with a focus on Biotech. In Chap. 15, he provides a reflection on the traits of DSM, which have contributed to its remarkable ability to transform itself, not once but twice. Reading only these chapters will provide you with a perspective on this amazing company history. The even-numbered chapters, written by Jean-Pierre, complement the story by focusing on the interactions of DSM with business schools throughout this time period. He shows how this unusual collaboration proceeded in four waves, starting in the field of Marketing and proceeding on to issues of strategy, culture change, and innovation. Thus, the even-numbered chapters detail how the business schools responded to the evolving requirements of a highly demanding customer, giving valuable contributions to the transformation trajectory of DSM. If you read the chapters in sequence, you will alternate between the authors, thus experiencing a different style from chapter to chapter.

We hope that the alternating chapters provide you with some variation, but there is a more fundamental reason to adopt this method—not only to approach it from two different styles, of course, but to combine two different perspectives. Hein wrote his chapters from the DSM perspective, as an insider, and Jean-Pierre wrote his from the perspective of a business school faculty member and an outsider to the company. While we were both involved in a number of important events over the years, inevitably, much of what we describe in this book was experienced by only one of us, so that those parts could only be reported from a singular perspective.

Since we both had to go back many years to report about the circumstances that brought us together, a considerable amount of digging up of old sources was required. Fortunately, neither of us delete old files easily, giving us access to a store of documents from which many illustrations in the book are derived. Beyond the usual desk research and consultation of personal files, the authors conducted a large number of personal interviews with involved parties. For a list of these interviewees, see the **List of Interviewees**. We are grateful to all who so generously gave their time and shared their insights. When possible, both authors attended the interview sessions. From these sources, and from our own memories, we have reconstructed history as best we can. We are fully conscious, however, that the story told in this book is what we ourselves experienced and perceived. Other participants in this story would undoubtedly have chosen different elements to convey or might have emphasized different angles within the narrative. Therefore, it is possible that we may have omitted one event or another or an individual participating in this extensive 25-year collaboration. Again, a selection had to be made and we have attempted to report the main events. Our apologies to anyone who has been left out.

The authors recognize that different readers may be attracted to separate parts of the book. On the one hand, there is the audience of business leaders who may primarily have an interest in learning about the marvelous transformation undertaken at DSM. Reading the uneven-numbered chapters of the book in sequence will give you an excellent rendition of the strategic redirection of the company and can provide an interesting read in itself.

On the other hand, for the audience of business school representatives, Deans, and faculty members, the even-numbered chapters carry the story about how academic institutions contributed to the transformation of DSM. The academic side of the story was complicated by the fact that there were two main business schools involved—IMD Institute in Lausanne and Babson College near Boston in the USA. But, additional institutions contributed and these were mentioned where possible. We may have overlooked one institution or another as the focus was on the collaboration involving the strategy of DSM.

Aside from business leaders and business school Deans, we hope to entice young academics and business school professors into an active participation in the area of executive education. We believe that the book provides helpful insights about how one could become an active participant in such efforts. We can imagine that this book might even serve as background reading when faculty are teaching Strategy, its implementation, and the role of business leadership over time.

Similarly, we hope there is an audience of strategy practitioners who may derive inspiration from the detailed account of how DSM proceeded to develop its own approaches to strategy formation, both at the business and corporate levels. We are both firm proponents of the participative "dialogue" mode of strategy formation as described in this book, although we recognize that each company will have to adapt any approach to its own circumstances and culture. Reading about the evolutionary transformation of DSM through the execution of "strategic learning cycles" hopefully provides strategy practitioners globally with food for thought about how they may design approaches that are "fit for purpose" in their own circumstances.

Finally, there is a wide community of academicians and practitioners who are interested in fostering more intensive and effective collaboration between the business and academic worlds. To this community, we hope to offer a fascinating case study, as well as our reflections on the factors contributing to its success.

Needless to say, this book could never have been completed without the active support of many. First of all, we would like to thank DSM, and in particular its CEO Feike Sijbesma, for having given us the support to complete this manuscript without any "strings attached." We would like to thank all former DSM executives who gave freely of their time, spoke openly about their roles and the company's strategy, and refreshed our memories when we experienced a lack of documentary evidence. We would also like to thank the IMD faculty members who helped us stitch together the remarkable transformation from IMEDE's early foundation to the IMD of today and, thus, shared with us their own recollections and personal files. All of these contributions were important to us. We are indebted to our Text Editor, Anita Hussey-Koschat, who not only carefully scrutinized the manuscript created by two non-native English speakers, but also encouraged us to keep our two different style formats to maintain our original voices. At Springer, Martina Bihn fulfilled her role as Editorial Director with great enthusiasm, professionalism, and warmth: we are grateful for the guidance and support we received from her throughout the publication process.

Finally, we would like to mention that we thoroughly enjoyed the collaborative effort required to create this text. For both of us, what is reported here represented a—if not the—major professional thread in our lives and both of us obtained significant enrichment from having been able to participate in this collaboration. We thought that this story needed to be told for its uniqueness. No matter how you read the book—whether you peruse just the even- or uneven-numbered chapters, or address just one part of the story or another—it is our hope that you will find it not only interesting but also stimulating.

Belmont-sur-Lausanne, Switzerland — Jean-Pierre Jeannet
Maastricht, The Netherlands — Hein Schreuder

Contents

DSM: From Dutch State Mines to Chemicals Company 1

As on previous occasions, the Managing Board (MB) of Royal DSM was assembling at Kasteel Ter Worm for one of its occasional off-site retreats. Kasteel Ter Worm happened to be the first DSM headquarters when the company was founded in 1902, as De Staatsmijnen (Dutch State Mines), with the purpose of ensuring energy security for the Netherlands. Today, it is a hotel and restaurant and still occasionally used by DSM's Managing Board for off-site retreats (see Fig. 1.1). In 2010, more than 100 years later, DSM had undergone a remarkable transformation, from a mining operator to a global Life Sciences and Materials Sciences company, generating revenues of more than EUR 8 billion, with operations across the globe and employing about 22,000 people. The MB was proud of DSM's achievements in recent years. An ambitious strategy program—spanning 5 years—had been brought to a successful completion, marking the end of a second period of transformation in the company's history. Before the Board was a proposal about how to communicate this in a press release and announce the new company strategy for 2010–2015. The proposed headline of the release: 'DSM finalizes portfolio transformation and enters era of focused growth.'[1]

1902: The Founding of Dutch State Mines

Founded in 1902, the company's name in Dutch was De Staatsmijnen and in English, Dutch State Mines. So, conveniently, the same acronym, DSM, could be used in both languages.

Why did the Dutch government establish a state-owned mining enterprise? After all, there were already a number of private mining companies active in the Limburg area. There are three motives that can be distilled from the parliamentary

[1] See DSM Press Release of 23 September 2010.

J.-P. Jeannet, H. Schreuder, *From Coal to Biotech*,
DOI 10.1007/978-3-662-46299-7_1

Fig. 1.1 Kasteel Ter Worm: the first DSM headquarters

discussion.[2] The first, and dominant one, was to achieve energy security for the Netherlands and its industries; in times of scarcity, the private enterprises could divert their sales to neighboring Belgium and Germany and there would be little that the Dutch government could do to prevent that. The second motive was financial; the exploitation of the 'national treasure' of natural resources should be done in a way that would benefit both national and regional communities. The third 'social' incentive was remarkable; having surveyed and evaluated the development of coalfields in Belgium and Germany, the government explicitly chose to proceed with the 'gradual' development of the remaining Dutch coalfields. The government had come to the conclusion that rapid development would only be possible by attracting a number of foreign, migrant workers, which was felt would be disruptive to local communities.

2014: Transformation into a Life Sciences and Materials Sciences Company

Fast forward 112 years. With the exception of Kasteel Ter Worm, boasting a Wenkebach room—the very room used by the DSM's MB for its off-site meeting—everything else had changed. DSM had become a Life Sciences and Materials Sciences company, employing 24,349 people all over the world (5,484 in the Netherlands alone) and generating EUR 9.6 billion in net sales.

It was already unusual that DSM still existed; most companies don't survive that long.[3] Few make it through the first 10 years of existence—'infant mortality' is quite high in the corporate world. And those companies that do make it to the

[2] See DSM, *Staatsmijnen in Limburg: Gedenkboek bij gelegenheid van het vijftigjarig bestaan* (1952). Many of the historical facts recounted in this chapter are based on this commemorative volume, published by DSM on the occasion of its 50th anniversary.

[3] See Arie de Geus, *The Living Company* (1997), as well as Hannah (1999) and Ormerud (2005).

Fortune 500, or so, only have an average life expectancy of 40–50 years.[4] Most companies that are 100 years or older are family-owned and of limited size. When Arie de Geus (Shell) went out to look for large-sized companies that were 100 years old, he only found 40 of them—a very select group. The group includes American companies, such as DuPont and Kodak; Japanese companies like Mitsui and Mitsubishi; and European companies, including Unilever and Stora Enso.

In order to reach an advanced age, most of these companies had to completely transform themselves. DSM has transfigured itself twice in its history. After 60 years of existence as a mining company, it shut all its collieries and became a Base Chemicals company. The success of this first transformation allowed the subsequent privatization of the company in the late 1980s. Recently, it has completed its second transformation from Base Chemicals into the Life Sciences and Material Sciences company it is today; a change, which started in the mid-1990s and took roughly 15 years to complete.

Transformation is a risky journey; it fails much more often than it succeeds. There are very few large companies in the world that have managed to transform themselves twice and prosper. DSM is a rare case.

Four Strategic Episodes

This first chapter includes a summary of some of the main events in DSM's history and development, until the late 1980s when it approached IMD, the business school in Lausanne, Switzerland, to collaborate on an Industrial Marketing program. Rather than a step-by-step account of the company's 80-year history, the focus will be DSM's characteristics in the late 1980s and early 1990s. This sets the stage and provides the initial context for the story, in subsequent chapters, of DSM's second transformation. It is useful to divide the company's history into four different episodes (see Table 1.1).

The first two episodes are covered here, continuing through most of the third episode (until the late 1980s, early 1990s, which will be continued in Chap. 3) and the next three sections deal with these time periods in some detail. There is a short summary below, allowing the reader with little interest in further detail about company history to jump from the end of this section to the final section in this chapter.

The next section describes the initial success of the mining activities and will elucidate how gas-based chemical activities evolved naturally within this mining company to constitute about one-third of DSM's revenue in the early 1960s and one-half in the mid-1960s. In terms of manpower, however, the mining and cokes activities provided employment for over 30,000 people in the late 1950s and continued in 1965 with 23,000 people (out of the total number of 35,300

[4] Corporate life expectancy may be trending down. Professor Richard Foster from Yale University believes it has decreased by more than 50 years in the last century, from 67 years in the 1920s to just 15 years today. See: http://www.bbc.co.uk/news/business-16611040?print=true

Table 1.1 Four episodes in DSM's history

1902–1965	*Mining* (with gradual build-up of chemical activities)
1965–1975	*First transformation*: 'hurry up' from mining to base chemicals
1975–1995	*Diversification and expansion*
1995–2010	*Second transformation*: from base chemicals to life sciences and materials sciences

employees). It was during this period that the company began to persuade the government that mining would not remain a viable economic activity in the Netherlands or provide a sustainable future for the firm. When the government acted in 1965 to announce the closing of all mines, DSM was faced with two challenges: (1) the orderly dissolution of about half of the company in terms of revenue and two-thirds of the employment numbers; and (2) to build its future on recently built-up chemical activities. This ushered in the 'hurry up' phase of a rapid expansion in Base Chemicals that was to constitute, over the next 10 years, DSM's first transformation.

The rapid ('hurry up') expansion of DSM into base chemicals can be described around two core businesses: (1) the Gas-based core with its historical roots in cokes gas from the mining activities; and (2) the added Petrochemical core based on naphtha, a feedstock originating from oil refineries. Just as these activities had reached a certain scale in the early 1970s, the 'oil shocks' hit. Feedstock prices soared and economic activity slumped. The company was severely bleeding. It was a period of extreme uncertainty for the management, who realized that the volatile nature of commodity chemicals provided for a shaky foundation of a company the size of DSM.

As a consequence, beginning in the mid-1970s, management embarked on a journey of expansion (scaling up the Commodity Chemicals), as well as diversification (broadening the base of the company). Expansion entailed both the scaling-up of plants, in line with the rapid technological progress in various areas, as well as the overall expansion of the Gas-based Industrial Chemicals and the Petrochemicals. Diversification was sought:

- Around the Gas-based and Petrochemical cores of the company, also using the 'side streams' of Base Chemical production (concentric diversification)
- Along the value chain toward the end markets (forward integration)
- By developing new products from own research or licensed-in technology (technology-push diversification)
- By acquiring new activities with hardly any connection to existing activities (unrelated diversification)

One could say that DSM was 'feeling its way' to a new future by exploring different routes for further development. However, as a consequence, DSM was also becoming a less homogeneous company and more of a 'conglomerate', encompassing diverse activities under one corporate roof.[5] The realization emerged that different competences were required to manage the new activities well. For instance, while DSM had strong capabilities in the fields of chemical research and operating large-scale production plants, it was relatively weak in industrial marketing and in operating smaller-scale (multi-purpose or batch) plants. Perhaps, this was one reason why many of DSM's diversification attempts were turning out to be less than successful, leading to uncertainty about the right strategic direction, as well as the desired future shape of the company. This was fuelled further when the cyclical nature of the base chemicals drove DSM into losses in the early 1980s and again in the early 1990s. Although the recovery was also steep in the subsequent years, there remained an existential anxiety in the company during the mid-1990s.

The period of the late 1980s to the mid-1990s will be addressed in the next two chapters about DSM (see Chaps. 3 and 5). First, however, the following provides more detail to the broad-brush summary of the company's history presented above.

1902 to 1965: Mining (with Gradual Build-Up of Chemical Activities)

For more than five decades, mining was a successful business for DSM. Mines were gradually opened: the Wilhelmina Mine (1909), the Emma Mine (1914), the Hendrik Mine (1918) and the Maurits Mine (1926), all named after members of the royal family. Production rose from 23,573 tonnes in 1907 to 6,959,387 tonnes in 1930. Employment rose correspondingly, passing the 5,000 people mark in 1915 and reaching the 20,000+ level in the late 1920s. Only in the post-World War 1 period was it necessary to recruit large numbers of migrant workers. When the employment figures reached 35,000 in the early 1950s, only around 2,000 of these were non-Dutch. As such, the 'social motive' of the Dutch government to gradually develop the mines and provide employment to Dutch workers had been realized well.

These early years did not develop without any volatility. Coal markets were competitive, both nationally and internationally. In the early 1920s, and again in the early 1930s, coal prices collapsed. The low point was reached in 1934 at Dfl 5.76 per tonne. At such a price level, DSM could only continue producing profitably by constantly lowering its costs. This led to a permanent drive for efficiency. Scale economies were sought, production techniques were improved and the organization 'rationalized' as much as was possible. Nevertheless, there were also inevitable wage decreases—one in 1932 of 10 % and another in 1934 of 3 %. During the second half of the 1930s, conditions improved. The average miner's wage increased again from the low point of Dfl 5.60 in 1934 to Dfl 6.35 per shift in 1939.

[5] Diversification was a trend for many companies in the post Second World War period.

Of the coal mined by DSM, only a minor part was anthracite, which is directly useable for household energy. By far the largest part was so-called ‘fat,’ or bituminous coal, which needs further treatment in order to be used economically. This type of coal can best be upgraded to metallurgical cokes, used for the smelting of iron ore in blast furnaces. It is no wonder, then, that in 1914 DSM decided to build a relatively large cokes plant next to the Emma mine. The cokes plant began operation in 1918. Cokes production does not only yield the primary product (cokes) but also ‘cokes gas’ as a secondary product and various ‘fatal’ products, like tar and various hydrocarbons. The cokes gas was used for gas distribution in the southern part of the Netherlands but also later for the production of gas-based chemicals. The hydrocarbons formed the (research) basis for the later expansion into petrochemicals. Looking back, one can say, as a result, that the disadvantage of mining lesser-quality coal drove DSM to broaden its production base to chemicals at a relatively early stage. Thus, the once disadvantage turned out to be an advantage when coal mining had to be phased out in the 1960s.

Cokes production took an enormous flight: the original capacity was doubled in 1922–1923 and tripled again in the next 2 years. In subsequent years, new technologies were introduced on ever-larger scales. In the early 1950s, DSM owned about 600 cokes ovens where 1,500 people were employed. As a result, the company was also producing ever-larger amounts of gas. It started distributing this gas to the local municipalities of Sittard (1921), Heerlen (1925) and Hoensbroek (1927). By 1934, a gas distribution system had been developed consisting of 240 km of pipelines and spanning the two most southern provinces of The Netherlands: Limburg and Brabant.

The gas was also used internally by DSM; initially, only as a source of energy. However, technological progress in the 1920s had made it possible to produce hydrogen from the cokes gas with such purity that it could be used to couple with nitrogen to produce ammonia, the feedstock for (nitrogen-based) fertilizers. The company decided to build a Nitrogen Works (het *Stikstofbindingsbedrijf*), which came into operation in 1930. Under the difficult economic circumstances of the early 1930s, DSM succeeded in increasing its capacity from 6,000 tonnes in 1929 to 60,000 tonnes in 1939. The increased production easily found its way to the agricultural market, which had come to appreciate the benefits of fertilization. In 1939 about one-third of the 456,000,000 m^3 of cokes gas produced was used for ‘upgrading’ into fertilizers. The schematic development of DSM in the period from 1902 to the early 1930s is shown below (see Fig. 1.2).

One element that would prove to be of vital importance for DSM’s further development is research.[6] Initially, research developed as a direct support for the various mines (Emma, Maurits) and plants (Nitrogen Works): its main tasks were production and quality control, as well as process support and improvement. Gradually, awareness grew that industrial research of a different caliber, one more systematically based on the frontiers of science, was also needed. In 1928,

[6] See *Research tussen vetkool en zoetstof* (ed. Lintsen, H., 2000).

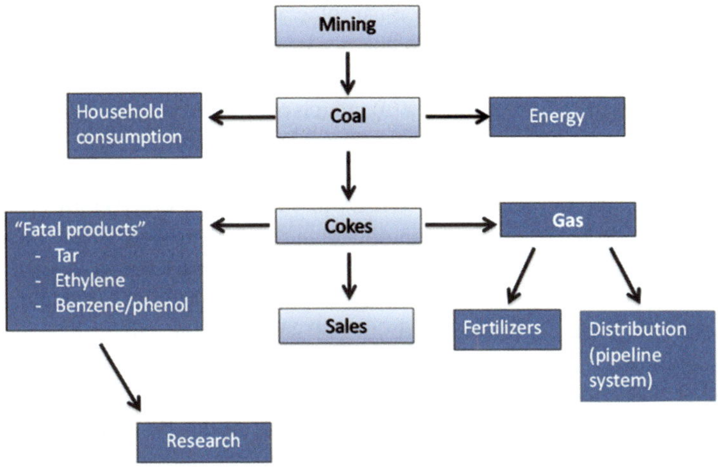

Fig. 1.2 Schematic development of DSM: 1902 to the 1930s

the Emma Mine research laboratory was upgraded to the 'Central Laboratory of the Staatsmijnen.' Here, more fundamental research could be undertaken 'in the grand hall' and 'when time was available.' The laboratory of the Nitrogen Works developed in similar fashion. Later, in the 1930s, the plan developed to combine these laboratories into one 'Central Lab' organization. A new building was constructed where, according to the plans, just over 200 persons would work. While the implementation of these plans was somewhat delayed by the Second World War, industrial research at DSM really took off after the war. In 1950, the Central Lab had 421 employees and in 1960 this number had grown to 750; by 1967 there were nearly 1,600 people working there (of which 700 were directly involved in research activities). At that time, DSM was spending about 8 % of its chemical revenues on research.

The 1930s and 1940s saw the expansion of existing activities, the limiting factor being the in-house production of cokes gas and, of course, the wartime conditions of 1940–1945. Over this time period, the research-driven knowledge base of the company expanded to the extent that in 1947 DSM decided to establish a separate company, Stamicarbon, to commercialize its patents by licensing to third parties. In 1952, DSM's research established a unique process to manufacture urea from cokes gas. This not only gave DSM a strong foothold in urea production, enabling the subsequent entry into melamine but it also boosted the licensing activities of Stamicarbon, since DSM decided to make the urea technology available for third parties. Over time, more than 250 urea plants all over the world have used DSM's technology. Thus, Stamicarbon provided a 'window on the world' for DSM and significantly contributed to its later international orientation and development.

After the Second World War, the Allied forces split up German company IG Farben into its former constituent parts, including BASF, Bayer and Hoechst, making IG Farben's technology available to interested companies. DSM took advantage of this by concentrating on caprolactam, a fiber intermediate that could be based on the phenol coming from cokes gas. Encouraged by the Dutch government, it entered into an exclusive supply arrangement with AKU ([*Algemene Kunstzijde Unie*] predecessor of AKZO), which obtained the nylon (PA6) polymerization technology. DSM started its first caprolactam plant in 1952, subsequently upgrading the technology and building its second plant on the basis of new caprolactam production technology (HPO) in 1977. Over time, DSM became the world leader in caprolactam, operating plants in the US, as well as in China. Since the 1960s, this 'division of labor' with AKU was repeatedly the trigger for merger explorations that, however, were never to be successfully completed. DSM acquired the Engineering Plastics activities of AKZO in the early 1990s, including the PA6 nylons.

Another 'fatal product' from the cokes gas was ethylene. This could be used for the production of polyethylene, a booming product in the 1950s and 1960s. DSM decided to construct its first (low density) polyethylene plant based on technology licensed from ICI in 1959. Again, over time, DSM Research managed to upgrade this technology significantly. To enable the further foreseen expansion of low density polyethylene (LDPE) and the entry into high density polyethylene (HDPE, 1962), the company had to relax its feedstock constraint: the limited supply of cokes gas. It was therefore resolved to add naphtha as a feedstock and in 1961, DSM built its first naphtha cracker (NAK-1).

The capacity of NAK-1 was 25,000 tonnes of ethylene. The naphtha, an oil refinery product, had to be transported to the DSM site by barge and road. These logistics and the small scale of the operation meant that it was only DSM's 'toe in the water' regarding petrochemicals. Under these conditions, the operations would not be competitively sustainable. Nevertheless, it enabled the later significant expansion of the company into petrochemicals, one of its subsequent core businesses next to the gas-based chemicals (see Fig. 1.3).

A lot of attention has been paid thus far to the gradual build-up of DSM's chemical activities because these prove to be invaluable in the further development of the company. However, it's important not to forget that in the late 1950s and early 1960s mining was still the company's prime activity, by far. It is during this period of time that the company started to realize that, in the Netherlands, mining might not be sustainable in the (near) future. Several factors contributed to this growing awareness. In the late 1950s, the sellers' market for coal was confronted with an oversupply, leading to a 'coal crisis.' Under these circumstances it became clear that coal imported from the US and Poland was at a significant cost advantage because it could be extracted with open-pit mining. Additionally, oil production expanded significantly in the Middle East and took market share from coal. And finally, a death blow was dealt to Dutch mining operations with the 1959 discovery of enormous natural gas reserves in the northern part of the country (Slochteren). Some people in the company, particularly Mr. Bogers (later a chairman), started to realize that drastic action was needed.

This, of course, was not a shared conclusion within the company straight away. It took until the fall of 1962 before the DSM Board notified the Dutch government

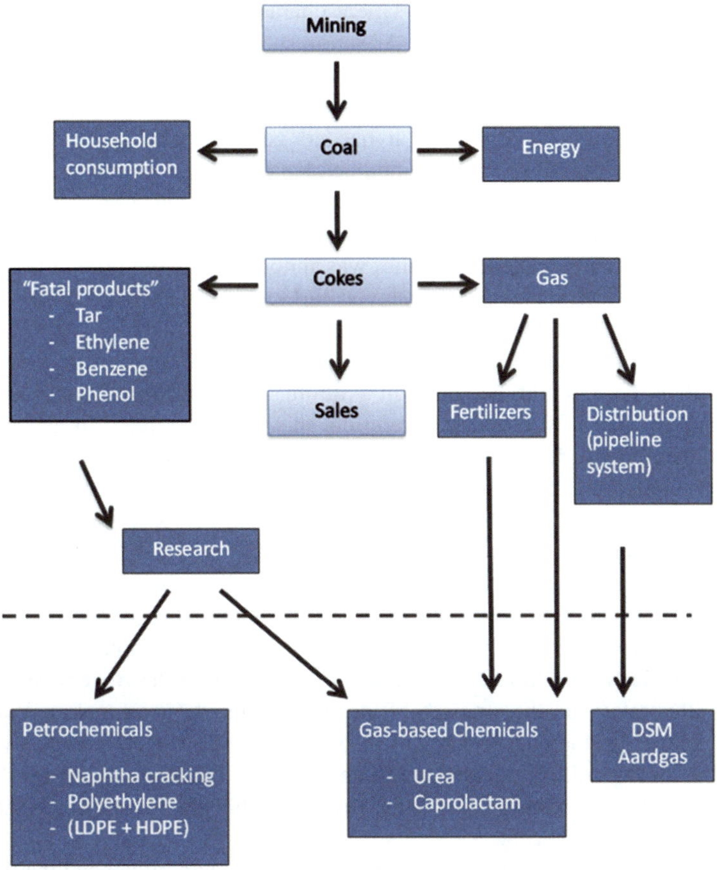

Fig. 1.3 Schematic development of DSM, 1902–1965

that it no longer saw any possibility for profitable mining operations in the Netherlands. The government also needed time to let the facts and figures sink in and come to the same conclusion. It was in 1965 that Parliamentary approval for the closing of all mines was obtained. At that time, more than 35,000 people worked for DSM, of which 23,000 were in mining activities and 7,400 in chemical activities. Mining generated revenues of about Dfl 400 million and an operating loss of Dfl 31 million. The chemical operations (including Fertilizers) contributed revenues of about Dfl 440 million and an operating profit of Dfl 84 million. The scale of the company's chemical activities was far below its European and American competitors. The company realized it had to 'hurry up' in order to catch up with those giants.

DSM's 'hurry up' phase, initiated by the decision to close the mines, will be addressed in the next section. Here, we want to provide a brief sketch of other DSM features in 1965: What were some salient characteristics of the company at this crucial juncture in its development? Attention should be drawn to the following:

- Although the company was still a state-owned enterprise, it was largely run as a private company. Nevertheless, it needed governmental approval for major projects and decisions, which sometimes led to delays. Moreover, whether by implication or by choice, the company was very conscious of its 'social responsibility,' particularly with regard to employment in the province of Limburg. When the decision to close the mines was announced, an important message was that the government and the company would seek, as much as possible, 'alternative employment' opportunities.
- The gradual rise of chemical activities in the company, and the growing awareness that these might be the firm's future, had introduced frictions in the Managing Board. In the Dutch tradition, this Board operated in a 'collegiate' style, meaning there was a collective responsibility for Board decisions. This did not preclude, however, that there were starkly different perspectives about the company's future. In 1964, the working group-Mines was unable to come to shared conclusions. The working group split into a group-Hellemans (the Board member responsible for Mining) forecasting a slight positive result, and the group-Bogers (who was head of the Economic department at that time and later chairman) predicting large cumulative losses. When it came to a Managing Board decision, the Board voted unanimously to adopt the Bogers perspective. This illustrates: (1) the strength of the 'collegiate' decision-making culture at Board level (in the end, Hellemans also voted for the Bogers perspective); and (2) the strong role of analytical reasoning in the 'engineering culture' of the company. Bogers won the day on the strength of his arguments, not as the result of political maneuvering.
- Bogers was one of a number of remarkable people who influenced the future of the company. He had studied business economics and econometrics at Tilburg University, graduating 'cum laude' in both subjects. After a short stint at Tilburg, he joined DSM, first in the Statistical Department and later in the Economic Department. He is credited with setting up a Planning Department at DSM and instilling a long-term perspective as the context for major decisions. Another remarkable person at DSM was Dr. D. W. van Krevelen, who laid the foundation for science-based research at DSM. Joining DSM in 1940, he became chef of the Central Lab in 1955. He authored the internationally-renowned, *Coal Science: Aspects of Coal Constitution*. Van Krevelen was no proponent of a tight coupling between research and commercialization: "I have learned one thing: no-one is such a short-term thinker as a commercial person. He. . .doesn't grasp the potential long-term developments."[7]
- The commercial side of DSM was indeed underdeveloped. In large part, this can be explained by three factors: (1) many of its main markets had been sellers'

[7] Quoted in Lintsen (2000, p. 28). Translated from Dutch.

markets requiring little marketing effort from producers; (2) the products had a commodity character, making price the dominant buying criterion; and (3) selling had even been organized at an arm's-length basis in a consortium of producers. As early as 1935, DSM had joined other fertilizer producers in establishing the C.S.V. (*Centraal Stikstof Verkoopbureau*), a joint sales organization, which would operate until the 1970s.[8] For its other chemical products DSM joined three other Dutch chemical producers to jointly establish the N.V.C.P. (*Nederlandsch Verkoopkantoor voor Chemische Producten N.V.*) in 1947 to offer a more complete range of chemical products than each could muster separately. The rationale at DSM was that otherwise it would have to establish a 'Trading Department' for the missing products in its own range and that such trading was beyond the company's statutory limits. In 1965, the N.V.C.P. was still operating and moved to a new office building in Amsterdam from where it sold DSM's chemical products, ranging from cyclohexanon to caprolactam. In fact, DSM had 'outsourced' its (operational) sales function to these organizations at arm's length.

- DSM's corporate organization was indeed along functional lines: Production, R&D, Finance, Personnel and Sales (co-ordination). Through these functions, there was a strong system of centralized control. This made sense for the mono-product (coal) company that DSM was originally. As the chemical part of the company grew, however, the functional organization came under pressure. The 1970s would bring the first attempts to adjust the organization to the new reality of being a diversified, multi-product company. Culturally, DSM has been described as a strong hierarchy with a 'German type of (autocratic) leadership.'[9] There was a strict separation between the blue-collar and white-collar workers, with strong cohesion within the two groups. It is fair to say that the international orientation had, thus far, been quite limited. Management looked with awe and respect to large peers like BASF, ICI, DOW and DuPont. It realized that it had to hurry to catch up with this peer group.

Finally, it must be noted that DSM experienced a tremendous amount of uncertainty during the mid-1960s. It was by no means clear that the gradual build-up of chemicals would provide a solid foundation for the further growth of the firm. It is, therefore, not surprising that various ways and means were explored to strengthen the company, including the possibilities of a merger. The prime candidate, as indicated before, was AKU, with which DSM had good commercial relations, existing through the supply arrangements of caprolactam to AKU's Polyamide-6 plants. In 1965 a proposal for a three-way merger between AKU, DSM and KZK (*Koninklijke Zout-Ketjen N.V.*) led to severe disagreement within the DSM Managing Board. Since DSM was still a state-owned enterprise, the

[8] Ernst Homburg, *Groeien door kunstmest: DSM Agro 1929–2004*, Uitgeverij Verloren (2004).

[9] *DSM Organisatie*, brochure by Arie de Jong (Head of Corporate Organization) for the Middle Management Course, 1997.

Minister of Economic Affairs would have also have to be in favor of it and he was not. Hence, the merger proposal was not followed up on at the time. KZK turned elsewhere and found a merger partner in *Koninklijke Zwanenberg Organon:* in 1967, KZO (*Koninklijke Zout–Organon N.V*) was formed. The discussions between AKU and DSM were reopened in 1967 with new key players on DSM side (Mr. Bogers and Mr. Kretzers); the codename of the project was BRIZE. This time, the Managing Board of DSM was unanimously in favor and the proposal was brought toward the Supervisory Board. On the Supervisory Board it came to a vote: five members were in favor and seven members were opposed. As a result, DSM would have to find its own way toward a sustainable future. AKU, on the other hand, decided that a merger was in its best interest and in 1969 merged with KZO to become AKZO. It is understandable that some observers inside and outside of the company felt that DSM had missed out on good opportunities to participate in the merger wave of the 1960s, which was also playing out internationally. Hans van Liemt, later the Chairman of the Managing Board, looked back at the situation: "DSM, AKU and KZO should have become one large chemical company. Why did it not happen? For a great part, because there were persons involved who did not get on well together. For another part, because DSM was still a state-owned company it was regarded with suspicion by those in favor of private enterprise. We had few friends at the time." Whatever the reasons, a merger did not come to pass. DSM would have to chart its own course to catch up with the major players in the chemicals industry.

1965 to 1975: Hurry-Up from Mining to Base Chemicals (First Transformation)

DSM's perceived need to catch up with major chemicals producers led to an aggressive expansion policy.[10] Expansion entailed both the scaling-up of plants, in line with the rapid technological progress in various areas, as well as the overall expansion of the gas-based industrial chemicals and petrochemicals (for an impression of the rapid technological progress enabling plants to be built at ever larger scales see Table 1.2). While DSM's first naphtha cracker had a design capacity of 25,000 tonnes of ethylene per year in 1971, and had been 'debottlenecked' to a capacity of 30,000 tonnes, 10 years later NAK-3 was built with a more than tenfold design capacity; in 1979 NAK-4 started with a design capacity of 450,000 tonnes. Moreover, these design capacities were only the start of a gradual capacity expansion of each plant by debottlenecking. Together NAK-3 and NAK-4 started with a design capacity of 800,000 tonnes and were stretched by debottlenecking to a joint capacity of about 1,250,000 tonnes in 2011.

The naphtha crackers produced a vast increase of hydrocarbons, which could be used in further 'downstream' production. The major outlet for ethylene, the largest

[10] See Arjan van Rooij, *The Company that Changed Itself*, (2007) who calls this phase "the Large Leap Forward."

Table 1.2 DSM's naphtha crackers

Naphtha cracker nr	Start	Stop	Capacity (tonnes of ethylene/year)
1	1961	1971	30,000
2	1967	1975 (explosion)	135,000
3	1971		350,000
4	1979		450,000

Source: Van Rooij (2007: 102)

fraction of hydrocarbons, was the production of polyethylene. DSM built LDPE plants at a furious pace, first with autoclave technology and also since 1975, with tubular technology. Again, the scale increased quickly: the second tubular plant, on stream in 1979, had almost twice the capacity of the first one. HDPE capacity doubled in 1972 when a plant was built using 'Compact' technology that was developed in-house. In 1967, the first plant was built to produce EPDM, a synthetic rubber requiring ethylene and propylene as feedstocks and in 1970 the second plant was constructed. This second plant, in 1974, could be debottlenecked and boosted to twice its design capacity. DSM became quite adept at both debottlenecking and plant modifications to produce 'special grades' of polymers.

Such large-scale expansion of petrochemical capacity was, of course, not possible without an appropriate logistic infrastructure. Here, DSM was faced with a potential competitive disadvantage: logistically, petrochemical complexes are best placed near refineries at the coast.[11] However, DSM had decided to expand on its inland site at Geleen, the location of the Maurits mine. It was inconceivable that the required amounts of naphtha could be shipped in by barge and truck. Therefore, in 1965 DSM created a special company DTM (*DSM Transportmaatschappij N.V.*) that would operate a pipeline of about 200 km, connecting the DSM site with the refinery complex in Rotterdam. Later, a similar pipeline was built to Antwerpen. While these pipelines enabled the inflow of naphtha, there were also large amounts of produced ethylene to be handled. DSM could not instantly use all its ethylene production on-site. Moreover, the production and maintenance stops at DSM plants would potentially cause a major mismatch between production and consumption of feedstocks. To ensure more flexibility, the company established an ethylene pipeline company called ARG (*Aethylen Rohrleitungs Gesellschaft mbH & Co. KG*), in conjunction with five German chemical companies, and became the managing partner of this new pipeline company. Through the construction of these feedstock (naphtha) and product (ethylene) pipelines, DSM was able to turn its inland location from a competitive disadvantage into an advantage. It created great flexibility for feedstock and product flows and was located at the center of chemical activities and end markets in northwestern Europe.

DSM was not unfamiliar with operating pipelines; it already had a gas distribution network in the southern part of the Netherlands to market its cokes gas. About a

[11] For some time in the late 1960s the option to build a refinery near the DSM site was explored together with Shell. However, this project never came to fruition (see Messing, 1988: 125–127).

quarter of total Dutch gas distribution flowed through DSM pipelines. In 1959, Shell and Esso (through their joint venture NAM (*Nederlandse Aardolie Maatschappij*) found an enormous natural gas field in the northern part of The Netherlands. The Dutch government was reluctant to grant NAM a license to exploit this gas field, since it did not want the gas exploitation and public supply to be totally controlled by private enterprise. Moreover, DSM convinced the Dutch government that: (1) it had the required expertise of gas purification and transport, while (2) it also had the necessary gas distribution system of pipelines in the southern part of the Netherlands. In the end, the Dutch government appointed DSM as its trustee in a partnership to exploit the gas. DSM had a 40 % ownership share in this partnership, but a 50 % governance (control) share. The partnership paid the government a profit share of 10 % and sold through a distribution company (*N.V. Nederlandse Gasunie*), in which DSM also participated for 40 %. DSM handed over its own gas pipelines, thus becoming connected to the 'northern gas' in 1964. It provided an enormous boost to the Gas-based Chemicals production, while enabling the phasing out of the cokes gas during the closing of the mines. Moreover, DSM benefited financially in two ways:

- As trustee of the State, it received a yearly dividend stream between Dfl 125 and Dfl 140 million, which continued until 2006
- Until 1987, the gas revenues were consolidated on the DSM accounts and the company was able to keep the interest earned on these amounts

It is not unfair to say that these cash flows helped DSM carry out its 'hurry up' strategy and have dampened the volatility of its earnings, due to the cyclical nature of base chemicals.[12]

The secure and increasing supply of gas enabled DSM to expand its gas-based chemicals production next to the petrochemicals production. Caprolactam production went from around 40,000 tonnes in 1964 to 100,000 tonnes in 1966. DSM also developed new HPO technology, which enabled it to expand internationally and build plants in both the UK and US. In 1964, a phenol plant was opened in Rotterdam. In 1967, a melamine plant came on stream in Geleen, followed by an acrylonitrile plant in 1969 and a second one in 1971. The production of acrylonitrile enabled DSM to construct an ABS polymer plant in 1974. In Petrochemicals and Gas-based Chemicals alike, expansion was often feedstock-driven. Making optimal use of feedstocks and of side-streams of the large Base Chemicals production was an important driver. Moreover, an integrated site was justifiably regarded as a stronger site, also in an economic sense (For a summary of DSM's main historic lines of development until 1975, see Fig. 1.4).[13]

[12] See interview with A. P. Timmermans in *Het Financieele Dagblad* (9 Oct 1993: 3): "Aardgasbaten bieden DSM garantie-inkomen."

[13] BASF would call this concept of an integrated site *Verbund* and also make it into a foundation of their expansion and site policies. See Fig. 1.10 for an overview of DSM's site integration by the early 1990s.

Optimization of feedstocks was one reason why some researchers had become interested in 'fine chemicals'—chemical products sold in small volumes but often at attractive margins. They had some early successes and managed to sell, for instance, 3.6 tonnes of L-pyrrolidone carboxylic acid to Unilever in 1968. There is no wonder that these products were referred to as 'small products' in the bulk mentality of DSM! In 1969 the researchers published a report entitled, *Small products: hobby or cornerstone?* in which they discussed whether DSM should diversify into fine chemicals. Apparently, this was regarded to be an interesting experiment and the group was awarded a small budget of Dfl 2.5 million for 2 years. Ruud Selman was appointed to manage the Small Products group, renamed Special Products in 1971. The Special Products group proved to be the birthplace of DSM's later drive into fine chemicals and Ruud Selman has been a driving force of this development, especially in his years as a member of the Managing Board from 1979 to 1997.

In the 'hurry-up' phase DSM had also started some experiments with:

- Diversification into products emanating from its own research. The primary example in these early years was lysine, an amino acid that could be produced with caprolactam as a starting-point. Hence, the project was feedstock-driven with a technology push. DSM Research worked out a synthesis process that was the basis for construction of a plant in 1968, which was closed again in 1969. The high hopes of supplying lysine mainly to food and feed markets (also in developing countries) had proven to be unfounded. DSM found out the hard way about how difficult it is to find and develop a market.[14] Paul van der Grinten comments: "The dramatic failure of lysine was very unfortunate, because this experience for many years severely dampened DSM's quest for new organic products and new markets. It was only with the much later acquisition of Gist-Brocades (1998) that the company fully recovered from this shock."
- Forward integration from plastics into companies producing plastic products. A prime example is Curver, a producer of household plastic products, in which DSM took a 40 % stake in 1966, expanding it to 100 % in 1972.
- Taking participations in, and acquiring, construction companies. This was apparently driven by the (correct) belief that synthetic materials would increasingly replace natural materials in construction and the (incorrect) assumption that acquiring construction companies would enable DSM to drive and accelerate this substitution. Since this did not materialize, DSM's foray into construction turned out to be a case of unrelated diversification rather than forward integration.
- Providing job opportunities for the miners who became unemployed. DSM had always felt a social responsibility for providing employment in the southern

[14] Based on De Rooij (2007: 114–125).

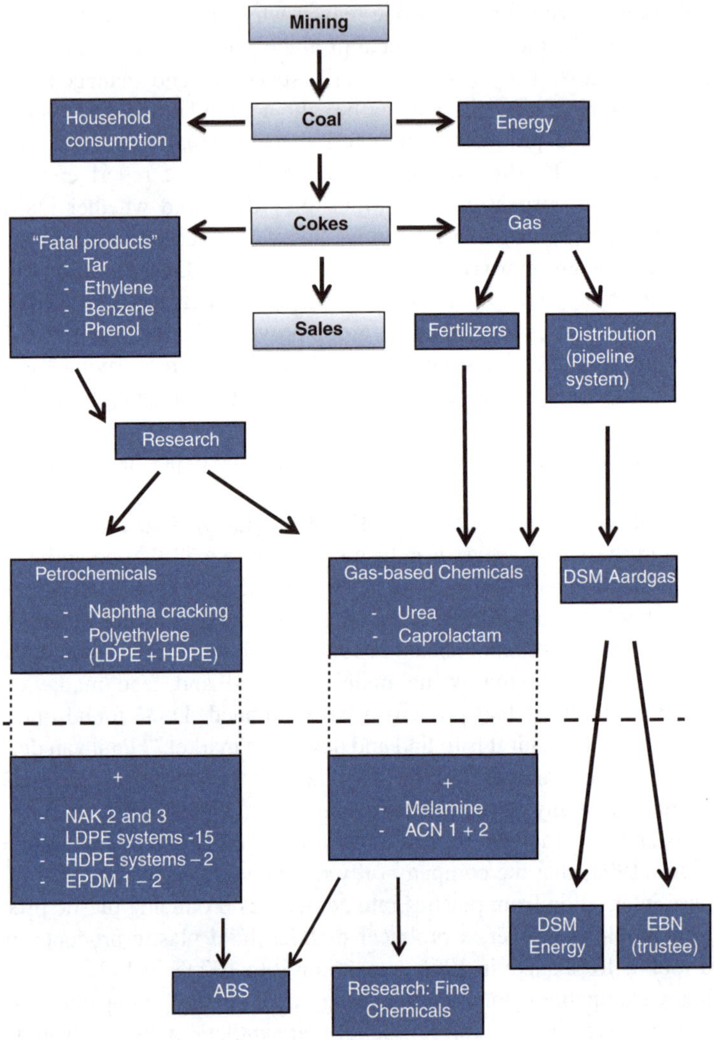

Fig. 1.4 Schematic development of DSM 1902–1975

province of Limburg.[15] The mine closings suggested the need to relocate more than 25,000 people; this led to a major effort to retrain mine workers to work in chemical activities, and for positions outside the company as well. In this context, for instance, DSM helped the Dutch car and truck producer DAF in 1967 create a new plant in the province of Limburg.

[15] In 1929 and 1932 the company had, for instance, created two clothing workshops where the wives and daughters of the miners could be gainfully employed. This initiative grew out to produce the retail company Macintosh that is independently listed today on the Dutch stock exchange.

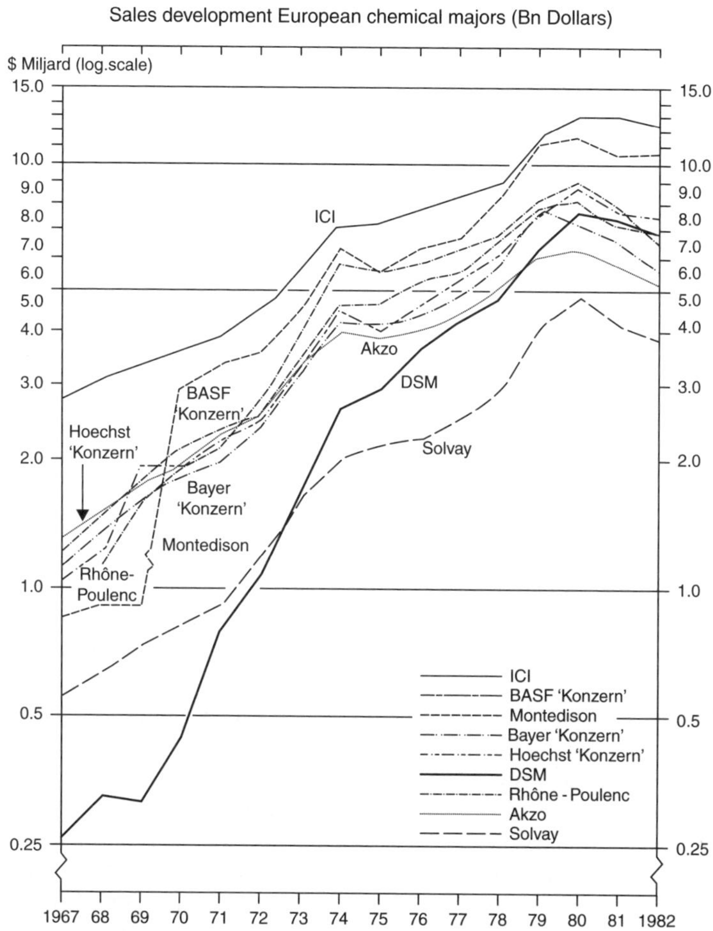

Fig. 1.5 Sales development European chemical majors (in USD billion)

DSM attempted to grow as fast as possible to catch up with the chemical majors, mainly by the vast expansion of its gas-based and petrochemical core activities, and in the other ways described above. Was this 'hurry-up' strategy successful overall? To convince the outside world that it was, for many years DSM updated the graph reproduced in Fig. 1.5.

At first glance, it indeed seems to show that DSM had indeed caught up with its chemical peer group in the late 1970s. However, to interpret this graph correctly, two observations should be made:

1. DSM's sales still include the gas revenues that it records on behalf of the Dutch government. These were only to be deconsolidated per 1987 (For the effect of the deconsolidation, see Fig. 1.14 at the end of this chapter.).

2. The chart uses a logarithmic axis to show the sales development of these companies. The effect of a logarithmic axis is that the peer group is shown as a rather compact group. In reality, ICI sales were nearly USD 7.5 billion in 1975, compared to DSM's USD 2.8 billion (Dfl 7.6 billion, including its energy revenues) or USD 1.7 billion (Dfl 4.7 billion, excluding the energy division). While DSM had shown an impressive growth, and had caught up with companies like AKZO and Solvay, it was still far behind the chemical majors of the time.

DSM's development, through expansion and diversification in chemicals and other activities, necessitated a fundamental rethinking of the corporate organization. For this, the Swiss consultancy firm of Knight Wegenstein was hired; it recommended decentralization by introducing a divisional structure. In 1971, four Main Groups were established and soon to be followed in 1975 by a real divisional structure with six divisions (see Fig. 1.6). With this decentralization, DSM shifted the responsibility for Marketing and Sales to the divisions. Sales offices were opened in Paris and Düsseldorf. Within the corporate structure, the staff Corporate Planning and Development group embodied what today would be called the Strategy Function. An important part of its function was to ensure the optimal planning of the expansion, including in terms of the balancing of upstream (feedstocks, like naphtha) and downstream (Chemical products) production. Since 1969, it was charged with producing a multi-year plan for the next 5 (detailed) to 10 (forecasted) years. Planning methodologies included input—output modeling and cybernetics, later supplemented by portfolio planning techniques. For many years, the department was headed by Paul van der Grinten (1978–1993), who was also a part-time Professor of Control Systems at Eindhoven University.

So far, no attention has been paid to external developments during the period of 1965–1975. In hindsight, it can be said that the decision to close the mines in 1965 had been taken 'just in time.' The second half of the 1960s provided a favorable economic climate for expansion. Investment projects could be justified on the assumption of continued, double-digit growth for many chemical products. That changed drastically with the advent of the first oil crisis in 1973, leading to a severe recession in the Netherlands from the fourth Quarter 1973 to the first Quarter 1976. At a time when DSM was applying full throttle to its chemical expansion, uncertainty struck. Even the question of whether it would be wise to delay the closing of the mines crept up (this, however, turned out to be technically infeasible). Similarly, the economics of many chemical projects were affected significantly (for the dramatic change in growth figures before and after the first oil shock, see Fig. 1.7). Whereas chemical production had historically shown a multiplier of 2 above (an already healthy 5 %) industrial growth, petrochemical production had enjoyed a multiplier of 4. But, this was never to be the same again. Growth figures declined dramatically, although (petro)chemicals did still enjoy a modest multiplier.

Moreover, the chart in Fig. 1.7 shows an important qualitative change. In the sellers' markets of the 1960s, supply had trouble keeping up with demand: additional capacity was absorbed quickly by market growth. The first oil shock caused

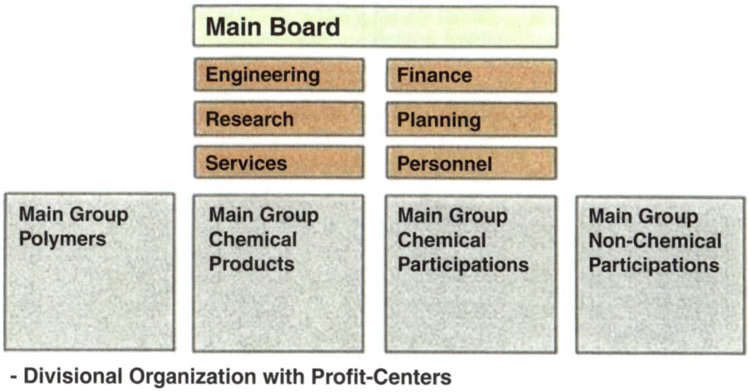

Fig. 1.6 First decentralization of DSM: main groups (1971), divisions (1975). *Source:* From the brochure, *DSM Organisatie: Geschiedenis, Organisatie-ontwikkeling, Organisatie-filosofie*, authored by Arie de Jong (1997)

Fig. 1.7 Growth curves with the trend breaks in the early 1970s as a result of the oil shocks. *Source*: CEFIC, BAK Oxford Int.

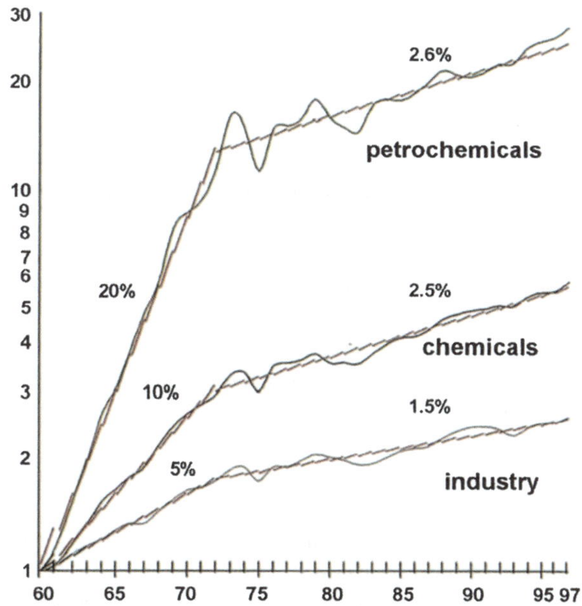

demand to fall to the extent that many plants (that were built on the assumption of the historic growth rates) became underutilized. The chart below shows the cyclical 'growth swings' of chemicals, particularly base chemicals like petrochemicals, since the early 1970s. As a result, DSM's results became volatile as well: after 1974, which was still good, net profit plunged 72 % in 1975. Results remained very low for the remainder of the decade at an average of 3.4 % of equity from 1976 to 1980. As one can imagine, this led to intense scrutiny of all capital projects. Looking back at this period, one can say that DSM was extremely fortunate to

The Maurits Mine The Emma Mine

Fig. 1.8 Demolition of DSM mines

have the Dutch government as a 'patient shareholder' with industrial and social policy objectives. This allowed DSM to continue investing in its future despite unsatisfactory results in the short-term. It also enabled DSM to realize the closure of the coalmines in a socially responsible way, despite the short time period available. The last coalmine was shut down in 1973 (Fig. 1.8).

1975 to 1995: Diversification and Expansion

The first oil shock of 1973 was followed in 1979 by a second one. These profoundly changed the (petro)chemical landscape. The growth mentality of the earlier era became overlaid with the necessity to rationalize and consolidate the bulk chemical activities. It became increasingly clear that in cyclical troughs only the most cost competitive players could hold their ground. Unfortunately, the main driver of cost was scale:

- Scale of the individual plants, which could still be increased significantly due to technological progress
- Scale of the site, leading to lower infrastructure (for example, utility and site services) costs per unit
- Overall scale of the (petro)chemical business. Dependent on the type of player this could lead to higher bargaining power on input markets, better logistics, etc.

Most petrochemical players were caught in a 'prisoners' dilemma'—to stabilize the cyclicality prudent investment in further capacity was called for, but prudence was counterproductive if this implied that other players could get ahead of you on the cost curve. As a result, there was a constant tendency to overinvest in capacity, thereby reinforcing the supply-driven cyclicality. Figure 1.9 shows the relentless drive toward lower costs in LDPE. It also shows how cyclicality increases over time with the swings around the experience curve becoming ever more pronounced. The

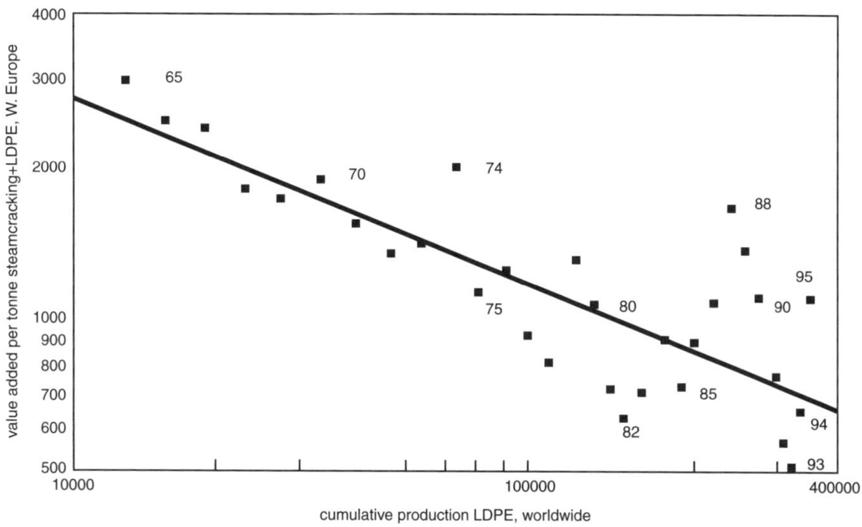

Fig. 1.9 The experience curve in LDPE

low points of 1982 and 1993 also mark the loss years that DSM would still face during this time period.

As Paul van der Grinten, Director of Corporate Planning and Development at the time, explains: "We realized already in the '80s, but certainly in the early-90s that our main products (fertilizers and polyethylene) were becoming 'mature', if not already 'old-aged.' We could not grow them anymore organically in terms of market share. Therefore, you would have liked to have sold them or otherwise merge the company, in order to then rationalize the combined portfolios. However, both these routes turned out not to be viable. Hence, DSM had to continue increasing the productivity of its base products, while at the same time attempt to broaden and rejuvenate its portfolio of activities."

Therefore, DSM also continued its expansion of petrochemicals. In conjunction with the naphtha-cracker nr 4 coming on stream in 1978, a further LDPE plant (system 16) and a third HDPE plant were built and DSM entered the production of Linear Low Density Polyethylene (LLDPE) as well (the first plant in 1980; the second in 1987). Polypropylene production was added in 1977, with a second plant in 1990. In the Gas-based cluster, a second melamine plant and a second methanol plant were both added in 1978, as well as a third ammonia plant in 1984. Further expansion came from debottlenecking existing plants. At the same time DSM actively sought 'diversification' to broaden and rejuvenate the base of the company and counter the cyclicality in its base chemical activities and results. Diversification was pursued along a number of very different routes:

Within and around the gas-based and petrochemical cores of the company, also using the 'side streams' of base chemical production (concentric diversification)

An example is Ultra High Molecular Weight PolyEthylene (UHMWPE), the base material for DSM's strong fibre Dyneema. Starting from acrylonitrile, DSM Special Products was successful in producing, for instance, phenylglycine, alpha-picoline and pyridine. Within the polypropylene production, DSM focused on special copolymers instead of the standard homopolymers. Looking back on these developments in a Corporate Strategy Dialogue (CSD) in 2000, DSM recognized it had built a 'tinkering culture' (*knutselcultuur*), where it differentiated itself from low-cost competition by adapting plants and developing 'special grades' that set its products apart from the mainstream offerings on the market. All in all, these diversifications and optimizations of side streams led to a strong and highly integrated (*Verbund*) site in Geleen (see Fig. 1.10).

Along the value chain toward the end markets (forward integration)

In part, this was done organically, for instance by building a Specialty Compounds plant in Genk. In this plant, DSM could apply a compounding step (adding, for example, glass fibre or additives) to its own polymer grades instead of leaving this to compounding companies in the next step of the value chain. More often DSM integrated forward by acquisition, for instance buying companies that produced plastic products, like Fardem (plastic packaging) and Polymer Corporation (engineering plastic products). Forward integration by acquisition was an important element of DSM's strategic repertoire in the 1980s and 1990s. The conviction was that this took the company 'closer to customers and end markets', thus boosting its marketing and sales capabilities. In hindsight, it is clear that an important acquisition was made when DSM Special Products bought Andeno, its customer for phenylglycine, from the printing company Océ-Van der Grinten. Andeno had itself diversified from chemicals for reprography into the production of pharmaceutical intermediates. The acquisition of Andeno doubled DSM Special Products' sales, brought additional technological and marketing capabilities to the company, as well as new channels into the pharmaceutical market. This laid the foundation for the later expansion in Fine Chemicals.

By developing new products from own research or licensed-in technology (technology-push diversification)

Over time DSM had built a capability to develop products from its own research or to modify licensed-in technology to such extent that differentiated products would result. In 1984, this diversification route received a strong boost when DSM's top management decided to start a number of ambitious 'corporate development programs.' These were separately funded, taking DSM's research expenditure from 1.6 % of chemical turnover in 1985 to 4.2 % in 1990. Important products coming out of this technology-push diversification included Aspartame (Holland Sweetener Company, founded 1985, production 1988), Stanyl (1990), Dyneema (1990) and SMA (1993). Several of these products were also based on side streams at the Geleen site (see Fig. 1.10).

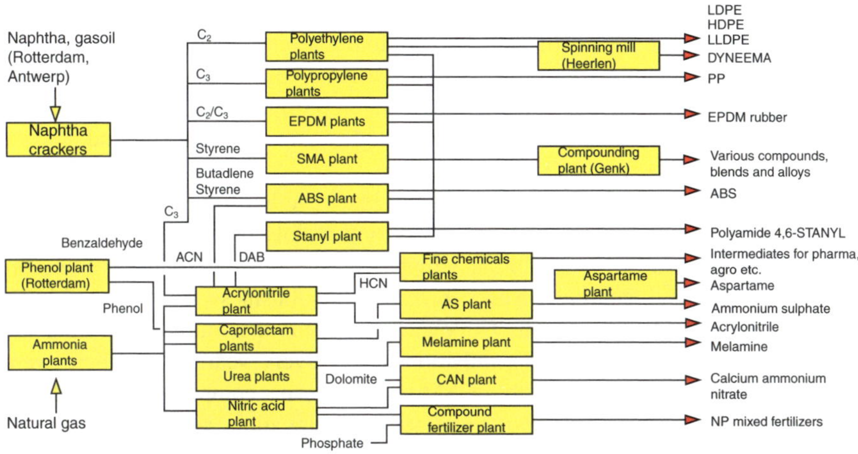

Fig. 1.10 The Geleen site

By acquiring new activities with hardly any connection to existing activities (unrelated diversification)

Expansion of the Construction activities continued with the acquisitions of a.o. Mosa (tiles, porcelain) in 1975, BetonSon (concrete) in 1976 and the creation of Coban (window panes) in 1979. The Construction division was discontinued in 1984 after the loss year of 1982. DSM also enlarged its share in Macintosh (textiles), until it agreed with a management buyout in the early 1990s. In 1977, DSM Special Products bought Chem-Y, a surfactants business, hoping to enter the personal care market. It was an underperforming business that DSM aimed to turn around by doubling its capacity, among other things. A new plant was built by DSM, which not only cost more than twice the initial budget but was also designed as a 'bulk chemical' plant (with a central control room) rather than allowing for the flexibility that true specialty production required. Chem-Y has always struggled in DSM's portfolio (see number 14 in Fig. 1.12) until it was sold in 1992.

By continuing to explore possibilities to join forces in some way or another with other companies.

As Hans van Liemt, a member of the Managing Board since 1973 and chairman from 1984 to 1993, told us: "We have had many, many discussions with other companies. With AKZO there were numerous contacts and several explorations. To Esso and Shell we have said: buy DSM's bulk chemicals but give us the time to build other activities. Even to Gist-brocades we put out our feelers. But DSM was not a favored partner at the time. I do recall that my predecessor, Wim Bogers, was once very near a deal with OGEM, the widely diversified Dutch conglomerate. When my colleague Schepers and I heard about this, we threatened to resign, because we saw no merit at all in this combination. The deal was subsequently shelved. All in all, no deals were possible in the

Netherlands, because DSM lacked friends in the industry and was viewed with suspicion because it was still state-owned. International deals were similarly out of reach: the chemical industry was at that time still a very much nationally driven industry. As a result, DSM had to develop organically. Its own diversification moves must be understood as inevitable against this background."

Some of DSM's diversification moves fall into several of the categories above. For instance, it built a (thermoset) Resin division mainly by acquisition. This had already been started in 1973 with the acquisition of Synres, a producer of unsaturated polyester and coating resins. In 1983, this business was merged with Unichema/Scado, bought from Unilever. Between the mid-1980s and the mid-1990s, DSM made a resin acquisition nearly every year. While there were again some feedstock linkages from DSM to these resins companies, it could also be argued that this was a case of unrelated diversification, since technological, production and market synergies were negligible.

Of course, within DSM all of these diversifications introduced substantial diversity of business operations. Moreover, it was felt that the divisional structure was not operating close enough to its markets. As a result, DSM introduced business units within the divisions in 1984. This was accompanied with a second wave of decentralization within DSM, in which formerly centralized functions were brought to the divisional and business unit level (for an illustration, see Fig. 1.11).

DSM had thus grown considerably in breadth and variety by the early 1990s when it conducted a strategic study (*DSM 2000*), followed by an organizational study (*Concern 2000*). The strategic study used the conventional portfolio techniques of the day to map DSM's businesses. With the help of the consultancy firm A.D. Little, Fig. 1.12 resulted. Several features of this portfolio overview and the study *DSM 2000* are striking:

- The breadth of DSM's portfolio as compared to 25 years earlier when the decision to close the mines was announced
- The classification of 86 % of DSM's businesses as operating in mature to aging industries
- The classification of 95 % of these businesses as having a favorable to strong competitive position (which was already regarded as quite 'diplomatic' at the time and later proved to be unfounded)
- The fact that only one business (adhesives) would have to prove its viability, while all others would be further developed

The latter observation is all the more striking, since the study *DSM 2000* itself concluded that:

- We should obtain more leadership position
- Consolidation of our current position to achieve the required critical mass will require substantial financial and human resources and great efforts in the fields of marketing and research

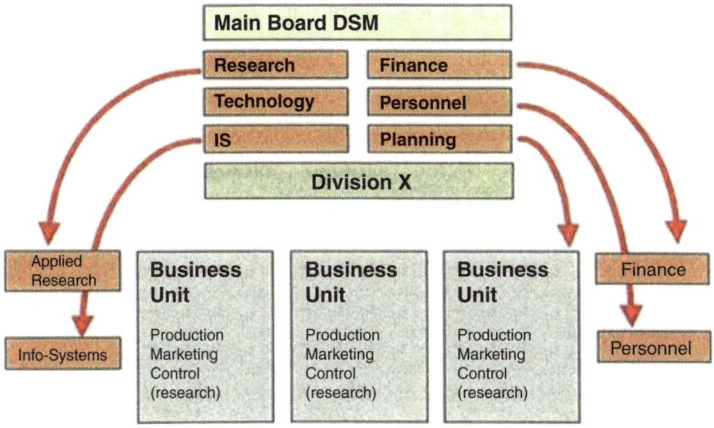

Fig. 1.11 Second decentralization of DSM (1984): business units

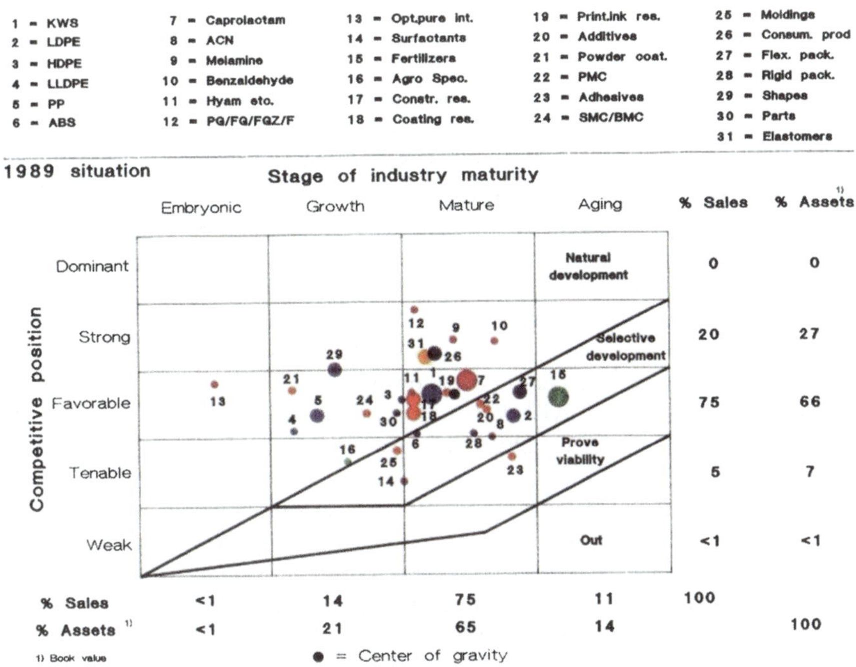

Fig. 1.12 DSM portfolio of businesses in 1989. *Source:* DSM, Special Issue of Management Letter, *DSM 2000 Strategy*, November 1990

- Notwithstanding our financial reserves, our resources are limited
- All this makes it necessary to focus on a limited number of core areas with critical mass

Against this background, it is remarkable that the 'forward projection' of the portfolio to 2000 is based on the same seven broad areas as in 1989, all forecasted to have become stronger. One reason why no firmer conclusions were drawn from the analysis may have been that financial results were high in 1988–1989. While, rationally, most managers agree that a company should 'repair the roof while the sun shines', psychologically it is difficult. Another reason may have been the particular composition of the Managing Board in the late 1980s and early 1990s. As Hans van Liemt confided: "It was very hard to come to shared conclusions together." Thus, no substantial strategic action had been undertaken when DSM plunged into loss again in 1993, as a result of the simultaneous downcycles of Petrochemicals and Base Chemicals. In the meantime, however, the Dutch government had taken advantage of the financially strong years of the late 1980s to bring about 70 % of its shares to market in 1989, effectively privatizing DSM.[16] When Hans van Liemt resigned as chairman of the Managing Board in mid-1993, the Dutch financial newspaper *Het Financieele Dagblad* ran a farewell interview with the nasty heading 'The wrong assessments of Van Liemt; DSM fails its stock exchange exam,' noting that DSM's shares had been brought to market at prices of Dfl 108 and 125 per share, and had subsequently risen to Dfl 140 per share, but were now trading Dfl 60 lower. Van Liemt acknowledged that he had not foreseen that the economic cycle would turn down so quickly and that the stock listing of the company came to be "an exam we failed in absolute terms."[17]

The follow-up *Concern 2000* study focused on the organization and concluded, not surprisingly, that further decentralization was called for. Courageously, DSM took as its motto 'decentralization, unless' (there are very good reasons not to do so). Building upon the earlier introduction of business units within some divisions, *Concern 2000* first established, in 1994, nine divisions and 23 Business Units. It brought all business-support functions to the lowest level possible, which often meant the BU. Divisions were initially regarded either as Operators, Synergy Coordinators or Span Breakers. Note, however, that the former and the latter essentially mean that the division and the business level coincide. In 1995, the divisional and BU-levels were collapsed into one and named Business Groups (for a summary, see Fig. 1.13). In the *Concern 2000* reorganization, DSM also aimed to take out considerable overhead costs by delayering and scrutinizing the value added of staffs and services. The Business Group is essentially the structure that DSM has maintained until today.

In the context of *Concern 2000*, the question also arose whether strategy could be decentralized. Until the early 1990s, the company had employed a corporate-wide Strategic Multi-year Planning (SMP) process, spanning all businesses and relevant functions (such as, Research and HR). There was dissatisfaction with the SMP-process, which was regarded as having become dysfunctional. Similarly, the

[16] The remaining shares were sold in 1996.

[17] Interview with H. B. van Liemt in *Het Financieele Dagblad* (19 June 1993: 16): "De verkeerde taxaties van Van Liemt; DSM–concern gezakt voor beursexamen."

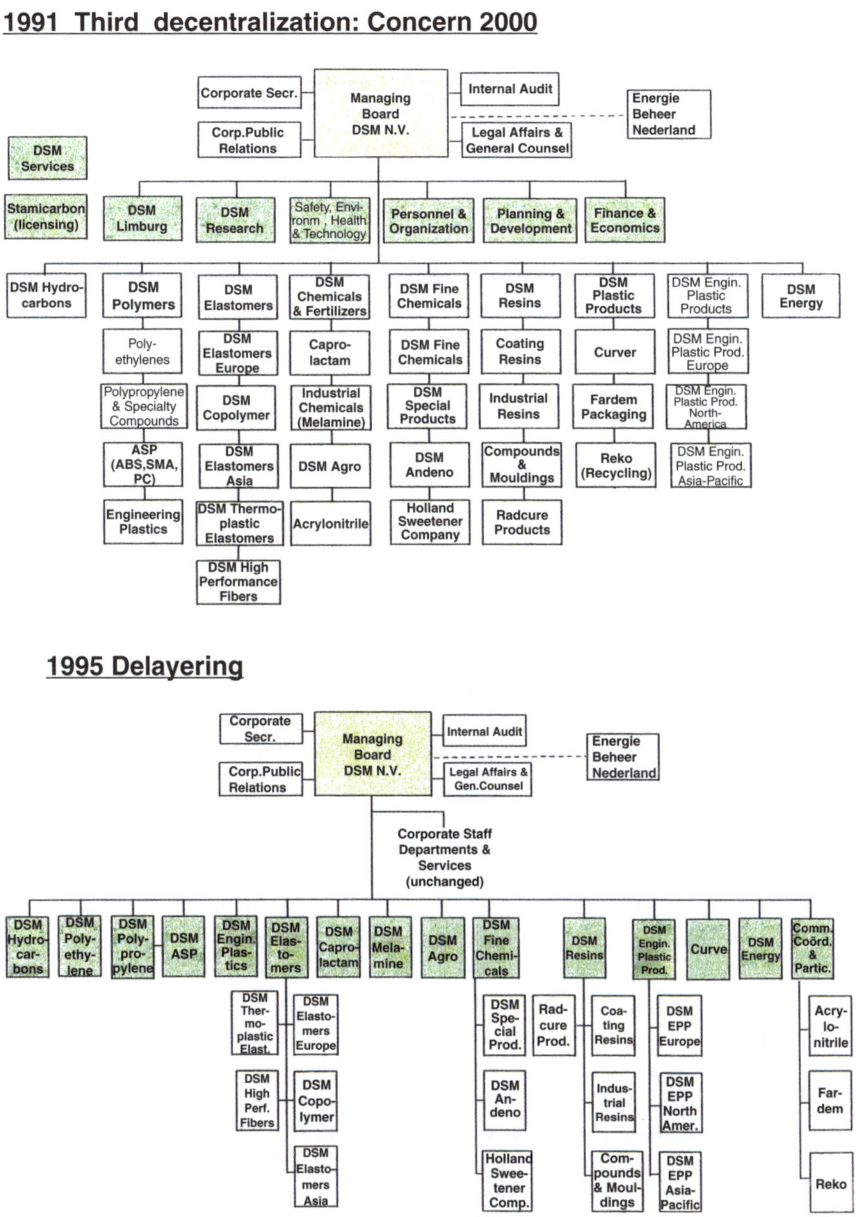

Fig. 1.13 Third decentralization of DSM: Concern 2000 with subsequent delayering

outcomes of portfolio analyses were regarded as less than satisfactory. As the businesses were being empowered as a result of *Concern 2000*, it was natural that DSM management asked themselves, 'Can we decentralize (business) strategy to the business level?' (a question addressed in Chap. 5).

DSM in the Early 1990s

Subsequent chapters will pick up the story from the early 1990s but how can the state of the company be summarized at this point in time? Here are some salient features:

- DSM had explored many strategic routes to broaden the base of the company beyond the gas-based and petrochemical cores.
- While some of these routes did bring success, many failed (including many acquisitions and unrelated diversification) or had not (yet) led to the desired leadership positions.
- As a result, the contribution of 'new businesses' was not (yet) very significant. DSM's results continued to be dominated by the cyclicality of the commodity chemicals.
- The relentless diversification had led DSM to become a 'conglomerate;' containing a portfolio of two core clusters and many otherwise unrelated businesses.
- Organizationally, the company had tackled the increasing diversity by three waves of decentralization, ultimately aiming to 'empower' the businesses to maximum effect.
- Strategically, the fundamental question involved the trade-offs between 'scope' versus 'size and scale' of the company and its businesses.
- It could rely on strong capabilities in base chemical (process) research and production skills for large-scale operations, including debottlenecking. It was much weaker in the capabilities required for smaller scale, more flexible operations like fine chemicals and specialty chemicals. In addition, there was an awareness that industrial marketing skills were insufficient.
- The company had a decidedly long-term orientation, as reflected by the *DSM 2000* study, which projected portfolio development 10 years out. Due to its history, people at DSM were proud to say, 'transformation is in our genes.'
- Nevertheless, the recent track record was one of stalling growth (see the mid-1980s to mid-1990s in Fig. 1.14). Whereas in the financially strong years of 1988–1990 revenue had surpassed Dfl 10 million, the level had dropped below Dfl 9 million in the years 1991–1994. In 1993 the company was loss-making.

Against this backdrop DSM's 'Concerntop' (the Managing Board with its top business and staff directors) met in February 1993. It discussed a memo regarding the strategic situation of DSM, which summarized the strategic dilemmas and concluded that choices had to be made. The memo did contain a number of actions, including initiating discussions with Shell and Exxon about a potential partnership in petrochemicals. The memo did not, however, come to clear choices regarding DSM's corporate strategy. This led the divisional and main staff directors to the

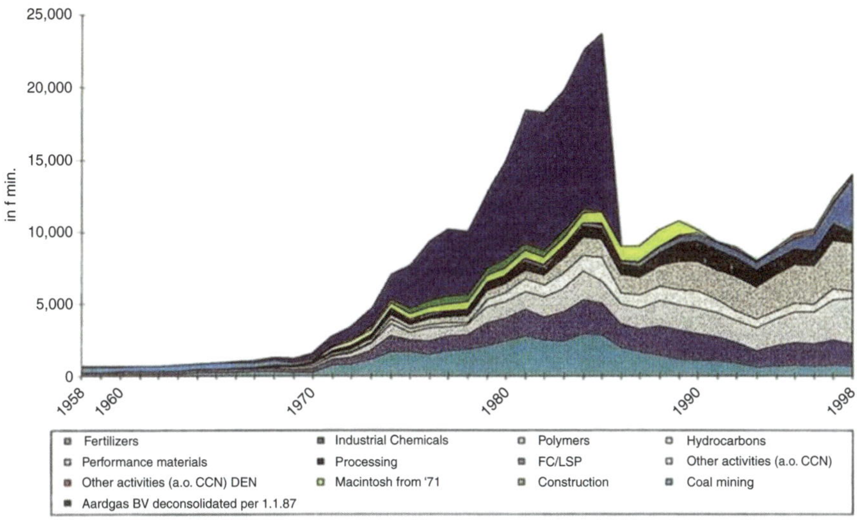

Fig. 1.14 Turnover DSM 1958–1998

unprecedented action to convene a meeting of their own to come up with such choices.[18] They produced two scenarios:

- Swap (a stake in) the petrochemicals for more stable business with preferably global leadership positions and synergy, or
- Merger

While the group of directors had different preferences regarding these scenario options, the summary of their meeting ended with the observation that, "none of the directors believes in hanging on."

References

DSM, *Staatsmijnen in Limburg: Gedenkboek bij gelegenheid van het vijftigjarig bestaan,* Heerlen: DSM, 1952

Geus, Arie de, *The Living Company: Habits for Survival in a Turbulent Business Environment.* Boston, Harvard Business School Press, 1997.

Hannah, Leslie, Marshall's "Trees and the Global Forest: Were Giant Redwoods Different?," in: N.R. Lamoreaux et al (eds), *Learning by Doing in Markets, Firms and Countries.* National Bureau of Economc Research, 1999.

[18] This group of about ten people included divisional directors like Dick van Waes (Chemicals and Fertilizers), Just Fransen van de Putte (Polymers), staff directors like Peter Elverding (Corporate Personnel and Organization) and Paul van der Grinten (Corporate Planning and Development). Paul van der Grinten recalls: "This meeting took place just before I retired. It was, of course, very unusual and a strong wake-up call."

Homburg, Ernst, *Groeien door kunstmest: DSM Agro 1929–2004,* Hilversum: Uitgeverij Verloren, 2004.

Lintsen, H., *Research tussen vetkool en zoetstof: zestig jaar DSM Research 1940–2000,* Stichting Historie der Techniek, Zutphen: Uitgeverij Walburg Pers, 2000

Messing, F.A.M., *De Mijnsluiting in Limburg*, Leiden: Martinus Nijhoff, 1988.

Ormerud, Paul, *Why Most Things Fail: Evolution, Extinction and Economics*. London: Faber and Faber, 2005.

Rooij, Arjen van, *The Company that Changed Itself*, Amsterdam: Amsterdam University Press, 2007.

Transforming a Business School 2

In 1955, a meeting took place in a hotel room in New York City bringing together the two senior-most executives of Nestlé—Jean C. Corthesy (Swiss) and Enrico Bignami (Italian), joint-managing directors of the Swiss-based food multinational—and two faculty members of the Harvard Business School—Professors C. Roland Christensen and George Albert Smith, Jr.[1] It is unlikely that the four participants in that hotel room could imagine then that out of their meeting would eventually emerge the creation of an executive development institute, IMEDE, located in Lausanne, Switzerland, which would become one of the most respected management development institutes anywhere in the world. The initiative would, some 30 years later, attract international firms for the delivery of special In-Company seminars aimed at specific strategic initiatives. How this capability was developed at IMEDE, and how it eventually would come to the attention of the Dutch company, DSM, will be the focus of this chapter.

Creating a New Management School

The View from Within Nestlé

Nestlé, based in Vevey, Switzerland, had already grown into a global company employing some 150,000 people and reaching sales of about USD 12 billion. During a senior management meeting in June of 1955 in Frankfurt, Germany, the need to develop more general managers to run this growing company was raised.

The purpose of Chap. 1 was not to create a detailed, all-encompassing history of IMEDE and its successor Institute, IMD. Instead, emphasis was put on the steps, developments, decisions and conditions that eventually lead to and contributed to the creation of capabilities for In-Company programs that later became the main reasons for DSM to pursue a collaboration.

[1] Harvard Business School website.

J.-P. Jeannet, H. Schreuder, *From Coal to Biotech*,
DOI 10.1007/978-3-662-46299-7_2

Jean Corthesy and Enrico Bignami, both present, supported the idea and arranged for a discussion with some younger managers. Following the meeting in Frankfurt, Corthesy and Bignami traveled to Australia together and used the long trip to discuss the suggestions made by their German managers. Although Nestlé had organized many internal courses, the company soon realized that the existing effort was not going to address the pressing need for more managerial talent.[2]

It was at this point that Corthesy, who had spent much of the Second World War period with the Nestlé operations in the US, utilized his contacts with the Harvard Business School (HBS) to reach out to its Dean, Stanley F. Teele. The pair traveled another 10,000 km from Sidney to Boston. Their idea was to enlist the faculty of the Harvard Business School as consultants for the management courses; it was not the original intent to have any active teaching involvement by HBS faculty.[3]

The Situation of the Harvard Business School

At the time of the Nestlé initiative, HBS was still a largely US-centric business school and the majority of its MBA students were from the States, with the intent of joining large US firms. Likewise, the HBS faculty consisted almost entirely of US citizens with teaching and research focused on the country's firms and economy. Dean Teele was known to consider this a weakness as he observed that US companies were increasingly becoming international in response to Europe emerging from the war's devastation. Apparently, a number of HBS faculty had seen military service in Europe during the Second World War and were eager to help. Thus, when Corthesy from Nestlé contacted HBS, Dean Teele was already wondering how he might engage his faculty to "think across borders."[4]

Agreeing on a Concept for an Executive Development Institute

According to several sources, there were some initial contacts between senior HBS faculty and senior Nestlé executives.[5] Several models were discussed and the HBS faculty advised Nestlé about how to structure such a program. HBS indicated that the school could not involve itself directly but was prepared to give advice on the educational philosophy, notably its case study method. Because it proved difficult to find HBS professors willing to relocate to Switzerland for an extended period of time, it became clear to Nestlé executives that they needed to push HBS into a more

[2] Source: HBS and interview with Pierre Goetschin.

[3] Enrico Bignami, "Birth and Development of IMEDE," comments made on the occasion of the 20th Anniversary of IMEDE. Enrico Bignami was Managing Director of Nestlé and Vice-Chairman of the Board from 1953 to 1968.

[4] Source HBS, and interview with Pierre Goetschin.

[5] Source HBS Centennial website, and interview with Pierre Goetschin.

extensive involvement and beyond a mere consulting relationship. Because the company was prepared to self-finance the effort, there was a turnaround and HBS was convinced to make at least some core faculty available, as an initial start-up and for a limited period.

It was at this time that HBS appointed a young faculty member, Professor C. Roland (Chris) Christensen (1919–1999), to step in. Christensen had been on the HBS faculty for less than 10 years.[6] He had not yet reached tenure or promotion to full professor and quickly came to an agreement with Nestlé's Corthesy and Bignami. He agreed that some HBS faculty would come to Switzerland to teach in the program but not exclusively, thus opening up the opportunity for faculty to join from other US business schools. As later reported by HBS, Nestlé accepted three points that were important to the Harvard professors. First, Nestlé agreed that at least one-third of the participants were going to be from companies other than Nestlé to more closely resemble the idea of an HBS open-enrollment seminar. Second, the program would be strong regarding basic managerial and functional skills and not only focus on topical issues. Third, the program would employ the case method as the main instructional methodology. Finally, Christensen also insisted that the envisioned program could not be just 1 or 2 months long, as initially planned, but had to be much longer; eventually a period of 9 months was agreed upon. Professor Pierre Goetschin has said:

> C'est à ce moment-là que Christensen est apparu. Il était jeune professeur, il n'était même pas un professeur ordinaire, il était ce que l'on appelle un chargé de cours ici chez nous, il travaillait déjà dans le General Management, mais ce n'était pas le principal responsable du General Management, mais enfin apparemment, c'était un homme avec un avenir. Et le Doyen pensait que c'était une bonne chose d'associer ce garçon qui déjà était enthousiaste de la méthode des cas et l'appliquait fort bien dans ses cours.[7] (Translation: It was at this moment that Christensen suddenly appeared. He was a young assistant professor, not one of those senior full professors. He was someone we would call a course assistant. He was active in the area of general management, and yet he was not the Department Chair for the area. However, this was clearly a person with a future. The Dean at Harvard thought that it would be a good idea to bring this young lad into the project who was already an enthusiastic supporter of the case method and had already become quite adept at teaching it in his own courses.)

The school, named Institute pour L'Etude des Methodes de Direction de L'Entreprise (IMEDE) opened in Fall 1957 for its first class of participants.[8] And finally, what is often forgotten, and came almost as an aside, the language of instruction had to be English as none of the invited faculty would be able to teach in any other language—no small issue as the school was to be located in the French-

[6] Christensen Foundation website. C. Roland (Chris) Christensen, 1919–1999, Faculty 1946–1990, full professor 1958, visiting IMEDE 1963–1964, 30 years on Advisory Board. Source: http://www.hbs.edu/teaching/about-the-center/c-roland-christensen.html (accessed November 28, 2014).

[7] Pierre Goetschin, Professor IMEDE/IMD (1923–2000), interview conducted by Dominqiue Turpin, Professor and current IMD President).

[8] The first programs ran from Fall through Spring and the first cohort started in Fall 1957 and graduated in Spring 1958.

speaking part of Switzerland. This, as it turned out, was a major advantage for the development of IMEDE in attracting international participants from all over the world. Christensen was to remain close to IMEDE, joining as a visiting professor in the 1963–1964 academic year and serving on its HBS Visiting Committee for many years.[9]

The conditions imposed by Christensen and the HBS faculty was to shape much of the later development of IMEDE. The insistence on the case method meant that the school's entire pedagogy was based on discussion and oriented towards real, practical business problems. The emphasis on functional issues, rather than solely on current affair topics, also led to a strong managerial orientation, but from the view of the general manager. The managerial orientation, the practical focus and the general management approach were substantial departures from how business had historically been instructed, both by the majority of the newly emerging business schools in the US, as well as the economics and business universities in Europe, largely dominated at the time by the economics and law disciplines. The learning style of the case method engendered an interactive teaching style very much appreciated by participants, even though most had been formerly taught with the traditional lecture style.

Defining the IMEDE Mission

Reflecting on the school's mission from its inception, Derek Abell (IMEDE Dean from 1981 to 1989) commented at the 25th anniversary celebration in the school's alumni magazine:

> The Mission of IMEDE is no different today (1982) then 25 years ago when the school was founded. It is to serve the international business community by developing management resources and by furthering the state of the art of management. IMEDE is committed not only to the teaching of managers, but also to developing solutions to management problems. This second and important part of our mission signifies a substantial commitment to understanding management problems through a distinct and extensive process of research and heavy investments in the development of teaching materials.[10]

From this mission flowed the emphasis on the use of teaching as a way to communicate with the management community, while at the same time learning from them. It was obvious that an interactive teaching style based on case discussions would be a key element of that teaching mission.

---

[9] IMEDE used academic years for its contracts, similar to the custom in the US. Most dates mentioned in this chapter also refer to academic years.

[10] "IMEDE's Mission and Activities," by Derek F. Abell, *Size-Up Alumni Magazine*, May 1982: 8–11.

The Creation of the IMEDE Campus and First Expansion

Because the new school could not be housed near the Nestlé head office in Vevey, a site in Lausanne-Ouchy was selected.[11] The site at Bellerive, very close to Lake Geneva, provided an ideal start. A villa, dating back to the eighteenth century, sat on a large property, which had been acquired in 1956 by the City of Lausanne, as a result of an inheritance (Fig. 2.1). In 1961, the Canton (state) of Vaud and IMEDE could acquire the property and in 1969 IMEDE became the sole owner, which included a large carriage house.[12] The villa, or 'Residence' as it was later called, was converted to house in one wing a classroom that initially accommodated some 40 participants. To make room for the large blackboard space necessitated by the case-teaching faculty, this classroom had the curious arrangement of a large board that, when pulled down, covered the entrance so that any latecomers had to enter the room through the windows! The rest of the building was converted into faculty and staff offices.[13] The carriage house was used for the restaurant and kitchen and study group rooms, as well as a small library.

From this humble beginning, the campus was later expanded. In Spring 1971, the Corthesy building was added behind the residence creating space for one large amphitheater style classroom seating about 60 participants and a smaller classroom on the third floor (Auditorium C) for about 30 participants, plus additional faculty offices and group meeting rooms.[14] This infrastructure, allowing the housing of two large programs simultaneously, and one smaller group, was to remain the IMEDE campus until 1989 when the Bignami building, containing three new classrooms and faculty offices, was inaugurated.

IMEDE operated on a day-campus format: participants arrived in the morning for their classes, had lunch on campus and returned to their hotel rooms or rented apartments after the end of the afternoon sessions. Since there were several hotels with sufficient room capacity in the Lausanne-Ouchy area, all within walking distance, IMEDE benefited from a type of 'walking campus' that included a radius of about 15 min. The proximity of these hotels created a US campus-like condition but, in contrast to US executive programs, participants could enjoy hotel-quality residences.

[11] It was rumored that Bignami from Nestlé heard about the property through his dentist.

[12] "History of Property on Chemin de Bellerive," by Frederic Paux, General Secretary of IMEDE 1970–1979.

[13] The term 'Residence' was introduced by Dean Derek Abell (Dean 1981–1989).

[14] The building received its name 'Corthesy' after one of IMEDE's co-founders, J. C. Corthesy, passed away in 1976. The buildings dedication in Corthesy's name took place in 1977 when his son Henri attended the MBA program as a participant.

Fig. 2.1 The Bellerive Property 1950 (approx.). *Source:* Copyright© 2014 IMD

Governance at IMEDE

There were three main elements to IMEDE's governance: (1) the faculty and school administration, (2) the advisory Board with mostly HBS professors, and (3) the Board of Trustees. Administratively its Dean, in turn supported by an administrative officer, led IMEDE. The Dean was usually a faculty member, often coming from HBS, such as Harry Hansen (1979–1981) or Derek Abell (1981–1989).[15] The head of administration, or Director of Finance, was frequently recruited from the Nestlé staff.

IMEDE's Board of Trustees was usually chaired by the Chairman of Nestlé's Board or its CEO, and joined by a senior executive from Roche, as well as some members of the Cantonal administration and local university community. And finally, the separate Board of Advisors (Visiting Committee) always included several HBS professors, such as Roland C. Christiansen or John McArthur, who was part of this group for several years. Since members of this group tended to serve for many years, and were intimately acquainted with IMEDE and its culture, there was a high degree of stability and consistency, which in turn contributed towards a very particular culture, steeped in executive education.

Established under the patronage of, and in cooperation with, the University of Lausanne, IMEDE was nevertheless financially and administratively independent.

[15] Previous IMD Deans were: Clark Myers (Ohio University) 1957–1960; Thomas A. Graves (Harvard Business School) 1960–1964; Chaffee Hall 1964–1966; Pierre Goetschin (ad intermim, IMEDE) 1966–1967; and Luigi Dusmet (University of California) 1967–1978.

Its association with the University was more symbolic and supported the validity of its MBA degree. IMEDE had always maintained its own revenue stream based on program fees. However, there was a regular annual deficit and it was Nestlé who balanced the books each year.

> We were fortunate to have been beneficiary of major contributions over the years from the Nestlé Corporation. In recent years, these have been supplemented by funds generously donated by a number of other institutions. But if we are to fulfill our mission effectively, these needs will be growing over the years ahead. It is a fact that investments in the underpinnings of management education have been far less in Europe than have been in the United States[16] (Derek Abell).

During the 1980s, the IMEDE Board expanded considerably. By 1989, the Board included CEOs from some 18 companies, including firms from Switzerland, the US, the UK, Denmark and even Japan, as well as academic representatives and members of the Cantonal Government.

The IMEDE Executive Education Programs

The Annual and PED Programs

> For the first ten years or so, IMEDE only offered one program for future general managers (Derek Abell).[17]

In line with the initial plans, IMEDE's first program consisted of a 9-month Annual Program (AP).[18] The opening class in September 1957 consisted of 35 participants from 15 countries. In this program, a single cohort, eventually growing to 60 executives were admitted annually and spent the next 9 months together in the same classroom with a small number of faculty members in residence. With a focus on general management, the AP program remained the major activity until Spring 1971, when the last class of 62 participants graduated (Fig. 2.2).

In line with changing expectations of sponsoring companies, the program was converted to the 19-week long session named Program for Executive Development (PED) with the first running taking place in the Fall 1971. With the shortened program, IMEDE could now offer two sessions annually, although the overall focus and orientation remained unchanged.

[16] Ibid.

[17] "IMEDE's Mission and Activities," by Derek F. Abell, *Size-Up Alumni Magazine*, May 1982: 8–11.

[18] The name Annual Program (AP) came in use only after it was changed into a shorter PED (Program for Executive Development) in 1971. Prior to that, the program has simply been known as 'IMEDE.'

Fig. 2.2 IMEDE Annual Program Class First Classroom in Residence Building (early 1960s). *Source:* Copyright© 2014 IMD

The MBA Program

In 1972, another major step was taken in IMEDE's development—the start of its MBA program.[19] As Professor Xavier Gilbert remembered, the program started rather small[20]:

> Since IMEDE at that time did not have the authority that it could launch an MBA program, its leadership at that time decided to call it Program for Junior Executives (PJE). Conceived as a 12-month program running from January to December, the first class was relatively small, something less than 30 participants. Only as of 1975 did IMEDE use MBA as

[19] Dusmet, Luigi. "IMEDE: An Historical Sketch." *Insights into the History, Activities and Aspirations of IMEDE (1957–1977)*. IMEDE, Lausanne, 1977: 13–18.

[20] Interview with Xavier Gilbert, Professor at IMEDE and IMD, 1972–2008.

program title, and the graduates of the first three years were offered certificates changed retroactively that carried the MBA title. The idea for the MBA program came from the Harvard Visiting Committee and both Harvard and Nestlé believed that such a program would connote academic respectability.

Equipped with two new classrooms in the Corthesy Building, the parallel running of a PED session with a 12-month MBA program became possible. The MBA program took over the smaller classroom on the third floor of Corthesy, while the PED program moved to the larger amphitheater-type classroom, named Corthesy Auditorium, on the ground level.

"When we started with the MBA program on the third floor of Corthesy, it was a flat room with those chairs-tables typically used in US college education. Once the cohort exceeded the capacity of that room, we moved back to the former AP room in the Residence as it could house up to 50 participants with improvements"[21] (Gilbert). The MBA program graduated 28 participants in 1972, 29 in 1973, 26 in 1974 and 46 in 1975.[22]

IMEDE Program Philosophy

Its foundation as an Executive Development Institute for experienced managers always set IMEDE apart from other management programs that were grown out of MBA programs. It also meant that the underlying interest, orientation and teaching mission remained focused on managers rather than students. This practical and managerial orientation, going back to the very beginning of IMEDE in 1957, would become an important ingredient in the later transition to company-specific executive education programs described later in this chapter. Equally, the IMEDE MBA program was heavily influenced by the history of IMEDE's AP and PED programs and was always characterized by a strong managerial orientation.

The educational philosophy always concentrated on assembling, in the classroom, multinational, multicompany, multifunctional and multicultural groups of participants assuring a unique blend and quality of IMEDE programs.[23]

In the late 1966, a shorter summer Program for Senior Executives (SEE) was added and ran during the summer month when the AP Program was not in session. A review of that program content provides a sense of the orientation of the IMEDE faculty.[24] The main topics covered were:

[21] Initially, the classroom in the Residence could hold only about 40 participants. The capacity was enlarged in the late 1970s when the MBA cohort expanded.

[22] Source: 1988 IMEDE Alumni Directory.

[23] Dusmet, Luigi. "IMEDE: An Historical Sketch." *Insights into the History, Activities and Aspirations of IMEDE (1957–1977)*. IMEDE, Lausanne, 1977: 13–18.

[24] Source: IMEDE SSE Brochure (1969).

- Financial Controls
- Marketing
- Environmental Analysis for Top Management Decisions
- Planning Corporate Strategy
- Organization and Leadership
- Quantitative Tools

This material was taught with an integrative point of view from top management, or what IMEDE faculty referred to as a 'general management viewpoint.' The listing of these course streams was similar to the 19-week PED middle-management program.

Functional Programs (MMS, Sales, Finance, M&A)

In the late 1960s, IMEDE began to add a number of functional programs to its portfolio. The first such program was the Marketing Management seminar offered in 1968, followed by several other 1- to 2-week long offerings. Regularly offered were Marketing programs and some in the areas of Finance, Operations and Merger and Acquisitions (M&As). These programs were typically staffed with faculty who were teaching in those functional areas, augmented with former visiting faculty who were familiar with the IMEDE approach and its audiences.

Building the IMEDE Faculty

The initial faculty team that started IMEDE was recruited largely from HBS and Stanford University in the US. This group was small, only about a half a dozen faculty members in residence for 1 or 2 years at a time. Soon, faculty members were recruited from other business schools with similar orientations and teaching approaches to HBS. Western Ontario was such a school, and some faculty members were also recruited from other US universities who either had close ties to HBS or had been in its MBA or doctoral programs. This ensured that the teaching philosophy of the core faculty team remained consistent and true to the original ideas as laid down by Christensen and his founding colleagues.

Following the initial start-up years, some faculty were recruited for longer periods, but it was not until the mid-1970s that IMEDE began to recruit recently graduated European faculty with a strong 'Boston connection.' Those professors were quickly integrated into the IMEDE teaching style and became the core of the IMEDE faculty during the 1980s. With the expansion into the MBA program, the faculty team in residence doubled and stabilized to around 15–20 professors. In 1971, there was only one permanent faculty member, the rest were all visitors who stayed 1 or 2 years. By around 1980, the annual visiting professors group accounted for less than half of the faculty. Later, some of the early visiting professors returned

Fig. 2.3 IMEDE Faculty 1987. *Source:* Copyright© 2014 IMD. *Pictured from Left to Right:* Joe D'Cruz, Visiting Professor from University of Toronto (Marketing and Strategy). Xavier Gilbert, IMEDE Professor (Strategy). Marcel Dunant, IMEDE Professor (Communication). Jack Wood, IMEDE Professor (Organizational Behavior and Leadership). Jim Ellert, IMEDE Professor (Finance). Pierre Goetschin, IMEDE Professor (Business and Economic Environment). Jan Kubes, IMEDE Professor (Strategy and MBA Projects). Werner Kettelhoehn, Visting Professor (Strategy). Kurt Schaer, IMEDE Professor (Finance). Jean-Pierre Jeannet, Visiting Professor from Babson College, (Marketing). Chris Harling, IMEDE. Professor (Management and Organizational Behavior). Derek Abell, Dean of IMEDE. Chris Parker, IMEDE Professor (Organizational Behavior and Leadership). Peter Killing, Visiting Professor from Western Ontario (Strategy). Paul Strebel, IMEDE Professor (Finance). *Not pictured: Robert Collins (Manufacturing) and Kamran Kashani (Marketing)*

regularly to IMEDE and took on the role of adjunct faculty, and a few of those eventually returned to the institution full-time (Fig. 2.3).

This change from an all-visiting faculty to a permanent one did not take place without a struggle. Luigi Dusmet, Dean for the period of 1968–1978, was not keen on having 'permanent residents' on the faculty. With strong arguments both from the Visiting Committee and Nestlé management, IMEDE eventually changed its practice. Harry Hansen who assumed the Deanship in 1978 had the clear mission from the Board to turn IMEDE into a full-fledged business school with a permanent faculty.

"Over the years, the IMEDE visiting faculty alumni numbered nearly 100 visiting professors. Of these, 25 have come from Harvard Business School, 12 from the University of Western Ontario, seven from Stanford and an equal number from the University of Virginia's Darden School and from Dartmouth's Tuck School"[25] (Derek Abell). In 1971, five Europeans joined the faculty, three of them straight out of US Ph.D. programs. In mid-1970s, three additional European faculty members joined, some of them were to make IMEDE their careers.[26]

[25] Ibid.

[26] Professors Xavier Gilbert, Robert S. Collins and Kurt Schaer.

Faculty recruiting was in the hands of the Visiting Committee that always included some HBS representation. For decades, Professor Christensen was a member of this group, as was someone from the HBS Dean's office (John McArthur played this role for many years), a member of the IMEDE faculty-in-residence and a member of Nestlé's senior management team (Jacques Paternot was the representative for several years). This committee tended to invite candidates to the HBS campus in Boston and played a key role in assuring a consistent philosophy, even though by the 1980s there were no active HBS faculty members teaching at IMEDE.

Assigning Faculty to Programs

The faculty at IMEDE always worked in teams; the two core teams consisted of the MBA program faculty and the PED program faculty. Both joined in to teach the Seminar for Senior Executives (SSE) in the summer. Because the MBA program went on all year, and the PED had two 19-week sessions, the workload was judged to be about the same. Probably because the MBA program always started in January, and the visiting faculty had academic year appointments from June to June each year, the regular, or permanent, faculty tended to be centered on the MBA program and most visitors, coming for 1 or 2 year terms, were inclined to teach in the PED program.

For additional programs, such as a functional program in Marketing, IMEDE regularly invited back former visiting faculty who had returned to their own institutions, creating a cadre of 'permanent visitors.' Some, such as Professor John Murray (Trinity, Dublin) continued to return over the years. This allowed the faculty to be expanded when necessary and to assure that all faculty members in a given program were employing the same approach, resulting in more coherent and consistent programs.

As a result of a faculty decision, compensation had settled into a fixed annual salary for teaching; no additional compensation was made for the participation in other executive seminars. Visiting faculty invited for specific teaching in seminars, however, were compensated on a per-diem basis.[27]

[27] This policy was adopted in the mid-1970s and was maintained into the 1990s, when a more detailed workload control system was adopted that made it possible to better measure the workload of each faculty member and compensate some for teaching above a minimum required level. For more details on this, see Peter Lorange, President of IMD 1993–2008, *Thought Leadership Meets Business: How Business Schools Can Become More Successful*. Cambridge: Cambridge University Press, 2010.

The IMEDE Research Orientation

Research undertaken by IMEDE faculty members differed considerably from that done in typical European economics programs or universities at the time. The bulk of the activity consisted of writing detailed cases that were anchored in the European, or occasionally Latin American, environment. When IMEDE was founded, most teaching material was US-centric, written at HBS, and did not involve European business context. Over the years, IMEDE had assembled a body of several 100 cases.

Without the case-based research, it would have been difficult for the IMEDE faculty to achieve a considerable knowledge of European business environments and to become relevant in the eyes of the practitioners who populated their courses. Although there were some topics that tended to be more lecture oriented, the vast majority of the faculty was steeped in running lively case discussions, leveraging the knowledge and experience of the executive audience into the flow of the conversation.

While case research was institutionally supported, each faculty member carried out an individual research agenda aimed at more traditional publications—journals or books—and participation in academic conferences.

Recruiting IMEDE Participants

IMEDE participants were recruited from mostly European companies and sponsored by their firms. A typical class combined many different nationalities in one classroom, as well as different industries. Although Nestlé used to sponsor the most participants in any given group, these participants were themselves coming from different businesses, regions and were from a variety of countries. IMEDE faculty had developed a skill to teach across different nationalities, both in the executive and MBA programs; a skill that was well engrained in the faculty teams by the mid-1980s.

The necessity of teaching international executive audiences for whom English was a second language also had its effects on the organization of the daily teaching schedule. The typical longer-term IMEDE programs (PED, MBA) had all run with three sessions per day, often requiring participants to absorb three different class preparations each day (a schedule initially adopted in the functional programs). But in the early 1980s, it became clear that with managers for whom English was not their mother tongue, three preparations every day were not manageable. Subsequently, changes were made in several programs to move towards two longer, half-day sessions per day. This model was easily adopted into company-specific programs, where the time was very short and there was even less opportunity for self-reflection. Compared to the initial teaching approach, this represented a considerable shift.

Building In-Company Program Capability

Early Experiences with In-Company Programs

In line with HBS tradition, IMEDE did not initially offer any company-specific programs. Although in 1966, IMEDE ran a 1-week seminar in French for managers from the Swiss watch industry. This was the first time the Institute changed from its credo of multi-company offerings. Over time, and during the 1970s in particular, opportunities arose to offer courses—usually shorter than the standard IMEDE programs and often given in a series of five in a week—for one, individual company at a time; the materials and content subject matter where identical and were used for a variety of different firms.

"Possibly one of the first truly In-Company seminars held at IMEDE was for Shell around 1975. By that time the third floor classroom in Corthesy was available again, after having moved the MBA program back to the Residence. Pricing was less than CHF 10,000 per day. Little marketing was necessary as clients walked in the door" (Gilbert). Other programs were offered for McKinsey, ITT Europe, Airbus Industries and Dentsu. Alvar Elbing, on the faculty at IMD at that time, was a strong proponent of these programs.[28]

The first large program series was conducted for GE Europe; a contract for a Sales and Marketing program for their European sales executives was signed in early Fall 1980. This program was placed under the direction of Professor Kamran Kashani,[29] who had joined IMEDE as a full-time faculty member shortly after the contract signing. The program was designed for sales executives and was intended to broaden their perspective to Marketing and Strategy. The 5-day program ran about three times annually, for 3 years, and was priced at CHF 35,000 per week. Eventually, the program fee was raised to CHF 50,000 per week towards the end of the cycle. "At the initial fee of CHF 35,000 per week, we thought we were making money!" (Kashani).

Kashani believed that General Electric (GE), although known for its own internal management development center in Crotonville, NY, was one of the first large corporations who wanted to break out of only using internal training. Rather than sending all of its European sales executives to the US for programs, the European operations, based in Brussels, preferred to do this in Europe. Over the years, this became a strong trend and more and more companies turned to business schools for entire programs, not only for sending individual participants for personal growth.

The GE program not only represented the first large program series, it also resulted in significant of case material development. At the time, Dean Harry

[28] Professor Robert S. Collins even remembers a program in the 1960s for the Swiss watch industry association. This was for an industry association, however, and not a single company.

[29] Kamran Kashani, member of Faculty and Professor of Marketing and Strategy 1980–2012, since 2012 a Professor Emeritus.

Hansen negotiated funding for five cases and Kamran Kashani developed these cases in less than 4 months. One case, entitled *Mediquip SA* dealt with the situation of a lost sale of medical equipment that became a frequently used case in many programs at IMEDE and around the world.[30]

Indirectly, Alto Chemicals, another well-known case series, originated from the GE program series. After having successfully led several GE programs, Kashani had a discussion with Dean Abell about his future professional development. For Kashani, "sales seemed to be a hot topic" and worth pursing professionally as a Marketing professor. Abell wanted Kashani to think broader, beyond sales, in the direction of Sales Strategy and Marketing Strategy, a suggestion Kashani to this day considers pivotal in his professional development. Abell connected him to a former participant from the time when he ran the HBS Program on the Mont-Pelerin (above Vevey). This former participant was in a senior position at a European chemicals company and willing to connect Kashani to another executive who became the protagonist in a case, later published under the name of *Alto Chemicals*. It turned out to be a real winner and has been in use in business schools around the world to this day. "Today, we would list this case under Leadership. However, that terminology was not yet in common use in the mid 1980s" said Kashani. The use of this material added to the strength of the IMEDE executive programs and became an important element in attracting In-Company programs later on.[31]

> When I took over as Dean of IMEDE in 1981, I saw this collection of programs that were relatively low-priced. We were not making any money with them when allocating our full cost. I appointed George Taucher to take charge of this effort and to increase the revenue from them. One day he proudly entered my office and waved a document indicating that he did just have such a new client, the Abu Dhabi National Oil Company (ADNOC), who paid without questions asked, the new, much higher price of CHF 75,000 per week (Derek Abell).

Professor George Taucher, in his role as the first formal head for IMEDE In-Company programs, negotiated the contract with the Abu Dhabi National Oil Company in the early 1980s, and also became deeply involved with programs for Italian-based Olivetti. The ADNOC programs were delivered in Abu Dhabi, whereas the Olivetti programs started at IMEDE and were later moved to the company's UK training facility.

From 1984 to 1989, Professor Robert Collins took over from George Taucher and also assumed the newly created role of Associate Dean for the period 1985–1989. Thus, he not only became responsible for programs but also played an important role in the scheduling of faculty, programs and facilities. "My assignment was, among others, to fill the Auditorium C on the third floor of Corthesy with programs that were of longer durations, 2 weeks preferably, and

[30] Kashani, Kamran: *Mediquip S.A.* IMD case no. IMD-5-0395, 1988.

[31] This anecdote was conveyed in an interview conducted by co-author Jeannet with Kamran Kashani in January 2013.

contracted in series or annually recurring programs. For study group rooms, we could use the second floor of our restaurant building."[32]

The role of In-Company program director involved, primarily, contact and negotiations with prospective clients, program staffing, space allocations and other administrative tasks within IMEDE. Both Taucher and Collins accepted these responsibilities as part of their overall faculty roles. Program design, material selection and contact with the client organization, once the program was launched, was usually done directly by the respective program faculty teams in coordination with the In-Company Program Director. Since both Taucher and Collins were also members of the faculty, and were themselves part of many In-Company program faculty teams, the entire process remained largely faculty driven.[33] Collins referred to the IMEDE program management as a 'Triumvirate' In-Company program administration and its director, the assigned program assistant and the faculty team represented the three areas. Each was in touch with the client for its particular area of responsibility and internally they coordinated their efforts to create one single integrated delivery team. This prevented the creation of silos and yet made it easy for the client to interface with IMEDE.

Sulzer Seminar Series[34]

In mid-1984, Sulzer Brothers, a leading Swiss machinery and technology company, approached IMEDE, with a request for a series of seminars focusing on market orientation. "The Sulzer Program represented the first really large-scale contract for IMEDE," remembers Professor Collins who was then IMEDE Director for In-Company programs, responsible for any new client requests.[35]

Driven by one of its Management Board members, Peter Sulzer, who had studied management in the US, the company was looking for a way to instill more of a market orientation in its management and operation. Contacts with IMEDE were also made possible through the Sulzer Corporate Planning Officer who had been a graduate of the IMEDE PED program.[36] After an initial contact period, Sulzer requested to expose its top 250 managers worldwide across all business, functions and support departments to an intensive learning program. Since the physical

[32] Professor Robert S. Collins, Faculty member 1975–2005; now Professor Emeritus 2005 onwards.

[33] As the In-Company volume increased, in the early 1990s, IMD adopted a model of a full-time contracting office that handled most commercial contacts with prospective and existing clients. Once a program was agreed upon, it was the Program Faculty who were responsible for execution, including design.

[34] This section borrows heavily from the experience of co-author Jeannet who was part of the program design team and acted in the role of program director for most of the program series.

[35] Based upon interview of Professor Robert S. Collins by co-author Jeannet in January 2013.

[36] George Koehli, Head of Corporate Planning, IMEDE PED alumnus.

capacity of the IMEDE campus was limited, the program would have to be held in the third floor small classroom in the Corthesy building as the other two major classrooms were occupied by the main programs, PED and MBA for most of the year. With a seating capacity of about 30 participants, the initial request was to deliver a pilot and six programs, each 2 weeks long, within about 8 months. This was the largest single such contract IMEDE had ever dealt with and also stretched available faculty resources. To overcome the faculty bottleneck, IMEDE made heavy used of a cadre of former visiting professors, all used to the IMEDE teaching style, who could manage to fly in for parts of the programs. This group included Professors Murray and Jeannet, both of them would play later a key role in the DSM programs.[37]

Sulzer selected 'Sulzer Market Orientation for the 1990s' as the name for its program initiative. The formulation of the design mandate around the market orientation theme was significant and had wide-ranging effects. Many programs delivered by IMD up to that point had a largely functional, or general management, character as intended by the Institute's founders. With Sulzer arrived a company with a theme that cut across all functions and in several ways forced the faculty team to rethink its own contributions and much more tightly articulate them as part of the program. Cross-functional issues were included, and the notion of the 'market' as the guiding principle was introduced. While initially hardly noticeable, the change in program design from a typical PED mid-management program to the Sulzer programs amounted to a step-change. When the Sulzer program first came in, the faculty all thought 'marketing' but then learned to distinguish 'market orientation' from plain marketing, which, for many, was an important learning (Tables 2.1 and 2.2).

Delivering what turned out to be 13 two-week programs to a demanding audience of senior managers with international experience left its imprint on the faculty, who benefited enormously from the challenge. Starting at the end of 1984, the first six seminars were delivered within 6 months, significantly stretching available faculty resources. The initial (pilot) program was launched on 25 November to 7 December 1984. In 1985, six additional programs were delivered in January, February (two), March and June (two). Two additional programs were offered in 1986, two more in 1987 and one each in 1989 and 1990. Due to the tight delivery schedule, some programs had to be held at a nearby hotel where a classroom had been installed previously to satisfy IMEDE teaching styles.[38]

The flow of the program followed established IMEDE practice. Program opening was on a Sunday evening, commencing with an initial dinner participants seated with their first set of study group. During the first week, classes were held on Saturday morning. Saturday evening was always a social event organized by

[37] Eventually, Sulzer contracted for 13 two-week programs, with the last one delivered in May 1990.

[38] In the early 1980s, IMD was able to collaborate with the Hotel Royal, which was within walking distance of the IMEDE campus, to build a classroom with a seating capacity for about 30 people.

Table 2.1 Sulzer program block schedule for first week (11th program offered)

Sulzer Market Orientation for the 1990s
Week one: November 29 to December 5, 1987

Sunday November 29	Monday November 30	Tuesday December 1	Wednesday December 2	Thursday December 3	Friday December 4	Saturday December 5
	Introduction to market orientation	**Market choices and Marketing mix**	**Industry and competitive analysis**	**Market oriented pricing**	**Market choices and functional plans: Manufacturing**	**Market choices and functional plans: Research and development**
	Scott Air Corporation	Dominion Motors and Controls Limited (1980)	Crown Cork and Seal Company and The Metal Container Industry	Jan-Erik Dyvi Shipowners (A)	Searla Medical Instruments Group-Abridged	BobstGraphic Division (A)
	Prof. Jeannet	Prof. D'Cruz	Prof. Jeannet	Prof. Jeannet	Profs. Collins and Murray	Prof. Murray
	Lunch 12:00–13:15		Lunch 13:00–14:15			Afternoon free
18:30 Cocktails and light dinner at the hotel Royal–Savoy	**Market segmentation**	**Bringing new technology to market**	**Market choices and selling**	**Industry and competitive analysis**	**Market choices and functional plans: Technology**	
	Prime Computer Inc.	Kenics Corporation	Mediquip S.A.	Tissot: Competing in the Global Watch Industry	Maillefer S.A. (A)	
	Prof. D'Cruz	Prof. Jeannet	Prof. D'Cruz	Prof. Murray	Prof. Collins	
	Daily participant review session					17:30 Course dinner

Table 2.2 Sulzer program block schedule for second week (11th Program offered)

Preliminary program
Sulzer seminar
Nov. 30–Dec. 11, 1987
Week 2

Sunday, Dec. 6	Monday, Dec. 7	Tuesday, Dec. 8	Wednesday, Dec. 9	Thursday, Dec. 10	Friday, Dec. 11
		The strategy/ function interface	**Market oriented organisation**	**Putting it all together**	Exercise
		Soudronic	Perkins	Alfa–Laval	
	PC	JPJ	JD'C/PC	JPJ	
				Late Lunch	
Negotiation for market success	**Entering "Closed Markets"**	**Intra–preneurship**	**Selecting a competitive posture**	**Putting it all together**	
	Biral		Motofabrikwerk	Exercise	
PC	KS	PC	JPJ		

Legends for Professor Abbreviations
PC Pierre Case (Organizational Behavior)
KS Kurt Schaer (Finance)
JPJ Jean-Pierre Jeannet (Marketing and Strategy)
JD'C Joe D'Cruz (Marketing and Strategy)

IMEDE that included a cocktail or drinks at a wine cellar, followed by an informal dinner. Sunday was free and was often used by participants coming from different areas to explore the region. On the second week, classes ended at Friday noon.

Each day, classes started at 8:30 and ended at 17:00 h. There was a morning and an afternoon session, each with a clearly identified agenda or topic. One faculty member usually took charge of the session and had the freedom to organize the half-day. Most of the time, there was an opening discussion of a case, followed by a group session with a specified deliverable and ending with a debriefing and summary. Since the program had dedicated study group rooms available, the faculty member could set his or her own schedule as the material required. Flexible breaks were scheduled both in the morning and the afternoon and lunch was in the IMEDE restaurant at noon, with a break until 13:30. This created two equal three and three-quarter hour slots for both morning and afternoon sessions. After the end of the afternoon session, participants returned to their hotel. For Sulzer, and most other programs, the same hotel was chosen for the entire class cohort to provide for more personal contact. Participants then had two case preparations for the next day.

The majority of the Sulzer participants had engineering degrees, without formal management education. However, they had considerable management and marketing experience on an international scale. Given the nature of Sulzer's businesses, the faculty had to use many industrial marketing cases augmented by some material on technology management and strategy. This created depth in working with industrial marketing material at a time when many business school-based marketing courses were taught predominantly with consumer material.

An important aspect of the Sulzer program experience was the need of the IMEDE faculty to jointly develop a program that integrated several aspects that had previously been taught independently. In this, Dean Abell played an important role. The theme of market orientation was not one that the faculty had extensive experience with. Marketing faculty would understand marketing orientation but Abell convinced the group that market was different from marketing. He pointed out that there were several functions in the business and that Marketing was to play the lead role (he called it quarterbacking, using a US sports idiom), and that the interrelationships among the functions were of equal importance. For Abell, the market consisted of the '4 Cs'—customers, competitors, costs and company—which he used to illustrate with the Scott Air opening case. He used to call this 'part-to-whole' and 'part-to-part' relationships but behind his back, the Marketing faculty joked about this language, however, with the benefit of hindsight, it was clearly a conceptual step-change that led the faculty to a more powerful program design.[39]

An additional benefit of the Sulzer program series was the inclusion of strategy using the then emerging idea of value chain analysis. At IMEDE, some faculty members, Professor Kubes and Professor Gilbert among them, had begun using a significant amount of value chain analysis in the MBA program. This material found itself into the Sulzer program and became one of the prominent features of the program. At the beginning, Professor Gilbert taught this pivotal session using the well-known *Crown Cork and Seal* case.

Since many IMEDE faculty members also had experience with the MBA program, the knowledge about business systems was shared across a broader set of faculty and not restricted to the Strategy group alone.[40] As the Sulzer programs continued, teaching responsibility was assumed by Professor Jeannet who was able to use the Tissot/Watch Industry material he had developed at IMEDE while teaching in the PED program. As a result of joining some sessions taught by Professor Gilbert, he became familiar with the concepts of industry analysis, a fact that turned out to be of great value for other In-Company programs later on.

The teaching material chosen for the program consisted almost exclusively of IMEDE or HBS cases. Harvard cases were used in the area of Industrial Marketing and Strategy, such as Scott Air, Kenics and Motofabrikwerk. IMEDE-written cases, the majority of the cases, were from a variety of areas reflecting the need to teach both Strategy and Marketing, as well as the various functional interfaces, such as R&D, Finance and Operations. At the time, some of the more recent cases were

[39] This observation is a personal memory of co-author Jeannet and reference to Derek Abell's "Marketing as the Quarterback" in some IMEDE working paper/newsletter.

[40] It is important to note that IMEDE, and later on IMD, never used academic departments. Faculty members were loosely associated around certain clusters of interest and topics but the clusters had no formal structure.

Maillefer (operations), Alfa-Laval and Soudronic (strategy) and Jan-Erik Dyvi (marketing/pricing). Virtually all of these cases were in the industrial, or as it is called today, B2B sectors, and had been developed in the early 1980s about European companies and business situations.

In collaboration with the company, the faculty team (with Professors Jeannet and Sprague leading) developed an internal Sulzer case as the last exercise to be run Thursday/Friday of the second week. The case material dealt with a project about entering the Flue Gas Treatment space for exhausts at industrial sites or power plants. This case was about a project that had not yet been decided, adding tensions to the discussions. Participants received the material on Thursday afternoon and worked through the evening to prepare group presentations. These presentations were discussed on Friday morning, ending the program and bringing together most of the conceptual elements covered in the course. As it turned out, creating specific material for an ending exercise became a hallmark of many IMEDE In-Company programs.

Establishing a dedicated program administration team for In-Company programs was a practice adopted from the IMEDE public programs. Typically, this consisted of allocating an administrative assistant for all the logistic and administrative purposes—starting with booking hotels and producing the program documentation to seating charts, picture books and supporting the program while in progress at IMEDE. The program assistant worked closely with the Program Director at IMEDE, which was always the lead faculty member on the program. Contacts with the company were maintained both through the Director of In-Company Programs, the faculty member in the role of Program Director and the Program Assistant. In the case of Sulzer, the assigned company contact was Arthur Duesel, a senior manager in the training area, who worked closely with IMEDE on the first series of programs. Duesel, in particular, took care of sending mixed cohorts, both in terms of businesses, geographies and functional expertise, combined with a member of the corporate executive team to accompany each seminar. For the first wave of programs the Program Assistant was Christine Kaesermann. The role of Program Director was initially shared among several faculty members and later became the responsibility of Professor Jeannet who also taught in all 13 Sulzer programs. "With the Sulzer programs IMEDE started into a new era for In-Company programs and, possibly, for the first time we priced it right" (Collins).[41]

Exxon Chemicals

Exxon Chemicals, representing Exxon's worldwide chemicals business, through its European area office in Brussels, contacted IMEDE for a program to enhance the

[41] The weekly program price for the Sulzer series amounted to CHF 100,000 per week, substantially more than previous IMEDE In-Company programs.

marketing capabilities of its European operation. With the Sulzer program series under its belt, IMEDE assigned a faculty team led by Professor Kashani, and including Professor Jeannet, both professors of Marketing, to conduct a needs assessment. Following meetings with Exxon Chemicals' senior managers from various European operations, a program was designed (one and a half weeks in length) that brought several groups of managers to the IMEDE campus in Lausanne.

Although the program thrust was not too different from the Sulzer experience, the Exxon Chemicals engagement had the effect of giving the IMEDE faculty experience with a company in the industrial chemicals sector. Previously, participants from this sector had often appeared in the mix, or in open enrollment, programs where the teaching agenda focused on issues that pertained to all industry sectors. With Exxon participants, the faculty was confronted for the first time with experienced executives from the industrial chemicals sector across Europe. The result was an increased familiarity with the language and business of industrial chemicals, something with which the typical business school faculty were, at that time, not normally familiar. Clearly, this opportunity contributed to the experience base deemed relevant later when confronting the issues of Royal DSM NV (DSM), also an industrial chemicals company at the time, although active in different segments than was Exxon Chemicals (Table 2.3).

Discussions About the Role of In-Company Versus Open Enrollment Seminars

As the In-Company programs began to expand in scope and volume, discussions took place within the IMEDE faculty on the role of these activities versus the open enrollment PED and MBA programs. In-Company seminars were in competition for scarce resources, both faculty and space for teaching and group discussions. The business model applied to the In-Company seminars was based upon a fixed fee per instructional day, regardless of the number of participants, always assuming that the group could be taught as a single class cohort. By the end of the 1980s, typical fees charged by IMEDE amounted to about CHF 25,000 per seminar-day, which included use of all classrooms, meeting rooms, any technology required, lunch for all participants and the coffee breaks in the morning and afternoon.[42] For some other, shorter open enrollment seminars for senior managers, such as the established SEE or the rapidly growing Managing Corporate Resources (MCR), the collective revenue when run with 40 participants exceeded the revenue generated by In-Company programs. The defenders of the In-Company seminars pointed out that these programs represented an important incremental revenue stream for

[42] For Sulzer, seminars that were delivered in 1987, under older contracts when the seminar fee was still CHF 100,000 per week, or CHF 20,000 per day. Source: IMEDE billing records from 1987. This daily delivery fee was later raised to 25,000 in 1990 and 30,000 in 1991, or 125,000 and 150,000 per week, respectively.

Table 2.3 Exxon Chemicals Program block schedule

Exxon Chemicals International/IMEDE
Managing for Markets of the Future
November 20–28, 1989

Week 1	Monday November 20	Tuesday November 21	Wednesday November 22	Thursday November 23	Friday November 24	Saturday November 25
		Understanding the market	**Market evolution**	**Company analysis and strategy formulation**	**Getting organizational commitment**	Day Off
		Bavaria Manufacturing	Prime computer	DAAG	Alto Chemicals	
		KK	KK	PJ	KK/JBK	
	18:00 Opening Dinner Hotel	**Industry analysis**	**Industry analysis**	**Implementing strategic change**	**Managing in turmoil**	
		Crown cork and seal	Project teams	Johnson and Johnson	Donna Dubinsky	
		PJ	PJ	JBK	JBK	
Week 2	Sunday November 26	Monday November 27	Tuesday November 28			
		Prepare presentations	**"Exxon Day" Introduction**			
		Project Teams	Group Work			
		PJ	KK			
	Industry analysis	**Presentations**	**Group presentations**			
	Project Teams	Project Teams				
	PJ	Faculty	Faculty			

Faculty Abbreviations
PJ Per Jenster (Marketing)
KK Kamran Kashani (Marketing)
JBK J. B. Kassarjian (Management and Organizational Behavior)

IMEDE at a time of consistent operational deficits and that, contrary to open enrollment seminars, the marketing and sales activities required for this business were substantially lower. Furthermore, internally there were no special payments made for participating in such seminars. Eventually, the view that this was indeed important, that it contributed to the intellectual vitality of IMEDE faculty through the learning about new issues and thus would make a financial contribution that needed to be considered, gained the upper hand.[43]

> With weekly fees increasing steadily for In-Company programs combined with the constantly rising demand, IMEDE was able to book six to 12 months ahead.[44] This full order book was more predictable than the open enrollment seminars where participants had to be recruited one by one. It also added a sense of stability to our revenue stream that we had not enjoyed before (Collins).[45]

The Second Expansion of the IMEDE Campus Facilities

In 1984, the IMEDE Board of Trustees (Foundation) gave the green light for a major augmentation of the Campus. In order to have more of the modern, horseshoe and amphitheater type classrooms, a major expansion was considered (later to be named the Bignami Building). Together with the expansion of the office space for faculty and administration, a large structure was to be constructed on the lakeside of the old Residence, arranged in semi-circular fashion, with three modern classrooms put in underground. This expansion would allow the conversion of the old classroom in the Residence, used for MBAs, to be used for office space. With the Corthesy building behind the Residence, a total of four amphitheater classrooms of seating for about 60 participants would be available, while still having access to the smaller classroom on the third floor of Corthesy. Together with this expansion, a total of about 30 meeting rooms were to be added, bringing the IMEDE delivery capacity from running two and one-half programs simultaneously to four and one-half programs. The 'Ecurie,' where the restaurant and the library were located, had to be equally expanded to allow all participants, and staff, to have lunch in two 60-min sessions.

Since this project represented a substantial impact on the on-going operations, it was to be constructed in phases. As it turned out, the work in the Residence and the Bignami wing required the Residence offices, and the MBA classroom, to be vacated from the beginning of the construction. As a temporary measure, a square

[43] The reader should consider that during this time other leading business schools, such as HBS, had always declined such opportunities and were to enter them only at a much later time in the 1990s after IMD, INSEAD and others had already gained a substantial reputation for executing such programs.

[44] By 1990, the In-Company program fees had risen to CHF 125,000 per week, according to an IMD brochure published in 1990.

[45] Interview with co-author Jeannet, March 2013.

Fig. 2.4 IMD Campus (early 1990s) View from South/Lake on Residence (First Building) and Expansion Building. *Source:* Copyright© 2014 IMD

two-level building, informally referred to as 'Cube', was constructed. Beginning with the renovation of the restaurant, followed later by the administrative offices located in the Residence and the MBA classroom, were all moved to the Cube temporarily. The Bignami wing became operational in January 1989 and offices in the Residence were re-populated around this time. Formal inauguration of the Bignami wing took place on 26 May 1989 (See Fig. 2.4 for a view of the new Bignami wing).

But even with the construction of the Cube, not everyone could be housed there. The expansion of the programs required still more group meeting space. A 'Portacabin Village' with some 30 'Portacabins' was constructed that housed faculty, staff and group meeting space as needed. These construction site-type 'containers' were eventually removed once the Bignami wing became operational.

Exhibit 2–7: IMD Campus During Construction 1987 (see Fig. 2.5)

By 1990, the IMEDE campus facilities were able to run four large and one small program, had sufficient study group rooms to allocate to each auditorium to run independently, enough seating capacity in its restaurant and also enough office space for an increase in faculty, that would coincide with the growth of its programs. This would include a substantial increase in the delivery of In-Company programs that now could be offered alongside the major IMEDE open enrollment programs, such as PED and MBA.

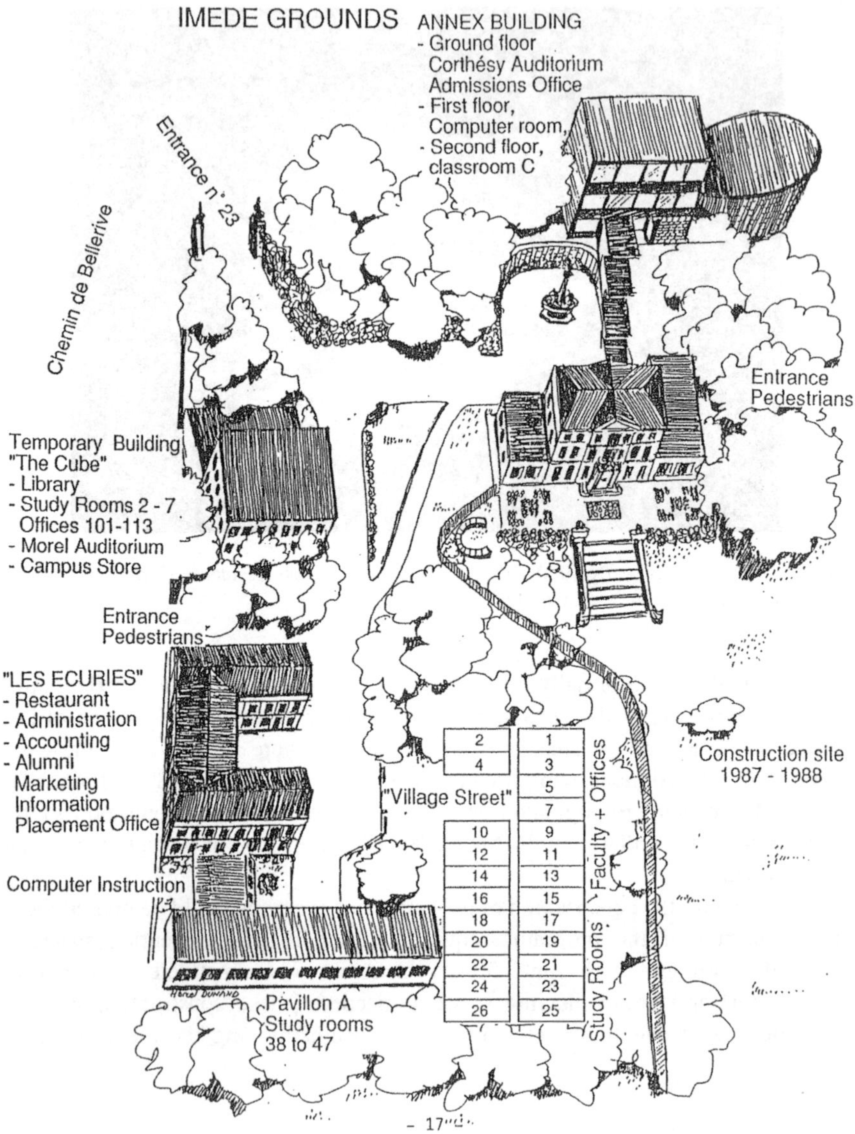

Fig. 2.5 IMEDE campus drawing during construction. Temporary building ('Cube') and Portakabin 'Village Street'. Status 1987 approx. *Source*: Copyright@2014 IMD

Summary

Although created for the specific purpose of bringing managers from many different companies together, by the end of the 1980s IMEDE had accumulated considerable experience in delivering company-specific seminars as a 'shock treatment' in a relatively short time frame. This was all the more impressive because the original founders, from Nestlé and Harvard, as the original academic partner, had agreed to create an Institute that would concentrate on public seminars for heterogeneous audiences. The partnership between business and academia was at the heart of IMEDE's foundation; it was an institution that had evolved into having the capability of doing precisely what it had originally planned not to do—namely, the company-specific seminars. These programs were emerging as a major source of revenue, as well as generating new ideas and an enhanced reputation, with a committed faculty able to deliver high impact seminars.

By early 1988, IMEDE had undergone a complete transformation of its program offerings, a major change towards company-specific seminars, and a complete overhaul and expansion of its physical campus. It was at this moment, in January 1988, that IMEDE was visited by a task force from the Dutch company DSM, looking for help in increasing industrial marketing capability.

Without such a complete transformation of its own IMEDE would most likely not have been perceived as an attractive partner when DSM first scouted for academic partners in late 1997. But more about this in Chaps. 3 and 4.

Moving from Sales to Marketing 3

Marketing was an unknown concept at DSM in the early days of fertilizer production. Sales were organized together with other producers via joint sales offices (Verkoopkantoren). The philosophy was 'home markets for home producers.' At the international level, Nitrex had been established as the European cartel, allocating the export to a.o. China and India among its membership of European producers.
—Willem Klaassen, interview, 2013

Sales at DSM: The Era of Cartels

To understand the origins of Marketing at DSM, one first has to go back to the Mining and Fertilizer activities. This is like taking a time machine to an era with different norms, customs and practices; back to an era when cartels were a customary phenomenon, both openly discussed and practiced. They weren't the secretive activity that they became later, vigorously pursued by the various competition authorities. We have to understand them within their own context and time—the history of the DSM sales of coal provides an excellent example.

An important reason to establish the mining company DSM was the wish to obtain national energy security (see Chap. 1). The role of the neighboring German cartel *Rheinisch-Westfälische Kohlen-Syndikat* (RWKS) was addressed in discussions within the Netherlands' Parliament: was the cartel using its market power to overprice its coal? Opinions differed. Representative Van Wijck stated that, "the German syndicate has not misused its power." The well-known Limburg industrialist Regout disagreed. He referred to "the terrible display of power of the coal syndicates, as we have not seen before. All countries and classes have been brought under the financial yoke of the owners of the coal mines, who have obtained perpetual concessions in times when syndicates were unknown." In the press a middle ground was taken, acknowledging that, "the German syndicate, in

J.-P. Jeannet, H. Schreuder, *From Coal to Biotech*,
DOI 10.1007/978-3-662-46299-7_3

view of the English competition, had been satisfied with *somewhat less* surplus profit than in Germany itself."[1]

The RWKS cartel was, of course, not happy with the newcomer DSM in the Dutch coal market. Through its Dutch agent, *Steenkolen-Handelsvereeniging* (S.H. V.), it initially tried to make life as difficult as possible for the new entrant. It lowered its prices to levels below cost and it forbid its wholesalers to list Limburg coal at the risk of becoming excluded from German coal. Nevertheless, DSM managed to secure the cooperation of a sufficient number of wholesalers to gain market entry. The outbreak of World War I changed the entire situation. Coal became (very) scarce in the Netherlands and a national distribution agency was established. When the distribution regime could be abolished in 1921, DSM established its own sales organization to sell coal. It set up shop in The Hague, where it established the *Verkoopkantoor der Staatsmijnen*.

In a brochure published in 1928, the mission of DSM is discussed in no uncertain terms:

> The significance of the State Mines for all of our people becomes clear when one knows that the total coal consumption for industry and households in this country amounts to 11 to 12 million tonnes per year. When one compares this with the total production of the four State Mines, which will amount to seven million tonnes in 1928, then it is clear that the Limburg mines delve nearly enough coal to satisfy the total coal need of our country. Owning our four State Mines will therefore protect our nation against a repetition of the misery, which everyone has experienced during the war years with respect to fuel supply. Already now it is certain that our country will never again have to feel threatened by coal shortages when (for whatever reason) coal supply from abroad might stagnate. The Limburg mines have forever made us totally independent of foreign supply.[2]

The Netherlands, however, remained a contested market, which attracted imports not only from Germany but also from England, Belgium and Poland. The resulting price pressure was exacerbated in the early 1930s by the rise of oil as alternative fuel. In 1933, this market situation led to a 'convention' between the Limburg producers and the importers of German coal. This convention aimed to regulate the Dutch market by establishing market shares. When this was insufficient to restore healthy market conditions, the Dutch government followed foreign examples by resorting to protectionist measures through import restriction. Again, the situation changed drastically with the outbreak of the Second World War, when distribution had to be re-established. It lasted until 1950, when DSM regained its commercial independence. In 1951, the European Coal and Steel Community (E.C.S.C.) was established by France, Germany, Italy and the Benelux countries. The E.C.S.C. would create the world's first international cartel agency. Although not immediately effective, this planted the seed for the later competition policy that was ever more vigorously pursued by the European Community (EC) and European Union (EU).

---

[1] See DSM, *Staatsmijnen in Limburg: Gedenkboek bij gelegenheid van het vijftigjarig bestaan* (1952: 57–58). Translations by the authors.

[2] Translated by the authors from *Staatsmijnen in Limburg*, a publication of the Verkoopkantoor der Staatsmijnen (1928: 4–5).

The Joint Sales Office for Fertilizers

DSM entered the fertilizer market in the 1920s. It's early product was ammonium sulphate generated by the Emma cokes plant. The surge in fertilizer products, however, occurred when the Nitrogen Works, *Stikstofbindingsbedrijf*, came on stream in 1930. Unfortunately, DSM was not the only company hoping to exploit the growth of the fertilizer market. Worldwide, expansion plans outpaced the steadily growing demand by a factor of two. In the Netherlands, three companies came to market almost simultaneously: Mekog in 1929 and DSM, as well as C.N. A., in 1930. It was an early example of supply-driven cyclicality that would characterize the commodity chemicals for decades to come. Of course, the three Dutch companies faced a difficult market entry, which was further complicated by the fact that a German syndicate regarded the Netherlands as its territory. Internationally, the fertilizer producers attempted to stabilize their markets by entering into the *Convention de l'Industrie de l'Azote* (CIA) for 1930–1931. This CIA agreement assigned production quota to each of the (many) participating countries. When it could not be prolonged in 1931, mainly due to differences of opinion regarding an increase in the Dutch production quotum, prices of ammonium sulphate crashed from a level of Dfl 9.50 per 100 kg to a level of Dfl 4.25. This led the producers to a renewed round of negotiations, which did produce a new CIA agreement, covering the 3 years from 1932 to 1935.

The year of 1935 proved to be an important year for the Dutch fertilizer industry. The CIA agreement was extended for another 3 years, in the context of which the Dutch producers established a joint sales office by the name of *Centraal Stikstof Verkoopbureau* (CSV). The CSV was to receive all fertilizer orders and to distribute these over the producers. Two-thirds of the Dutch market was reserved for Dutch producers and one-third for the German cartel. Export markets were also assigned in the CIA agreement. The Holland group received an export quotum of 8 % and was in charge of exports to the Dutch Indies and to the US. In practice, this implied that they had control over both export prices and sales terms for these regions. These arrangements indeed stabilized markets and led to increased profitability of the producers. In 1939, a DSM Board member was quoted saying that "We do not publish much about the Nitrogen Works these days. We do not ask too high prices, but when consumers would see what we earn, they would demand lower prices."[3]

Just like coal, fertilizers were also brought under a distribution regime during the Second World War, causing fertilizer production to decrease and, ultimately, dry up completely in the Netherlands. In 1948, the CSV was renamed *Centraal Stikstof Verkoopkantoor N.V.* by the three Dutch producers and resumed its tasks, adding an agricultural bureau (*Landbouwkundig Bureau*) for purposes of research, education and promotion. Willem Klaassen, later a CSV director, recalls that in the 1950s the CSV organized an annual formal dinner for the large Dutch fertilizer buyers,

[3] Translated by the authors from Ernst Homburg, *Groeien door kunstmest: DSM Agro 1929–2004* (2004: 79).

accompanied by their spouses: "At that dinner the buyers found a note containing the new sales terms and conditions under their plate. They then had two or three weeks to submit their orders." In 1962, 13 European fertilizer producers convened in Zürich to establish Nitrex AG, a central selling organization for the export markets. Within Nitrex, a quota system was agreed upon for exports to countries outside of Europe, the US and Canada; a central sales organization was created and a system for the division of costs and the pooling of proceeds was maintained.[4] CSV, and its counterparts in other European countries, were only allowed to export products to countries not covered by Nitrex.

This short description makes it clear that the fertilizer world was characterized by the existence of suppliers' cartels, both at a national level and an international level. Buyers often also organized themselves: Cebeco and Cehavé were two very large cooperatives in the Netherlands, which were among the largest CSV customers. In China, the largest export market, Sinochem was the central purchasing organization of the Chinese government. In this way, the fertilizer markets were "organized" to an extent that we have difficulty comprehending today. Over time, the word 'cartel' has also acquired a negative connotation. Of course, these cartels were aimed at regulating and softening competition. After the Second World War, however, they also played a role in the allocation of fertilizers, which were in very short supply. As supply increased, the cartels dampened the cyclicality of fertilizers: (1) volume-wise, by allowing transparency and coordination of capacity expansion and utilization among producers and, (2) pricewise by agreeing to minimum prices collectively. According to the norms of the day, the cartels avoided cutthroat competition and allowed producers to set 'reasonable' prices. They were perfectly legal operations. In the Netherlands, cartels were registered in the *Kartelregister*. Nitrex's articles of association were filed in 1962 and its entry into the commercial register in Zürich was published in 1962. In those days, it was public knowledge that cartels existed and that they were price-setters. It was only later that competition policy came to emphasize the harmful effects of cartels and they became known as price-fixers.

The Joint Sales Offices for Chemical Products and Polymers

The DSM Managing Board deemed the organization of fertilizer sales to be a successful model.[5] It is no wonder that the model was copied when the production of chemical products was started later. The *Nederlandsch Verkoopkantoor voor Chemische Producten N.V.* (NVCP) was established in Amsterdam, with three other chemical producers, in 1947. The wide diversity of chemical products was mentioned as an additional argument to form a joint sales office—no producer

[4] *Thirty-Five Years of Nitrex AG*, a book published by Nitrex AG in 1997.

[5] See *Staatsmijnen in Limburg: Gedenkboek bij gelegenheid van het vijftigjarig bestaan* (1952: 295–296).

could offer a complete range of those on its own. In 1958, DSM joined forces with AKU (a predecessor of AKZO) to jointly sell polymers through the *Verenigd Plastic Verkoopkantoor* (VPV), located in Utrecht. DSM withdrew from the NVCP and VPV in 1972 and combined its sales activities in a DSM Sales Office in Utrecht. In 1980, DSM's main sales functions were integrated, with their respective businesses, in Urmond, in the south of the Netherlands, where a former monastery was converted and named the DSM Marketing Center.

Throughout the 1950s, and until the 1970s, sales had been separated from DSM's production activities. At first, in joint sales offices, the separation had not only been geographical, it had also been in some sense hierarchical. The atmosphere at the time is nicely captured by Willem Klaassen's anecdote, of the time he was summoned to a meeting with Mr. Plusjé, the production chef of the Nitrogen Works, upon his appointment as director of the CSV in 1970: "Mr. Plusjé made it very clear to me that this was a nice promotion for me, but that I should not let things get to my head. It would remain the case that Production would call the shots." In those days DSM could be characterized as a technology- and production-driven company. The sales offices were regarded as playing second fiddle. The commodity nature of most of its products had not yet necessitated the development of new markets or product applications. Only when DSM diversified into more differentiated products, did the need for Marketing arise.

The Origination of Marketing at DSM

Simon de Bree, later Chairman of the Managing Board of DSM, points toward the polymer products as the origin of marketing at DSM. The first marketing plans were written for these products in about the mid-1970s. The polymer products were more differentiated than DSM was accustomed to; they needed to be tailored toward the particular applications of targeted customers. For DSM, this was quite a learning experience, as illustrated by Simon's story about Lego, the Danish toy company famous for its plastic building blocks:

> When DSM came on the market with its ABS polymer, we approached Lego to see whether we could supply them with our product for their building blocks. Lego explained to us that they had a problem with the color red. To produce the right color, so far cadmium had been added as the pigment. But Lego was terrified that mothers would learn about the addition of cadmium and would stop buying Lego products. Could DSM solve this problem? The DSM application engineers returned to their labs and revisited Lego several weeks later. In the meantime, they had fed finely grained red Lego blocks to rats and had established that it was no health problem at all! The Lego people were horrified. . .this would not convince mothers at all!

But DSM did learn from such experiences. The team went home and after great effort, were the first to develop the right cadmium-free color red. Somewhat later, DSM even received the prestigious Lego 'Supplier of the Year' award. Such experiences convinced Simon of the importance of Marketing, of listening in an unbiased way to your customers and remembering that "the customer pays your salary." He became chairman of an early working group Marketing at DSM and in 1979, the Marketing Director of the Polymers Division, before assuming the overall responsibility for the Group Polymers 1 year later.

The rise of Marketing at DSM exacerbated the tension between Geleen (Production) and Utrecht (Sales and now also Marketing). This led to the decision to bring these functions together in the Limburg area. The first appointments in Marketing were illustrative for the difficulties DSM experienced in staffing these positions. Frans van Helmond recounts the appointment of Dr. Roel Westrik (who came from DSM Research) as the first Marketing manager of Polyethylene: "Roel Westrik was a very sympathetic, good-tempered man with a good dose of humor and excellent contacts in the industry. These contacts were based on his exemplary social skills. A colleague of Hoechst once characterized him as the man with many supporters but no knowledge of the PE (Polyethylene) industry. When a potential customer (like a converter) was mentioned, he always asked 'How do you spell that name?' and 'Where is that company located?'. This shows that DSM then thought that Marketing meant the capability to build good contacts. This was the beginning of Marketing at our company." Similarly, Jan Hessel Kruit recalls his experiences in the early 1970s when he was offered the chance to gain commercial experience in the context of his Management development. "In 1973 the first oil crisis struck and there was a general panic. Our feedstock suppliers Esso and Shell, who we thought to be reliable, just tore up the supply contracts. We decided that we had to quickly chart the world of cracker feedstocks, of which we knew next to nothing. I was tasked to do so with the 'commercial people,' Pierre Schevernels and Fred de Jong. We traveled together by train to Switzerland where our first Middle East and Africa trip would begin. Upon arrival in Switzerland, Fred de Jong announced that he would travel back to the Netherlands. Because of a severe fear of flying, he never took a plane! He did offer me a pair of new shoes. Until this day, I cannot imagine why."

Nonetheless, the Marketing function came into being and began to organize itself within DSM. The *Branche Overleg Marketing* (BOM) was established—a platform of 'marketeers.' Within the BOM, the succession planning of Marketing functions was discussed, as well as the responsibility for communication and learning among the DSM 'marketeers.' The word marketeers appears between single quotation marks because not all members of the BOM initially felt they deserved the title. For instance, Gerard Duyfjes observed: "I was not a marketeer at all! I had not even done a business study, but originally worked as control engineer. I then moved into the purchasing function of Hydrocarbons before entering into commercial functions in Utrecht and Urmond. I had felt the need to educate myself and had participated in the nine-week International Management Program taught by the Harvard Business School in Mont Pelerin, Switzerland. When I returned to DSM, I promoted the IMP-course, but DSM felt it was too long and too expensive."

In fact, the career of Gerard Duyfjes, who later became Business Unit (BU) Director in the Resins area, was not atypical. Recruitment of (academically trained) 'higher personnel' in the 1960s and 1970s had usually focused on the Research area. The large majority of new recruits, therefore, had a chemical and/or engineering background, consistent with the technology- and production-drive of DSM. After the first step(s) in Research, a selection could be made between those who could further climb the Research career ladder and those who were more suited to business and staff functions. Simon de Bree recalls that he was also offered a first job in Research, although his own aspiration was to obtain a business function: "When offered this Research job, I replied that I would not stay there very long. My recruiter looked at me and said: 'That was not a very wise remark'." Simon did, however, move on quickly and was then fortunate to obtain a function at Stamicarbon, DSM's worldwide licensing operation. While most DSM functions in those days were still located in the Netherlands, Stamicarbon was an international training ground. It had been founded in 1947 to license out coal-washing technology and later broadened to offer fertilizer, urea and polyethylene technologies. Its urea technology, in particular, was a global leader and has remained so. This offered the opportunity for DSM managers to gain business experience in almost all regions of the world.

As Marketing became more widely recognized within DSM, a typical marketing career could take you from Research into Business Development and Product Application functions. A next step could be to become Marketing Manager, first for one product and later perhaps for a group of products. In the 1970s, most of DSM's divisions also introduced the function of Marketing Director at the divisional level. On the corporate level, however, DSM has long remained reluctant to establish a Marketing function in view of the wide diversity of products in the 1980s and 1990s. It was only in 2006 that DSM appointed a corporate director of Marketing and Communications.

Of course, DSM also recruited for Marketing functions on the external job market. In addition, later acquisitions brought in people with marketing experience at other companies. However, it is fair to say that in the 1970s and 1980s, the professional development of the Marketing profession within DSM had to be organized by the pioneers of these functions themselves. In some instances, this went remarkably well. Just Fransen van de Putte, who was recruited from the outside to become Marketing Manager of Polypropylene (PP), recalls one instance where Heineken had decided to replace its beer crates: "Heineken's existing crates were made of high-density polyethylene (HDPE), but they believed making them out of polypropylene might be cheaper. This involved potentially 45,000 tonnes of PP! They were seeking three suppliers for this volume. At DSM, however, we realized that potentially HDPE was the better material, also in cost terms. With Frans van Helmond, the HDPE marketing manager, I agreed to develop the new crate in PP as well as HDPE. We openly explained the pluses and minuses of our two competing materials to Heineken and left them the choice. They were flabbergasted with our openness. In the end, they chose the HDPE crate. DSM was awarded a supply contract of 20,000 tonnes of HDPE by Heineken."

The Marketing Initiative

Despite such occasional successes, there was a general feeling within the Marketing function at DSM that more professional development was in order. This was discussed in the BOM's typical self-organizing way. The BOM agreed that DSM had to develop its own marketing language, adopt uniform concepts and invest in training its marketing executives. It appointed a three-person working group to investigate the possibilities: Just Fransen van de Putte, Frans van Helmond and Menno de Vries, who was responsible at the time for Management Development and Training within DSM. They were asked to investigate the possible options and report back to the BOM.

The working group selected IMEDE and INSEAD as potential Business Schools to partner with, while Just Fransen van de Putte also recalls visits to both an English and a German institution: "They all had nice stories about their courses and expertise in Marketing. On that basis we could see little differentiation. I decided to test them on the spot. I asked 'Do you have a philosophy about Marketing and if so, could you get up and explain that to us, please?' I vividly remember how the German professor replied, 'I am not prepared for this,' the INSEAD professor said, 'Give me ten minutes to prepare' and only Jean-Pierre Jeannet at IMEDE jumped on his feet and explained his philosophy in a clear and straightforward way. We decided that this was the man we needed."

Achieving Market Orientation 4

Do you have a particular philosophy about marketing?
was the question posed to a team of IMEDE faculty and Dean
by a group of visiting executives from DSM.

On a wintry day, 29 January 1988, three executives from DSM arrived on the campus of IMEDE in Lausanne to have a meeting with Dean Derek Abell. The meeting, following lunch in the cafeteria, took place in the temporary office on the second floor of the 'Cube' building. For the discussions after lunch, two IMEDE faculty members were invited to join the discussion. The DSM team explained to the IMEDE faculty team its interest to move the dial on its Industrial Marketing capability and that they had already visited several other institutions and consulting companies to find a suitable partner for this important corporate initiative.

Around a small conference table in the Dean's office were three DSM executives: Just Fransen van de Putte (Head, Corporate Strategy and Development), Frans van Helmond (Engineering Plastics) and Menno de Vries (Corporate HR Development). Representing IMEDE were Dean Abell, Associate Dean Robert Collins (Professor and Director of In-Company Programs), as well as Professors Joe D'Cruz and Jean-Pierre Jeannet, both Visiting Faculty in the Marketing area and, at the time, on leave from their respective home institutions.[1]

Once the DSM team laid out the company's needs, they wanted to know if IMEDE had had any previous experience with similar assignments. IMEDE's experience with both Sulzer Brothers and Exxon Chemicals, both Industrial Marketing seminars in similar industry settings, were explained. There was one moment during this meeting when Just Fransen van de Putte turned to the IMEDE

[1] The first formal contact between DSM and IMEDE took place late in 1987 at the DSM head office in Heerlen (NL). Professor Bob Collins in his role as IMEDE Director for In-Company Programs had traveled to DSM to meet up with Menno de Vries and hear more about the DSM interest in a marketing program.

J.-P. Jeannet, H. Schreuder, *From Coal to Biotech*,
DOI 10.1007/978-3-662-46299-7_4

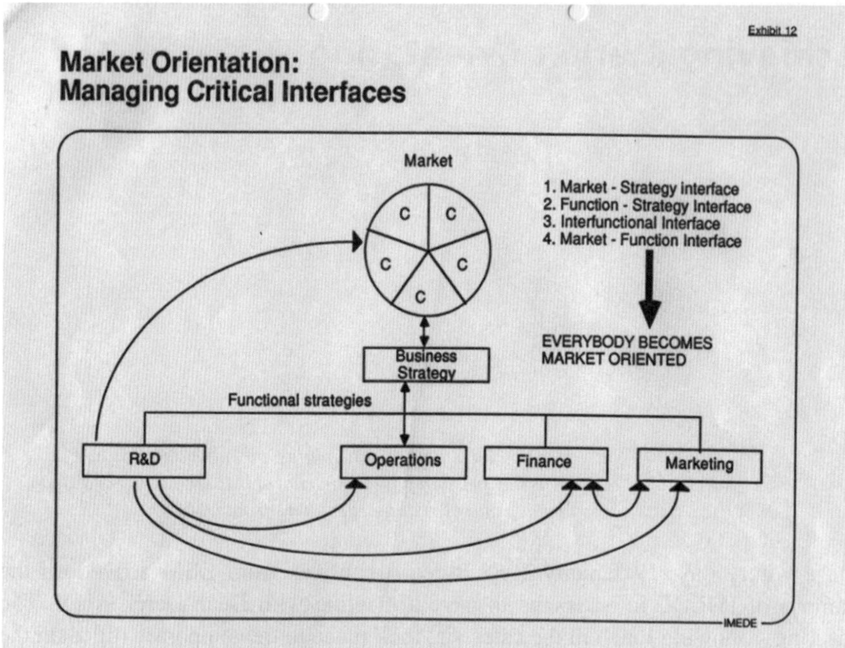

Fig. 4.1 Conceptualization of market orientation. *Source*: Jeannet, IMEDE SSE Seminar, 1986

representatives and wanted to know: "Do you have a particular philosophy for approaching such an assignment?"

It was at that point, after a short silence, that Jeannet stepped forward to the white board located on the wall behind Dean Abell's desk, grabbed a black white board pen and started to chart a graphic (See Fig. 4.1), with the following explanation:

> Based upon our experience with other programs in similar settings, we would not suggest that the effort be focused solely on marketing activities and restricted to Marketing professionals. In our view, we need to start first with a complete understanding of the market, which includes not only a company's customers but also its competitors, the entire industry context, the industry cost structure, and the company's own skills. Against this complete understanding of the market a firm can then craft its business strategy. This strategy, in turn, consists of several functional strategies such as Production, R&D, Finance and Marketing, all fitting together into a coherent business strategy. However, for this to succeed each functional strategy needs to be separately anchored and based on a direct and thorough market understanding. It is not sufficient to make Marketing executives good at Industrial Marketing. They have to become good at understanding the entire market environment. Equally, all of their colleagues, with whom they have to interface, need the same understanding. Only then can we expect to succeed with achieving a market orientation.

For the IMEDE participants in the discussion, it was difficult to ascertain anything other than satisfaction on the faces of the DSM visitors. It turned out, as was described in Chap. 3, this brief discussion in front of the white board was a pivotal moment in DSM's search for a provider for its intended seminar project. However, it would be disingenuous to portray this display as an impromptu exercise, created on the spur of the moment. The idea of conceptualizing market orientation had been in the works for some time. Its background and history is worth explaining because it shows how concepts were developed over time.

Background of Philosophy on Market Orientation

The conceptualization of market orientation goes back to the IMEDE Sulzer seminar series held during the years 1984–1986. As mentioned in Chap. 2, Sulzer approached IMEDE with a specific request for a program entitled, 'Sulzer Market Orientation for the 1990s.' Thus, the term 'market orientation' was first used by the company and not created, or advanced, by IMEDE. In the seminar, where Dean Abell led the faculty in the first session on Monday morning, he used what was familiar to him from HBS and known as a market's '4 Cs' (customers, competitors, cost and company). If a company wanted to understand its market, it had to analyze those four areas. By calling this the '4 Cs' it became memorable, just as the '4 Ps' (price, product, promotion and place) have been by countless Marketing students. The inclusion of industry analysis concepts, initially advanced and made well known by Harvard Professor Michael Porter, added an additional element to market understanding; this was reflected by adding the fifth 'C' to the list—for context—and how we arrived at the '5 Cs' (See Fig. 4.2).

In 1986, at just about the time that the first Sulzer seminar series was coming to an end, Jeannet taught a session in IMEDE's most senior program, the Seminar for Senior Executives (SSE). The slides used in the summary of that session featured the '5 Cs' as a clear articulation of the market. Additionally, the idea was advanced that market orientation was beyond just marketing orientation and that companies needed to engage in organizational changes in order to achieve this. In particular, the orientation of a business strategy towards the market, the need to connect each functional strategy to the business strategy, the requirement to interlink each functional strategy with other functional strategies (for example, functional interfaces) and, finally, the need to orient each function directly and independently towards the market were all included in the 13-slide summary. Since Jeannet was the only member of the Sulzer team teaching both functional and, eventually, strategy and industry analysis sections, it was evident that he would have to connect the dots between these sessions and articulate the message of what it would take to achieve a market orientation.[2]

There was one additional step required for the response to the 'philosophy question' posed by Just Fransen van de Putte, the lead member of the DSM task force looking for an answer from the IMEDE faculty. The DSM task force actually

[2] "Achieving Market Orientation," Presentation by Professor Jeannet, IMEDE SSE Seminar, 1986.

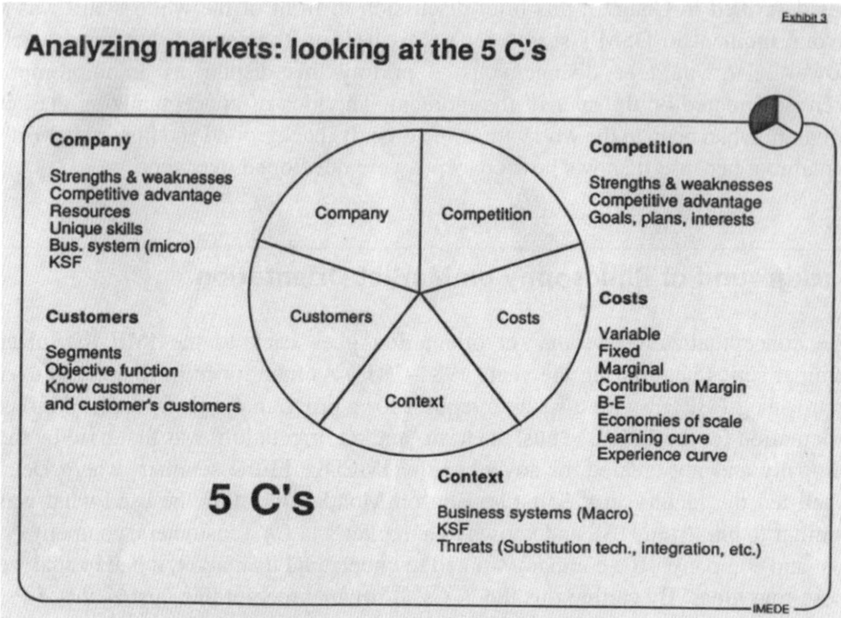

Fig. 4.2 Market analysis conceptualization used in DSM impact seminar: the five Cs. Jeannet, IMEDE SSE Seminar, 1986

came to IMEDE looking for a 'Marketing' program. The task force had not used the term 'market orientation' as Sulzer had. The moment arrived when Jeannet realized that, although DSM had inquired specifically about a 'Marketing' seminar, the underlying philosophy had to be driven by 'market orientation.' Previously having been with all ten Sulzer seminars, he could step forward quickly and make the argument. It not only satisfied the DSM team that IMEDE had a philosophy about how to deal with a Marketing initiative but also that through its experience and faculty had the capacity to take them a step further. By that time, all it took was a white board, a black pen and a couple of minutes to make the point. How the DSM team eventually viewed this explanation was addressed towards the end of Chap. 3.

Contracting with DSM for the IMPACT Seminar

DSM decided relatively quickly on contracting IMEDE for their program initiative. On 26 February, both Professors Collins (in his role as Director of In-Company programs) and Jeannet traveled to Heerlen, DSM's head office, to discuss further implementation of the initiative and to get a short briefing on the company's businesses. With the first program slotted for 8 August 1988, the time was short for implementation. The formal contract was issued by IMEDE on 26 May and another meeting took place on 21 June. With a CHF 250,000 per program fee, the revenue was getting closer to what IMEDE was receiving on public programs and exceeded the Sulzer fee (by CHF 25,000 per week from 6 years earlier). Included in the program fee: an opening dinner on Sunday evening, all lunches and breaks, use of the facilities and all instructional materials; no fees were charged for program development

From the outset, DSM expressed the need for five programs, which would include approximately 150 executives. The timing of delivery was an issue for IMEDE, due to both physical capacity and faculty availability. The shortening of the PED program from 17 to 12 weeks opened up the larger Auditorium Corthesy for August and January and again in summer (May and June). In addition, completion of the new Bignami complex, with three new auditoriums, was expected in early 1989. While physical constraints were suddenly gone with the inauguration of the new complex, IMEDE remained faculty constrained. Only 10 % of the teaching for the first program was taught by permanent IMEDE faculty; all other sessions were delivered by Visiting Faculty who were either committed to 1- or 2-year stays, or returning visitors who were familiar with the running of IMEDE. Those faculty members, still under contract from their home institutions in the US, were available only outside regular semesters.

Defining Program Objectives[3]

The contract described Industrial Marketing Power as a Competitive Tool (IMPACT) as focused on market orientation and marketing thinking throughout DSM. Listed were four objectives dealing with market dynamics: (1) choices relating to marketing plans, (2) functional interfaces, (3) organizational structures, and (4) integration of all these elements to achieve a market orientation.

In a program brochure foreword, CEO Simon de Bree reminded participants that, “In 1992, when borders, boundaries and barriers no longer will hamper business in Europe, a high level of professionalism in DSM’s Marketing (activities) will be even more crucial than now.”[4]

IMPACT Program Design

The faculty design team developed a program that kept the overall objectives in mind and grouped the sessions into five modules of 2–3 days in length. Each module was devoted to a certain theme and consisted of two sessions per day. Week 1 was grouped around two modules and the week 2 contained the other three modules. See Tables 4.1 and 4.2 for a representation.

[3] Proposal for DSM IMPACT Program, by IMEDE, 2 May 26 1988.

[4] IMPACT Brochure, DSM, 7–19 August 1988.

Table 4.1 DSM impact seminar block schedule (week 1)

Week 1: August 7–13, 1988

Sunday August 7	Monday August 8	Tuesday August 9	Wednesday August 10	Thursday August 11	Friday August 12	Saturday August 13
	Introduction to IMPACT: elements of market analysis	**Understanding the context of your business–industry analysis/key success factors**	**Leveraging distinctive competence**	**Selecting target markets**	**Managing distribution and market channels**	**Developing and launching new products**
	Ericsson do Brasil	The European pulp and paper industry	Scott-Air Corporation	Bavaria manufacturing international	Kenics Corporation	Jan-Brik Dyvi Shipowners (A) and (B)
		The tissue products industry in Europe				
	Prof. Jeannet	Prof. D'Cruz	Prof. Jeannet	Prof. Hayes	Prof. Hayes	Prof. Jeannet
	Lunch 12:00–13:00					Afternoon Free
19:30 cocktails and night dinner at the Mövenpick	Performing customer analysis—segmentation	Leveraging competitive advantage generic strategies	Managing vertical integration	Pricing speciality products	Pricing bulk products	
	Prime Computer Inc.	Mailler SA (A) and (B)	Cellulose Attisholz AG (A) and (B)	Cumberland metal industries (A) (B)	Knox Chemical Corporation	
	Prof. D'Cruz	Prof. Collins	Prof. D'Cruz	Prof. Jeannet	Prof. D'Cruz	
		17:15 Cocktails				17:30 Course dinner

Note: Professor Hayes Visiting Professor from the US who joined IMD for 1 year

Table 4.2 DSM impact seminar block schedule (week 2)

DSM impact program
Week 2: August 15–19, 1988

Monday August 15	Tuesday August 16	Wednesday August 17	Thursday August 18	Friday August 19
Managing the marketing/R&D interface	**Managing the marketing/ finance interface**	**Organizing for marketing effectiveness**	**Developing a marketing plan**	**Presentation of group work**
Teradyne, Inc., 1979	Daag Europe (A) (B)	Alto chemicals Europe (A) (B) (C)	Alfa–Laval	
Prof. D'Cruz	Prof. Jeannet	Prof. D'Cruz	Prof. Jeannet	Faculty
Lunch 12:15–13:30	Lunch 12:00–13:30	Lunch 12:15–13:30	Lunch 13:00–14:15	Final lunch
Managing the marketing/ manufacturing interface: manufacturing as a competitive weapon	**Managing the sales function**	**Expanding internationally**	**Integrative exercise**	
Sunwind A.B. (A) Sunwind A.B. (A) process flow chart	Mediquip S. A.	Stewart Manufacturing Ltd. (A) (B)	Sealed Air Corporation	
Prof. Collins	Prof. Hayes	Prof. Jeannet	Faculty	

Module 1 was devoted to the understanding of market dynamics and making market choices, comprising the first full 3 days of week 1.

- Elements of Market Analysis as an Introductory Session
- Performing Customer Analysis—Segmentation
- Understanding the Context of Business (Industry Analysis and Key Success Factors)
- Leveraging Competitive Advantage—Generic Strategies
- Leveraging Distinctive Competence—Company
- Managing Vertical Integration

Using a variety of IMD-developed and outside cases, the purpose of this module was to raise the participants' understanding of the market and the various elements that needed to be understood. This was referred to later as the '5 Cs' and gave the entire seminar a distinctive strategic outlook.

Module 2 was aimed at formulating the Marketing mix and had a decidedly more Marketing (functional) orientation. The five sessions comprising this were entitled:

- Selecting Target Markets
- Pricing Specialty Products

- Managing Distribution Channels
- Pricing Bulk Products
- Developing and Launching New Products

Using typical B2B Marketing cases, this module emphasized the tools of Marketing and how they should be combined to impact a given target market. The week usually ended on Saturday at noon and an dinner off-campus was organized for Saturday evening. Participants were free on Sunday.

Module 3 was devoted to critical interfaces and filled both the Monday and Tuesday morning sessions in week 2. Three interfaces were selected because they proved to be of major importance to DSM:

- Managing the Marketing/Research and Development (R&D) Interface
- Managing the Marketing/Manufacturing Interface
- Managing the Marketing/Finance Interface

It was important that participants from the Marketing functions be exposed to the impact they have on R&D, Manufacturing, and Finance by understanding what these other functions contributed to an overall business. By exposing them to such interfaces, Marketing executives were expected to become more effective at interfacing with other parts of the company. These sessions had to be taught from a Marketing perspective and were not geared towards teaching R&D to non-R&D managers. From a faculty perspective, this was clearly a difficult assignment.

Module 4 was devoted to the implementation of a market orientation within a firm or business and absorbed the three half-days from Tuesday afternoon through all of Wednesday.

- Managing the Sales Function
- Organizing for Marketing Effectiveness
- Expanding Internationally

In this module, the faculty stressed organizational issues of achieving a market orientation, starting with the sales force, then going to multi-segment coverage and eventually moving towards internationalization. It should be pointed out that for this module the faculty could fall back on materials developed by Professor Kashani (see Chap. 2), such as the cases Mediquip and Alto Chemicals.

Module 5 capped the program and was called, 'Putting it all Together' to provide some integrative discussions and exercises that were to be combined with actions plans in the form of a Marketing plan.

- Developing a Marketing Plan
- Integrative Exercise
- Presentations of Group Work

The module started with a case discussion on Marketing planning followed by an integrative group exercise. As there were no DSM-specific cases available for the start of the program, the faculty chose a proven Industrial Marketing case (*Sealed Air*) and each study group prepared a presentation that was presented on Friday morning. Attending the presentations were members of the program faculty who posed some questions to the presenting groups. To deal with six groups presenting on a single morning, the faculty divided the class into half, each consisting of three groups, and each presentation was chaired by two faculty members; all of the groups re-convened at the end.

Creating the IMPACT Faculty Team

In the DSM contract, the faculty team was to be comprised three professors who were primarily from the Marketing area (D'Cruz, Hayes and Jeannet), in addition to Bob Collins (Manufacturing) and Pierre Casse (Organizational Behavior). As it turned out, the IMEDE Marketing faculty taught most sessions with Bob Collins who ran two sessions related to his area of Manufacturing. This had to do with a preference for faculty who had an affinity with the participants (mostly from Marketing areas), as well as a deliberate choice not to fall back on Finance, Technology or Behavioral faculty for the interfaces.

Availability also had something to do with the choice of Marketing professors. All three were visiting professors at IMD, two of them were there for 1 year. Jeannet, who had been a visiting faculty at IMEDE from 1981 to 1983, was returning annually for specified periods when not under contract with his home institution of Babson College, in the US. Since the DSM program stretched limited faculty resources, IMEDE needed to make use of visitors who were well versed in the 'IMEDE way' of delivering programs. When Hayes returned to the US at the end of his visiting term, Per Jenster stepped in who had been recently hired by IMEDE on a permanent basis. D'Cruz had taught in the last of the Sulzer programs and in the Exxon Chemicals program, where much of the later Impact concepts had been conceived and tested.

DSM asked Jeannet to be program director and since this required being present at all of the seminars, date restrictions had to be approved by the company.

Organizing the Delivery of the IMPACT Seminars

The first, or pilot, seminar was held in August 1988 and was planned for 30 participants. The later seminars in 1989, and a trailer in August in 1990, were running with a group size of 42 people. The first 150 participants were drawn from the original profile of members of business teams and immediate succession candidates. As the intended group was expanded to 250 participants, the targets were broadened to include other group functions, such as R&D, Production and Finance. The coordination of sending a balanced cohort each time that reflected the overall target composition was DSM's responsibility (specifically, Menno de Vries

Fig. 4.3 IMEDE campus construction (1988). *Source*: Copyright@2014 IMD

from Executive Training and Development). De Vries not only created balanced cohorts, he also created the two rounds of discussion groups for weeks 1 and 2, as well as organizing travel groups from Holland, or other destinations, to make sure that the restriction of not allowing more than five or six participants to travel on the same plane was honored. DSM also produced its own program booklet, something that, at first, caused some consternation at IMEDE since this had always been the prerogative of the IMEDE program management group. Having a person on the company side who did all of the coordination, including the recruitment of each participant group, meant that the program could run smoothly with no wasted 'empty' seats.

On the IMEDE side, the IMPACT programs began at a time when the campus was being expanded but not yet ready (See Fig. 4.3 on campus under construction). Classes for the first program were still held in the Corthesy Auditorium in the Annex Building, where classes for the PED and SSE programs were being held. For study group rooms, however, participants had to walk to temporary 'Portakabins,' one per group, on the IMEDE grounds (See Fig. 2.5 for Campus Map). As classes ended at 17:00 h, DSM arranged its own group study room at the Hotel Mövenpick (next to the campus) where all the participants stayed. This was intended so that participants would get together after regular class hours to discuss cases and assignments; DSM also arranged for a separate lounge room—all of which was above and beyond what other companies did.

For IMPACT programs two to six, beginning in January 1989, classes could be held in the new Bignami Complex using one of the three auditoriums, combined with adjacent modern group discussion rooms just a few steps away.[5] The cohort was always divided into six study groups with six or seven participants per group and changed mid-way through the program.

Further programs were held as follows:

- IMPACT-1/7–19 August 1988 (Pilot Program with 30 participants)
- IMPACT-2/8–20 January 1989 (with 42 participants)
- IMPACT-3/21 May to 2 June 1989
- IMPACT-4/18–30 June 1989
- IMPACT-5/13–25 August 1989
- IMPACT-6/5–17 August 1990

Conducting Regular Review Meetings

At the request of DSM, all participants stayed back for a formal review session with the faculty on Friday afternoon, following the formal closing of the first program. Two members of the original task force that chose IMEDE (Just Fransen van de Putte and Frans van Helmond) were present for the feedback session, creating some immediate and relevant feedback. In a formal questionnaire distributed by IMEDE, and tabulated after the program, the program was ranked by participants and the ratings were excellent (11) and good (16), out of the 27 questionnaires collected. The internal view for the program back at DSM was very good and the company moved to continue without any changes in the program structure.[6] As part of the review, Jeannet traveled to DSM on 4 April 1989 for a review with Just Fransen van de Putte and Menno de Vries following IMPACT-2.

> Now that we have had five courses, we can only conclude that the choice (of IMD) was excellent. Not only does the institute employ professionals of a very high caliber; the underlying philosophy of the institute also appeals to us. All of which has contributed to the high quality of the IMPACT course (de Vries).[7]

The course administration was handled by a Dutch national who had been working and living in Lausanne for several years. She could not only handle all program matters with competence but was also able to deal with smaller personal issues for DSM participants in Dutch, thus facilitating the rapport with the company and its participants.

[5] DSM Impact was one of the first programs that took place in the new Bignami wing of IMEDE, which had opened for operation in January 1989.

[6] Among faculty a generally acceptable notion of program evaluations was that Dutch participants were far more critical in evaluations than other nationalities. The ranking of 4.4 would be considered good but not exceptional by current IMD standards.

[7] "IMPACT: To the Top," *DSM Magazine*, Fall 1989: 28–30.

IMEDE Merges with IMI-Geneva to Form IMD

Merger Discussions with CEI/IMI-Geneva (1988–1990)

On 6 September 1988, following a long period of intermittent consultation and discussion, the IMEDE and IMI Boards decided to merge IMEDE with IMI-Geneva, a management development institute with a similar history to IMEDE.[8] This decision was to virtually double the size of IMEDE since the operations of IMI-Geneva were transferred to the recently expanded IMEDE campus. The two institutes began operation as of 1 January 1990 under the new name of the International Management Development (IMD) Institute with combined operations at the Lausanne site of former IMEDE.[9]

The contract with DSM, signed under IMEDE with Professor Robert Collins as Director of In-Company programs, remained in force. All contractual terms, including scheduled dates, were maintained. The same faculty remained responsible for the programs. From DSM's point of view, nothing of relevance changed for IMPACT. What did change were the leadership positions with Juan Rada assuming the leadership role for IMD as Director General and Professor Andre Vandermerwe (formerly IMI) becoming the head of In-Company Programs. In the beginning of 1990, DSM requested one additional program (IMPACT-6), which was also contracted at the same terms as the previous programs.[10]

Background on IMI Geneva (Initially Known as CEI)

In 1946, some 10 years before IMEDE was founded, another management development institute, Centre d'Etudes Industrielles (CEI), was formed in Geneva. The impetus came from the CEO of Alcan, a leading Canadian international firm, who was enamored of the idea to create a school for its managers in neutral Switzerland. Alcan had operated an international management institute in Geneva from 1938 and stopped it during the Second World War. The Alcon effort was resumed in 1946 but then the company decided to form CEI.[11] The purpose was to gain an understanding of different cultures, international relations and the growing world economy. During its first 10 years of operation, CEI offered an annual course, over 11 months and with participants between age 26 and 40 years. In 1956, CEI became an independent foundation associated with the University of Geneva.

---

[8] The first DSM IMPACT program had been run just 1 month prior to this decision.

[9] The IMD name was registered on 13 April 1989.

[10] Letter sent by Andre Vandermerwe, Director In-Company Programs at IMD, to DSM on 21 February 1990 for a program scheduled 5–17 August 1990, for a fee of CHF 250,000.

[11] David M. Culver, The Centre D'Etudes Industrielles (CEI) Geneva in 1952, from their internal publication, as reported by Max Daetwyler, and in "The IMI-IMEDE Merger," 30 July 1988. David Culver, Alcan Chairman at that time, was a CEI alumnus.

When Bignami and Corthesy were in the process of creating IMEDE, they also visited CEI. It is reported that Bignami commented to CEI Director Paul M. Haenni that CEI appeared to be heavily focused on manufacturing sectors and not enough on consumer goods. Haenny was to have responded, "I don't tell you how to make Nescafe. Don't tell me how to run my school!" That was the end of any collaboration between the two institutes for a long time.[12]

Major changes took place at CEI, and in 1956 a new program was introduced, the 4-week Executive Course open to participants from many companies. In its first brochure, CEI described the purpose of the course as "an opportunity for executives of diverse backgrounds and nationalities to review together the impact of changing environments on executive functions and responsibilities."[13] The program had as its basic theme, the "Impact of Changing Environments Upon Management" and focused on changes in the economic and social environments, human behavior, shifting political and international environments, changing technologies and managerial techniques and developing patterns of management.

Around 1970, CEI was undergoing significant adjustments in its governance and funding structure. The name was also changed to International Management Institute (IMI) came in 1981.[14] The school was moving from a situation where Alcon carried some 80 % of the deficit funding to a self-financing model offering a broad range of executive education programs. However, since there remained a need to finance continued research and program development CEI, under its Director Bodan Hawrylyshyn, pursed the creation of a network of companies that would support the Institute by offering such firms special benefits for an annual support fee. The first firms joining the network, known as Business Associates (BA), were from Sweden, followed by a firm from Belgium. A Ford Foundation grant was received to help the expansion to 50 BA members. Within 10 years, membership had reached 60 companies from 18 different countries. By the end of the 1980s, membership had risen to 70 major international firms, all contributing an annual fee towards the Institute. These firms became active members of the Institute, participated in its programs and used a number of additional services.

It is helpful to reflect on the histories of both IMEDE and IMI at this point. Two major international firms, Nestlé for IMEDE and Alcan for IMI, had started both and, for a considerable amount of time, these two founding firms were also the main financial supporters of the respective institutions. Both institutes, by the end of the 1980s and leading up to their mergers, pursued the same target group, for example, managers from large international firms. But there were also significant differences between the two schools. IMEDE had a major focus on general management skills and relied on a singular instructional philosophy, such as the case discussion method. CEI was focused much more on the external environment and

[12] Reported by Xavier Gilbert, Professor at IMEDE and IMD, to the co-authors in February 2013.

[13] "CEI: First International Executive Course," Brochure, 1963: 3.

[14] Some people reported that the name change was triggered by the difficulty participants had with CEI and what it stood for.

understanding macro trends. As there was no singular academic partner, such as HBS for IMEDE, the faculty was recruited from different educational backgrounds and case discussion played a less important role. Although these differences were the source of many discussions between the faculties of the two institutes, their international corporate customers did not perceive a significant difference between them. Both institutes competed for the same participants and were active in the same segments for In-Company program contracts.

Despite what it seemed to insiders, such as faculty members, there were obvious differences between these two schools but the outside world, however, did not see them as being so divergent. Derek Abell recalled a conversation he once had with Pierre Liotard-Vogt, then IMEDE Board Chairman and Chairman of Nestlé, about IMI versus IMEDE, and the differentiation among schools. “Look, business schools are like bicycles! They all perform the same function and look alike.”[15]

When it came to organizing outside financial support, IMI had, at a much earlier stage, begun to diversify its funding by creating a large group of business associates when IMEDE was still largely dependent on Nestlé for financial support. As it turned out, the newly merged institute, IMD, was later to develop a similar network of Partner and Business Associates in the years following the merger.

With Nestlé under the new leadership of CEO Helmut Maucher, the company looked to broaden the financial support for IMD. It became clear that many international firms were not eager to support two institutions for executive education. In fact, some senior executives and companies were represented on both Boards. Paul Jolles, Chairman of Nestlé, chaired the IMEDE Board at that time, whereas Stephan Schmidheiny, a leading Swiss industrialist, chaired the IMI Board. Largely driven by concerns from both Boards, the momentum for a merger grew stronger as IMEDE began to expand its campus with the Bignami wing. The building activity under way at IMEDE helped to convince both Boards that there should be only one campus and that the IMEDE facility was better suited for the expansion of the combined institutions. This meant that all of IMI’s staff had to relocate their offices to Lausanne. In the end, not everyone made the move, and among the faculty about two-thirds moved to Lausanne with the others preferring to focus on other activities or join other institutions.

New IMD Governance and Leadership After Merger

With the merger decided upon in 1988, the new combined IMEDE/IMI Institute created a new governance structure. Both Boards appointed Kasper V. Cassani, Vice Chairman of IBM and Swiss native, to chair for the transition team. Cassani was supported in this effort by Louis von Planta, former Chairman of Ciba-Geigy and experienced in merger implementation, as well by Max Murbach who had been active for some time in management development at Ciba-Geigy and was familiar

[15] Conversation with IMD Board Chair as reported to the co-authors by Derek Abell.

with both institutes. Cassani assumed the chairmanship of the new IMD Foundation on 21 March 1989.

The IMD Board's new Executive Committee included, Cassani, Louis von Planta, Helmut Maucher, Richard Murray and S. van Houten. The Board was expanded to include representatives of both the former IMI and IMEDE Boards. As of 1 January 1990, the Board appointed Juan Rada (who formerly served in the same role at IMI) as Director General. Several changes in the governance and IMD leadership took place over the next 3 years with Professor Xavier Gilbert acting as interim Director General after Rada's departure at the end of 1991, until Peter Lorange assumed this position permanently in mid-1993. The IMD Board also saw a change in leadership with Fritz Leutwyler, formerly head of the Swiss National Bank and Chairman of ABB, assuming the chairmanship at the end of 1992.

From a program offering point of view, IMD had the opportunity to run all of the IMEDE and all of the IMI programs. Among those, the MBA programs were combined into one larger one with the expansion aided by the acquisition of a former École Polytechnique Fédéral de Lausanne (EPFL) building adjacent to the IMD campus that resulted in the addition of two auditoriums, each with a seating capacity of 90 participants. The expanded IMD faculty now included about 30 professors from both institutions.

The creation of IMD, resulting from the merger between IMEDE and IMI, was well-received by the client base of both institutes; after an initially difficult start, due to internal adjustments as a result of bringing two different faculty teams together, business started to expand putting IMD on a strong growth path.

> By 1993, In-Company seminar revenues had risen to 40 % of total at IMD and were critical to our economic success. The merger with IMI had essentially eliminated a competitor in this space and the market viewed our merger very positively. This buzz, combined with our tested and proven delivery models, allowed us to take advantage of this movement towards external programs. In addition, IMI had a successful program to make companies associates and make them contribute towards the growth of the Institute. This approach was then copied by the newly formed IMD with great success (Gilbert).

IMPACT Program Improvements

Although the structure of the program remained virtually unchanged, the faculty nevertheless made some changes in the material selection. Those changes were smaller than they had been for IMPACT-5 but became important for IMPACT-6, a trailer delivered 2 years after the pilot.

The most important change came through the inclusion of the first DSM-specific case (*DSM Resin*) that could be developed as a result of contacts made in IMPACT-5 with DSM Resins executives, Gerard Duyfjes in particular. In the early summer 1990, with the help of a student who was several weeks on location in Zwolle, the Netherlands, Jeannet developed a comprehensive case on (construction) resins, containing a full range of strategic and functional business issues.[16] This new material replaced the standard Sealed Air case exercise at the end of the program. Gerard Duyfjes, the BU Manager for DSM Resins, also attended the final group presentations. Freeing program material previously used at the end of the program allowed the faculty to re-shuffle other materials and discard some less ideally suited to the chemicals and process industries. Two cases formerly used at the end of the program were moved into the first week.[17] Experience had proven that affinity to the participants' own industry environment was a good predictor for a successful session.

A second change dealt with a strengthening of the module on industry context and industry analysis. Since the beginning of the IMPACT series, Jeannet had experimented with different material to create an exercise at the end of week 1, devoted to understanding and analyzing an industry sector, the topic addressed at the beginning of the program. At first, articles were collated from special issues of the *Financial Times* relating to DSM-relevant industries (both tires and paint). This material culminated into an IMD-written and released case on the World Paint Industry. Combined with the new end-of-program exercise (*DSM Resins*) the strategy and industry analysis part of IMPACT had grown to ten sessions, or half of the entire program. This occurred partially in response to the strong positive evaluations of the sessions relating to industry analysis. In addition to that, by IMPACT-6 the IMD- or IMEDE- developed cases had reached 60 % of all materials.

Reflections and Observations by IMPACT Program Faculty

As the IMPACT programs ran, the faculty considered the participants very active and interested in the course. DSM participants engaged vigorously in discussions and were eager to share their own professional experience as part of the case discussions. As participants, they liked it when the faculty was direct and responded well to cajoling or an occasional remark made in jest.

It was the first time that any of the faculty had any extensive experience with a largely Dutch group and it was realized, quickly, that Dutch participants reacted differently than Swiss German or German participants. Their directness when sharing views with each other, or with the faculty for that matter, was something that everyone had to get used to. Throughout the IMPACT programs there was one session that always grabbed the attention of DSM participants—a case series, Jan-Erik Dyvi (A) and (B), developed a few years earlier, that dealt with a Norwegian shipping company that had developed semi-submersible deck carriers for the transport of jack-up oil drilling rigs. The company got into direct

[16] *DSM Resins*, a case developed by MBA Candidate David Harrington from Babson College under the direction of Professor Jeannet. Unpublished case, IMD Institute, 1991.

[17] *Alfa-Laval* (ultrafiltration, process industry, global) and *Sealed Air* (packaging industry, US) were moved to first week, replacing cases dealing with a metal construction product and the telecommunications industry.

competition with a large Dutch player who also built like ships. DSM participants, with their affinity to the oil and gas industry, as well as their understanding of ocean transport, always got emotionally involved in what came to be referred to as the Norwegian-Dutch naval shoot-out. Nothing ever grabbed their attention as the Dyvi case series did.

DSM Launches a Follow-Up Program

With the last of six IMPACT programs successfully concluded, DSM decided to create a course that was not focused on Marketing as a discipline, but one that dealt largely with business and industry analysis and strategic decisions. By focusing on only the strategic topics, the original IMPACT course could be reduced to 1 week. A first such course, initially referred to as COMPACT, was scheduled to be delivered at IMD from 21 to 29 June 1991 by the same faculty team as the IMPACT series.

In addition, DSM communicated to IMD that the IMPACT project had run its course and that the follow-up program, COMPACT, would be structured as a regularly scheduled, in-house program. Since in-house programs at DSM ran under different budgets and could not spend the CHF 125,000 weekly fee demanded by IMD, the company wished to run such programs under its own name, near its head office in Heerlen, in the South of Holland. The program was to be called the Strategic Management Course (SMC). DSM informed IMD that the company intended to engage the same faculty team as they had for IMPACT.

What ensued was an intense debate, both between DSM and IMD and within IMD, about the move to take this program 'private,' as it was referred within IMD. Initially, DSM had approached IMD for a lower price for its planned COMPACT/SMC course but IMD was not willing to lower its prices due to a long-standing policy of standard prices for all companies. Moreover, in part due to the increased business as a result from the IMEDE/IMI merger, IMD had announced new prices for In-Company programs, raising the fee to CHF 150,000 per week. When the fee for delivering at the DSM site was quoted at that rate, DSM wanted to step back. When IMD (there were not have yet the firm rules on this subject imposed later) acknowledged through its In-Company Program Director, that there was nothing to prevent DSM from hiring IMD faculty directly, the case for taking the program in-house was made. Following additional communications and meetings that involved Juan Rada, IMD Director General, the two institutions agreed to have one more program at IMD (SMC-1) for a 1 week duration at the older, IMPACT period price of CHF 125,000 per week. After that, DSM planned to take the program in-house.

The discussions that began at this time, and will be addressed in later chapters, returned periodically and at times had a negative influence on the relationship between IMD and DSM. The conflict between the self-interest of the educational institution and the company, not to speak of the faculty, was a permanent source of irritation that could only be kept in check due to constant efforts of involved players on both sides.

Thus, DSM's SMC-1 began at IMD as scheduled in June 1991 delivered by the same faculty team that had been involved with the IMPACT program series. The role of this new program as part of DSM's transformation will be described in more details in Chap. 8.

DSM's decision to continue the ideas taught by IMD's IMPACT Program was just the first sign of a typical approach to new ideas. Once the "shock treatment" of the initial programs had been delivered, DSM wanted to continue the delivery of additional programs and not let things go dormant. The format to be chosen, namely a 1-week program to be delivered on an in-house basis was more sustainable in the long run. It signaled to the entire organization that the ideas coming from IMPACT were to be maintained and expanded to a wide array of participants, not just a chosen few at the top. That this mandate was to be entrusted to the IMPACT delivery team was only natural. That this working relationship should not be restricted to this new program series will be the focus of following chapters.

Developing Business Strategy Dialogues at DSM

5

I regard the Business Strategy Dialogues (BSDs) as one of the strongest cohesive factors within DSM. BSDs offer a joint language and frame of reference. As they were increasingly developed and refined within DSM, they provided discipline and rigor. They allowed the abandonment of the yearly planning cycle, giving us time for proper execution. In many other companies, the strategy process is too fragmented and driven only by superficial, directional statements

—Peter Elverding, interview, 2013.

1989 to 1990: Privatization and Its Effects

In 1989, DSM was privatized and became listed on the Amsterdam Stock Exchange (AEX), with the Dutch State selling 69 % of its shares in two steps.[1] The timing was impeccable: for the second year in a row, net sales surpassed the Dfl 10 billion mark, while for the first time in DSM's history, operating profit would rise above Dfl 1 billion and net profit totaled Dfl 1.38 billion. It was no wonder that the DSM shares were well absorbed by the financial markets. Whereas the first series of the DSM shares was priced at Dfl 108 in Spring 1989, by the Fall the second could already be priced at Dfl 125. Although DSM had always prided itself on being run 'like a private company,' Hans van Liemt, chairman of the Managing Board at the time, spoke honestly in a public interview in 1990 saying, "I confess that since we are publicly listed and the majority of our shares have come in private hands, we choose more sharply at DSM. We emphasize shorter term profitability more than in the past."[2] In his internal communication, Van Liemt was even clearer: "In the coming years we will have to execute a consistent dividend policy now that we are a

[1] The remaining 31 % was sold off by the Dutch State in 1996.

[2] "Beursnotering dwingt DSM tot scherper kiezen," *Het Financieele Dagblad*, 13 December 1990: 11.

J.-P. Jeannet, H. Schreuder, *From Coal to Biotech*,
DOI 10.1007/978-3-662-46299-7_5

listed company. This requires a balanced development of profitability, which is as urgent for us as the strategy itself and should really be part of the strategy. This used to be different. When DSM was still wholly owned by the State, the longer-term strategy could have priority above shorter-term matters. Our financing possibilities were also greater (cash flows from natural gas). Now we are publicly listed and we live, as it were, in a glass house."[3]

In order to prepare for the necessary choices, DSM had conducted a strategic review called *DSM 2000* in 1990. This strategic review (see summary in Chap. 1) concluded that DSM was in need of more leadership positions and would, therefore, have to focus on a limited number of core areas with critical mass. Nevertheless, the company had decided to go forward with substantially all of its activities in Base Materials, Performance Materials, Plastic Processing, Base Chemicals, Fine Chemicals, Resins and Energy. The Managing Board (MB) had explicitly concluded that, "the opportunities for improving DSM's profile by large divestments are exhausted or even undesirable." However, the financial projections did not show a rosy future. Costs were foreseen to rise, among other factors, due to a number of expensive, technology-push type projects that would only become profitable in the longer term (such as: Stanyl, Dyneema, Aspartame, SMA). Operating results for 1991 and 1992 were forecasted to decrease, both for these internal reasons, and for external ones (rising feedstock costs, for example). Now DSM had to become self-financing, it was not acceptable that four divisions, and nine additional business units, projected in their strategic plans that they would not conform to the corporate norm of a 15 % ROI. As a result, the MB announced that it would review all plans from the perspective of "the relationship between profitability and ambition." It further communicated that the organization would need to be reviewed. Did the chosen product-market combinations require a different organizational grouping? Were the various layers of management sufficiently effective and did they generate value added? What about the overhead of the different corporate units? In short: the strategic review 'DSM 2000' was to be followed by the organizational review 'Concern 2000.' This name was a clever play of words—'concern' is the Dutch term for corporation but the MB also wanted to signal its concern about the organization and its future financial performance.

'Concern 2000'

In 1991, the organizational review, 'Concern 2000' was kicked off. DSM had contracted McKinsey and Company for project support and execution. Internally, a 'Concern 2000 Implementation' team was established with Willem Klaassen as chairman and Director 'Concern 2000.' Peter Elverding, who served as director Corporate Personnel and Organization at the time, was an important driving force

[3] Nawoord van de Raad van Bestuur bij Strategie *DSM 2000*, Extra Edition Management Letter, October 1990. This quote and the following ones were translated by the authors from Dutch.

behind the project. The overall theme of 'Concern 2000' was to 'decentralize, unless...' (there is a very good reason not to do so). This theme was chosen for a number of reasons, including:

- A widely perceived need to increase the decision power of the businesses, in order to bring decision-making closer to market
- The feeling that DSM had grown an unwieldy bureaucracy and overhead structure over time, with 8,000 people in corporate staffs and services within a total number of about 25,000 employees
- The urgency to bring costs down in a drive to counter the pressure on profitability

McKinsey quickly produced a number of insightful analyses.[4] One revealing example pertained to the large differences between businesses in the 'home base' of South Limburg and those outside of this area. In South Limburg, corporate staff and service units were responsible for Personnel, R&D, Maintenance, Accounting and Control, Information Management, Safety, Procurement, Engineering, Environment and Health, Logistics and Utilities. Consequently, the autonomy of the business units located in the South Limburg area was, for a large part, constrained to operations, since their decision authority was restricted to 30–40 % of all activities performed by the business units. The contrast with business units outside of the South Limburg area was striking (see Fig. 5.1). Looking back, Peter Elverding observes: "Decentralization unless... implied that we wanted to enable the integral responsibility of the businesses for the short-term and the long-term. It was clear that this required the streamlining of staffs and services, particularly in the Limburg area. Historically, many of these staffs and services were located in the Limburg B.V., which had a strong local orientation. The businesses, however, had also grown staffs and services leading to significant duplication. It was our aim to clarify the value added by staffs and services to their users, either the businesses or the corporation. The expectation was that significant numbers could be involved in this streamlining process. In order to prevent subsequent unduly growth of the overhead again, we wanted to install a contracting system based on Performance measurement."

Given the interdependent nature of many of DSM's activities at the time (see Fig. 1.10), synergy management remained necessary to optimize the company's performance. These considerations led to an overall structure of the 'Concern 2000' project, comprised of four principal workstreams:

---

[4] For the description in this chapter how BSDs grew out of the *Concern 2000* project on performance measurement, the authors are indebted to Prof. Dr. Mariëlle Heijltjes who documented this process in her case studies, "Performance measurement at DSM: Linking the company's long term strategy with its short term actions" and "An Alternative Proposal to Performance Measurement" (1996).

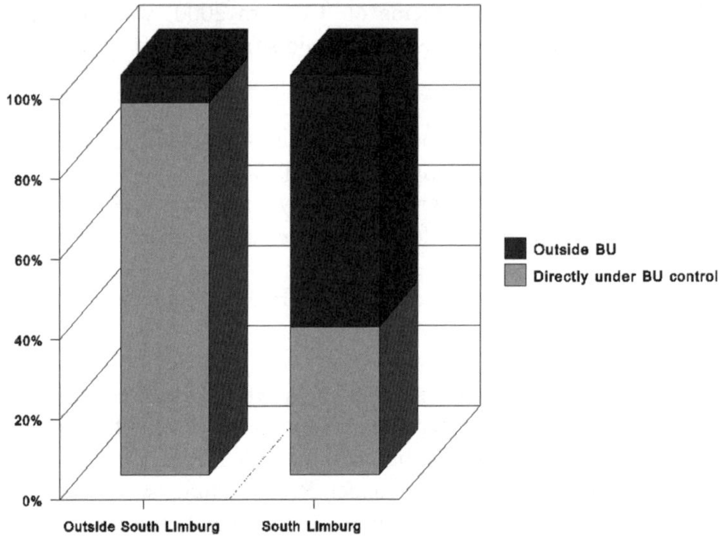

Fig. 5.1 Distribution of personnel involved in BU decisions

1. **Empowering the line**: decentralization of responsibility and authority for short- as well as long-term performance to business unit (BU) managers
2. **Adding value through staff and services**: linkage of staff and services to direct users (the BUs)
3. **Measuring performance and contracting**: development of a consistent set of controls which match the new, decentralized structure
4. **Realizing synergies**

The original expectation was that 1,200 employees would be affected by decentralization, another 1,000–1,500 by outsourcing and, finally, some 500 jobs would be lost overall. All in all, however, the total number of DSM employees during the period 1991–1995 went from 24,800 to 17,600.[5] This higher number was partly the result of the 'delayering' of the company structure, which had been enabled by 'Concern 2000.' After the decentralization of staffs and services, and the empowerment of business units in 1991–1993, the company executed a follow-up project 'Check-up Concern 2000' in 1994–1995, in which the remaining divisional structure was reviewed. DSM came to the conclusion that it could collapse the two layers (nine divisions and 26 business units) into one (14 business groups, albeit with four still containing BUs; see Fig. 1.13). The company structure with Business Groups as the main building blocks, corporate staffs serving the Managing Board and corporate services steered by the business groups, has essentially survived until today.

[5] See "DSM: chemie en polymeren (1930–2000)" on http://www.chemelot.nl/ (accessed 1 Dec 2014).

Table 5.1 Development of DSM net sales and net result 1989–1993 (Dfl million)

	1989	1990	1991	1992	1993
Net sales	10,772	10,164	9,347	8,907	8,040
Net result	1,380	859	516	224	−118

Source: DSM, Annual Report 1994

From this overview, it is clear that the years 1991–1995 represented a period of upheaval for DSM, symbolized by the abandonment of the familiar organizational structures and the significant reduction of the workforce. The uncertainty was further exacerbated by the development of results: sales had decreased year-on-year from the record level of Dfl 10.7 billion in 1989 to barely Dfl 8 billion in 1993. Net results had declined even more dramatically: from the record Dfl 1,380 million in 1989 to Dfl 118 million negative in 1993 (see Table 5.1). The main reason for this was the severe cyclicality experienced, simultaneously, in the Petrochemicals and Industrial Chemicals divisions. As a result of these financial developments, DSM had to lower its dividend proposal from Dfl 4.00 per share in 1992 to Dfl 1.50 in 1993. In its communication to shareholders, the company added that this proposal was possible thanks to its strong balance sheet position, meaning that dividends would be paid out of reserves.

The First Attempt at Performance Measurement: Shareholder Value

On 1 October 1991, DSM's Managing Board appointed Gert Koolman, director of Corporate Control and Accounting, as the project manager for the 'Concern 2000' workstream on the topic of 'measuring performance and contracting.' Following the McKinsey suggestions, the project's objective was twofold[6]: (1) that the value creating factors which could be influenced by the division, or BU, needed to be identified and, (2) that it was necessary to adapt the management reporting system in such a way that; (a) management attention was focused on the most important factors that drive value creation per business, (b) performance of staff and services could be measured and, (c) reporting would be simplified. McKinsey organized a workshop to present the approach they recommended DSM adopt. Basically, this approach later became known as the 'shareholder value' perspective and methodology.[7] The McKinsey meeting agenda focused on how DSM could implement a value-creation approach to 'performance measurement,' answering three questions:

[6] Based largely on "Performance measurement at DSM: Linking the company's long term strategy with its short term actions" (Heijltjes 1996).

[7] This shareholder value approach had just been published in the now well-known book *Valuation: Measuring and Managing the Value of Companies* by T. E. Copeland, T. M. Koller and J. Murrin (NY, 1990).

- Why should DSM focus on value
- How should value be measured
- What is a value creation mentality

McKinsey argued that DSM's recent stock market listing implied a responsibility to shareholders to maximize the value of all the businesses within the company, which should strive to earn for its shareholders a return above the cost of capital—the return the owners could earn elsewhere with investments of similar risk. Value should be measured by the use of free cash flows rather than accounting-based figures. Technically, this boiled down to a Discounted Cash Flow (DCF)—analysis, as already used for capital investment projects, now applied to the entire business. Essentially, a business was seen as a collection of such projects. A value creation mentality could then be instilled in the business by breaking down the components of free cash flow into 'key value drivers' and allocating the responsibility for these key value drivers within the business (see an example of the resulting 'value driver tree' in Figs. 5.2 and 5.3).

The McKinsey presentation met with a mixed reception in the DSM audience. Gert Koolman, the project leader, was intrigued by the possible opportunity to 'create an artificial stock market' for DSM businesses by simulating their value. Others, however, doubted whether DSM should follow this route. The objections included:

- DSM's experience with the reliability of cash flow forecasts as a basis for determining value
- The perception that this approach was tactical-operational rather than strategic
- The feeling that performance measurement and evaluation should encompass more than just financial numbers
- The absence of convincing (European) examples where the approach was put into practice with good effect

What perhaps also played a role was the less-than-harmonious relationship between Gert Koolman (director of Corporate Control and Accounting) and Paul van der Grinten (director of Corporate Planning and Development). The proposal of McKinsey was seen as too financially one-sided. In DSM's experience, strategic and technological factors were just as important to determine success. Most likely, it was not helpful that a financially-oriented approach was proposed by a project leader who was responsible for the financial discipline. In any case, DSM decided to abandon this approach[8] and to install a more balanced project team with a 'neutral' chairman in January 1992.

[8] It was revived a number of years later when Boston Consulting Group proposed using a Cash-Flow Return on Investment (CFROI) which DSM adopted for a decade until a new CFO (Rolf-Dieter Schwalb) decided to return to the more traditional financial measures like Return on Capital Employed (ROCE).

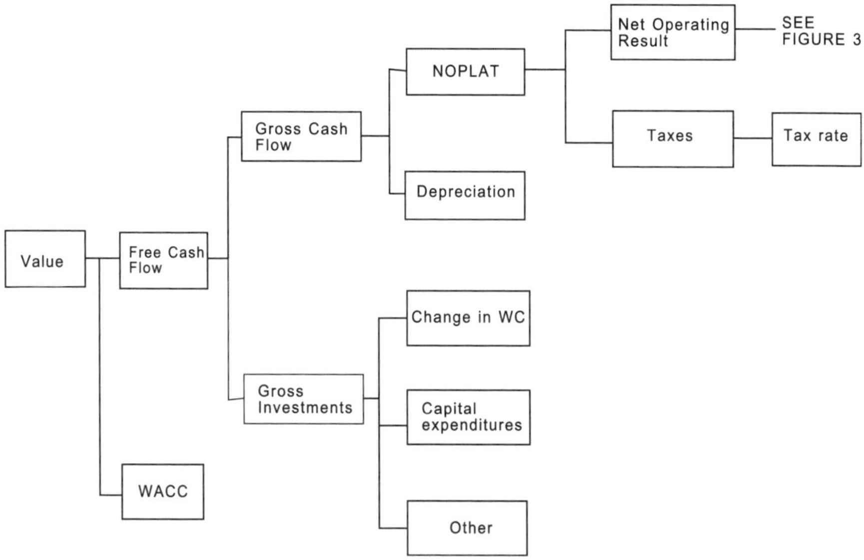

Fig. 5.2 The value driver tree. *Source*: M. Heijltjes, "Performance measurement at DSM: Linking the company's long term strategy with its short term actions", Case Study, 1996

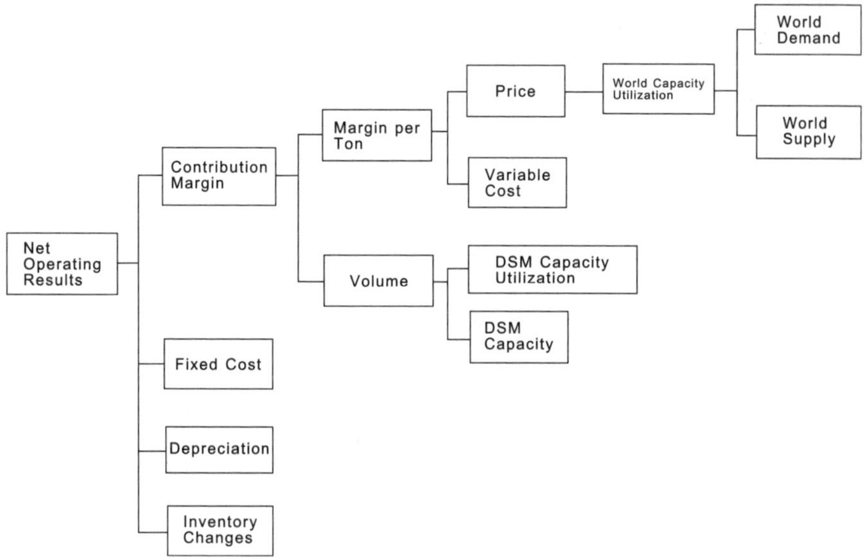

Fig. 5.3 Value driver tree: further breakdown of net operating result

Intermezzo: Hein Schreuder Joins DSM

On 1 September 1991, (co-author) Hein Schreuder joined DSM. He had been approached earlier that year, while enjoying a 'sabbatical' after having helped to create the new Faculty of Economics and Business at the University of Maastricht (1984–1991). Having always thought he would enter the business world, Schreuder had 'caught the academic virus' while studying Business Economics at the Erasmus University in Rotterdam. Hence, he had first embarked on an academic career becoming director of a research institute at the Free University of Amsterdam, where he completed his Ph.D.[9] At the research institute, he was responsible for a wide range of business research projects with a practical orientation, while academically he was most attracted to the emerging fields of 'social accounting and reporting,' as well as 'economic theories of organization.' The latter field included the new (industrial-)economic approaches to strategy, as exemplified by Michael Porter in the 1980s. At the University of Maastricht, Schreuder developed this interest further, eventually becoming the Professor of Business Economics, Strategy and Organization. During his sabbatical year, 1990–1991, he wrote, with Sytse Douma, the book *Economic Approaches to Organizations* (first edition 1991; fifth edition 2013). He also served as a visiting professor at Harvard Business School as a guest of Professor Robert Kaplan, who was at that time developing activity-based costing, as well as the balanced scorecard. At Harvard, he interacted intensely with both the Accounting and the Strategy faculty.

Schreuder joined DSM as member of the management team in the Polymers division and was responsible for Planning and Development, reporting to Just Fransen van de Putte who had been appointed as divisional president. As Peter Elverding recalls, Schreuder was specifically recruited into DSM as a potential successor to Professor Paul van der Grinten, then the director of Corporate Planning and Development: "But succeeding Paul van der Grinten, who had left a strong personal mark on DSM's strategy, would not be easy. In any case, Schreuder's first task would be to get to know DSM's businesses" (Elverding). There was an urgency in becoming familiar with the Polymers division: DSM's results were sliding quickly, as a result of supply-driven overcapacity. This had caught the division by surprise, since its business intelligence had been primarily focused on Europe, with some attention given to the US. In the early 1990s, however, Asian producers joined the fray: the South Korean *chaebols*[10] all decided to integrate backward from automobile and electronics production into hydrocarbons and polymers. As a result, capacity utilization rates plummeted all over the world. This also caused severe

[9] His Ph.D. dissertation dealt with Corporate Social Responsibility and Corporate Social Reporting (*Maatschappelijke Verantwoordelijkheid en Maatschappelijke Berichtgeving van Ondernemingen*, Leiden, Stenfert Kroese, 1981), which perfectly matched DSM's convictions about People-Planet-Profit and Sustainability. In the dissertation an indicator-approach to Corporate Social Reporting was proposed.

[10] Although there is no direct translation of the term *chaebols* in English, the essence is a conglomerate of businesses in Korea, usually owned by a single family.

margin pressure at DSM. In addition, the Polymers division, home to two of DSM's expensive technology-push projects (Stanyl and SMA), had just executed a swap with AKZO, bringing in a new Engineering Plastics unit, and was one of the focal points of attention of the 'Concern 2000' project. Schreuder's plate was more than full. It was, therefore, with mixed feelings that he received the invitation to contribute to DSM's second attempt to devise a new system of performance measurement.

The Second Attempt at Performance Measurement: Performance Indicators Derived from Business Strategy Dialogues

There were two leading questions for a new working group set up to elaborate this element of 'Concern 2000': "Is it possible to decentralize strategy?" and "Is it possible to link performance measurement to decentralized business strategy?". This time, the working group had a more balanced composition with these key members: Martin Aertsen (Corporate Control and Accounting), Paul van Eijsden (Technology and Corporate Planning) and Hein Schreuder (Polymers division) and headed up by a 'neutral' chairman (Theo Vermeegen, head of DSM Consultancy and member of the 'Concern 2000' implementation team). What had been initiated in October 1991 as a project to be carried out under the management of Corporate Control and Accounting, had now been transformed into a project with a broader scope emphasizing strategic, as well as control, issues.[11] The working group was appointed in January 1992 and was expected to present a proposal to the Managing Board in June, which the members of the group did not regard as being a very generous time frame.

The working group quickly converged around the idea of using, as much as possible, methodologies that already existed within DSM. Hence, not introducing new techniques in the financial area and maximally using the IMPACT concepts in the marketing field. However, the implementation of IMPACT had, until 1992, been non-committal. Just Fransen van de Putte had organized the Marketing Day because he observed that, "marketing planning had become a rain dance: filling out forms." He wanted to re-invigorate marketing discussions. As Schreuder's new boss, he had invited the latter to attend the Marketing Day in September 1991, just after his arrival at DSM. This was a nice co-incidence, since Schreuder thus had the opportunity to hear the presentations from IMD's Jeannet on 'IMPACT Revisited' and 'Managing the Strategy Dialogue.' Colleagues Aertsen and Van Eijsden had followed the IMPACT courses. Therefore, it wasn't difficult for all three of them to agree to take the IMPACT marketing kernel and develop this into a full-fledged strategy development approach. Similarly, Jeannet's plea for Strategy Dialogues

[11] Based on *An Alternative Proposal to Performance Measurement* (Heijltjes 1996) and on H. Schreuder, "Strategic Monitoring at a Chemical Company," *Long Range Planning*, Vol. 28, No. 6, 1995: 69–77.

had resonated with Schreuder, who had led a number of 'participative' strategy exercises as a Strategy professor, including with Curver, a DSM subsidiary. But, the working group felt that significant modifications were necessary to make the approach applicable to DSM and make it a suitable basis for performance measurement.

The In-House Proposal Presented to the Managing Board

All members of the working group recall the arduous work to come up with a proposal that would fit DSM's specific needs. There were numerous iterations and the related discussions were not without tension, despite amicable relationships. There were five areas that were the particular foci of both attention and contention:

1. **The functions**. The previous attempt at performance measurement had been dominated by the financial function, while IMPACT originated from the marketing function. A true strategic dialogue would, however, have to include all relevant functions. But how to determine the relevance of functions? Are all functions equal or are some more equal than others? The latter conviction existed, for instance, in the Research and Technology (R&T) community and not without reason given the importance of technology for the strategic successes of DSM (summarized in Chap. 1). The R&T community had probably felt underrepresented in the previous discussion but they now had an advocate in the person of Paul van Eijsden. To the surprise of other members of the working group, Van Eijsden produced a competing concept to the Business Strategy Development (BSD): a Business Technology Analysis (BTA). The concept had been worked out with the support of Arthur D. Little, a consultancy firm with a specialization in technology. Van Eijsden argued that strategic success for DSM's businesses depended so greatly on their technology position, that the BTA—and not the BSD—should be the leading instrument for strategy development.

   This challenge led to heated discussions in the working group where the majority view was that the BSD should lead and the BTA should provide important input to strategy. Van Eijsden, however, put up a good fight for his dissenting view. The Chairman, Theo Vermeegen, remembers his late-night discussions at Van Eijsden's home to "keep him aboard." In the end, however, the proposal to the Managing Board regarded the Business Strategy Dialogue as the overarching process and approach, to which all relevant functions should contribute. Relevance was to be determined by the strategic issues at hand: BSDs were not to be pre-formatted (also to avoid that the process degenerate into 'filling out forms') but should be driven by the prime strategic issues to be determined up-front.

   For the functions this was a clear signal to prepare their potential contribution to BSDs. Following the example of the Technology function, which had prepared the BTA, other functions followed suit. As will be covered in the next chapter, many departments developed their own functional instruments. However, all these instruments were clearly coupled to the BSD, either for providing input (Marketing, Emerging Technologies, etc.) or translating the BSD outcomes into functional implementation (Communications, M&A, etc.). All were mentioned in the *Guide to Business Strategy and (long term) Performance Measurement*, the booklet that was developed by the working group to outline the BSD approach and which was regularly updated to incorporate DSM's learnings. Through this process, the BSD became the clear integration mechanism for the functions to contribute to the successful development of DSM's businesses.

2. **Strategic concepts**. The working group wanted to retain as many concepts, which had been previously adopted by DSM, as possible. In order to develop the 'business strategy dialogue' into a true strategic exercise, however, a number of new concepts had to be introduced. We will mention two such concepts here, which played a particularly pivotal role in the final design of the BSD:
   a. *The 'Strategic Group' concept.* In the IMPACT methodology, a good deal of attention was directed toward industry analysis. The results of this analysis were then captured in the formulation of Industry Key Success Factors (KSFs).

   With his background in Industrial Economics, Schreuder felt that this approach was too general to produce really sharp KSFs, clearly expressing the factors on which the business had to excel. Generally, in any industry, there are a variety of ways to compete. Michael Porter had provided an early example by making a distinction in his writing and teaching between low-cost competition versus differentiation.[12] These two competitive strategies implied very different KSFs. Such insights led to a vast amount of literature on the existence of different 'strategic groups' in almost all industries and distinguished by very different dimensions like technology, global versus local, market segments covered, economies of scale and scope, etc. Schreuder had just co-authored an overview of the research on such strategic groups[13] and was convinced that the adoption of this strategic tool would enable DSM businesses to define their competitive strategy more sharply. This was important because the working group wanted to base performance measurement on 'performance indicators' derived from the KSFs. Therefore, these KSFs had to be defined as precisely as possible. The working group came to view that the KSFs had to be based on the strategic group in which the business chose to compete. These KSFs were further to be distinguished into the following:

[12] Michael Porter was professor at Harvard Business School. His book *Competitive Strategy* (NY: The Free Press, 1980) was the leading textbook at the time on applying Industrial Economics to Business Strategy.

[13] See P. van Cayseele and H. Schreuder, "Strategische Groepen: Een Overzicht van Het Onderzoek," *Maandblad voor Accountancy en Bedrijfseconomie*, Vol. 63, No. 11, 1989.

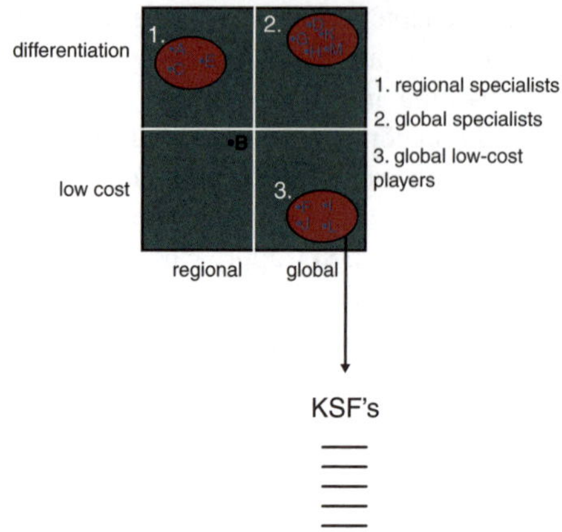

Fig. 5.4 Strategic groups

- Qualifiers = entry tickets to compete in a strategic group, and
- Differentiators = those KSFs that give you a competitive advantage if you are performing better than the relevant competition

The more precisely qualifiers and, particularly, differentiators could be identified, the sharper the competitive strategy could be defined (and, therefore, the performance measured).

Identifying the strategic groups in your industry became the summary of the external analyses in a BSD (see Fig. 5.4). If done well, it provided a very useful overview of the competitive landscape for any business. Moreover, it provided the basis for a sharp definition of KSFs. For example, there would be very different KSFs for the global low-cost players than for the group of regional specialists. Strategic group analysis often proved to be the turning point of a BSD. Jos Wassen, who would become one of DSM's most experienced BSD facilitators, observed: "Strategic group analysis was more of an art than a science. The BSD team would often wrestle with it for considerable time, trying out different drivers of competition to find the right dimensions of the competitive map. But when the 'right' map had been constructed, it was as if all pieces of the puzzle came together."

b. *Introduction of a 'Process' view.* As mentioned above, it was a challenge for the working group to give all relevant functions their 'proper place' in the BSDs. Initially, many businesses would want to list their functional strengths and weaknesses. Strengths and weaknesses are never absolute, however: they are relative to the strategic mission that a business would aspire to. Moreover, lists of functional strengths and weaknesses treated the functions in isolation, whereas identified 'strategic gaps' would hardly ever have a mono-functional cause.

One effective solution had been to design the BSD as issue-driven. The place of the functions in the BSD process could then be derived from their contribution to the resolution of the main strategic issues. However, this still did not provide a

Fig. 5.5 Process concepts

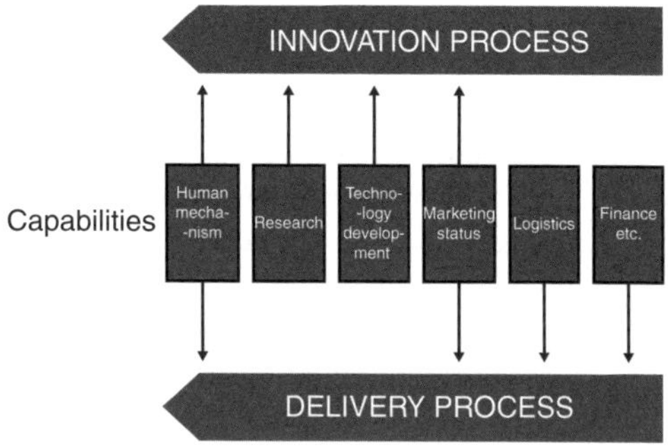

structured approach to the functional contributions to business strategy. This structured approach evolved when a 'process perspective' was adopted. It was recognized that DSM businesses generically operated by utilizing two main business processes:

- The 'innovation process' (or, prospect-to-order)
- The 'delivery process' (or, order-to-cash)

Adoption of this process perspective allowed BSD teams to determine the contribution of the various functions to these overall business processes. Furthermore, it led to the recognition that the business capabilities (or competences, whether distinctive or not) were most often not due to any particular function, but instead to the interplay and complementarity of various functions, as these played out in the innovation and delivery processes.[14] Quite often, the reverse also held true: the ineffectiveness of any process could be due to the insufficient quality of any particular functional contribution, but more often could be traced to insufficient cooperation of functions from the process point-of-view. Hence, the process perspective contributed to the breakdown of 'functional silos' within DSM (see the discussion of the ABS pilot later in this chapter).

3. **Strategic logic and flow**. The IMPACT methodology had at its core the '5 Cs' analysis: analyzing and understanding in depth the Customer, Competition, Costs, Company and Context of a business, together representing 'the five elements of market knowledge' (as presented in Chap. 4). While all of these elements were, of course, major pieces of a BSD, the working group felt it was necessary to bring more strategic logic and flow to the analysis. In the IMD classroom many IMPACT participants had observed how Jeannet had been capable of bringing the '5 Cs' analysis to logical conclusions. As Marthijn Jansen remembers: "Jeannet acknowledged the various contributions made by

[14] Again, there is a link to the strategy literature, in particular on the 'resource-based view of strategy, dynamic capabilities and business models.' See: S. Douma and H. Schreuder, *Economic Approaches to Organizations*, Chapters 9–12, 5th edition (London: Pearson, 2013).

IMPACT participants by noting them on a seemingly random spot of a gigantic whiteboard. Only in the end could we see that it all fitted magically like a puzzle." However, when DSM teams were supposed to go through a BSD exercise, they could not be relied upon to bring disparate analyses of the '5 Cs' to similarly logical conclusions.

The working group decided to enforce a certain flow of a BSD along the following lines with specific DSM terminology for each step:

a. *Business characterization*: the requirement that the business should first invest time in gathering the necessary data for a BSD and its main issues. Pilots showed that businesses were often not up-to-par with their business intelligence and needed time to collect the necessary data. The working group developed a first draft of a 'Strategic Data Checklist' to assist businesses in evaluating the quality of their existing business intelligence and identify any gaps that need to be filled before meaningful discussions could take place.
b. *Macro analysis*: the prescription that a BSD would commence with external analysis by 'looking outside' and analyzing the industry 'from the outside in.' This was necessary to counter the natural inclination of the business to start with its own situation, and ideas, and to proceed to 'from the inside out.' The external analysis should be concluded with a strategic grouping, leading to specific KSFs.
c. *Micro analysis*: only then should the business conduct internal analysis, look 'from the inside out,' apply the process perspective and come up with their capabilities.
d. *Strategic choice*: here the working group adopted the classical strategic logic of confronting—often with some iterations—the results of the external analysis with the internal analysis. Within the DSM BSD-methodology this was enabled by sharp definitions of (external) KSFs and (internal) capabilities. Essentially, this boils down to a 'brutally honest' confrontation between:

   - What does it take to compete (in a chosen strategic group)?: the KSFs
   - Do we have what it takes?: the (process) capabilities

   The final strategic choice of the business can be formulated in a 'strategic mission,' expressing both:

   - To which strategic group we will belong, and
   - Our ambition level: the aspired place within that group

   Examples of strategic missions include: being a top-three global low-cost player, an innovation leader in second generation biofuels, or the first choice supplier of the XYZ industry.

   The next section will address how the strategic choice—formulated in a strategic mission—provided the basis for performance measurement, the original task of the 'Concern 2000' working party (for a summary overview of the BSD steps thus far, see Fig. 5.6).

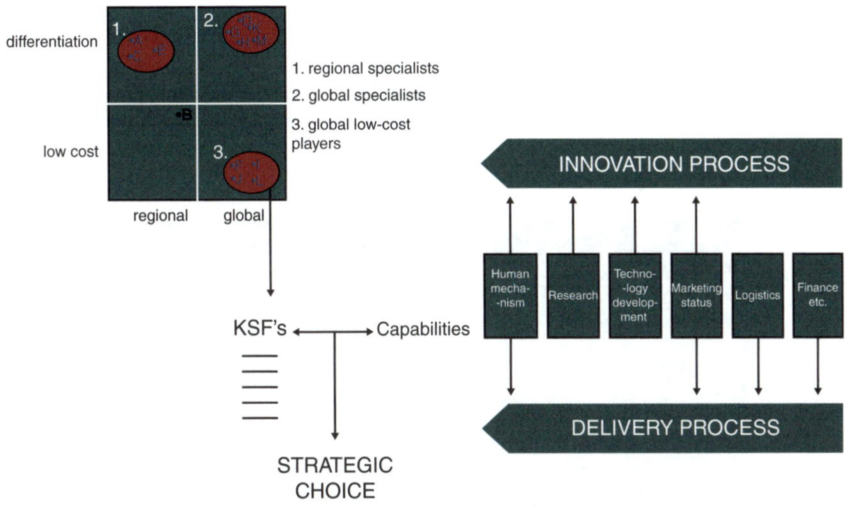

Fig. 5.6 Strategic choice

4. **Performance measurement**. Within the context of 'Concern 2000', the working group's main task was to come up with a system for the workstream named, 'measuring performance and contracting.' This was defined by McKinsey as "The development of a consistent set of controls which match the new, decentralized structure." The working group felt strongly, however, that any proposal should primarily reflect the main aim of 'Concern 2000': the empowerment of the business. Hence, the objective was to propose a performance measurement system of which the businesses could feel the true owner. It was determined that the system should also reflect the wide variety of businesses within DSM at the time: it should be possible to tailor the system to the specific needs of such different businesses. Hence, the working party did not work toward a 'consistent set of controls' from a corporate perspective, which implied standardization and uniformity. On the contrary, it emphasized consistency with the specificities of the business strategies evolving from the BSDs (for a summary of the proposed performance measurement format, see Fig. 5.7).

   The first step is to decompose the Strategic Mission into specific objectives. For instance, if the mission is to 'Gain market share through increased focus and low costs,' then it could be translated into specific objectives, such as:

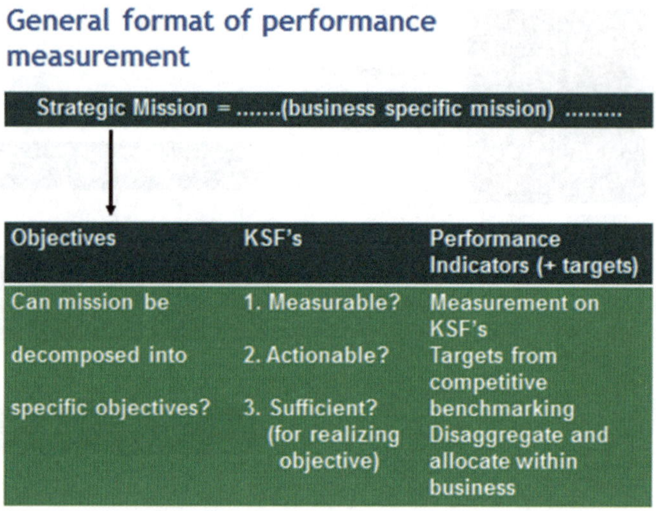

Fig. 5.7 Performance measurement

- Market share
- Focus on:
  - key products and applications
  - key areas
  - key customers
- Low cost

Subsequently, these specific objectives are to be translated into KSFs and KPIs. The main requirement for the KSFs is, of course, that the selected set of KSFs corresponds well with the chosen strategic mission; for example, there should be a reasonable expectation that the mission will be realized if the KSFs are met. Furthermore, KSFs should be measurable and actionable. If they are actionable it will also be possible to assign an action owner. An example of how a low cost KSF can be broken down into specific components with performance indicators assigned to various levels of responsibility is shown in Fig. 5.8. While the Business Group manager is responsible for the overall costs per tonne, the component of manufacturing costs can be broken down to the level of plant managers, production managers and even day foremen. A similar 'performance indicator tree' can be developed for the other cost components. Needless to say, such a clear insight into the composition of costs and a corresponding assignment of responsibilities contributes demonstrably toward achieving the objectives.

This can also be seen in Fig. 5.9—a translation of the objective of a business to achieve more focus in its product and application development. The example

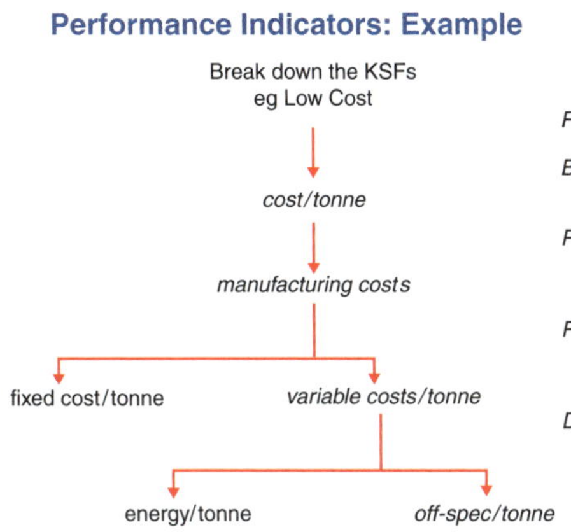

Fig. 5.8 Breakdown of a KSF (Low Cost)

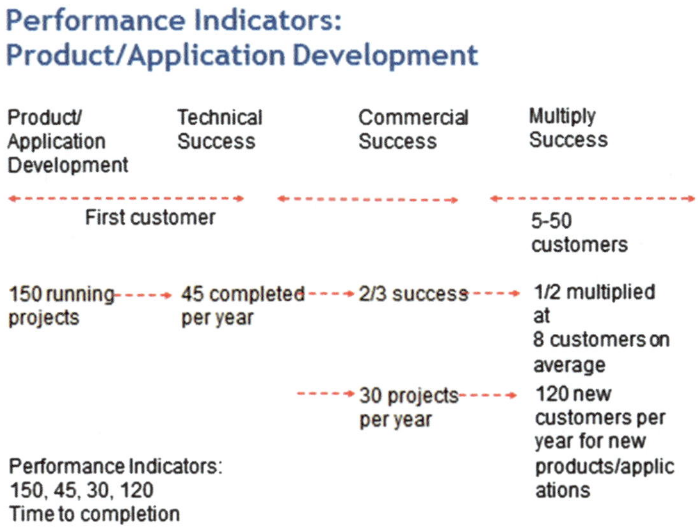

Fig. 5.9 Performance indicators for product/application development

comes from the first BSD of Stanyl, a new engineering plastic (Polyamide 4.6) developed by DSM. Stanyl could potentially be used in a multitude of applications. The business was pursuing many of these, in a rather scattered approach, with the intent of quickly generating cash flows for this product development. The BSD showed that there was not enough co-ordination across the stages of the product development pipeline to potentially focus on 'big wins.' For example, technical people were focused on achieving technical successes without sufficient input from the commercial people about what the potential customer base for these technical successes would be.

As an outcome of the BSD, the decision was made to focus on projects where technical and commercial successes could be multiplied to a sufficiently wide range of customers. In this stylized example, the business would focus on 150 projects, of which at least 45 per year would be regarded a 'technical success' by the customer; two-thirds of those successes were expected to result in commercial orders from that first customer. Half of those 30 commercial successes should then be replicable for eight customers, on average, leading to 120 new customers per year. Combined with time indicators, such as average lead times per development stage, this performance measurement system allows effective management and control by the business.

As the examples make clear, the working group opted for a decentralized 'strategic monitoring' system next to the standard financial measures. The proposal was to enable the business to primarily monitor the success of its own strategy execution. The main indicators could then also be used to report to corporate, next to the regular financial reporting. Only later, when the system had been sufficiently tested and adopted within DSM, were both reporting sets integrated into one 'strategic value contract', which covered the strategic KSFs and KPIs, as well as the financial 'promise for performance.'

5. **Facilitators and Challengers**. In the 1980s and early 1990s, DSM had hosted a number of consultancy firms. While they had been very useful in gaining insight into best practices outside the company, a drawback had been that various approaches and terminologies existed next to one another. It may also have been that an over-reliance had developed on outside support. In any case, DSM resolved to use this opportunity to not only adopt its own systems of strategy development and performance measurement, but also to train an internal cadre of people who could support these processes at the business level. The working group proposal was to distinguish the following roles:

   - Facilitators: people trained to support the business in ensuring the quality of the BSD process
   - Challengers: people invited to provide an 'outside-in' perspective

   The facilitator role was especially demanding because the BSD process was intended to be a genuine dialogue. This implied that hierarchical relationships needed to be 'suspended' in order to allow equal participation by the members of the BSD team. To foster this participative atmosphere, the facilitator was encouraged to introduce himself by saying: "We are all equal here, but when it comes to the BSD process, I am more equal than others."

   This amounted to quite a culture shock within DSM, which was still evolving from the more centralized and hierarchical company that it had been in the past. In order to enable the facilitator to concentrate fully on the process, the challenger was invited to focus on the content of the discussion, in particular on any 'taken-for-granted assumptions' or 'dominant logics' prevailing within the business. Thus, a typical introduction by the challenger could be: "I am here to ask the stupid questions!" In the DSM experience, it was not productive to combine these two roles: a challenge on content could often be construed as taking a stance. If a facilitator was seen as having his own position, this could undermine his process guidance role.[15]

June 1992: The Managing Board

In the January 1992 Managing Board meeting, it had been decided to grant the new working group the time until June to come up with an alternative proposal to decentralize strategy and to base performance measurement on such decentralized strategies. The working group decided to work along two lines:

1. The development of an overall approach to BSDs that fitted DSM's needs
2. The execution of a pilot project to try out these new ideas, simultaneously, in a real business setting within DSM

The working group also recognized that it was fine to train DSM executives in this new BSD approach, but that it was equally important that the Managing Board became familiar with the approach itself. As the saying goes, "the bottleneck is at the top of the bottle." It would be potentially disastrous if business came up to the Managing Board for a strategy discussion along these new lines only to find them resorting to traditional questions and discussions with which they had become familiar over time. Therefore, the working group proposed to train the Board prior to the first BSD discussion and, to its credit, they accepted this proposal. On 1 June 1992 the Board training was held, also in preparation for the first BSD discussion, which was scheduled for the next day. The business unit ASP[16] had offered to act as a guinea pig and to be the pilot project.

The overall process of Strategy Development and Performance Measurement as proposed by the working group is summarized in Fig. 5.10. Some salient features include:

- The recommendation to invest sufficient time to prepare for a BSD. The expectation was that the businesses would often not have the required data readily available. The preparation time also allowed the execution of a market study, benchmarking exercise and/or a Business Technology Analysis (BTA) if these were deemed essential for addressing the strategic issues.

[15] What did happen occasionally was that two people would take turns at fulfilling these two roles. We use only the male gender in the text, because the first generations of facilitators and challengers were indeed all male.

[16] The Business unit ASP consisted of three products: ABS, SMA and PC (Polycarbonate).

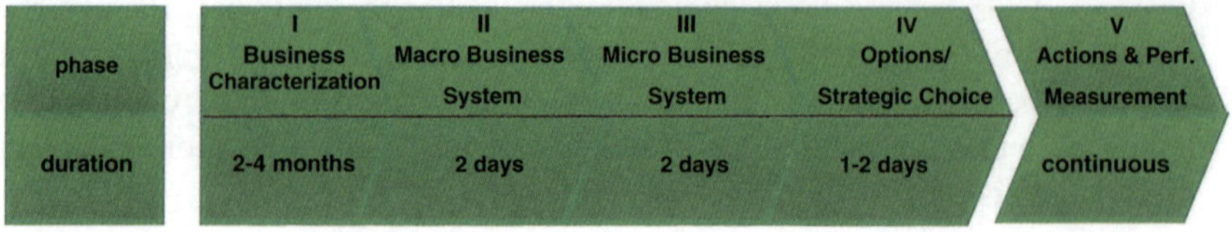

Fig. 5.10 The strategy development process and performance measurement

- The BSD itself was split into three phases: external (macro) analysis, internal (micro) analysis and options with strategic choice. There would be several weeks between these rounds, again allowing sufficient preparation. Each segment would typically consist of two full days of intense, off-site discussions.
- The BSD would be finished with the strategic choice, to be presented to the Managing Board for approval, together with a preliminary set of performance indicators to monitor strategic progress. Detailed performance measurement and strategic action planning was then left to the business to complete and to agree with its particular Board Delegate at a later point in time.[17]
- All in all, the process could take about 6 months to complete—a considerable amount of time. On the other hand, once completed the focus could be entirely on execution until the business felt that a next BSD was in order.[18]

On 1 June, the Managing Board willingly engaged in a discussion of this approach with Jeannet, Koolman and Schreuder. While there was certainly a positive attitude toward the proposals, the Board kept quiet on the question whether DSM would adopt the BSD approach but Board members were eager to discuss the results of the first pilot project (ABS) the next day. Some doubts remained, as Simon de Bree explained: "In those days, DSM had a tendency to develop many things in-house, even if perfectly acceptable solutions were available on the market. An example were the information systems, where we had a very large department working on systems that turned out to be cumbersome and costly, whereas better alternatives could have been bought from outside suppliers. I was a bit afraid that these proposals would work in the same direction. So, I decided to give it the benefit

[17] It was not unusual that this follow-through was less than seamless for businesses, which just came out of intense discussions and were glad that their strategic mission had been approved. Later, the BSD was to be finalized by the Strategic Value Contract, which also served as a very useful device to summarize the main elements of the BSD (see Chap. 7).

[18] The average frequency within DSM turned out to be every 3 years or so.

of the doubt and allow further development, but to keep my ears closely on the ground to hear whether our internal users were happy."

ABS as a Pilot Project

The polymer ABS is a terpolymer of acrylonitrile, butadiene and styrene. Compared to more commodity-type polymers, like polyethylene and polypropylene, it is more expensive to produce. However, for certain applications it is a very functional material, due to its properties like impact and heat resistance, toughness, colorability (gloss) and electrical insulation. It is widely used in applications where these functional properties are essential, but it is always under attack from lower-cost polymers trying to upgrade into these higher-margin applications. ABS was mentioned in Chap. 3 when Simon de Bree recalled an anecdote of DSM trying to convince Lego to use its ABS for the famous Lego building bricks. DSM had started ABS production in 1974 by taking a technology license from Japan Synthetic Rubber (JSR). The decision to enter ABS was probably driven to a large extent by DSM's desire to diversify, as well as the fact that it produced the feedstocks in-house (see Figs. 1.4 and 1.10).[19] In terms of the markets to be served with this material, DSM was often a novice, as illustrated by the Lego anecdote. Nevertheless, it had built up a credible market position over the years, often serving demanding customers with special grades. DSM had also developed a special competence in coloring. Production of ABS for the market occurred in two steps: (1) the production of the polymer and (2) a 'compounding' step in which additives and colors were blended with the polymer. At DSM the compounding step took place in a separate plant called the 'the coloring factory' (kleurenfabriek). Here, the customer requests for special colors were accommodated. This required not only the expertise of highly skilled 'colorists,' but also the ability to schedule production according to a 'color cycle'—a sequence of colors that caused minimal switching costs. Although DSM had successfully developed such competences, ABS had not proven to be a financial success in the 1980s. As the ABS industry entered the maturity phase, DSM's position was regarded as slightly more than tenable in the 1989 portfolio review and the strategic classification of this business was 'selective development' (see Fig. 1.12).

Some in the company argued that the main reason for this marginal performance was because ABS was only one of the required products for the markets in which it operated. There was a lot of 'inter-material competition' for its main applications. For instance, in the markets for heat-resistant applications, other so-called engineering plastics, such as polyamides and polycarbonate, could also be used. This

[19] See also De Rooij (2007: 139–140). De Rooij explains the decision to acquire external ABS-technology by the fact that DSM wanted to diversify fast and needed "large plants," which had been proven externally on a large scale. As will become apparent in the main text later, the Japanese technology was to become sub-scale quite rapidly despite the best efforts of DSM Research to improve the process.

line of thinking was adopted in the 'DSM 2000' strategic review, conducted in 1990, leading DSM to pursue a portfolio of engineering plastics, building on ABS as a 'cornerstone for the multi-product Engineering Plastics strategy of DSM.' Another driver of this multi-product strategy was probably DSM's wish to incorporate two of its own development products with an engineering plastic nature (Stanyl and SMA) in a portfolio with more mainstream products, which had already gained market acceptance. In September 1991 this strategy led to the execution of a swap with AKZO: AKZO acquired DSM's Powder Coatings business, while DSM acquired AKZO's Polyamide 6 (PA6) business. DSM combined this mainstream PA6 product with its development product Stanyl (a Polyamide 4.6) into a new BU called Engineering Plastics. ABS was combined with another development product, SMA, and a fledgling business in Polycarbonate, creating the business unit ASP. Both business units were part of the Polymers Division.

Wim Donners was appointed BU Director for ASP in the 'Concern 2000' wave. Until then, he had pursued a career in DSM Research. He recalls the confusion he encountered in the BU about its strategy: "Wim Dohmen, the marketing manager, came to me and said: 'I hope that *you* will listen to me; ABS is not as strong as DSM believes it to be.'" Donners also noticed that the BU was not in favor of allowing 'outside interest' from the headquarters and the functions. He decided to "open the windows and let some fresh air in" and to volunteer the ABS business as the first pilot project for a BSD. It particularly appealed to him that the BSD had outside-in challenge built into its design.

The BSD was conducted in three sessions, 3 days each, with a core team of about eight people. Key members were from Controlling, Marketing, Production and Research and Technology. Particular attention was first focused on the 'Strategic Data Set:' did the BU have the required information to conduct a strategic dialogue? As was often the case in other business units, the answer in this initial BSD was no. Donners said, "We had to make pragmatic decisions which data gaps to fill, because that knowledge was absolutely essential, and which data gaps to leave for the time being. We invested heavily in, for instance, an activity-based costing exercise and in a technology analysis, which both proved crucial elements for our strategic choice. Just like other business groups we found that the first BSD was the hardest, particularly because of the lacking data and analyses up-front. Later, DSM businesses invested in keeping such information up-to-date and therefore found it easier to start up a new BSD."

A particular incident highlighted the cultural change that the BSD could bring to a business. Dohmen, the Marketing manager, was convinced that the main problem was the high cost level of the business. He complained that the ex-factory costs were so high that he could not give commercially attractive propositions to potential customers. At this point, the Production Manager Wim de Vries, who was normally a composed and reflective man, exploded: "Do you know why the costs are so high? Because Marketing chases all these different customers and accommodates all their special requests for different grades and different colors! Do you know what havoc that creates for my production schedules? This is the reason our costs are high!" Activity-based costing confirmed that ABS had a few highly profitable customers but also a long tail of unprofitable customers. This information was new to the business. Production and Marketing had operated as 'silos' with insufficient communication between these functions. The BSD broke down these walls and stimulated cross-functional dialogue and subsequent coordination. The activity-based costing information was used to enable Marketing to make more informed decisions on which customers to pursue and which propositions were financially attractive. Marketing could still make 'special requests' on behalf of the customers; in the future, however, the extra costs would be charged to the Marketing budget and thus be made transparent.

The Production function itself was also made more transparent. The two steps of polymer production and compounding were formally separated and each given their own responsibilities. This enabled a more rigorous cost control of, in particular, the compounding step with its complicated 'color cycle' production schedules. Donners commented, "Formerly, the compounding step had been the 'poor cousin' of production and the whore of Marketing. They were too eager to please. When given their own responsibility and budget, they were basically given the possibility to optimize the compounding step and thus contain costs." Cost containment turned out to be absolutely essential. The main reason was that DSM's ABS business operated on a too small scale. Its factories had become sub-scale in the early 1990s as compared to its European and Asian competition. This impeded it to vie for the mainstream applications with large volumes, where cost competition was the name of the game. It had, therefore, been 'forced' into niche positions, with highly demanding customers and smaller volume applications. This tended to drive costs further up, a spiral, which had to be broken.

The business solicited from its employees 23 strategic options to be investigated. Of these, ten options were deemed interesting enough to warrant deeper analysis. Unfortunately, none of these options were financially viable without a very serious cost drive: the preliminary indication was that the fixed cost base of Dfl 100 million had to be reduced by at least Dfl 16 million. These ingredients became the proposed strategic choice to DSM's Managing Board:

- A better market positioning toward customers who would be profitable on an activity-based costing basis
- More transparency in the production steps necessary to execute customer orders, particularly those with 'special requests'
- A substantial cost drive with the aim to reduce the fixed cost base with at least Dfl 16 million[20]

[20] With this strategy the business obtained a longer 'lease on life' but it also recognized that life would, in the end, probably be limited. However, the strategy was implemented successfully and eventually led to an even further cost reduction of more than Dfl 30 million. In 1999, one of the main competitors in the ABS business—BASF—made an offer to acquire the business, which DSM accepted.

The strategy proposal to the Managing Board was accompanied by a set of performance indicators that would enable the business and the Board to monitor strategic and financial progress. The Board approved the proposed strategy and concluded that in the strategic discussion, "all aspects had been dealt with in a balanced way and that the real issues and dilemmas had been brought into the open. Further application to other BUs must be stimulated... The use of this methodology for the formulation of performance indicators has indeed led to very specific, actionable and measurable parameters... There is every reason to continue on this path."[21] Basically, the Board was encouraging the working group, as well as the DSM businesses (all BU directors would read these official Board minutes), to bring it more evidence that this new BSD approach would work well in practice.

Reflecting on his first BSD experience, Donners noted: "Of course, the strategic outcome is important, but the process is even more important. The BSD process led to a unity of approach and a resolve to execute the strategy that was remarkable. For instance, I did not have to worry at all that the members of the core team would communicate the approved strategy each in their own light, something that otherwise often happens. It was clear to all of us what was required and we were eager to execute. In that sense, I meant that process was even more important than outcome. I would rather have a second-best outcome implemented with this enthusiasm and resolve than a first-best outcome executed lousily... I regard the BSD process as one of the best products of DSM. I had to work 100 hours per week to get the first one done but I regard it as one of the high points of my career."

References

Copeland, T.E., T.M. Koller and J. Murrin, *Valuation: Measuring and Managing the Value of Companies,* NY: John Wiley, 1990

Douma, S. and H. Schreuder, *Economic Approaches to Organizations*, 5th edition (London: Pearson, 2013).

Heijltjes, M., "Performance measurement at DSM: Linking the company's long term strategy with its short term actions" and "An Alternative Proposal to Performance Measurement" Case studies, University of Maastricht, 1996.

Porter, M., *Competitive Strategy*, NY: The Free Press, 1980

Schreuder, H., *Maatschappelijke Verantwoordelijkheid en Maatschappelijke Berichtgeving van Ondernemingen*, Leiden, Stenfert Kroese, 1981

Schreuder, H., "Strategic Monitoring at a Chemical Company," *Long Range Planning*, Vol. 28, No. 6, 1995: 69–77.

Van Cayseele, P. and H. Schreuder, "Strategische Groepen: Een Overzicht van Het Onderzoek," *Maandblad voor Accountancy en Bedrijfseconomie*, Vol. 63, No. 11, 1989.

[21] Minutes of the 24th meeting of the Managing Board, held 2 June 1992. Translated by the authors.

6 Enhancing Business School Impact

How much do you think our participants really remember, or apply, of all the concepts you taught them?
(Senior DSM executive)

Following the end of IMPACT, Jeannet made several trips to DSM's head office in Heerlen to discuss how the learning from the course could be further implemented. In one of these meetings a challenging question was posed: "How much do you think our participants really remember, or apply, of all the concepts you taught them?" Without preparation or detailed evidence, but based upon scattered discussions with participants and given previous experience with programs at IMD, he responded, "I think it is 20 %!" Assuming that the next comment would be something about waste of effort and poor return for DSM's money, the following question was a bit of a surprise, "And what would you propose to do to raise this percentage?".

This exchange cannot be placed definitively in time and location but has been remembered vividly by Just Fransen van de Putte, then serving as President of the Polymers Division at DSM. "The development and creation of Marketing plans tended to become routinized. It was becoming more of a rain dance, just filling out forms," he commented.[1]

At that time, Jeannet's response dealt with a need for upper management to pull through the IMPACT concepts from lower levels of management. It would be hard to apply these newly acquired Marketing concepts consistently if senior leaders were not specifically asking for their application and engaging upper and middle management in such a way that that type of thinking had to be utilized. By requiring or demanding their use, top management would also signal that these were important concepts. How could this be implemented? This was the new challenge posed by DSM.

[1] Interview conducted with Just Fransen van de Putte, by the co-authors on 29 January 2013.

J.-P. Jeannet, H. Schreuder, *From Coal to Biotech*,
DOI 10.1007/978-3-662-46299-7_6

Previous Experience with Strategy Workshops

Before the DSM engagement, Jeannet had led a series of strategy workshops at Sulzer, following the Sulzer Seminar series at IMEDE (see Chap. 2). These workshops, each with a 2-to-3 day duration, resulted from the Sulzer Market Orientation seminars; usually initiated by the respective Division or BU head, who contacted Jeannet directly and arranged the appropriate dates. The meetings were generally held off-site and the number of participants was restricted to the key executives of a business representing all the main functions, with no more than about ten executive participants. Pre-assignments were requested of the participating team—they were asked to have some of the key business facts, as they understood them, on hand; these included related business statistics, market statistics, customer lists, key account information, information on competitors and other readily available data or information. There was no deliberate effort to prepare special material for the meetings.[2]

In all of these meetings, Jeannet worked as the moderator and discussion leader. All of the facts, or data, about the business were in the heads of the participants; the moderator's job is to guide them through conceptual understanding. The agenda usually began with a review of the customers and market trends; although it was communicated to all workshop participants, the agenda timing was left open, since progress through the topics could not be pre-determined. The workshop usually began with a review of the market and its segments. Included was the competitive advantage of the business unit ("Why would any customer buy from you"?), as well as the distinctive competence of the business ("What are you really good at?"). The competitors were also part of the discussions and at the end, participants were driven to some conclusions about action of a strategic nature. This could include the development of new products, changes in the marketing structure, or entering new segments. Since the Sulzer seminar series at IMEDE/IMD had more 'Marketing' as content, the workshops put more emphasis on those topics.

The experience gained from these sessions with the various Sulzer businesses talking through their business and, thus, deepening of their conceptual understanding by applying it to their own context led Jeannet to propose a similar initiative for DSM.[3] Again, with the assistance of van de Putte (Corporate Strategy), feelers were

[2] It is perhaps important to point out that in the late 1980s companies did not have readily available presentations on their businesses. This is the pre-PowerPoint era. The most a company might have had was a strategic plan, usually heavy with financial goals, and not yet what we later came to know as a business plan that also included the rationale for the action and the expected results.

[3] As this initiative was entirely open to the initiatives of various Sulzer businesses, only a handful of workshops were held within 2–3 years after the program. One Sulzer Division, later organized as Sulzer Infra and dealing with building services and technologies, held a series of workshops that were repeated over the years including meeting for a week in Boston to have Jeannet lead the workshops from Babson, his main teaching position. Together with another faculty colleague from IMD, Jeannet also participated in a number of workshops held under the auspices of Sulzer Corporate Development and aimed at developing managerial talent for Sulzer.

put out to various interested parties. With the IMPACT seminar series fresh in their minds, two businesses volunteered. The first one was DSM Construction Resins, located in Zwolle, Netherlands and headed by Gerard Duyfjes, an early eager supporter of the DSM Marketing initiative. The second was the DSM Caprolactam business, then headed by Jacques van Goolen. Both workshops offered valuable experience, eventually being taken on board to create the later DSM initiatives concerning business strategy.

The DSM Resins Pilot Workshop

The workshop for DSM Construction (Structural) Resins took place from May 6 to 8, 1991 in Zwolle, a small town located in the middle of the Netherlands. Jeannet traveled from Lausanne to meet with the business team. He was already familiar with the Resins business, having worked there during the previous year, in order to create a case that could be used in the last IMPACT courses. Through IMPACT, Jeannet had also met Gerard Duyfjes, the Business Unit (BU) Director and initiated the pilot workshop. Duyfjes was new to this business and he thought this workshop would provide an excellent way to learn the business and see his new team in action and said, "I wanted to sit back and learn and get to know my own people in the process."[4]

In addition to Duyfjes, the group included the Divisional Director of R&D (John Prooi), the then heads of functions such as Manufacturing (Michel Loubry), Marketing (Paul Wigmann), Technical R&D (Adri de Koning), Finance (Melle Beverwijk), the head of DSM Resins UK (Tony Criddle) and head of Planning (Peter Meyer). This small group met for 3 days in a conference room in the Zwolle Manufacturing site.

DSM Resins was one of eight DSM Divisions at that time and was headquartered in Zwolle. Formed in 1983, following a merger with DSM Synres and Unilever Resins, the division employed some 2,700 people, had sales of Dfl 1,400 million and operated some 20 profit centers in Holland and internationally. A new BU structure was implemented as of January 1990 to replace the former one based on functions across the entire division. BU II (Construction Resins) accounted for about 30 % of the divisional turnover and was responsible for unsaturated polyester (UP) resins, as well as printing inks. DSM was sharing the leadership in this sector with BASF and had achieved sales of about Dfl 300 million with positive operating results. Although there were some 2,200 customers, most of the sales were made to a few larger accounts. The business was large, and considerably complex, due to many products, batch manufacturing of many different grades and a complex logistic system.[5]

---

[4] Conversation of Gerard Duyfjes with the co-authors on January 31, 2013 regarding his reflections of the entire IMPACT and BSD development process.

[5] *DSM Resins B.V.*, unreleased case written by Jean-Pierre Jeannet (IMD and Babson) with assistance of Paul Harrington and Ted Farnham, both MBA candidates at Babson College. 1991.

Since Duyfjes was new to this business, he took a back seat in the discussions. Led and moderated by Jeannet, the major contributions were made by those members of the team who had had a longer experience in the business segment, in particular Wigmann (Marketing) and Loubry (Manufacturing). But even 'longer' did not mean decades. With none of the participants having a dominant knowledge of the industry sector and the business, discussions tended to be open and free flowing. The staff director was tasked with keeping minutes and notes of the meeting, which were later shared in typed format although there were a number of important elements in the discussion that had not been fully captured in the minutes; a learning that, under similar circumstances, note-taking is a critical element.

The agenda followed the then tested approach Jeannet had been used in previous assignments, with the exception of a more detailed view of the business system or value chain. For 3 days, the business data and industry realities were organized on flip charts and work was done to draw conclusions for future competitive behavior. With the records of those days lost, there are just a few key moments that remain at top of mind—the discussions around R&D projects and how they had helped the business, or not, as well as the manufacturing set up with the various types of plant configurations. Both of these areas were reviewed in detail in light of the changing market and competitive structures. Without all the functions in the same room sharing their perspectives and reviewing the market realities together, these insights would not have occurred.

The DSM Caprolactam Workshop

About a month later, on 12 and 13 June, 1991, Jeannet was asked to run a second workshop for DSM Caprolactam. In many ways, the Caprolactam business in 1990 was the opposite of Resins and more typical of DSM commodity chemicals businesses. Given that it offered less complexity, the strategy workshop was scheduled for 2 days and held near DSM's Heerlen complex.

Caprolactam was an intermediate chemical, a precursor to Nylon 6 and a widely used polymer. DSM was the largest merchant producer of this material, which was sold as either 'dry flakes' or 'liquids' to converters that made Nylon 6 fibers or engineering plastics from this. DSM operated plants in the Netherlands and the US and the company's largest customer base for this, by far, were converters for Nylon 6 fibers used in either carpets or textiles. There were, therefore, few customers buying large amounts of this material.

Participants in this workshop included the BU Director (Jacques van Goolen) and Director of Marketing and Sales (Herman Polak), both graduates of the IMPACT seminar and familiar with the conceptual approach of analyzing strategy. Similar to the Resin workshop, Jeannet was the moderator, guiding a small team of participants over the 2 days. The issues centered mostly around competition, due to a number of Eastern European companies having begun to enter the world market. The uncertainty regarding major customers was another major program topic, as well as under which circumstances those customers might turn captive, preferring to make their own Caprolactam for use in their downstream Nylon fibers operation.[6]

Because the immediate pressures on the business included a response to the changing realities in Eastern Europe, the workshop was less focused on general strategies and Key Success Factors (KSFs) for this business. Having pressures to respond to regarding possible acquisitions can easily monopolize a discussion. This was in stark contrast to the Resins workshop where no immediate large single issue dominated the discussions.

The Learning from the Pilot Workshops

Discussions were held with Just Fransen van de Putte, who had been promoted to Division President of Hydrocarbons, after the workshop experience. Based upon internal discussions, the drivers behind the IMPACT seminar (DSM's Branch Marketing Committee, or BOM, members) and Corporate Planning issued an invitation to Jeannet to come to DSM on the company's 'Marketing Day' to present both a summary of all the key IMPACT seminar concepts and the learning from the pilot strategy workshops.

The DSM Marketing Day 1991[7]

On 26 September 26 1991 about 75 senior DSM Marketing and business managers gathered in the Moretti Auditorium at Vaalsbroek, the castle owned by DSM (see Fig. 6.1) and used for its management education programs.[8] The arrangements of the meeting were in the hands of BOM who took responsibility for the improvement of Marketing throughout the company. Members of the BOM, under the chairmanship of Hans Dijkman, had all recently attended the IMD IMPACT program and were now eager to improve Marketing thinking throughout the whole company.

In the morning, Simon de Bree, DSM Executive Board member responsible for Marketing affairs, opened the meeting with Hans Dijkman, head of BOM. About 70 senior executives from across all DSM business and divisions were present, most

[6] DSM is still in this business and Caprolactam is now in the Business Group Fiber Intermediates. It is a basic feedstock for DSM's Stanyl branded engineering plastic (Nylon 6) and Dyneema fiber.

[7] Source for this section: 'DSM Marketing Day,' 26 September 1991, Vaalsbroek Castle, Vaals, DSM Program Brochure.

[8] 'DSM Marketing Day,' September 26 1991, Vaalsbroek Castle, Vaals, DSM Program Brochure: 13.

Fig. 6.1 Kasteel Vaalsbroek, Vaals, Netherlands. *Source*: DSM

with marketing, sales or business unit responsibilities. After Dijkman's opening remarks by on the objectives, tasks and activities of the BOM, Jeannet was asked to provide a summary of the key IMPACT Program concepts. While most of the meeting attendees had participated in IMPACT, it had already been some 2 years earlier for most of them. Also part of this afternoon group was Hein Schreuder who had just recently joined DSM (and it was the first time that Jeannet and Schreuder met). In the afternoon, two businesses presented their experience and strategy. One of the presenters was Gerard Duyfjes, Head of the BU Unsaturated Polyester Resins, who detailed his recent experience with the 3-day strategy review of his business that had been completed using concepts from IMPACT; he was joined by the entire team that had been part of those discussions 6 months earlier.

Following Duyfjes, Jeannet presented ideas about 'Managing the Strategy Dialogue,' a result of intensive discussions and workshops that had recently taken place. The concepts behind this are described in more detail later in this chapter. The presentation was followed by a panel discussion that included a group of senior DSM executives: Simon Dingemans (President DSM Resins), Dick van Waes (President DSM Chemicals), Gerard Duyfjes (Business Director Coating Resins and Additives), Jacques van Goolen (Business Director Fiber Intermediates) and Hans Dijkman (Business Director DSM Elastomers Europe). The panel was chaired by Just Fransen van der Putte (Deputy President Polymers and Hydrocarbons). With the exception of Dingemans, all of the panelists were IMPACT alums.

In hindsight, this Marketing Day 1991 was a pivotal event in DSM's development because it led, eventually, to the adoption of several stepping stones that impacted and contributed to the company's development over the next several years. In particular, DSM did not favor one particular approach to development over another; instead, a number of approaches were developed. These will be described in more detail in following chapters.

The Concepts of 'Managing the Strategy Dialogue'

The 'Managing the Strategy Dialogue' presentation was introduced to a DSM audience for the first time. Jeannet presented an assessment after his exposure to DSM businesses and having had some pilot workshops on the business strategy processes. There were five parts to the presentation.

Part One covered the purpose of holding a strategy dialogue at all. The argument was made that traditional approaches at DSM to strategic planning did not yield maximum impact as most planning exercises tended to deteriorate into budgeting exercises only. Functional strategies were rolled into functional budget requests, which, in turn, were accumulated into strategic plans and resulted in a budget submission to the corporate entity. Additionally, the existing level of strategic planning at the business level made only partial use of the IMPACT concepts, such as business systems, KSFs, competitive advantage and market segmentation, to name but a few. The use of IMPACT concepts, where found, represented only partial and isolated attempts. Concepts were used superficially and were not thought through. On top of that, the practice of strategic planning took place without sufficient senior management involvement at the corporate and divisional levels and was restricted largely to reviewing budgets.

But how could the typical strong link between budgeting and strategic planning be cut so that each element would be given sufficient attention? How could the process be changed so that the strategy exercises did not deteriorate into simple budgeting exercises? What needed to be done that strategic questions were given the attention they deserved? This was the question that was put before the DSM audience that day.

The idea of establishing a strategy dialogue was advanced to enhance the quality of strategic thinking at DSM. The dialogue was described as an extensive exchange of ideas where no single person combined all the facts required and where business teams pooled their market knowledge, submitting to intensive questioning and resulting in a well thought out and coherent strategy.

In Part Two of the presentation, the content of the dialogue was laid out. All steps, from diagnosis to options and alternatives, leading to a complete business strategy should be encompassed. As part of the diagnosis, increased emphasis was to be placed on what at IMPACT was called the '5 Cs' (context, costs, competition, company and customers) a complete view of the industry business system or value chain, a thorough competitive analysis of the relevant players and a company analysis that was clear about the businesses own strength and weaknesses. In so doing, the business would offer a clear definition of the KSFs as a cornerstone of the diagnosis, offering a coherent picture of the industry context. Key points included being 'brutally honest in the assessment of your competitive advantage' and 'don't confuse distinctive competence with competitive advantage' for the business.

Following the diagnosis, the business could formulate its own strategic intent. Starting from the present position, a vision could be formulated and a strategic gap identified. A list of alternatives could be drawn up that could serve to close the gap. The resulting strategic plan could become a living document where business strategy was both internally linked to functional strategy and externally linked to the industry and market environment.

In Part Three, suggestions were offered about how to prepare for a fruitful and productive dialogue. Following the experience with DSM Resins, Jeannet argued for a group of seven to nine participants covering the key functional areas of the business (R&D, Production, Marketing, Finance, Sales, etc.) with some participation from the 'field.' Each participant was asked to prepare their own industry view, although some tasks might be assigned to individuals who had the best factual knowledge. The BU head might bring some documentation on the business system (value chain); the Head of Marketing a list of segments and market information, in addition to a chart on the sales structure of the business; the R&D head could come with a list of key technology trends and a list of current R&D projects and similar assignments were suggested for other functional heads and participants. None of this was to be complicated and most likely each participant would be able to draw on readily available materials.

The running of the dialogue was addressed in Part Four of the presentation. Based upon the experience with other workshops, 3 days was thought to be a good amount of time for a first pass through, starting with the diagnosis and ending with convergence towards a strategy. Periodically, time between workshops could be useful to summarize each step. Venue preference was given to off-site locations.

Some additional observations were made on the role of key individuals involved in the dialogue. Business unit managers were encouraged to foster a shared vision of the business, as opposed to dictating a strategy, creating a broader basis for strategy making. Should the division manager participate (still in place at DSM at that time), they were to challenge the business team to a better thought out plan. Early involvement in the process by senior managers was preferable to reactions or judgments after the fact. Some special words were addressed with potential moderators whose role was to 'keep everyone honest.' This meant challenging prevailing assumptions, asking hard questions, checking the logic and the implications of what was said. And finally, the business' strategic planner was tasked with note taking and documentation.

Behind presenting the strategy process as a dialogue lied the intent to move from a random application of a number of different business strategy elements towards a clear, concise, and well thought-out business strategy where all the linkages between concepts would become clear. Through discussions and dialogues the dynamics of the industry would yield Key Success Factors that needed to be addressed by the business. That would then be tested against functional strategies such that each of the functions would find their place within the overall business strategy. This approach placed great emphasis on the interpretation of an industry sector that was relevant to a business and could be described as "Outside-in" vs. "Inside-Out" for most of the existing exercises. Without the strong industry

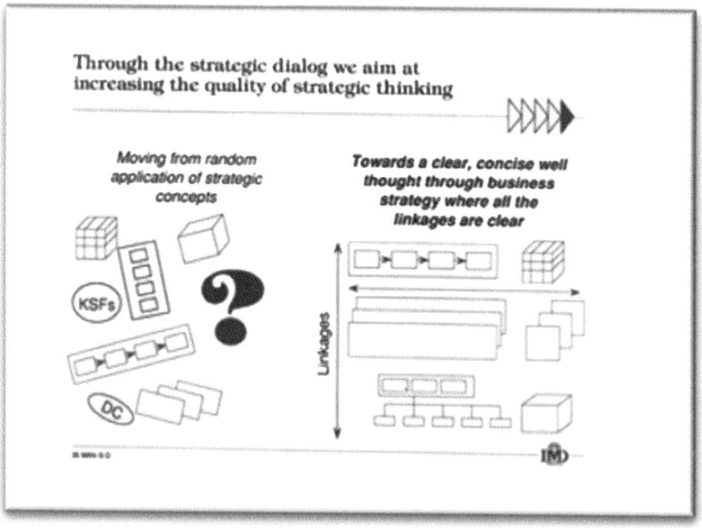

Fig. 6.2 Summary slide of strategy dialogue. *Source*: J.-P. Jeannet

analysis elements part of the IMPACT program which served as a common language to the DSM audience that day, the message might not have been fully understood nor appreciated.

The informed reader might search here for business strategy concepts that might be completely new, or invented for the purpose of DSM use. Neither was the case. It was not the particular concepts and their application to strategic processes that were new. What was new and different was the proposed process. During the IMPACT seminars the participants, and most of the Marketing Day participants were IMPACT alumni, had been in several discussions and exercises that approached the dialogue format proposed and thus could connect to this type of format. Without IMPACT, both content and format of the strategy dialogue presentation would have fallen on deaf ears.

The summary presented at the DSM Marketing Day was a complete blueprint and proposal about how to conduct 'strategy dialogues.' The proposal to DSM management triggered a lively dialogue within the company; it focused on business strategies and not on DSM's corporate strategy, which was in line with the content and mission of the IMPACT seminar series. See Fig. 6.2 for summary slide of the presentation.

It is important to reflect here on a change in DSM's collaboration with the business school community. While in the first part of the collaboration, the focus was on delivering educational programs tailor-made to DSM's strategic needs, the company now proceeded to involve the program faculty into a deeper collaboration proposing and testing new strategic planning processes. The outline and proposal for the strategy dialogue came at the request of DSM and was beyond the typical work performed by business school faculty for other companies. Such a deeper involvement would not have been possible without the previous program delivery that exposed hundreds of DSM executives to the concepts part of the strategy dialogue. The behavior displayed by DSM furthermore shows a company that was not willing to stop at mere educational delivery but wanted to make sure that the lessons learned would also become an inherent part of company culture.

7 Embedding Business Strategy Dialogues as a Core Process

Although development of a theory of dialogue was far from complete, by 1994. . .dialogue began to be seen as a breakthrough of major significance in a number of emergent fields of human activity: in organizational learning, in the process of collective inquiry, and, significantly, in the way humans might govern themselves. . .Dialogue does not require people to agree with each other. Instead, it encourages people to participate in a pool of shared meaning that leads to aligned action.
—Joseph Jaworsky, from his book Synchronicity (1996: 110–111)

When the Managing Board of DSM decided on 2 June 1992 that, "further application (of Business Strategy Dialogues [BSDs]) to other Business Units (BUs) must be stimulated," it did not specify how it envisaged the further adoption of this new approach within the company. It had, however, signaled quite strongly that, "There is every reason to continue on this path." Simon de Bree, then the Chairman of the Managing Board (MB), had basically decided to take a wait-and-see approach, curious to observe whether the businesses would voluntarily try out the BSD approach and what their experiences would be. As will become clear, de Bree was not disappointed. In this chapter, the process of adopting the BSD and its further institutionalization within DSM will be addressed—institutionalization in terms of the embedding of BSD as a core process within the DSM organization, inextricably intertwined with other processes and routines. How the process, which was developed in practice, became incorporated in DSM's formal systems and how it further evolved over time, spanning a time period of about 15 years, will also be covered.

J.-P. Jeannet, H. Schreuder, *From Coal to Biotech*,
DOI 10.1007/978-3-662-46299-7_7

A Second Pilot Study: Polyethylene

In 1991, Just Fransen van de Putte, one of the originators of IMPACT on the DSM side, became President of the Polymers Division at DSM. This division was comprised of four business units: Polyethylene, Polypropylene, ABS/SMA/PC and Engineering Plastics. The Polyethylene (PE) business unit was by far the largest of the four. With the Hydrocarbons division (which supplied all the cracker products, including the largest, ethylene), it formed the heart of DSM's Petrochemical operations. Petrochemical activities were undergoing a cyclical downturn in the early 1990s, driven mainly by overcapacity, due to the many new plants coming on stream. The division was facing mounting losses. In this context, the PE business was selected by Van de Putte, in 1992, as a worthwhile site for a second pilot study of the BSD approach. Jeannet and Schreuder[1] were asked to act as facilitator and challenger.

The PE management team arrived at the BSD meeting with an enormous pack of slides. It was clear that they wanted to convey that they were fully on top of their industry and its markets; it also seemed clear that their intent was not to have an open dialogue. On the contrary, they wished to impress divisional management and get approval for their preconceived plans (which were further capacity expansions). To be fair, this was an experienced team with many members having spent a long career in the PE business. They were well informed about many strategic and operational aspects of their business but not all aspects.

Content-wise, the main realization from this BSD was how the petrochemical industry had evolved to become a truly global industry. Historically, the competition had been mainly on a regional basis. Both the Hydrocarbons division and the Polyethylene business knew their European competitors very well. Due to the long lead times for constructing new crackers and PE plants, there had always been some transparency about expected supply conditions. Now, however, DSM had been taken by surprise by new capacities coming on stream in other continents, including the Asian newcomer, South Korea. This had depressed utilization rates on a worldwide basis, leading to considerable margin erosion, including in Europe. It was clear that the business intelligence function had to be expanded to cover competitors across the globe. The main question continued to be how DSM was positioned for low-cost competition in these commodity products, but now on a global basis. Important derived questions involved product mix (LDPE, LLDPE, HDPE), corresponding technology choices, capacity decisions and geographical coverage.

The second pilot study was memorable due to an incident that took place about halfway through the BSD. At the instigation of the PE Business Unit director, Frans Noteborn, a piece of paper was passed around among the members of the PE management team. When it was returned to Noteborn, he smiled when he saw the

[1] At the time, Schreuder was member of the Management Team of the Polymers Division, responsible for Strategy.

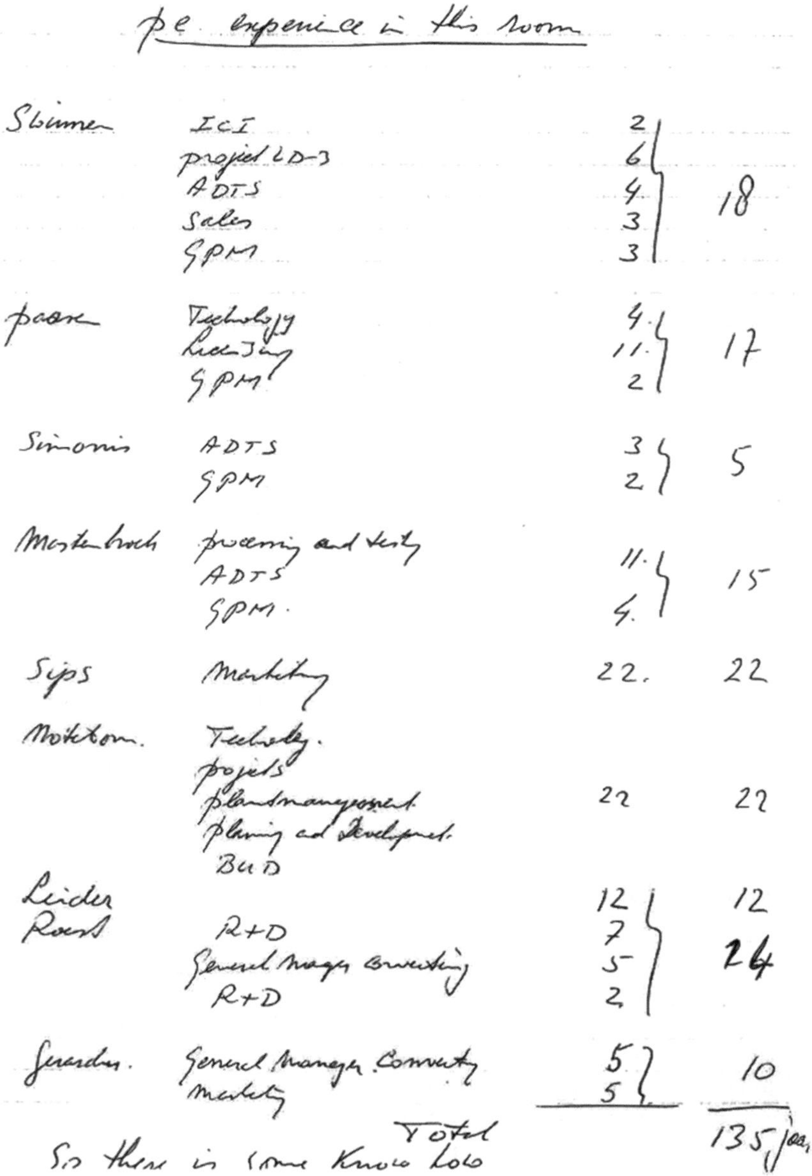

Fig. 7.1 135 years of experience in PE Management Team. *Source*: personal archive J.P. Jeannet

results of what his team members had contributed. Everyone, of course, was curious to know what that might be. At the end of the session, Frans asked to Just Fransen van de Putte: "Just, how many years of experience do you have in the PE business? And how many years of PE experience do the facilitator and challenger have?" We don't know the exact answer by Just anymore, but we do remember that Noteborn came back to say: "In our management team, we have over 135 years of experience in Polyethylene!" (Fig. 7.1). It was a clear attempt to undermine the authority of the divisional president and also of the BSD 'outsiders'. Just Fransen van de Putte later recalled: "Of course, I should have thrown Frans Noteborn out of the room, but I was too flabbergasted to do so." Upon reflection, the appropriate response to the "135 years experience" remark at the time would have been: "That's exactly the problem, Frans!" Time and again, in mature products where low-cost competition was driven by the race to achieve scale economies, business teams 'set in their ways' and were blindsided by developments (like geographical or technological shifts) that did not fit with the 'dominant logic' they had come to adopt over the years.

This PE anecdote bears some resemblance to the experience of Marthijn Jansen (Corporate Planning), when he arrived at the Fibre Intermediates business to assist the facilitator Frans Baraké with the first BSD on Caprolactam, another mature commodity product. They entered the room where the management team was gathered around a conference table. The BU director opened the meeting and asked, "Do we all have last year's plan in front of us?" When that was affirmed he said: "Ok, turn to page one: has anything changed there? Page two? Page three?..." and so forth. The anecdotes illustrate that the acceptance of the new BSD process was not a foregone conclusion, nor was the legitimacy of the new BSD facilitator and challenger roles uncontested. Additionally, not all of the facilitators were immediately up to the task of enforcing the culture change that would result from strategies being developed in a participative dialogue mode. This was only to be expected in an organization that was itself going through a wave of decentralization and change ('Concern 2000') and which had lived for so long with its old strategy routines (the SMP process).

Training Facilitators

As discussed in Chap. 5, DSM resolved to use its own staff for the two new roles introduced to support the BSD process. It was, of course, important that the first group of facilitators were seen as a credible support to the businesses. They were chosen by the Managing Board and received a personal invitation letter from the Chairman, emphasizing the importance of the new role they were to assume in addition to their daily responsibilities. A special effort was made to train this group for their first assignments and Jeannet was invited to lead the training session. Initially, the focus was as much on the 'process' of the BSD approach as on the 'content.' Facilitators had to be trained in the art of 'appreciative inquiry' and prepared for potentially difficult process issues, such as the ABS, PE and Caprolactam examples have shown. Moreover, the facilitators should be able to support the businesses with the proper understanding and application of the new BSD concepts. Having completed the training, the facilitators were congratulated by the Chairman of the MB, de Bree, who awarded them a specially designed 'facilitator tie' as a token of appreciation (and authority?) (Fig. 7.2).

Fig. 7.2 Facilitator tie

As the BSD approach became accepted over the years at the company, the facilitator training increasingly incorporated experiences and examples from within DSM. In addition, the training was used to make new strategic emphases operational. For instance, in 2005, DSM formulated a very ambitious Innovation target in its 'Vision 2010' corporate strategy—an additional EUR 1 billion sales from innovation, to be realized in the next 5 years. In order to support this strategic target, a new DSM Innovation Center was set up under the leadership of Rob van Leen, the first Chief Innovation Officer (CIO). Rob participated in the January 2006 training of facilitators to explain and discuss the new innovation approaches and best practices within DSM. His colleague Eric Rutten, from the DSM Innovation Center, explained the new 'Innovation toolbox' that was under construction. In this way, it could be ensured that BSDs within DSM could incorporate the latest available concepts and tools within the company.

The facilitators were recruited from all parts of DSM: Business, Research, Finance and Corporate staffs. Of the first groups, many people later reached higher positions in DSM, including Business Group Director, Executive Vice-President of Research, Executive Vice-President of Corporate Strategy & Acquisitions, Group Controller and Managing Board Member (for the 2003 list of facilitators, see Fig. 7.4). This is no co-incidence because it reflects both the selection criteria at the time and the experience that could be gained through this role. Until that time, to get to know the full breadth of DSM and focus on the really important issues required many years of internal rotation across businesses and functions, as well as promotion to positions of increasing responsibility. Several 'generations' of facilitators were trained (together with Professor Jeannet who ensured that best practices from outside DSM were brought into the facilitator training).

In 2012, the list of active BSD facilitators, which the businesses could choose from, numbered more than 30 people. Using internal people as facilitators, and challengers, had several other consequences, which had not all been anticipated at the time of the proposal. It was, for instance, a mechanism by which experience could be accumulated within the company and best DSM practices could be disseminated across the businesses. This happened in a formal sense (see Fig. 7.3 with the 'Strategic Data Checklist'), but perhaps more important were the enhanced opportunities for strategic discussions across the boundaries of DSM's businesses and functions. Where a 'silo mentality' had previously still existed, the BSD helped to break this down. Furthermore, with so many facilitators trained from among the own ranks, DSM had much less need for the support of outside consultants in the strategy processes. During the 1980s, DSM had extensively used firms like Arthur D. Little, McKinsey and the Boston Consulting Group. But, from the mid-1990s onwards, these firms were used only occasionally to delve into specific strategic topics (as well as for organizational projects), but they were no longer employed for strategic process facilitation. In this respect, DSM had become a 'learning organization,' developing and further refining its own ways and means of conducting strategy dialogues.

The Diffusion of BSDs Across DSM

A survey was held in 1994 among the DSM business in the context of monitoring the progress of *Concern 2000*. Several questions probed how the businesses perceived the BSD and satisfaction scores that were quite high resulted. The main reasons were: (1) satisfaction with the sharper content of the strategies, (2) the ownership they felt for this decentralized strategy process and (3) their finding that a BSD would act as a team-building exercise by 'rallying the troops' around the main strategic issues and actions. It was clear that the adoption of the BSD as a voluntary initiative by DSM businesses had gained considerable momentum. Nevertheless, it came as a surprise that "By the end of 1994 nearly all BUs had gone through this process" (Schreuder 1995). Apparently, the momentum had become self-sustaining and the process was reaching even the most (initially) skeptical businesses. There may have also been a bandwagon effect where business managers did not want to be perceived as lagging behind the adoption of a successful new approach. Be that as it may, Simon de Bree's wait-and-see approach had paid off—he did not have to wait long to see that businesses were voluntarily embracing this new way of crafting business strategy.

The widespread adoption of the BSD allowed DSM to start accumulating its own experiences and best practices from these strategy exercises. In 1995, all the business units and business groups had conducted a BSD. On this basis, the *Guide to Business Strategy and (Long-term) Performance Measurement* could be

Contents

Fig. 7.3 Contents of the 'strategic data checklist' (2008). *Source*: strategic data checklist for the business characterization phase of the BSD, DSM corporate strategy & acquisitions, April 2008

updated to incorporate the learnings from this first cycle of BSDs. A companion booklet, the 'Strategic Data Checklist,' was compiled to support the businesses in preparing for BSDs. It also contained examples from DSM's own BSDs to illustrate particular approaches. In 2008, the booklet had grown to 130 pages of strategic topics, tools and examples (for the contents page see Fig. 7.3).

In the Executive Letter of 16 January 1996 it was announced that the Managing Board had decided "to base DSM's planning processes on the BSD approach and to include the main performance indicators resulting from the BSD in the periodic management reports." What had begun as a voluntary, informal process of adoption had now become a formal, institutionalized process. The BSD was now a core process within DSM and had become 'the way we do business strategy around here.' Increasingly, other organizational processes and routines would be based on the BSD foundation. This pertained, first of all, to other functions (see next section). Over time, the BSD became the bedrock of the DSM approach to evaluating, developing and monitoring its businesses, as well as deciding whether the businesses themselves would remain part of the portfolio. The success of the BSD also led DSM to explore whether such an approach could be equally applied at the corporate level (as will be discussed in Chap. 9, the 'Corporate Strategy Dialogues' becoming the main instrument by which DSM decided on the steps to take, leading to the company's second transformation).

Linking to Other Functions

Once it was clear that the BSD had been adopted as the company's core process for strategy development, the other functions advanced related tools and services to link in with the BSD process (for the 2003 overview, see Fig. 7.4). These related tools were partly aimed at securing the right functional 'input' to BSD processes. Examples in this category include, the 'Strategic Data Checklist,' the' Organizational Scan' and the 'Emerging Technologies Module.' The functions also contributed to a proper (functional) implementation of BSD results in fields like Communications, M&A and Intellectual Property Management. The fact that all these functions referenced to the BSD as a core process greatly enhanced the possibilities for coordination between these functions. The BSD provided the strategic direction for such functional coordination and helped determine the proper priorities.

Another interesting development was that the functions started raising the question about whether the BSD approach could be applied to their own groups. Would it be possible, and worthwhile, to hold a 'Functional Strategy Dialogue'? Various functions started experiments, assisted by the BSD facilitators. For instance, Pieter de Haan, DSM's General Counsel and Director Legal Affairs, started a Functional Strategy Dialogue (FSD) in 2006, assisted by Harrie Boumans, who was an experienced facilitator. Looking outside, BSD's Legal Affairs team noted the ongoing legalization of society, increasing need for compliance, mounting regulatory pressure, globalization of markets, increasing complexity and speed of transactions, more M&As projects, the need for risk management, etc. Confronting this outside analysis with their own organization, Legal Affairs concluded that their old structure would no longer be able to cope with this new context. They decided to change the organization of the legal function by creating one integrated global legal function with a small corporate department (specialists) and a number of regional support centers (generalists) for each BG—a Business Group Legal Lead Counsel. As Pieter de Haan told us, "The BSD process was excellently applicable to the legal function. Questions like, What is our market? Who are our customers? What is the competition?, etc., are just as relevant for functions as they are for businesses." Over the years, many functions, such as Purchasing, IT, Intellectual Property Management and others have held their FSDs and come to the same sort of conclusion.

Revamping DSM's Planning: First Design

Until the formal adoption of BSDs as tool for business strategy, the company operated with a planning process called the Strategic Multiyear Plan (SMP [*Strategisch Meerjaren Plan*]). Many companies still operate today with such a planning process (for its main features, see Fig. 7.5). The SMP was initiated by the Corporate Planning department, which issued 'planning guidelines' during a particular month of the year; in the early 1990s, this happened in March. The

List of facilitators

The following persons have been trained as facilitator over time. Please contact Corporate Planning to discuss specific support for your new BSD.

M. Aertsen	A. Gratama van Andel	T. Stikkers
G. Algra	P. Greidanus	F. Teeuwisse
R. Atsma	E. Meijer	J.P. de Vries
F. Baraké	E. Meinders	J. de Visser
T. Bormans	G. Mooren	J. Wassen
H. Boumans	R. Poldermans	B.Welten
E. de Brabander	L. Radix	
W. Dohmen	K. Rietveld	
R. Gerards	J. Roels	
N. Gerardu	J.Schneiders	
H. Gielkens	J. Scholz	
J. Goessens	H. Schreuder	

Related tools and services

Field	**Tools or service**	**Inquiries**
1.Business Intelligence	Strategic Data Checklist	Corporate Planning & Development
2. Communication	Communications Strategic Development	Corporate Communications
3. Divestments	Divestment Manual	CPL/CFE
4. Human Resources	HRM's contribution to the BSD	Corporate Human Resources
5. Intellectual Property	Intellectual Property Management	DSM Intellectual Property
6. Logistics	Integrated Chain Management (BLA)	Corporate Technology
7. Mergers & Acquisitions	Guideline to manage the M&A process	CPL
8. Marketing	Guide to Marketing Planning	CPL
9. Organization	Organizational Scan	CHR: Consultants
10. Performance measurement	Strategic Value Contract	CPL/CFE
11. Technology	Emerging Technologies Module	Corporate Technology
12. Technology	Business Technology Analysis (BTA)	Corporate Technology
13. Value creation	Value Based Business Steering	CFE

For information:

Corporate Planning & Development
P. Meyer tel. 045-5782911
H. Schreuder tel. 045-5782340

29

Fig. 7.4 List of facilitators and related tools and services (2003). *Source*: guide to business strategy and (long term) performance measurement, DSM corporate planning & development, August 2003

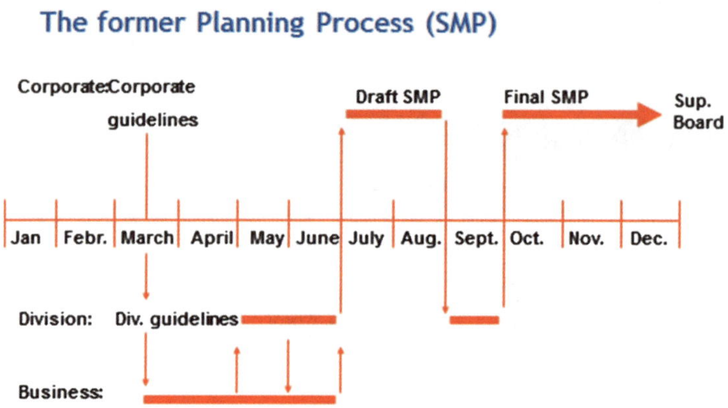

Fig. 7.5 The strategic multiyear plan (SMP)

guidelines covered topics such as expected economic world growth, currency exchange rates and forecasted oil and gas prices as well as strategic themes, which had to be addressed. The guidelines also provided certain templates that were required to be filled in. This standardization was of course aimed at (1) ensuring comparability of the business plans and (2) allowing for consolidation at the corporate level. On the basis of the corporate guidelines the divisions and businesses then started their planning cycle and submitted their preliminary plans to 'corporate' before the summer. After a first consolidation on the corporate level, feedback sessions were held after the summer where divisions could be requested to amend, or further elaborate on, their plans. After having received the final divisional plans a 'corporate SMP' could then be drawn up and discussed by the Managing Board. The MB then submitted its final SMP to the Supervisory Board for approval in a meeting usually held in February/March.

This SMP process may have been productive in earlier times but had become dysfunctional in the early 1990s. The major reasons included:

- After its first transformation, and the subsequent wave of diversification, DSM had changed as a company from a single core business (mining and related chemicals) to a multi-core business with very different businesses in its portfolio. Planning processes that were appropriate for Petrochemicals were not fit for a consumer household products business like Curver. Moreover, DSM wanted to further decentralize in the early 1990s and to 'empower' its businesses. A centrally directed process like the SMP no longer corresponded with this organizational philosophy.
- The SMP attempted to serve too many purposes. Its aim was to produce business and divisional strategies, as well as a corporate strategy. Also functional

strategies (like R&D and HR) were incorporated. The SMP was the basis for internal and external communication. If a process serves so many purposes, it serves none of these purposes very well. The end result was more of a compromise between the different strategic perspectives than an instrument allowing sharp choices. As a result of the many discussion rounds and the ultimate presentation to the Supervisory Board, the final SMP document presented a rather optimistic and 'polished' story rather than an explicit recognition of strategic issues and dilemma's.

- It is perhaps inevitable that a process, which had been used for a great number of years can become 'routinized' over time. This is particularly true if the process is standardized and repetitive to the extent that the SMP was. The standardization generates the risk that the process degenerates into a 'numbers exercise' rather than a strategic discussion. The repetitive character leads people to take last year's plan as the starting-point and to think only of amendments to that plan. As a result, a degree of 'incrementalism' is difficult to avoid.
- The SMP was an example of 'calendar-driven planning.' The process was initiated annually because it was March, not because the businesses perceived a great need to start the process at that point in time. Having to start a planning process because the calendar and 'corporate' say so, generally leads to a lack of motivation at the business level. The businesses themselves felt little ownership of the process; it was seen more as a corporate requirement than as a useful tool for their own purposes.

The successful development and adoption of the BSD allowed DSM to revamp its business planning systems. The Strategic Multiyear Plan was abolished and substituted by the BSDs (see Fig. 7.6). This entailed a number of drastic changes in the way in which DSM operated:

- The responsibility for developing business strategy was effectively decentralized. It was no longer the calendar or 'corporate' requiring the start of a new strategy round, it was left to the businesses to determine the start of their own BSD. In that sense, they were truly 'empowered' and they were (and felt) the owner of their own strategy process.
- Similarly, it was left to the businesses to determine when to start up a new BSD. Reasons to do so could include, (1) that the previous strategy had been fully executed, (2) that the strategy was not working as anticipated, (3) that unexpected developments necessitated a fresh look, or (4) that a new manager had arrived. Whatever the reason, it was felt that the businesses themselves could best judge when a new strategy was in order. This implied that for some businesses, for example in slow-moving, mature markets, there could be quite a while between strategy rounds. In other businesses, for example with new products in newly emerging markets, the interval between strategy rounds might be a lot shorter. On average, DSM's 'cycle time' for business strategy turned out to be about 3 years.

Fig. 7.6 Business strategy dialogues as building blocks of DSM's planning process

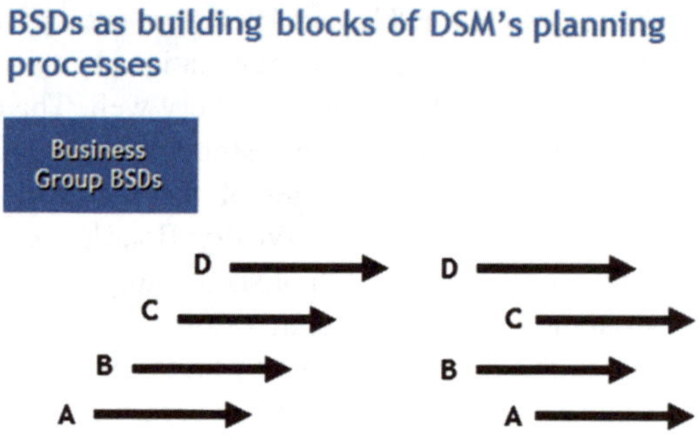

- Since BSDs were designed to address all significant strategic issues and dilemmas in a dialogue mode, they took, on average, half a year to complete. This is a very significant investment in time and resources for a business. However, in combination with the cycle time of 3 years, it implied that businesses could thereafter focus for 2½ years on the 'execution' of their strategy without being 'bothered' by another strategy round. This 'strategic rhythm' suited DSM's businesses much better than the previous annual cycle.
- Of course, a potential drawback to the new planning system was that at any point in time DSM's businesses would be in very different stages of strategy development and execution. Some businesses might be involved in a new strategic dialogue, while others would be in various stages of implementing their BSD. This presented challenges at the corporate level about how to maintain a comparable and consistent overview. However, it was felt that the advantages of the new system at the business level far outweighed such potential disadvantages at the corporate level. As it turned out, the corporate planning challenges were a 'blessing in disguise' because they forced DSM to rethink its corporate planning systems as well.

In the first design of the new planning systems it was felt that DSM could suffice with one additional process being an Annual Strategic Review (ASR). The idea was to ask the business groups once a year how well they were executing their BSDs (note the terminology—the ASR was explicitly a 'review,' not a new strategic exercise). The approved BSD and Performance Indicators were the given context against which the business should report its progress. With the ASRs of all business groups as input, DSM could then construct its Corporate ASR (see Fig. 7.7). While in principle this design could be appropriate for a fully decentralized (financial holding) company, in practice it did not suffice. In hindsight, the reasons are obvious:

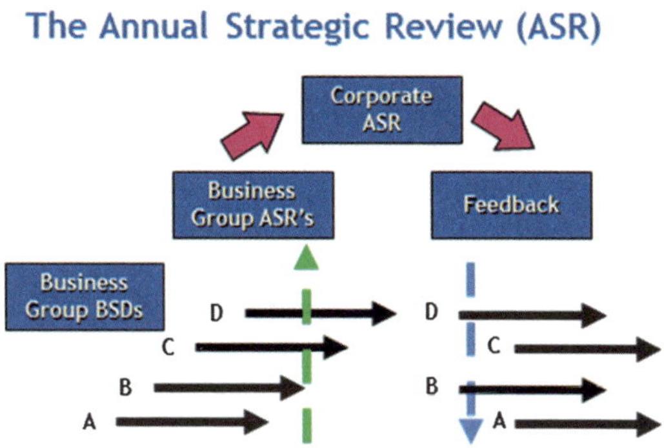

Fig. 7.7 The annual strategic review (ASR)

- DSM was not a financial holding company; it aimed to be a strategic holding company.
- For such a company, corporate strategy is more/different than the consolidation of business strategies.
- As has already been illustrated in Chaps. 1 and 5, DSM was in dire need of a clear corporate strategy in the early to mid-1990s. After the loss-making year of 1993, the confusion about the overall corporate direction had to be addressed. The 1993 memo, summarizing the meeting of a number of business and staff directors, had concluded with the sentence: "None of the directors believes in hanging on."

How this state of affairs led DSM to conduct a strategy dialogue at the corporate level called 'Clarifying the Corporate Strategy' (*Aanscherping Concernstrategie*), in 1994, will be addressed in Chap. 9.

BSDs and Strategic Value Contracts

A better Performance Measurement system was one of the reasons why DSM embarked on the course of developing BSDs (as seen in Chap. 5). After the McKinsey proposal to implement a 'shareholder value' approach at DSM had been rejected, the company developed its own system of Performance Measurement, which entailed the formulation of Key Performance Indicators, or KPIs, derived from the KSFs for realizing the specific Strategic Mission of any business (see Fig. 5.7). Thus, DSM had opted for a decentralized 'strategic monitoring' system next to the standard financial measures.[2] The primary purpose of the new system was to enable the businesses to monitor the success of their own strategy

[2] In the terminology of Goold and Campbell (1987) or Goold and Quinn (1990), DSM was a "strategic control" company.

execution. Next to that, the KPIs could also be used to report to corporate, in addition to the regular financial reporting. Thus, the expanded set of financial numbers and strategic indicators would be part of the regular (quarterly) review meetings between the business and the MB.[3]

This system required a large amount of discipline from the businesses to focus on these KPIs. It is fair to say that this discipline was not always abundantly present. In some cases, a business was so glad to have concluded its BSD that it went to the MB with an incomplete set of KPIs and a promise to finalize this set at a later stage. In some other cases, a complete set of KPIs was formulated but not always adhered to when it came to management reporting. As a result, this initially designed system, which relied heavily on voluntary discipline, was never completely implemented across all DSM businesses to the satisfaction of the MB. It had, however, been sufficiently tried out and adopted within the company's businesses and appreciated for its value regarding the monitoring of strategic progress.

Hence, in 2002, the MB decided to enforce more discipline, deciding to integrate the financial and strategic metrics into one 'Strategic Value Contract' (SVC), to be drawn up after completion of the BSD. Another reason to do this was that during the previous year, DSM had adopted 'Value-Based Business Steering' with new financial metrics. The brochure, "Strategic Value Contract and Reporting Procedures" summed it up:

> About every three years, each DSM Business Group holds a Business Strategy Dialogue (BSD) to determine its strategic direction. . .The BSD is the starting-point for all planning and control processes within DSM. . .In 2001 we have experimented with Strategic Value Contracts, which should capture the main 'promises for performance' from the Business Group, as approved by the Managing Board. These Strategic Value Contracts will henceforth be the end result of a BSD and will form the basis of the ASR as well as the quarterly reporting within DSM. . .The future performance of the business will be monitored against the agreed Strategic Value Contract.[4]

The SVC, which in practice would constitute a six- or seven-page document (Table 7.1), was an innovative way to formalize Performance Management in DSM for two main reasons:

1. The SVC contained both the financial and strategic performance measurements in a format approved by the MB at the conclusion of a BSD. Thus, it brought together these two different perspectives on the performance of the business and allowed for an 'integrated' evaluation.
2. The SVC was conceived as a true two-sided contract; it was signed by the Business Group Director, as well as the member of the Managing Board

[3] Initially called Board Delegate Meetings, because the business would formally meet with one (or two) Board Delegate(s) from the Managing Board. At these meetings, and also at the later Quarterly Review meetings, a member of the financial and the strategic staff would usually participate as well.

[4] From the brochure *Strategic Value Contract and Reporting Procedures*, issued by DSM Corporate Planning & Development and DSM Corporate Finance & Economics in 2002.

Table 7.1 Content of the Strategic Value Contract (SVC)

1. Main assumptions BSD
2. Strategic mission
3. Financial performance (3 years)
4. Value drivers
5. KSFs and KPIs
6. Strategic actions and milestones
7. Required resources
8. Sensitivities

responsible for that business at the MB level. The signature of the BG Director acknowledged the 'promise for performance' of the business. The signature of the MB member acknowledged the approval of the BSD and the expected (financial and strategic) performance of the business. It implied that the MB would enable the execution of the contract by providing the required resources, as long as the 'promise for performance' was kept. The SVC was the last step in the institutionalization of the BSD, as well as the Performance Measurement and Management system based on the BSD, and became the context for the reporting processes and routines within the company. In addition, DSM developed a rhythm of evaluating the progress of the business in meetings of the full Managing Board, twice a year. The SVC was the formal context of evaluation in the spring and the draft Annual Strategic Review (including the Budget) provided this context in the fall. With these rhythms and processes in place, DSM had concluded a journey of about 8 years, developing a sophisticated way to evaluate and monitor its businesses. In Chap. 9 we will step back to the beginning of this journey (1994) to see how the pathway to an evaluation and monitoring of 'corporate' strategic progress developed. As we shall see, this was much less a matter of design. In fact, with hindsight it can be seen that DSM found its way at the corporate level by a process of 'trial—and—(luckily not too much) error.'

References

Goold, M and Campbell, A. *Strategies and Styles: The Role of the Centre in Managing Diversified Companies*. Oxford: Basil Blackwell, 1987.

Goold, M. and Quinn, J.J. *Strategic Control: Milestones for Long-Term Performance*. London: The Economist Books Ltd, 1990.

Jaworsky. J., *Synchronicity: The Inner Path of Leadership*. San Francisco: Berrett Koehler, 1996

Schreuder, H. (1995), "Strategic Monitoring at a Chemical Company." *Long Range Planning*, Vol. 28, No. 6, 1995: 69–77.

8 Contributing to Business Strategy Dialogues

In your past experience with BSD pilots for DSM, what have you learned and can you share this experience with us!
(DSM executives' questions on discussing strategy dialogues)

This was the question posed to Jeannet after stepping into a meeting room at the Dusseldorf Airport in April 1992, with 11 pairs of searching eyes focused on the facilitator[1]

Realizing immediately that much had happened at DSM since his presentation on strategy dialogues the previous September, Jeannet recognized many of the faces present in the room as former participants of DSM's IMPACT Program held at IMD and the follow-up Strategic Management Course (SMC), which had started the previous year. The group, under Hein Schreuder's leadership, were all members of a special 'Task Force,' assembled to propose the best way to adapt the Business Strategy Dialogues (BSD) methodology to DSM's strategy process and present their findings to the Executive Board. Only a few of these people had been at the Marketing Day presentation the previous Fall and most were from non-Marketing functions. They were, however, all familiar with the strategic concepts utilized in the IMPACT courses (but less so with the strategy dialogue concept outlined at the Marketing Day). See Table 8.1 for a list of Dusseldorf Meeting Participants.

[1] The meeting at the Duesseldorf Airport took place on 23 April 1992.

J.-P. Jeannet, H. Schreuder, *From Coal to Biotech*,
DOI 10.1007/978-3-662-46299-7_8

Table 8.1 Participants Düsseldorf Airport Meeting 1992

Participants and their connection to "IMPACT" program concepts
Martin Aertsen (IMPACT-5, August 1989)
Frans Baraké (DSM Marketing Day 1991, IMPACT-2)
Paul van Eijsden (IMPACT-4, June 1989)
Arnold Gratama van Andel (IMPACT-6, August 1990)
Theo Gremmen (SMC-1, 1991)
Boy Litjens
Reinier Maarschalkerweerd (IMPACT-4, June 1989)
Emmo Meijer (DSM Marketing Day 1991)
Geert Mooren (IMPACT-4, June 1989
Hein Schreuder (DSM Marketing Day 1991), Chairman of Group
Theo Vermeegen (SMC-1, 1991)

Contributing to the ABS BSD Pilot[2]

During a trip to Heerlen earlier in 1992 to coordinate future meetings, Jeannet was confronted with another opportunity to conduct a second pilot for the BSD process. Wim Donners, an IMPACT alumnus and recently appointed head of the ABS business, was familiar with the concepts from the program and eager to try out the BSD process on his new business. Having been transferred from research, it was his first experience as a business unit (BU) head and, in his view, a perfect opportunity to learn the business together with his management team. A date was set for a 3-day meeting in early April.[3] Different from the Construction Resin pilot held a year earlier, it was agreed that Schreuder would join the meetings and that he and Jeannet would jointly moderate the sessions.

The determination to have a strategy dialogue on ABS, Donners' business, came on short notice. It was determined that there needs to be a coordination meeting with Donners and Jeannet to help him prepare his team for the session. Due to very tight travel schedule, this meeting happened in a taxi on the way to the Brussels Airport, giving the two a 75–90 min time frame in which to discuss the preparation. During the ride to the airport, about a dozen points, or items, were covered that the ABS business team should bring to the meeting; these were derived from the DSM Resins pilot BSD experience, including the following items:

- List of top customers
- List of R&D projects
- Market data on volumes

[2] Hein Schreuder's impressions and recollections of the ABS Pilot BSD meetings have been summarized in Chap. 5. This section summarizes Jean-Pierre Jeannet's recollection as the outside moderator.

[3] The actual data was 12–14 April 1992, held in the vicinity of Heerlen.

- Market data on segments
- List of key competitors
- Production cost data
- A segmentation of ABS market
- P&L for the business
- Draft outline of the industry business system
- Etc.

This list was based upon the idea that, if all of these items were available in the ABS meeting, dialogue could develop around them. Additionally, it was assumed that this preparatory work could be distributed among the participants from the business and that each person was only responsible for a part of it. Each functional area head was likely to know this material regarding their areas. This would be enough to jumpstart discussions on those topics and drive deeper where necessary.

As requested, the meeting was held offsite in a hotel near Heerlen. The meetings were long, lasting well into evening hours and some of the time slots were left open, for members of the business team to advance the agenda without moderation or intervention on the part of either the team leader, Schreuder, or the facilitator, Jeannet. As the business team was relatively new to their jobs, not all members had experience working together. It was soon clear that tensions would, and did, emerge. Particular strain between functional heads and their conflicting goals began to surface. Managing such tensions would be par for the course for any moderation team if these dialogues were to continue on a DSM-wide basis.

The ABS business also had some very tough strategic challenges. ABS was a small player in the field, competing mostly in the European market. Although the company had some prestigious clients, such as Lego, it was not easy to locate a strong and distinctive competitive advantage.[4]

Jeannet remembers pushing for reasons why DSM would get the business and what made it attractive to buyers. After hearing many reasons of a technical nature, none of them could fully explain the sales results. Finally, the notion of the color team was brought up. After further probing, it was concluded that DSM had a particularly strong color-matching group that was able to outperform competitors when color was crucial to the application. Thus, color matching became a distinctive competence for DSM's ABS business.

This strategy dialogue with the ABS business team was quite different than the earlier experience with the DSM Resins team,[5] due primarily to the longer business experience that the Resins team had brought to the table. Often, the ABS strategy dialogue was left open-ended, with speculative conclusions; there was also a lack of depth in terms of business experience to verify these insights against business and industry knowledge. While the Resin team could be more certain of its conclusions,

[4] DSM eventually divested its ABS business after it was concluded that it would not ever reach sufficient scale.

[5] See Chap. 6 for details on Resin BSD Pilot.

have greater confidence and could move towards strategy and business implications, there were still many unanswered questions for the ABS team. As Schreuder recalled, there were a number of follow-on meetings with Donners, the business head. This experience significantly contributed to DSM's view that it would be difficult to run these sessions as a single meeting and that it would be more valuable to space them out over 3 days, each with a dedicated topic. As it turned out, this was to become common practice for future BSD's.[6]

DSM's top management continued to closely monitor the BSD pilots and Jeannet was asked to join Schreuder to report on their experience at a DSM Executive Board meeting.[7]

Contributing to the DSM Polyethylene (PE) BSD Pilot

For 2 days in August 1992, a BSD exercise was arranged for the Polyethylene (PE) business, one of the major business units in DSM's hydrocarbon cluster. The PE business had a well-established leadership team, many of the executives having served long tenures in the business. Thus, preparation and conduct of the BSD workshop were different from the other business units dealt with previously. The business team preferred to present their business and segments using a large number of formally prepared overhead slides. Professionally done, the slides gave the impression of certain 'finality,' making points that were not to be open for discussion. As a result, it had the feeling of a long business briefing where the business team was informing a group of visitors about the status of their business, performance and sales developments. It turned out that it was much more difficult to apply the lenses of IMPACT concepts on the business and industry in this situation, despite the fact that several of the participants had previously attended IMPACT. Although there was enough time for discussions, they actually took more the form of answering questions about presentations rather than the searching type dialogues that were typical of the previous BSD pilots for Resins and ABS.

While the team of moderators came to the meeting with the intent of broadly exploring the PE industry, and review DSM's competitive position in that industry sector, the PE business team primarily wanted to sell its strategy, calling for a major capacity expansion. Clearly, the starting point for the moderator and the business team were different and reduced the business team's willingness to question past practices or to get to the fundamentals of how to compete in the PE industry. A list was circulated during the meeting detailing, 'The PE industry experience in this room' of each of the business team members. The nine team members had a combined 135 years of PE experience; this number was then promptly compared

[6] For a detailed description of the ABS BSD pilot workshop see Schreuder's descriptions in Chap. 5.

[7] The meeting with the DSM Executive Board took place on 1 and 2 June 1992, in Heerlen (as per the co-author's calendar).

to the moderator team's experience with the implied question, "What do you know about this industry?"[8]

The experience with the PE business team demonstrated that good dialogue was assured only when all participants joined the discussions with open minds and did not arrive with previously completed strategies, or answers. While it useful to have market data and internal sales and performance data at their fingertips, it was not helpful to the principle of dialogue if minds were already made up. One of the main elements of the ideas behind the strategy dialogue was to let the analysis take its course and not to second-guess it with preferred alternatives. Even though five of the nine PE business team members had been to the various IMD IMPACT programs, their conceptual knowledge was not sufficient to guarantee an open discussion. And, the fact that the business head had not been participated in IMPACT didn't help either.

In the previous two pilots, with Resins and ABS, the Business Strategy Dialogue process had been activated by BU heads new to their businesses; in both cases, they had been IMPACT alums and more open to new ideas. However, in terms of PE the management team had been in place for some time, had their own pre-conceived notions as to what the strategy should be and were involved in negotiations with the DSM Managing Board on a major capacity expansion. This expansion was dear to the hearts of the PE management team so that no open discussion could take place that just might, in the end, endanger their preferred outcome. This signaled that a business team could also be 'over-experienced,' and that the conditions for a thoughtful outcome of the dialogue had to be carefully set to avoid that the process would get undermined by a pre-set agenda.

Contributing to the DSM Curver-Rubbermaid BSD

In early 1993, Jeannet again teamed up with Schreuder, on a strategy exercise for Curver-Rubbermaid. The company represented a forward integration for DSM. The European firm Curver, in conjunction with its joint venture (JV) partner Rubbermaid in the US, were producing and Marketing plastic products for home and kitchen use. Rubbermaid was a well-known firm with major brand recognition in the US market. In the European market, Curver was more widely known, particularly in Germany. Participating in Curver allowed Rubbermaid to explore the European market and DSM was able to obtain a foothold in a major customer of some of its basic plastic materials (PP, PE and ABS). Despite the strategic logic for both firms to be owners of Curver-Rubbermaid, the business had been struggling for some time to reach satisfactory profitability and the need arose to subject the business to a BSD-type exercise.

[8] For the original see Fig. 7.1.

The Curver BSD process differed from other previous BSDs. The process called for a support spread over time (Jeannet was to support Schreuder's business and corporate planning efforts). Several different meetings were held and it was the first time that a BSD had been extended that way—all previous BSD exercises had been executed in one go, with some subsequent internal follow-up. After a first meeting with the Curver CEO, in order to settle boundary conditions and the scope of the exercise, two 3-day meetings were held, followed later by a summary meeting. Participating were the usual small number of direct reports to the CEO.[9]

The additional time needed for Curver's BSD process may have been related to the fact that Curver was not a core business for DSM. Representing a forward integration, DSM was not active in any other consumer products. As a result, little knowledge existed internally about the sector. Also, as a JV company Curver was probably less tightly controlled by DSM and, as a result, the parent company was less a part of the typical strategy processes. In addition, Curver executives were not included in the original IMPACT courses. This lack of conceptual experience necessitated longer breaks between sessions, in order to obtain needed facts about issues that had surfaced during the meetings. As pointed out earlier, the Curver meeting format was to become, over time, the model for all BSDs at DSM. The new set-up would also render it more difficult for outside moderators to participate. Faculty, or consultants, might be available for single 2 or 3 days sessions but it would be more difficult to schedule them for multiple sessions.

Assisting DSM in the Creation of Its Own BSD Process

In the course of about 18 months, valuable experience had been acquired surrounding the BSD process as it might be crafted around the DSM realities. Jeannet had moderated the first pilot alone (Resins), and teamed up with Schreuder for a series of differently positioned businesses (such as PE, ABS, and Curver-Rubbermaid); these experiences represented a diverse background of business units with radically different strategic imperatives, sets of managers with more or less industry experience in their businesses and units with varying levels of strategic clarity of their strategy.

DSM was a company that favored well-developed methodologies and was disposed towards manuals and documentation that covered content, as well as approach. The Task Force that Jeannet had met in April 1992, at the Dusseldorf airport, was asked to document the BSD process. A brochure entitled, "Guide to Business Strategy and (Long Term) Performance Measurement" was the result.[10]

[9] DSM Curver-Rubbermaid CEO at the time was Antony Lenders. A first meeting with him took place in January 1993, with the first 3-day meeting in April and then on 2 May. The follow-up meeting was held 2 weeks later.

[10] Internal company document entitled, 'Guide to Business Strategy and (Long Term) Performance Measurement,' DSM, 1992, publication and printing February 1993: 27.

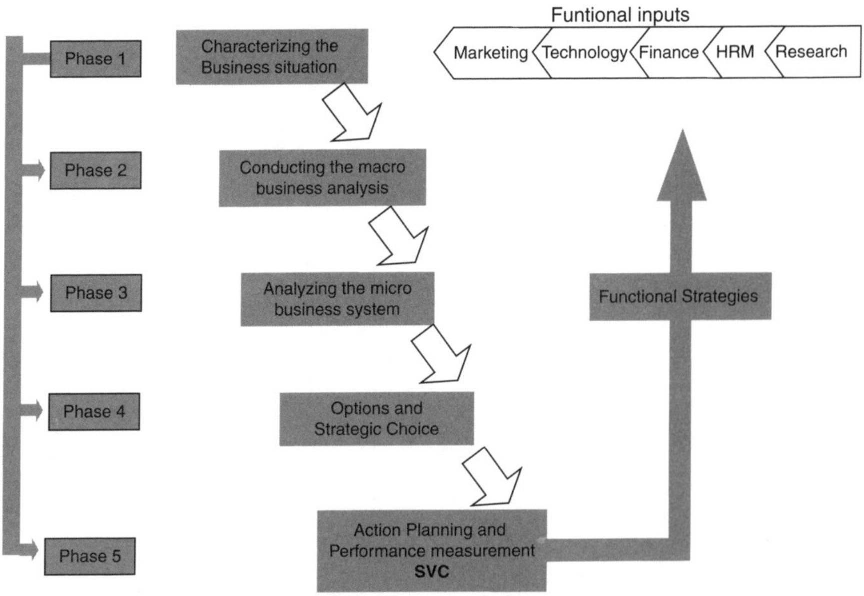

Fig. 8.1 DSM five-phase strategy process with functional inputs and strategies. *Source*: DSM guide to business strategy, 2008

On some 25 pages, the group proposed to the DSM Managing Board a process that incorporated the IMPACT concepts and extended these with some further strategic concepts, adopted Jeannet's idea of a strategy dialogue and also created a five-phase process of which the business strategy dialogue was but one of the phases. A working group (consisting of Vermeegen, Aertsen, van Eijsden, Schreuder and Maarschalkerweerd, all part of the Dusseldorf meeting) proposed that it was Jeannet's role to ensure that the IMPACT concepts were correctly displayed and described in DSM's draft Guide to Business Strategy and (long-term) Performance Measurement. DSM changed the phasing of the BSD process and had extended it to include Performance Measurement. These and other additions went beyond the original IMPACT concepts. For the faculty, this marked a shift from concept supplier to co-creator. Several later additions to this guide were also published and it remained in regular use for a number of years.[11] See Figs. 8.1 and 8.2 for details on the DSM Process.

[11] Additional publications of this guide took place on 1995, 2001, 2003, 2008 and in 2011. In addition, a 'Strategic Data Check List' was issued in 1996 to guide the data collection aspect of BSD exercises.

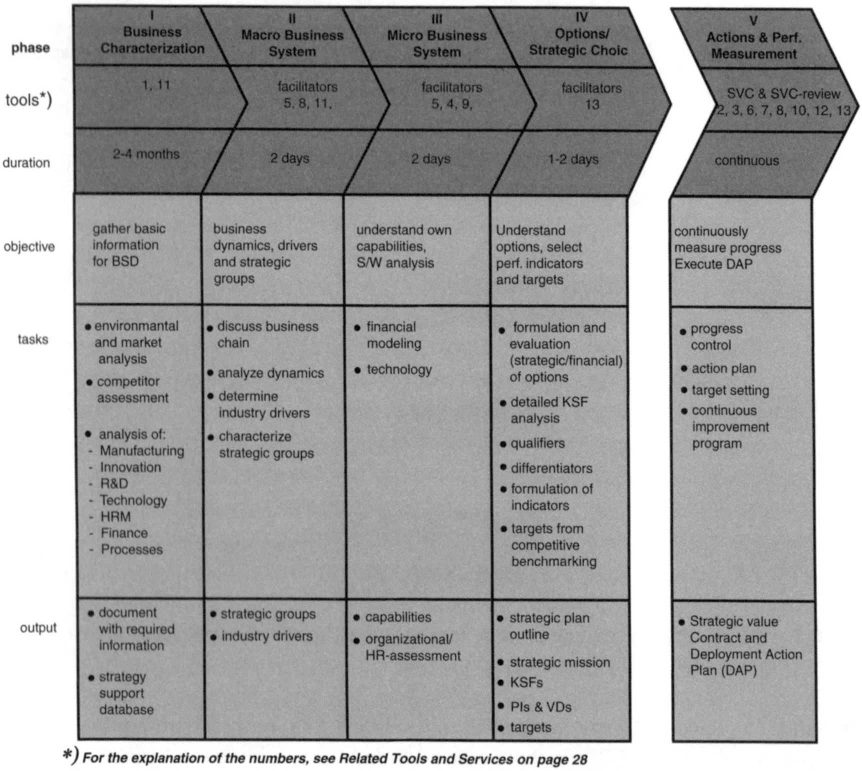

Fig. 8.2 DSM strategy development process and tasks. *Source*: DSM guide to business strategy, 2008 (for the content of Strategic Data Checklist please refer to Fig. 7.3)

DSM's Need for More Trained Managers and Moderators

The experience of the above-cited BSDs with Resins, PE, ABS and Curver-Rubbermaid demonstrated that a sufficiently trained cadre of managers was required to carry out the process. Both the conceptual understanding around the concepts taught in DSM's IMPACT courses, as well as the role of dialoguing and moderating, needed to be understood to make it a fruitful and valuable exercise.

The IMPACT courses were originally oriented towards Industrial Marketing. However, the BSD exercises that had already been carried out showed that it was necessary to have all the business functions present, not just Marketing. A gap existed in functions such as Research, Production and Finance, all of which were needed to contribute to a successful BSD. This lead to an extension of the IMPACT program and the launch of a program named Strategic Management Course (SMC). Equally important, however, was the availability of a group of individuals who could moderate these sessions. They needed to be steeped in the IMPACT concepts, as well as have a sense of how to guide a management or business team through the process. For that purpose, a Facilitators Course was created.

The DSM Facilitators Course

Early in the BSD rollout process, DSM had asked for support in creating a special course for facilitators who could be called in to assist the business in the process of running a BSD. DSM had developed its own approach to the BSD process and, in particular, had gravitated towards a model including both a facilitator and a challenger.[12]

The splitting of the facilitator and the challenger roles showed some differences in the discussion cultures between business schools and company settings. In business schools—IMD was a typical example of this approach—the faculty member has always served in both roles of moderating the discussion and challenging participants to a higher level of insights. It was a natural role for faculty members and the use of the large black boards to keep up with the discussion was part of this. In setting such an environment up for DSM, the comment, "Well, when you stand in front of the group you make it all come out so easy! We cannot do this!" was often heard. Although Jeannet had done the first pilot BSDs functioning as moderator and challenger, the sentiment among the early cohort of future facilitators was clearly that they would not be able to perform both roles in parallel. If DSM wanted to pursue this process with internal talent, an accommodation for their preferences had to be reached.

With the company deciding to staff its own facilitating and challenger roles from internal resources, and not to rely on outside consultants, there arose a need to bring in a group of senior staff and executives to facilitate the process. The program was under the responsibility of Corporate Planning and Development (CPL), such as Schreuder and his staff.

The facilitator workshops were taught by a team, which included both business school professors and CPL members who had accumulated some experience conducting BSDs. The course was increasingly driven by DSM staff and was held in the Limburg region. Selection of candidates for the program was undertaken by CPL. An invitation was also issued by DSM's CEO, a clear signal that it was an important program for the company, taught by its senior executives and managers.

The role of the academic partner consisted of teaching a refresher module of the major strategic concepts taught previously during IMPACT; initially, it took about 1 day. A second day was devoted to facilitating skills, also taught in conjunction with the academic partners. A third day was devoted to examples, or best practice, and documented and instructed by CPL members.

The facilitator course was offered every other year or so—at less regular intervals than other DSM management courses. Over time, the review of strategic

[12] See Chap. 7 for detailed descriptions on facilitator and challenger models.

concepts tended to be reduced because many of those elements were absorbed by the DSM planning and strategic culture. More time was focused on some difficult elements of the strategy process and on sharing experience from previous BSDs. What began as a 3-day workshop was eventually reduced to 2 days.

When DSM first started with the facilitator program, most participants were culled from the group of IMPACT seminar alumni. In later years, many other participants were recruited and some did not have IMPACT experience—they were alumni of the SMC program, launched as a follow on for IMPACT.

Developing the Strategic Management Course

The idea of a follow-up program to IMPACT started early and was fielded towards the end of six programs held in 1990. Even before DSM had embarked on a larger effort to institutionalize BSDs, the company and its leadership realized that although successful, the company still had a considerable need to form younger talent in a fashion similar to what IMPACT had achieved. DSM was particularly keen to emphasize the business and environmental analysis, and less so the classical, industrial marketing topics. The idea then arose to strip IMPACT of its pure marketing content and to create a shorter course focused on strategy. Originally termed 'Compact,' due to its shorter duration, the course was eventually launched as Strategic Management Course (SMC) to emphasize the strategy focus.

A first group of 36 managers was sent to IMD in June 1991. The course was aimed at upper level managers of all business functions, such as Business managers, Marketing managers, Plant managers, Research managers, Controllers, HR managers and other support disciplines. This was a clear departure from the IMPACT that was squarely focused on Business and Marketing managers; this cohort was quite diverse in containing all business functions.

In the internal DSM program brochure, the objectives included four elements that the program was expected to encompass:

1. Introduce participants to the business and environmental analysis concepts that could be employed to assess the competitiveness of their own business
2. Provide a framework that could be employed throughout DSM for the development of business plans by utilizing the concepts taught in the IMPACT course
3. Enhance participants' understanding of how competitiveness could be created in their own businesses
4. Help create a personal network for participants to exchange ideas and reinforce the DSM corporate identity

In terms of content and sessions, the program contained sessions with the following titles:

- Developing a Business Plan
- Understanding Your Industry (The Business System)

- Leveraging Key Success Factors
- Assessing Generic Strategies
- Developing Strategic Options
- Assess Industry Dynamics
- Managing Technology

Not included were the more 'Marketing-oriented' topics, such as pricing, distribution and some issues dealing with negotiation. See Table 8.2 for SMC-1 Block Schedule.

The teaching material utilized for the SMC-1, as it was later called, included some DSM-specific materials that had not been utilized in earlier IMPACT programs where the faculty relied more on existing, publicly available materials. For SMC, a first case on the Polyethylene (PE) industry was developed, focusing on the industry sector as a whole. A second case was developed for DSM Construction Resins, the business unit that was the subject of the first BSD pilot—an integrated case requiring participants not only analyze the entire industry sector but also follow through on functional strategies, such as application for Production, Marketing and Research. The DSM Resins Business manager attended that session to create a more realistic atmosphere. This was a model that was used later in many later programs run for DSM.

Regarding faculty, DSM had insisted on the same delivery team that had led IMPACT (Jeannet and Joe D'Cruz who was a visiting faculty member on leave from University of Toronto when the original IMPACT series began). In order to cover new technology topics, the faculty team was enhanced with Jean-Philippe Deschamps who had joined IMD from the consulting company ADL.

On the business side, IMD delivered a 1-week SMC program for the fee of CHF 125,000, or half the price of the 2-week IMPACT programs—a price that was agreed upon after some intense negotiations between IMD and DSM. After the last of six IMPACT programs, that had been contracted under the original fee of CHF 250,000, or CHF 125,000 per week, the IMD fee structure changed, in part a reflection of stronger business and increased demand for In-Company programs. The school's daily rate was increased to CHF 30,000 and the program was 'labeled' a 6-day program, resulting in a potential fee of CHF 180,000 for the week. These policy changes came at the time of the IMEDE/MI merger into IMD (see Chap. 2), and with the appointment of a new head for the In-Company programs to replace Professor Collins. For a while, DSM considered taking the program out of IMD but after discussions it was agreed that the first SMC program would be run under the old fee structure and that DSM reserved the option of taking the program privately after that.[13]

[13] Based upon detailed analysis of correspondence between DSM (Menno de Vries for DSM Corporate Management Training), Juan Rada (IMD's newly appointed Director General), Andre Vandermerwe (IMD newly appointed head of In-Company Programs), Robert Collins (IMD outgoing head of In-Company Programs), and Vijay Jolly (Professor who followed Andre Vandermerwe as head of In-Company Programs).

Table 8.2 SMC-1 program block schedule

DSM strategic management course (June 23–29, 1991)							
Program Director: Jean-Pierre Jeannet				Auditorium Bignami 3			
Program Administrator: Claire Zwerner							
Sunday, June 23		**Monday, June 24**	**Tuesday, June 25**	**Wednesday, June 26**	**Thursday, June 27**	**Friday, June 28**	**Saturday, June 29**
	08:30–12:00	**Developing a business plan**	**Understanding your industry The business system**	**Assessing generic strategies**	**Assessing industry & technology dynamics**	**Managing technology for competitive advantages**	**Group presentations**
		Alfa-Laval	Paint Industry	Cellulose Altisholz	European PE Industry 1990	Technology management	Faculty
		Prof. Jeannet	Prof. Jeannet	Prof. D'Curz	Prof. Jeannet	Prof. Deschamps	
						Put it all Together	
	12:00–13:30	Lunch	Lunch	Lunch	Lunch	Lunch	Lunch
Cocktails and opening dinner IMD Restaurant	13:30–17:30	**Segmenting the market**	**Leveraging key success factors**	**Developing strategic options and managing interfaces**	**Developing an integrative business strategy**	**Continued**	
		John Deere	The tissue products industry in Europe	Jeanneau (1986)	DSM PE	DSM Resins	
		Prof. D'Cruz	Prof. D'Cruz	Prof. Jeannet	Prof. Jeannet	Prof. Jeannet	
19:30						Farewell dinner	

Source: DSM/IMD

It is interesting to note that DSM had originally called on IMD to deliver an Industrial Marketing program. The earlier experience at IMD with Sulzer Brothers, a Swiss engineering company (also see Chap. 2), who had come to IMD for a program on market orientation, had resulted in IMD's faculty team to consider the value of applying Strategy and Marketing at the same time. So when DSM launched IMPACT, the requested Industrial Marketing program had evolved in a market orientation program with a strong emphasis on strategy. The very positive experience, and exposure to those strategy topics, caused DSM to then specifically request a strategy program in the form of the SMC. Having enhanced the strategic capabilities of its executives, it was then possible for DSM to pursue the BSD idea and roll it out throughout the company.

The virtuous learning cycles from the Sulzer experience to DSM IMPACT and then on to BSD concepts, facilitator workshops and SMC programs, would have been much more difficult to achieve had not the same faculty team with a coherent educational philosophy been employed. The faculty consisted mostly of IMEDE/IMD-based professionals although by and large the recurring visitors delivered the majority of the sessions. Jeannet, John Murray (Trinity) and D'Cruz (Toronto) were teaching many of these programs, with the steady support of permanent IMD faculty, such as Collins (also In-Company program director for much of this time) and some Marketing faculty. For a period of about 7 years, these faculty members were working closely with one another, facilitating the learning from program to program and from company to company.

Taking the SMC Program In-House

In August 1991, 2 months after the successful launch of the SMC at IMD, DSM informed IMD of its intention to bring the SMC program in-house and no longer use the business school's services anymore.[14] DSM reasoned that the original IMPACT programs were part of a special project with a corresponding budget but that continuing programs, such as the SMC would have to be funded by regular budgets and could not support the relatively high fees of IMD. Since DSM had already taken out an option to do that, the path towards an internal program was clear. After IMD confirmed that there was no impediment to hire its own faculty, DSM engaged the same faculty team that had run previous courses for them.[15]

[14] Letter by Menno de Vries (DSM Corporate Management Training) to Juan Rada, Director General of IMD, dated 1 August 1991.

[15] The cost savings for DSM were substantial. Using two faculty each day, even accounting for their travel expenses and paying for the rental of the venue, amounted to about CHF 15,000 per day, which was about half the daily fee for IMD that included free use of facilities and food during the day. In addition, most participants where from the Limburg region where the program was placed, thus saving travel costs for about two-thirds of the cohort. Also, hotel costs in Holland were below Lausanne hotel costs.

The decision to make the SMC an in-house program was much debated at IMD. The school had lost a major client and with its faculty being asked to teach in the in-house programs, some at IMD were concerned that its faculty was going to compete with the institution. The rules were interpreted at that time differently than they would be today; under the same circumstances today the faculty team would normally be forbidden to engage in such teaching activity.

With the SMC being run in-house at DSM's Vaalsbroek facility, its head office in Southern Holland, a number of changes were instituted. The program became even more focused on business unit strategy; the following topics remained part of the program for many years:

- Industry Dynamics
- Strategic Priorities
- Generic Strategies
- Industry Key Success Factors
- Analyzing Competitor Strategies
- Industry Vision
- Strategic Options
- Strategy Dialogue
- Ending Exercise

The program opened on Sunday, in the late afternoon, with a full opening session, ran the entire week and ended on Saturday noon, following an intensive industry analysis exercise. About 60 % of the teaching material consisted of publicly available cases but related to the chemical process industry and had been tested in previous DSM programs. The final part of the program used DSM cases on relevant industries, such as the PE and Resins industries. The entire program was focused on the ending exercise, which ran as a simulated BSD group exercise with presentations to senior managers from that particular BU. Participants worked every evening on case preparation. To an audience today, this might sound rather harsh but this was a time without email or mobile phones and faxes were not so easily sent to seminar venues. Once the participants rolled in, they became a captive audience for the duration of the program. Starting on a Sunday afternoon and going through the following Saturday resulted in a very intensive and complete strategy program.

DSM utilized its company-owned Vaalsbroek Castle in Limburg as a venue, close to the German and Belgian border. It was a lovely old manor house with a large park-like garden, a pond and an attached old mill with restaurant and hotel facilities. Although only about 30 min by car from DSM's Heerlen head office, the town of Vaals was a 60- to 90-min taxi ride from the nearest airports of Brussels or Dusseldorf. This serene château was about a 30-min walk outside the town of Vaals and became the location for a whole series of DSM seminars until DSM sold the property to an international conference management company. From there on, many of the DSM seminars were relocated to hotels in the general Maastricht and Heerlen area.

The building, however, was not ideal from a teaching point of view and the group rooms were distributed all over the château. The main classroom had limited technology and couldn't be compared to IMD's modern facilities. The faculty, used to huge blackboards and tiered classrooms in horseshoe shaped arrangements, had to get used to running discussions around much smaller boards rolled in the room for each program and to adapt to the flat room settings.

Evolving the SMC Faculty Team

Once the SMC program had moved in-house, program planning and timing had to consider the availability of faculty since all of them were affiliated with different institutions.[16] At the beginning of the program, there was an 'opening crew' for the first 3 days and a 'closing crew' for the next 4 days; with two faculty members needed for each day, the program involved initially four people. As time went on, arrangements were made for three faculty members to participate; Jeannet teamed up with a colleague for the beginning and then was joined by a second colleague for the end. The team members would switch roles so that there were always three people with experience for the entire program. The SMC team included experienced faculty from the IMPACT program series (including Joe D'Cruz and John Murray) and, over time, younger faculty who were new to the IMPACT seminars.[17] By 2008, some 19 SMC programs had been delivered and due to the consistency of the team, continuity was assured. See Table 8.3 for a SMC course listing.

When a program is run on an institutional basis, with a formal contract with a business school, the school is responsible to staff the program, even in case of emergencies or illness. In contrast, when a company runs a program on its own by hiring individual faculty from the outside on a consulting basis, the risk is on the company to make sure that the program can be run even in case of emergency.

SMC Expansion Abroad

For the period 1991–2004, a total of 16 SMCs had been delivered in the Limburg area. Initially, they were all in Vaalsbroek Castle, and later on also held in other hotels in the region. With DSM's internationalization progressing rapidly, particularly with the acquisition of the Roche Vitamins business in Switzerland, the company suddenly found that many of its target groups were located outside the Limburg area. The DSM Business Academy (DBA), the organizational unit that

[16] Jeannet took the lead in line with his previous experience with IMPACT at IMD and since he was based in the US at Babson College during the regular US academic semesters (Fall and Spring), the timing had to be such that it fit his schedule and that of other faculty involved.

[17] John Murray (1948–2010) was a great friend, colleague and contributor to many DSM programs and participated in virtually all SMC programs.

Table 8.3 DSM SMC program dates and venues

• SMC-1: IMD, 23–29 June 1991
• SMC-2: Vaalsbroek 1–6 June 1992
• SMC-3: Vaalsbroek: 4–10 April 1993
• SMC-4: Vaalsbroek, 18–23 April 1994
• SMC-5: Vaalsbroek 17–23 April 1994
• SMC-6: Vaalsbroek 2–7 April 1995
• SMC-7: Vaalsbroek 21–26 April 1996
• SMC-8: Vaalsbroek 20–25 April 1997
• SMC-9: Vaalsbroek 19–24 April 1998
• SMC-10: Vaalsbroek 19–23 April 1999
• SMC-11: Vaalsbroek 9–14 April 2000
• SMC-12: Vaalsbroek 14–19 May 2000
• SMC-13: Vaalsbroek 9–13 April 2001
• SMC-14: Vaalsbroek 15–19 April 2002
• SMC-15: Vaalsbroek 19–23 May 2003
• SMC-16: Vaalsbroek 10–14 May 2004
• SMC-17: CEIBS, Shanghai, 13–18 March 2005
• SMC-18: Babson College/Boston 20–24 March 2006
• SMC-19: Basel/CH: 26–30 March 2007
SMC program faculty:
Jeannet (Babson/IMD) SMC 1–19
Joe D'Cruz (Toronto/IMD) SMC 1–16
John Murray (Trinity Dublin/IMD) SMC 2–17, 19
Dan Muzyka (Insead) SMC 3–10
James Henderson (Babson) SMC 11–16, 18–19
SMC program administrators (DSM business academy)
Menno de Vries SMC 1–6
Joop Joosen SMC 7–9
Christiane Thielens SMC 11–13
Rob van Tilburg SMC 13–18
Mark Oskam SMC 19

had become responsible for all executive education programs, in conjunction with the Corporate Planning Group committed to take the SMC 'on the road' and to have only every third program in Europe. This was a considerable departure from past practice.

In March 2005, SMC-17 was held at the Shanghai campus of China Europe International Business School (CEIBS). DSM had begun a major effort to make many of its businesses active in China and thus had a large number of potential participants. However, there was also a considerable group flying in from Europe who wanted to use this opportunity to learn more about the Chinese business realities. The program was essentially structured in the same as previous versions that had run in Europe. A special China module was added up front and the ending exercise was focused on one of the DSM businesses in China.

In Spring 2006, the SMC-18 was held at the Executive Education Center at Babson College (Wellesley, MA in the US). The material and the content were largely similar and participants came both from US and European businesses. In 2007, SMC-19 was held in Basel to accommodate the large number of participants from the DSM Nutrition cluster (formerly Roche Vitamins) located in that area. This turned out to be the last SMC program in its original format. A new format for the same content was launched at the end of 2007 (see Chap. 10).

Program Management and Organization at DSM

At the time of SMC's inception, the program was managed by DSM in the same way that the IMPACT programs had been. The same individual (Menno de Vries) was responsible for the process at DSM, which included contracting the program with IMD, recruiting and selecting participants, coordinating the logistics with IMD concerning hotel arrangements and collaborating with the faculty team regarding content. De Vries, who was heading DSM's Corporate Management Training, was also in charge of bringing the program in-house and conducting all of the negotiations with IMD. For the faculty team, little changed, because the same professionals were at DSM with which to interact. De Vries continued to be responsible for the program until his retirement in 1996. From that moment on, the organizational responsibility changed intermittently and involved four DSM program managers.[18] The corporate management training organizational set-up also changed. With the inception of DBA, additional responsibilities were added to the program management unit. However, despite these changes, the commitment of the DSM program managers remained the same and from the faculty team perspective there remained a consistency which covered commitments made from year to year. Since the company also had a long-term commitment to the program, dates were proposed to the faculty a year or more in advance, allowing for forward planning and coordination.

Responsibility for Program Content

The content of the SMC programs remained the prerogative of DSM Corporate Planning Department. Schreuder headed that department for almost 20 years (until his retirement in 2011) and took a strong personal interest in program design and visited the program each time to give participants an overview of the DSM strategy process. Since he was intimately involved in the BSD strategy process (serving as Chief Strategy Officer [CSO]), the content reflected the changing needs of DSM. DSM's Business Academy did not influence the content of the SMC programs but

[18] Joop Joosen (SMC 7–9); Christiane Thielens (SMC 10–13); Rob van Tilburg (SMC 14–18); Mark Oskam (SMC 19).

restricted itself to program logistics. There was a close cooperation, however, between DBA and Corporate Planning and all the responsible executives knew each other, making for effective personal interactions. Additionally, it was certainly of great importance that the person in the CSO role did not change over the period, assuring consistency regarding the DSM strategy outlook and process.

Making the SMC Sustainable

An executive education program running for over 16 years is rather unique. It is important to reflect on some elements that have contributed to that long run. Although the faculty and the CSO were the same over the entire period 1991–2007, DSM as a company underwent enormous changes. These changes (see Chap. 9) included a massive reorganization through divestments and acquisitions. Although the program structure underwent few changes over the years, the teaching material changed as the DSM business portfolio evolved. The early SMC programs were dominated by Hydrocarbon and Base Chemical businesses and the teaching material, in the form of cases, reflected that composition. As DSM divested its basic chemical businesses, one by one, and then acquired more and more Life Sciences companies to transform into a Materials and Life Sciences company, teaching materials related to the new industry sectors had to take the place of older ones, even if the underlying concepts to be taught remained constant. The responsibility and initiative for this change remained with the program faculty whose self-interest was to remain current in the eyes of participants.

The program's ending exercise serves as a good example of these material changes. Originally, the program ended with materials on the PE and Resins industries. At a later stage, material was included about DSM's other chemical sectors. In a next phase, the Melamine industry became the focus for a while, while, finally, the focus moved to the Food and Nutritional sectors, which had become a major part of DSM's portfolio. As part of this transition, the participant profiles changed and the geographic locations of the business shifted away from Southern Limburg and even from Holland. In order to remain fresh in the eyes of participants, the teaching material was constantly undergoing changes and the faculty was always challenged to demonstrate relevancy by learning new industries and business sectors. Despite such efforts to remain current, the SMC program underwent substantial changes in 2007, caused by the enormous transformation that took place at DSM, which also brought about a geographic shift. The last of the 19 SMCs was delivered in Basel, in March 2007, due to the large number of managers brought in through the DNP acquisition.

Role and Contribution of SMC Programs

The importance of running the SMC program for such a long time cannot be underestimated. DSM, by maintaining the program and expanding it internationally, assured itself a continued supply of new recruits for the many BSDs run on a regular basis for its businesses. Some BSD exercises had involved as many as 50 participants at different levels and could only be carried out successfully if an extended cadre of informed participants understood and appreciated the underlying approach and concepts.

In addition, the changes in the DSM business portfolio over time meant that every time a business was divested, trained executives left the company. Equally, with every acquisition, a new group of executives had to be exposed to the principles of its BSD approach. Maintaining the role of the BSD process while changing the corporate portfolio could only be accomplished through an intensive management development effort carried out consistently over all the years.

The faculty team responsible for delivering the SMC programs had remained largely unchanged over time and could provide consistency for younger generations of managers. It was not the role of the faculty to direct or influence DSM strategy. Instead, the faculty's role was to ensure that there would be a sufficient management talent who understood the principles of strategy and could engage, together with senior management, in the transformation of individual businesses and thus DSM as a whole. Without this pedagogic contribution, DSM's ability to carry out its strategic transformation through a number of crucial dialogues might have been more difficult.

Role and Contribution of SME Programs

Experimenting with Corporate Strategy Dialogues to Focus and Explore

9

If strategy dialogues are successful at the business level, can we also conduct them at the corporate level?
—Simon de Bree

The Chairman of DSM's Managing Board asked this question in 1993. This chapter will chart the answers DSM formulated over time to this question and show how DSM embarked on an exploratory journey to find its way to a corporate strategy that dealt with the major uncertainties that the company faced during the early 1990s. It will also be illustrated how, over time, DSM became increasingly confident that it could develop and execute a strategy allowing it to determine its own future. This confidence enabled the company to follow through with the major steps that constituted its second transformation. However, what was the context within which the company operated when De Bree posed the question?

DSM in 1993

At the time, DSM was in a state of some disarray and the reasons were threefold.

First, the company suffered a loss in 1993: the net result at the end of the year would amount to Dfl −118 million. It had again become clear that DSM's main businesses were highly cyclical. They could generate enormous cash flows and profits in 'the good years,' but these would inevitably be followed by another downturn. The Petrochemicals business, which had already had an operational loss of Dfl −53 million in 1992, slid further down to a loss of Dfl −183 million in 1993. The Base and Fine Chemicals saw their results dive into an operational loss of Dfl −105 million.[1] The results of other activities (including Energy) were

[1] The results of Fine Chemicals were grouped with those of Base Chemicals at the time because: (1) Fine Chemicals was still a rather insignificant part of DSM and (2) the results of Fine Chemicals were not yet at a level that could be shown separately.

J.-P. Jeannet, H. Schreuder, *From Coal to Biotech*,
DOI 10.1007/978-3-662-46299-7_9

positive but could not compensate for these heavy losses. DSM did not pay an interim dividend in 1993 but decided instead to pay a final dividend of Dfl 1.50 per share (1992: Dfl 4.00), which it therefore had to finance by borrowing. During the year there was no visible 'light at the end of the tunnel.'

Second, attempts to increase the scale of DSM had floundered. Two routes had been attempted: (a) an overall company merger and (b) a potential partnership in Petrochemicals. The overall company merger was explored with AKZO (again) in 1992 by a joint task force.[2] The idea was to create a 'NewCo' and to jointly determine:

- what should be the core of NewCo?
- which activities (in both companies) should be divested?
- what would be the future strategy of NewCo?

The task force reached agreement on all three issues and there was an expectation that the groundwork had been lain for the Boards of AKZO and DSM to proceed toward joint conclusions; a dinner meeting was arranged. But, Aarnout Loudon, Chairman of the Board of Management at AKZO, had a nasty surprise for DSM's Board when he arrived for the dinner and announced that he had had "a bad night's sleep" and come to the conclusion that, "we better not do this." The DSM delegation was taken totally by surprise; such behavior was just 'not done.'

In the NewCo merger with AKZO concept, DSM's Petrochemicals had been categorized as a business to be divested. When these discussions floundered, DSM was therefore 'back to square one' in deciding how to deal with this business. There was a widespread feeling that DSM could not afford the wide swings of results caused by the cyclicality of Petrochemicals. There were also doubts whether DSM could continue to compete successfully in a business driven by the need to achieve economies of scale and increasingly within a global context. This led the company to initiate discussions with Exxon to explore the viability of a European joint venture in Petrochemicals. Significantly, the code name for this discussion was 'Project Scale.'[3] With help of a third party, both companies submitted their assumptions and forecasts into a valuation model that would then indicate the value of both contributions to the joint venture (JV). It turned out that the two companies had widely diverging views of the business, which led to great differences in the value they attributed to their own and to the other's business. The gap proved to be insurmountable. During an interview with the authors on this topic, de Bree still became indignant about what he saw as a misrepresentation by Exxon of their own competitive position and their disregard for DSM's strengths.

[2] The DSM members were Jan Wolters (Corporate Planning) and Gert Koolman (Corporate Finance & Economics). The AKZO members were Mr. Van Oosterom (Strategic Planning) and Mr. Den Hoed (Finance).

[3] Simon de Bree and Louk Ligthart supervised this project at the Managing Board level. Project leader was Jan Wolters, with the assistance of a.o. Pieter Nederstigt and Siemen Groen. The third party involved was Arthur D. Little, with Eric Léon as project leader.

At year-end, for 3 years after the JV discussions had failed, he asked Jan Wolters to calculate how the Petrochemicals business of both companies had fared, as compared with the predictions both companies had put into the valuation model. To his great satisfaction, he could then write a Christmas card to Mr Wilson, his negotiation partner at Exxon, saying: "Merry Christmas and a Happy New Year! By the way: you will have noticed that, based on the actual performance of both our companies, the decision not to enter into the JV was clearly beneficial for DSM."

The discussions with Exxon did have a side effect: they revealed that internally, DSM was not aligned about the future of the company. The Scale JV would have been part of a scenario where DSM would 'hang on.' But how exactly was this scenario foreseen to unfold? Would the JV last for another 5 or 10 years? If DSM wanted to exit Petrochemicals, wasn't it better to sell the business for cash in order to re-invest the money in other activities? Wasn't the JV, in fact, a 'bear hug' with a much larger partner that could force DSM to exit at any point in time in the future? And if so, would DSM then be ready to continue with its remaining businesses? As Wolters explained, "The Scale discussions revealed that DSM could not explain its corporate strategy. We were not ready for that. It was as if you would take a first step without an indication of the road ahead. This left me with a distinct 'double feeling' when the talks collapsed."

Thus, the third reason why DSM was in a state of some disarray was probably the most important: there was widespread skepticism within the company about the medium-term sustainability of its portfolio—initially, something not openly discussed with the Managing Board (MB). Simon de Bree's style of conducting meetings with the 'Concerntop' (the top-20 or so, including the MB and divisional managers, as well as staff directors) was less participative and inclusive than that of his predecessor, Hans van Liemt. Therefore, the skepticism went 'underground' as it were, but surfaced after a meeting of a number of the company's most important divisional and staff directors. They produced a memo painting DSM's predicament as follows[4]:

- DSM's short-term results were insufficient to finance necessary investments. Some activities would need to be sold (like fertilizers)
- Longer term, DSM would remain too cyclical. The 'culprits' were in the Petrochemical sector: Hydrocarbons and Polyethylene. These should be swapped against more stable business, or
- A merger was inevitable, since
- None of the DSM directors believed in 'hanging on'

However, as mentioned above, neither the merger discussions nor the Petrochemicals discussions had produced the desired solution. This had only

[4] *Beraadslaging Directeuren N.V. DSM betreffende scenario SMP 1992–1997*. Copy in possession of H. Schreuder.

reinforced the internal skepticism: apparently, the outside world did not value DSM and its businesses sufficiently to be able to execute such strategic options.

It was clear that the MB had to address these concerns. Hence, De Bree's question about the ability to conduct a strategic dialogue at the overall company level? A simple question but not one with a simple answer. Conducting 'corporate strategic dialogues' was largely uncharted territory. It was not at all clear whether this could be done, and if so, how it should be done. There was no other way to find out but to try it.

1994–1997: Clarifying the Corporate Strategy

In June 1993 DSM announced that Professor Paul van der Grinten would retire at the end of the year as Director of Corporate Planning & Development, when he reached the age of 60. He was to be succeeded on 1 January 1994 by Dr. Jan Wolters and (co-author) Professor Schreuder would be appointed deputy Director and 'successor of Mr Wolters.'[5] This long lead time between the announcement and appointment allowed Schreuder to begin a wider orientation of DSM's portfolio of businesses. Wolters had had a career in Research, as well as the Industrial Chemical and Fine Chemical parts of DSM and thus far, Schreuder's experience was in Petrochemicals. It was Wolters' ambition to return to a business position within 3 years.

The first analyses of DSM's strategic situation showed that the company had gone through 20 years of diversification and expansion (see Chap. 1). Diversification had been pursued along all of the following routes:

- Within and around the gas-based and petrochemical cores of the company, also using the 'side streams' of base chemical production ('concentric diversification')
- Along the value chain toward the end markets ('forward integration')
- By developing new products from own research or licensed-in technology ('technology-push diversification')
- By acquiring new activities with hardly any connection to existing activities ('unrelated diversification')

[5] *Benoemingen directeuren bij chemieconcern DSM,* 10 June 1993. This was an unusual press release for two reasons: (1) announcing these changes so far in advance and (2) for the cryptic formulation that Schreuder was appointed "as successor of Mr Wolters," while Jan Wolters was not the deputy Director of Corporate Planning & Development at the time. He was introduced earlier in the press release as Director of Corporate Strategy within the Corporate Planning & Development staff. DSM excelled in such cryptic formulations at the time, particularly in Management Development reports. A running joke was that you needed a Kremlinologist to interpret the exact meaning of such reports. In this case, the meaning of the press release was that Schreuder was foreseen to succeed Wolters as Director of Corporate Planning & Development after some time.

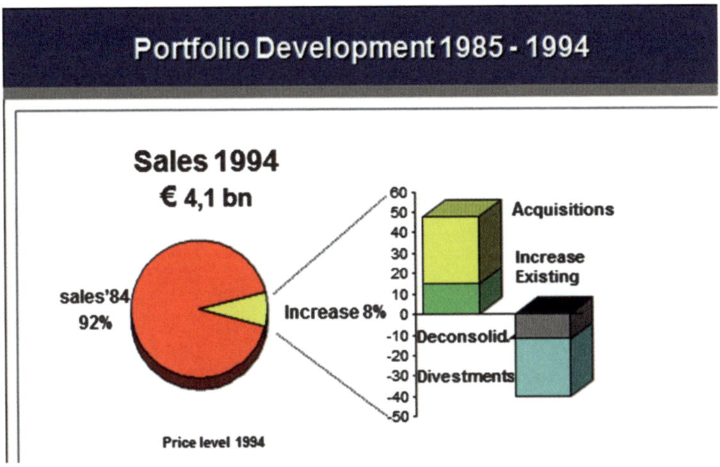

Fig. 9.1 Portfolio development 1985–1994. *Source*: Company presentations

As a result of the activities along all these diversification routes, DSM had become a quite widely diversified 'conglomerate' type of company, without clear focus areas. Strategic priorities were unclear, since so many different growth paths were being tested. Moreover, the net result of all these activities was disappointing (see Fig. 9.1). Real growth had only amounted to a cumulative 8 % over the 10-year period of 1985–1994. This was the net effect of a respectable gross growth of 48 % (for a large part by acquisitions),[6] which was, however, counteracted by the necessity to divest and deconsolidate about 40 % of sales over this same time period. Such a large program of divestments was the result of unsuccessful diversifications, for instance into the construction sector. Hence, the overall net growth of the company, just like its financial performance, was unsatisfactory.

How could this situation be dealt with while regaining a sense of purpose and direction? With this objective in mind, a project named 'Clarifying the Corporate Strategy' (*Aanscherping Concernstrategie* [ACS]) was initiated in the first Quarter 1994 and Corporate Planning & Development (CPL) was asked to propose a project set-up. In April, the outline of the project was agreed upon with the MB (see Fig. 9.2). The goal would be to develop a vision regarding the corporate portfolio. There was a clear preference to develop an own-strength scenario and there was the realization that the company could only achieve this by starting to 'focus.' To enable that process, the concept of 'clusters' was introduced and defined as:

[6] Organic growth of the activities that DSM had kept for these 10 years was therefore not very impressive. A major factor was that the volume increases in Industrial Chemicals and Petrochemicals were compensated by price decreases as a result of the experience curve (see Fig. 1.9).

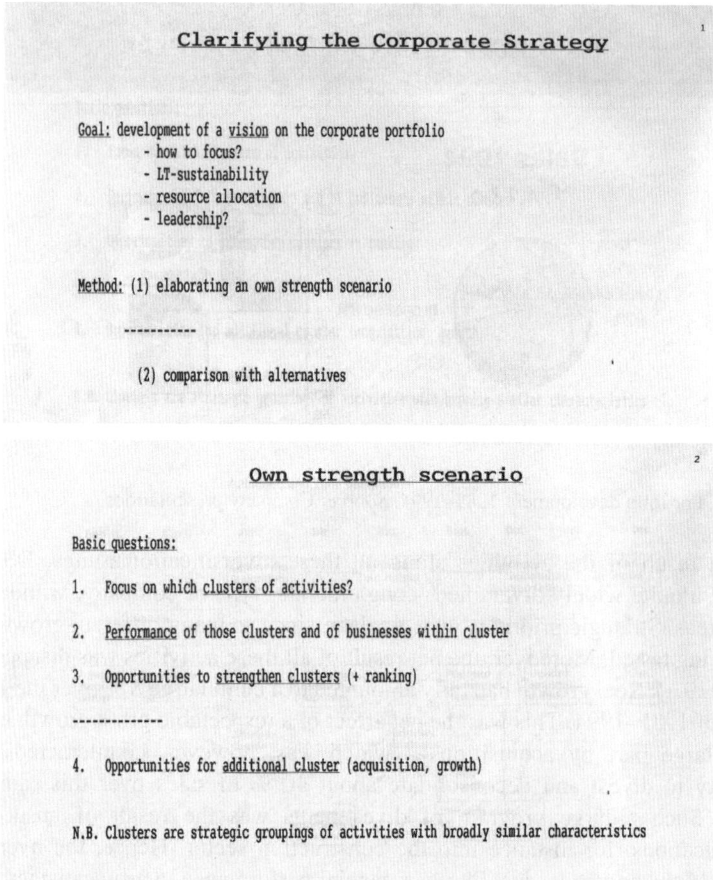

Fig. 9.2 Clarifying the corporate strategy: goal, method and basic questions. *Source*: *Clarifying the corporate strategy*, presentation to the Managing Board, Corporate Planning & Development, 1994 (personal archive of H. Schreuder)

strategic groupings of activities with broadly similar characteristics. DSM would have to find out how many clusters of activities it actually had, whether these clusters had long-term sustainability and whether businesses in that cluster could achieve leadership positions. Resource allocation would be directed toward clusters and businesses which, based on such leadership positions, could achieve good, sustainable performance over time. In some, if not all, cases this implied that the chosen clusters and businesses would need to be strengthened. Clear priorities and rankings were needed in order to avoid DSM 'spreading itself too thinly' again. While the approach's main direction was clear, there were lingering doubts about, (1) whether DSM could achieve such an own-strength scenario and (2) whether the existing clusters would provide sufficient basis for sustainable, profitable growth (see Fig. 9.2). Hence, these doubts were expressed below the dotted lines—an honest 'reality check' was required to address these issues.

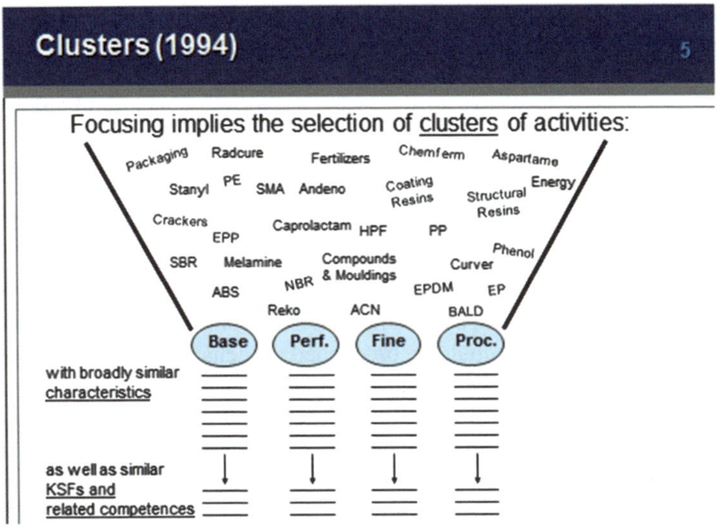

Fig. 9.3 Determining DSM's clusters of activities in 1994. *Source*: Company presentations

The first question was how to come to reasonably homogeneous groupings of DSM's activities into 'clusters.' The company had amassed a wide array of businesses, ranging from the large-scale crackers to small companies like Fardem (packaging) and Reko (recycling), as well as start-ups, such as Dyneema (a fibre), Stanyl (an engineering plastic), SMA (a polymer) and Aspartame (a sweetener).[7] Fortunately, in the meantime, Business Strategy Dialogues (BSDs) had been held for most of these businesses. This had increased the transparency of the competitive positions of these businesses and had also resulted in the application of a common approach and terminology. The essence of the strategic choice any business was facing had been captured (see Fig. 5.6) in the confrontation between its:

- Key Success Factors (KSFs) answering the question, 'what does it take to compete?'
- Competences (or Capabilities) answering the question, 'do we have what it takes?'

This common approach allowed DSM to group its activities into clusters with broadly similar characteristics and, in particular, similar KSFs and related competences. Thus, the BSD results provided the building blocks for the first Corporate Strategy Dialogues (CSD) in 1994. This process of determining DSM's business clusters (see Fig. 9.3) revealed that the initial assumption was that there

[7] It also still had its Energy interests: participations in oil and gas fields on the North Sea (in addition to being the trustee of the Dutch government in Energie Beheer Nederland).

would be four clusters (with a number of businesses, like Energy, falling outside of these categories):

	% of DSM sales 1993
Base chemicals and materials	44
Performance materials	32
Fine chemicals	4
Plastic processing	16

Thus far, DSM's department of CPL had been in the lead to drive the process of working out an approach to focusing and clustering. Once this common framework was established, the process could be broadened to include many more participants and become a true 'Strategy Dialogue.' Working groups were established to apply the common approach to the various clusters and, if validated, then to come up with proposals about how to strengthen the clusters. In addition, a 'Sounding Board' was set up to act as a sparring partner for CPL and provide its independent opinion on the results at various stages. All in all, about 40 people from across DSM were actively involved in CSD roles. In addition, the 'Concerntop,' intensively discussed interim results in several meetings.

An initial surprise in this process was that application of the common approach showed that in reality, only three homogeneous clusters could be established; the fourth cluster, Plastic Processing, was internally too diverse. It consisted of two different large businesses: (1) Engineering Plastic Products, a forward integration of engineering plastics into intermediate products and parts[8] and (2) Curver, a branded, non-food consumer products company,[9] as well as a collection of smaller businesses like Reko, Fardem and Mouldings. It turned out that the KSFs of these businesses were too different to continue thinking about the Plastic Processing activities as one cluster—an ominous sign for the future of them as part of DSM, which wanted to focus on clusters of activities. Indeed, over the period of 1997–2001, the Plastic Processing activities were sold off step-by-step. For the characteristics, KSFs and related competences of DSM's three 'real' clusters in 1994, see Fig. 9.4. Note that the first two clusters represented over 75 % of DSM's sales at the time and that Fine Chemicals contributed only 4 %.

In this first CSD, focusing was already foreseen to be a process over time. The process consisted of four steps, as Table 9.1 shows. The first three steps should be taken in the CSD. Monitoring the success of the focusing process by determining whether the business and cluster performance lived up to expectations, would be a continuing task after the CSD results had been implemented.

[8] DSM companies like Erta and Polypenco were later sold to Quadrant, now part of the Mitsubishi Plastics group of companies (see: http://www.quadrantplastics.com/eu-en/our-company/history.html, accessed 1 December 2014).

[9] The Curver brand now belongs to the Israelian Keter Group (see: http://www.curver.com/nld/brand-history, accessed 1 December 2014) after having been sold by DSM in 1997 to Rubbermaid, which later became part of the Newell Rubbermaid group (see: http://www.fundinguniverse.com/company-histories/newell-rubbermaid-inc-history/, accessed 1 December 2014).

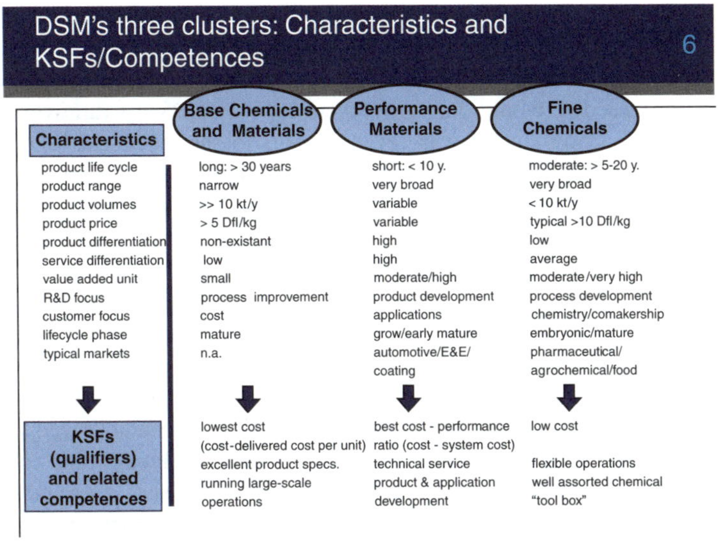

Fig. 9.4 DSM's three clusters in 1994. *Source*: *Clarifying DSM's corporate strategy*, final presentation to DSM Managing Board, Corporate Planning & Development, December 1994 (personal archive of H. Schreuder)

Table 9.1 Focusing involves four steps (ACS, 1994)

Focusing is a process:
1. The selection of clusters of businesses with broadly similar characteristics and Key Success Factors: *Focusing on clusters*
2. The clarification of the strategic mission of each business and grouping these for corporate purposes in strategic categories: *Focusing on particular businesses*
3. Setting priorities for (long-term) resource allocation: *Focusing the resource allocation*
4. Monitoring whether the expected performance of businesses is realized: *Focusing on performance*

Source: *Clarifying DSM's corporate strategy*, final presentation to DSM Managing Board, Corporate Planning & Development, December 1994 (personal archive of H. Schreuder)

After the clusters had been established, the strategic priority ranking of the businesses within each cluster was the second step in the CSD that needed to be determined. For this purpose, DSM assigned its businesses to the following four strategic classifications:

	Strategic posture and financial criteria
Grow/build	Grow to critical size. Be patient with returns
Actively maintain	Maintain position versus competition. Insist on profits and net cash
Maximize cash	Maximize profits and net cash. Accept long-term vulnerability
Retrench	Prepare divestment. Maximize divestment value

This analysis produced a rather stunning result. In the first category of Grow/Build, the category that represents a company's 'hope for the future,' only 5 % of DSM's sales could be classified. Moreover, giving these businesses all the resources they needed, would only grow them to 7 % of DSM's turnover in 1997. A full 88 % of DSM's sales was (evenly split) in the categories of 'Actively Maintain' and 'Maximize Cash.' Their share was predicted to grow to 90 % in 1997. Clearly, this was not an attractive picture. The financial projections were also not very encouraging. This was partly due to the fact that DSM adopted the discipline of requiring its cyclical businesses to take the volatility of their business into account while planning, which was done by requiring all these businesses to assume that the next dip in their cycle would occur at the end of their 7-year planning horizon (in 2000). For that year they had to assume that the 'worst historical conditions' in their industry would reoccur in terms of utilization rates and margins. This abolished the 'hockey sticks' that characterized previous projections in the Strategic Multi-Year Planning rounds. Having thus enforced a more realistic financial picture for these cyclical businesses, it turned out that average return on investment (ROI) between 1993 and 2000 (the next assumed trough in the cycle) would be in the range of 10.6–14.2 %, a range fully below the corporate ambition of at least 15 %.

It was not (yet) an option for DSM to dispose of the large cyclical businesses in Petrochemicals and Industrial Chemicals. As the previous analyses showed, there was simply not (strong) enough other business upon which the future of the company could be built. This made it clear that DSM's overriding corporate strategic objective would need to be to build such other strong business. Only if the company would succeed to substantially strengthen the other part(s) of its portfolio, would it one day be able to exit its large cyclical businesses. Creating this strategic option was paramount for the company's ability to follow an 'own strength' scenario and not to be hostage to the willingness of other companies, such as AKZO or Exxon, to partner.

Fortunately, the projections showed that DSM would generate a substantial amount of cash, more than was required for the 'necessary investments.' Moreover, an additional sum of about Dfl 2 billion could be made available by divesting or swapping designated businesses (eight of these were identified). Therefore, funds seemed available to strengthen the portfolio but where were these to be invested? How would DSM be prevented from once again 'spreading itself too thinly?' In other words, how to ensure that the third step of the focusing process—resource allocation—would be applied with rigor (see Table 9.1)?

Firstly, the answer to the question of investing funds was to have a very clear priority ordering and to rigorously rank all investment proposals in three categories:

	Priority classification and its meaning
Top priority:	These projects will be funded as soon as they can be realized
High priority:	These projects will be realized to the extent that funds can be made available
Opportunities:	Will only be realized if an attractive opportunity presents itself and additional funds are available

Secondly, the answer to preventing the spreading of resources too thinly was to create a very sharp selection process regarding 'Top Priorities.' Strategically, these priorities would have to contribute significantly to the overriding objective to enhance DSM's strategic flexibility over time. Hence, no Top Priorities could be accepted in the Base Chemicals and Materials cluster.[10] Financially, the Top Priorities would have to improve the expected earnings profile of the company and reduce its exposure to cyclicality. Proposals for the Top Priorities came from the cluster working groups, a New Business Development working group, a Sounding Board group and from the plans submitted by all of the businesses. After rigorous application of the strategic and financial selection criteria, two Top Priorities survived, one in Fine Chemicals and one in Performance Materials[11]:

- Increase the share of Fine Chemicals to 15 % of DSM sales, by alliance or acquisition(s), preferably with a major step
- Expand Polypropylene to a European leadership position (Top Four), by building new plants and executing acquisitions to increase the business scale to 800 kton

In essence, DSM chose to significantly strengthen the two clusters that could provide the new 'core of the company,' if the Base Chemicals and Materials were to be exited over time. It was, however, by no means a foregone conclusion that the Top Priorities could be achieved. In Fine Chemicals, the ambition was to 'triple' DSM's presence. Only a few possibilities were available for a 'major step' to achieve this, the foremost being the Swiss company Lonza. If such a 'major step' would not materialize (and indeed Lonza turned out not to be available at the time), it would be a long and difficult road for DSM to achieve this ambitious goal. Similarly, in Performance Materials, the ambition was to 'nearly triple' DSM's capacity in polypropylene. In part, the company could achieve this on its own strength by building a third plant. For the rest, it would be dependent on opportunities to acquire additional capacity. Highest on the list were the European activities of Amoco, located in Geel (Belgium), which would also give entry to Amoco's new production technology. Subsequent discussions with Amoco,

[10] Given the conclusions about the heterogeneity of the Plastic Processing cluster, also no Top Priorities could be accepted here. Initially, a third Top Priority was considered: Specialty Compounding. This could have provided a bridge between the Performance Materials and Plastic Processing clusters. In the communication about the CSD in the Executive Letter dated 13 February 1995, it was announced that, "In addition, it will be studied how DSM can translate its competences in processing and compounding into an attractive and profitable position" (p. 2). This study showed that the competitive position and financial results of "specialty compounders" would be under pressure in the medium term already. DSM abandoned the idea to expand here.

[11] DSM's strength in Polypropylene (PP) had been built on its technological capabilities. In particular, it had developed production processes and applications geared toward the polypropylene co-polymer market, which gave higher margins and more protected positions than in the homopolymer market. At the time, this justified regarding PP for DSM as a performance material.

however, showed that it would not be possible to acquire Amoco's European business or to create a joint venture with them.[12]

Nevertheless, the DSM Top Priorities were executed from 1995 to 1997. This took some luck, a lot of hard work and a considerable amount of courage. 'Luck' was needed because the 'obvious' top-of-the-list acquisition candidates were not available. Therefore, DSM was dependent on other opportunities to arise. It helped, however, that DSM had clearly communicated its strategic priorities, a lesson that was to be repeated in next rounds of CSDs. Other companies now knew that DSM was in the market as a potential acquirer. Some of these companies approached DSM to have a discussion. 'Hard work' was required, first of all, to execute a substantial investment program that was also part of the CSD outcome (in total, an amount of Dfl 6 billion had been adopted for the period 1995–2000). But it was also hard work to make acceptable 'business cases' out of the acquisition opportunities that did arise. For Fine Chemicals, for instance, the activities of Chemie Linz could be acquired from the Austrian state-owned oil company ÖMV. Although the company had a number of attractive products and prospects (notably Roche's new weight loss product Xenical), it also had many 'legacy assets' and it had been managed in the context of a state-owned oil company, which is not the best environment for fine chemicals production, to say the least. It therefore took 'courage' on the part of DSM's management to be convinced that Chemie Linz could be developed into an attractive business.

Similarly, in Performance Materials, an acquisition opportunity was Veba Oil's Vestolen business. Here, the business was not up to DSM's standards and would require significant upgrading and expansion; the business came with complicated cracker contracts on the Gelsenkirchen site and even included a Second World War bomb that had not yet been unearthed! In this case, DSM management also had the courage to see the potential of this 'second site' for DSM, which already housed the fourth PP plant and could be used for the construction of the fifth. Finally, a more obvious acquisition target could also be incorporated—the Spanish company Deretil, which was a competitor of DSM Andeno in the production of antibiotic side chains. DSM's enlarged position in antibiotic side chains would lead to increased co-operation with Gist-Brocades, the world leader in antibiotics.

All in all, DSM was able to make very substantial progress with its Top Priorities during the period of 1995–1997 (see Fig. 9.5). The company's position had more than doubled in Fine Chemicals and good further growth was foreseen. Moreover, the company had established itself as a credible competitor in the field of Fine Chemicals, no longer as a company that was wondering whether these activities were a 'hobby' or a 'cornerstone' (see Chap. 1). In the Polypropylene business, the ambitious target was more than achieved by building PPF 3 (the third PP plant), acquiring PPF 4 in Gelsenkirchen and also planning that PPF 5 go on stream there in 2000. The company was starting to gain confidence that it was capable of setting

[12] DSM's third PP plant was built with Amoco technology, which gave opportunities for technological co-operation.

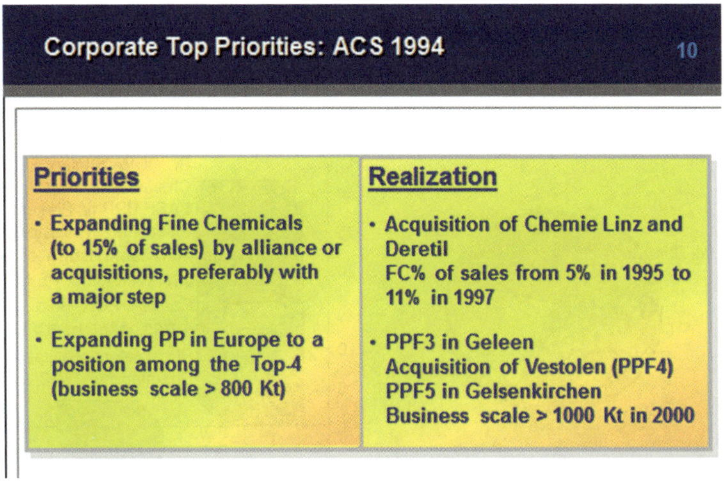

Fig. 9.5 Realization of the ACS top priorities in 1997. *Source*: DSM company presentations, 1997

ambitious strategic priorities and realize them within a reasonably short period of time and had experienced that 'focus' was a necessary ingredient for such success. By concentrating its efforts on a few top strategic priorities and clearly communicating these both internally and externally, the company had been able to achieve goals that were perceived in 1994 as being very ambitious. Therefore, it was only natural that Simon de Bree asked a follow-up question: "Now that we have been successful with this CSD, can we execute another one?"

1997–2000: Priorities for Profitable Growth

The Corporate Strategy Dialogue 1997, which was to be called 'Priorities for Profitable Growth,' started off in a very different constellation than had the previous round in 1994. The company had entered into a new growth phase. Whereas DSM had grown in the 10-year period between 1985 and 1994 with only 8 % (cumulatively, see Fig. 9.1), in the 3-year period between 1994 and 1997, this percentage was above 20 %.[13] This growth was partly due to acquisitions but, even more so, was caused by organic growth in the existing business activities (see Fig. 9.6). Another big difference between these two time periods was that DSM's

[13] Figure 9.5 was calculated during 1997 and used in the CSD itself. End-of year results showed that the 1997 sales of DSM even reached a level of Dfl 12.4 billion (see: *DSM Annual Report* 1997).

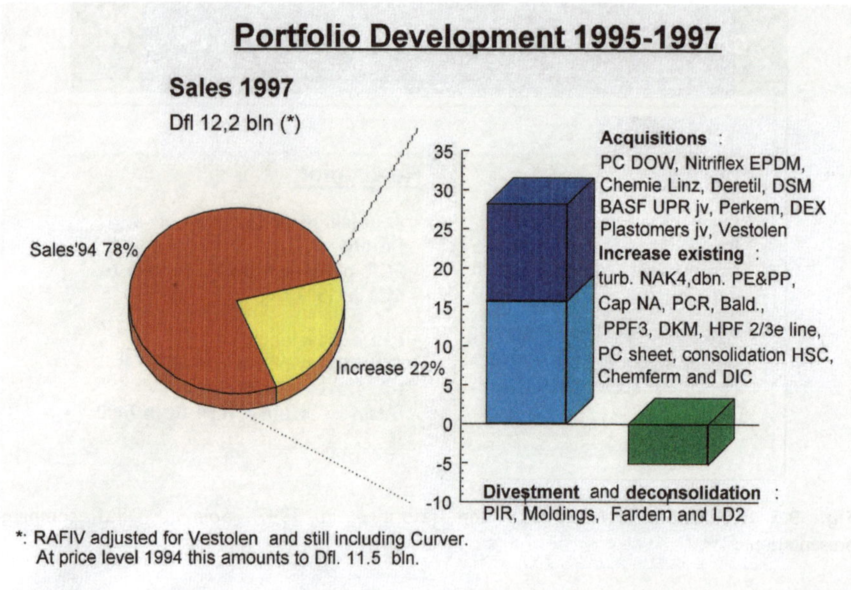

Fig. 9.6 Growth and portfolio development 1995–1997. *Source*: DSM company presentations, 1997

focus had been nearly entirely on growth; the divestments were negligible. As a consequence, revenues had risen from Dfl 8.9 billion in 1994 to Dfl 12.4 billion in 1997. Moreover, the years 1994–1997 had produced steadily increasing profits and cash flows, enlarging the scope for further strategic development.

Further strategic development was clearly needed. While DSM had found a growth path in Fine Chemicals, the overall composition of the portfolio had not yet shifted significantly. In fact, the relative weight of Base Chemicals & Materials had even increased due to the following: (a) 'upswing' prices for these cyclical products, also depressing the margins of some Performance Materials, (b) some organic investments and (c) the relative decline of the Plastic Processing 'cluster,' where first steps had been taken to phase out these activities. Together, Fine Chemicals and Performance Materials still made up 37 % of DSM's sales, just as they had in 1994:

	% of DSM sales	
	1994	1997
Base chemicals and materials	44	48
Performance materials	32	26
Fine chemicals	5	11
Plastic processing	16	10

With this starting position, it was felt that the prime task of the CSD 1997 was to come to a view on DSM's corporate portfolio as a whole. Assuming that Plastic Processing would be further phased out, would the remaining business be a logical and consistent whole? How would this portfolio continue to develop over time? What financial performance could be expected? Would it be a resilient package of activities if projected against different possible future environments? Would DSM then be a strong competitor against its corporate peers? And, finally, given the results of such analyses: which adjustments could the company make to position itself better for the future?

These main questions led to a totally different CSD process in 1997 than in 1994. Now, four working groups were installed to study DSM's entire portfolio from four different angles (see Fig. 9.7). In addition, there was again a Sounding Board, chaired by Jan Zuidam, which provided an independent view on all interim and final CSD outcomes. Again, Corporate Planning & Development (CPL) acted as the spider in the web and had the responsibility to conduct the process toward workable conclusions. Somewhere between 50 and 60 people were involved all together.

'Performance,' the working group led by Frans Pistorius, put the spotlight on the realized and projected performance of DSM's businesses. They began with the fourth step of the focusing process that DSM had embarked on in 1994 (see Table 9.1)—monitoring whether the performance of the businesses, as had been expected in 1994, had in fact been realized. This put a rather harsh light on the financial performance of DSM's portfolio. It turned out that more than 80 % of DSM's recent operating results had been generated by businesses representing 58 % of DSM's sales and 50 % of capital employed. The other side of this coin was that businesses representing 35 % of sales and 40 % of capital employed had contributed only 5 % to the company's operating results. It was for DSM somewhat 'countercultural' at

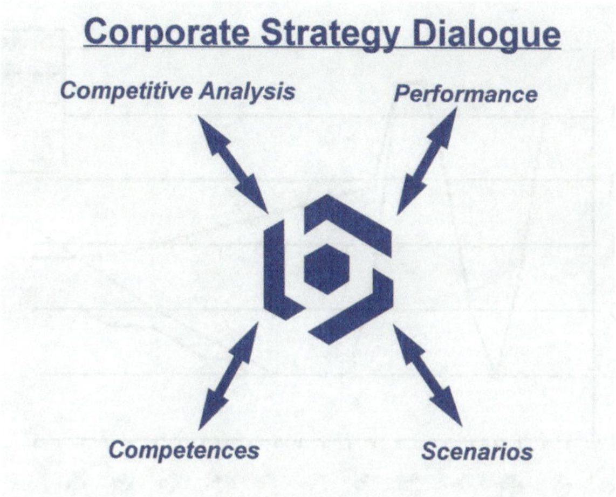

Fig. 9.7 The four working groups of *Priorities for Profitable Growth* (CSD 1997). *Source*: *Corporate strategy dialogue*, presentation S. de Bree/H. Schreuder to ConcernTop, December 1997

the time to so clearly name and shame businesses for their disappointing performance, but it clearly reinforced the message that performance would, henceforth, be a major element of the focusing process. The working group recommended that DSM initiate a drive toward 'Operational Excellence,' which has indeed led to significant performance improvement in the years that followed.

The working group 'Competitive Analysis,' led by Jan Dopper, selected 20 Chemical companies against which to benchmark DSM. Their study reinforced the conclusion that further focusing was necessary. The scope of DSM was still too large to excel in all activities. Leadership positions had to be further extended, as did geographic positions, such as toward the US and Asia. Also, the drive toward lesser cyclicality had to be continued. The working group 'Competences,' led by Dick Venderbos, did not contribute significantly to the end results of the CSD—they concluded that DSM's technological competences were in order and provided coherence between the various activities. In particular, they noted that Fine Chemicals should be able to benefit from this. The DSM executives surveyed by this working group responded that competences related to markets, entrepreneurship and adaptability should be at the top of the company's attention list.

The working group 'Scenarios,' led by Schreuder, split itself into subgroups that applied the Shell scenario planning methodology to four DSM business areas. As an example, for the Petrochemicals industry four scenarios were constructed dependent on whether (a) the global growth in demand for plastic would be high or low and (b) the European competitive position would be strong or weak. The margins on the Hydrocarbons (cracker) business would be entirely different under the four scenarios (see Fig. 9.8). Since the Petrochemical results still contributed very significantly to the overall DSM financials, this analysis illustrated that DSM's corporate financial performance was still rather dependent on external circumstances. Even more important were the results of the subgroup on the Pharma-

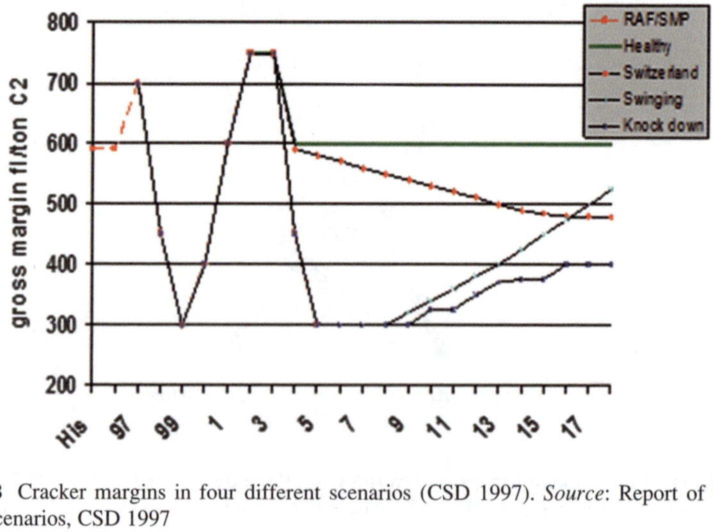

Fig. 9.8 Cracker margins in four different scenarios (CSD 1997). *Source*: Report of working group scenarios, CSD 1997

related Fine Chemicals. In this subgroup Emmo Meijer, later DSM's R&D director, played a very important role. Here, the scenarios revolved around the questions (a) whether societal 'willingness-to-pay' for new Pharma products would remain high or would decline and (b) whether new Pharma products would continue to be produced by chemical synthesis or increasingly also by biotech methods. It was concluded that the latter was likely and that DSM should therefore strive to augment its toolbox toward the Pharma industry by incorporating such Biotech methods as fermentation and enzymatic production. In summary, this entailed a step from Fine Chemicals to Life Science Products.

Looking across the results of the four working groups, there was quite a large degree of convergence toward the main conclusions of the CSD 1997, in particular to continue the drive toward leadership positions in the non-cyclical parts of the portfolio. A prime candidate was the Fine Chemicals cluster, which could be strengthened by adding chemical product trees and custom manufacturing; it was also thought that the scope of this cluster should be expanded to add biotech and become the Life Science Products cluster. DSM concluded that it would be best to do so by making a 'major step,' rather than by a string of smaller investments and acquisitions. Again, not many opportunities existed for such a move, however next to the 'old favorite' Lonza, a company like Gist-Brocades could now be added to the list. Both companies were analyzed extensively in the CSD. In the meantime, other activities had to be 'actively maintained' by securing their investments. If in the Performance Materials area, opportunities would arise to strengthen Powder Coating Resins or Engineering Plastics these would be considered but making a major step in the Fine Chemicals/Life Science Products arena was the undisputed Top Priority (see Fig. 9.9 for a summary of these conclusions).

Of course, such convergence was undoubtedly in great part due to the force of the analyses. There was, however, another force was at play as well—the force of momentum. For a long time, there had been proponents of further expansion into Fine Chemicals, such as Ruud Selman (see Chap. 1). Initially, these people were regarded as being 'hobbyists' by the majority of those involved in DSM's large-volume businesses. As recently as 1994, Fine Chemicals had only represented 5 % of DSM's sales, a marginal position. However, the initial success of the 1994–1997 growth path emboldened those who believed in Fine Chemicals to propose more radical steps. An 'informal coalition' of such proponents included Emmo Meijer, Jan Zuidam, Dick Venderbos, Jan Wolters, Henk Numan and others. In the 1997 CSD, they had the momentum of first successes, such as Chemie Linz and Deretil, on their side. As it turned out, they had even more going for them than thought at the time.

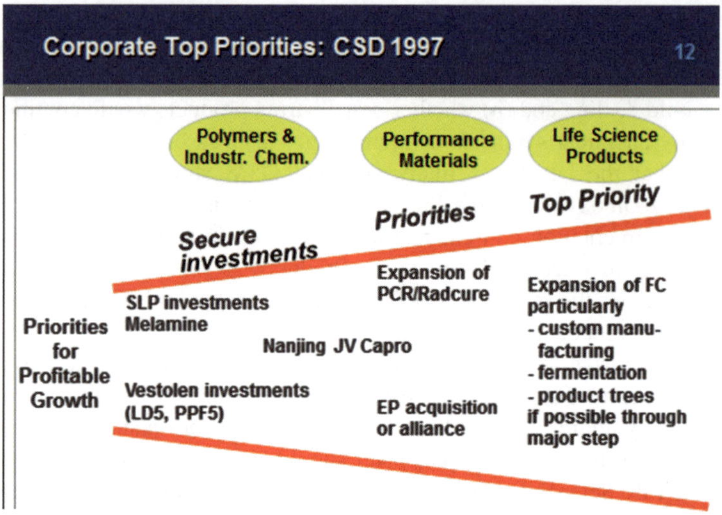

Fig. 9.9 The top priority of the CSD 1997: expansion of fine chemicals. *Source*: DSM company presentations

1998: Gist-Brocades

While DSM was conducting its CSD in 1997, management at the Dutch company Gist-Brocades was also doing some soul searching. At Gist-Brocades, the strategy process was less refined. Feike Sijbesma, director of the Food Specialties division at the time, recalls: "Strategy at Gist-Brocades was what the CEO occasionally devised. In the mid-1990s we were going through 'de toeter van Herman,'[14] being the objective of the CEO Herman Scheffer to first shrink the company by divestments in order to grow thereafter." In this context, the company had shed its Industrial Enzymes activities to Genencor in 1995 and was now contemplating how to grow again. In fact, it had many ideas how to grow. Among these was the construction of an innovative plant (the ZOR-f) at its main site in Delft in order to produce the antibiotic 7-ADCA by fermentative methods, further expansion of its fermentative capacity at its French site in Seclin and the addition of new products.

[14] This is difficult to translate into English; literally, it is "trumpet of Herman," but the image of an hourglass captures the meaning better.

Ideas enough but without sufficient financial resources to embark on an ambitious investment program; the risk profile of such a program was also considered to be too dangerous for a company the size of Gist-Brocades.[15]

Executives from DSM and Gist-Brocades had known each other for many years and had occasionally explored the idea of coming together, however to no effect. More recently, they had come to know each other even better due to a JV (Chemferm) they had created in the antibiotics field after DSM's acquisition of Deretil. After Chemferm board meetings, the topic of Gist-Brocades joining forces with DSM had occasionally been discussed over drinks. In 1997, acting upon these leads, DSM again put out feelers to the Gist-Brocades Board of Directors to determine whether such a discussion, which would be a perfect match with DSM's Top Priority, was possible. The initial reaction was not positive. When asked about the fit between the two companies, Ruud Selman, who was due to retire at the end of that year, gave a farewell interview to *Het Financieele Dagblad* (in December 1997) and said in reaction to the possibility: "Yes, that would be a terribly interesting combination of toolboxes." He added: "There has been speculation before. But it takes two to tango. DSM would favor this, but at Gist-Brocades they, of course, have the feeling that the game of Pacman is being played with them. Gist-Brocades is a very proud company. But perhaps one day the mood and time will be ripe for this."[16]

Of course, Selman's parting shot was far from cautious. When the stock market reacted, Gist-Brocades was forced to publicly deny any interest in such a combination. However, the interview also had an unanticipated consequence. As Feike Sijbesma explained: "At Gist-Brocades we realized that this time it was serious. An answer needed to be formulated, given our funding situation and DSM's strategic intent. In the end, we chose to join a Dutch combination although we were aware of cultural differences between the two companies." And so it happened that on 6 January 1998, when the DSM 'Concerntop' met at Rullingen Castle in Belgium to discuss the results of the CSD, De Bree could also take a poll among the top managers whether the invitation from Gist-Brocades to have exploratory discussions about a merger with DSM should be accepted. All were in favor.

Events unfolded quickly after that. Between the Managing Boards of the two companies, a joint intent was reached in January, allowing the Supervisory Boards to discuss these proposals in early February. In the subsequent weeks, rumors about a potential merger started to resurface on the stock market and the companies were forced to speed up their discussions. Over the weekend of 21–22 February, all of the final details needed to be hammered out. DSM could only perform a very limited due diligence. On Sunday evening, just before midnight, the deal was finalized.

[15] Indeed, the start-up of the ZOR-f, the single largest project, was far from flawless during subsequent years. Gist-Brocades would probably have had a hard time justifying the disappointing performance of the first few years.

[16] "In de schaduw van de technologie" and "DSM lonkt naar Gist-Brocades," *Het Financieele Dagblad,* 17 December 1997.

It was announced the next day and consummated in May. The Top Priority of DSM to expand Fine Chemicals, preferably with a single, major step, had been realized within a few months. As compared to the implementation of the CSD 1994, a lot more luck was involved in 1997–1998 in the ability to implement a deal so quickly. But, there is also the element that "luck favors the prepared mind," as Louis Pasteur said. Having gone through its CSD process, DSM was ready to execute the largest transaction in its history with sufficient confidence. It paid about Dfl 3 billion in cash and shares for Gist-Brocades and committed to execute an investment program of about Dfl 0.5 billion.

The acquisition of Gist-Brocades was transformative for DSM. Firstly, in one fell swoop, the company's strategic objective was realized in becoming 'more than a chemical company' when it entered the Biotech field. DSM had expanded its own field of Fine Chemicals into the broader area of Life Science Products, enabling a much wider offering to the Pharma industry, but this also gave entry to a broad range of other industries. Secondly, because the Gist-Brocades culture was different—more direct, rather confrontational, certainly more entrepreneurial than DSM and also quite opportunistic. As Feike Sijbesma put it: "At Gist-Brocades we played the ball recklessly, regardless of personal sensitivities. We had perhaps even a bit of a cowboy-style. At DSM, people expected to be treated with respect. They took challenges more personally. Processes were in place, which we often perceived as bureaucratic. We had to get used to each other." A very intensive cultural integration program was rolled out, which attempted to retain the best of the two cultures.[17] Certainly for DSM, this infusion of a more entrepreneurial culture turned out to be beneficial. Thirdly, and in hindsight, the acquisition of Gist-Brocades opened new strategic avenues for DSM to explore. Interestingly, at the time of the acquisition the (large) Antibiotics division of Gist-Brocades was the main focus of DSM's interest. The (much smaller) Food Specialties division was regarded as 'nice to have' but strategically of lesser importance, due to DSM's primary focus on Pharma. As events evolved over the following few years, DSM's perspective would change drastically.

Reflection: The Explorative Phase

Looking back at the two first Corporate Strategy Dialogues, it can be seen that these constituted an 'explorative phase' in DSM's strategy development in various ways[18]:

[17] DSM presented the acquisition of Gist-Brocades as a 'merger.' It was an attempt to treat the acquired company on equal footing and indeed to preserve 'the best of both worlds' in the integration. Culturally, this was probably beneficial but managerially this resulted in much more cumbersome decision-making processes than would have been necessary.

[18] See also: Henk Volberda et al. (2013).

1. First of all, DSM explored whether a strategic 'process' could be conducted in a dialogue format at the corporate level. The 1994 CSD could already be considered a success, from a process point-of-view, because it enabled the company to formulate a clear strategic vision with two top priorities, which were shared throughout the company. When the company subsequently was able to execute these two priorities successfully, it could leave the period of strategic disarray of the early 1990s behind.
2. In terms of the 'strategic mindset' and 'intent,' the perspective was changed from a diversification drive to an exploration of the ability to focus. Recognizing that DSM's portfolio had become too broad and diverse, the company embarked on a journey to determine the 'core clusters' of the future and to find out whether these could be sufficiently strengthened to one day allow DSM to exit the cyclical Base Chemicals & Materials.
3. Finally, the CSDs provided DSM with a 'strategic direction': an exploration of growth pathways in Performance Materials and Fine Chemicals, the latter to be broadened (with biotech/Gist-Brocades) to Life Science Products.

In 1994, DSM was basically trying to 'find its way' in terms of process, mindset/intent and direction. In that sense, the CSD of 1994 can be seen, in hindsight, as an experiment to allow DSM to learn whether the new approach could work. The experiment could have failed. The outcomes of the CSD were considered very ambitious, involving the tripling of the selected priorities in the core clusters. When it turned out to be possible to execute these priorities within the CSD's 3-year timeframe, the company gained confidence in this new way of working. Hence, a momentum was built up to further explore the new pathways and to continue with setting clear priorities along the way. In 1997, it was again not obvious that the preference of a 'major step' in Life Science Products was achievable. When DSM was fortunate enough to be able to initiate discussions with Gist-Brocades so quickly, the momentum was, of course, strongly reinforced. Subsequently, DSM shifted its focus from exploration to 'exploitation' of its new strategic repertoire.[19]

References

Douma, S. and H. Schreuder, Economic Approaches to Organizations, 5th edition, Harlow: Pearson, 2013

March, J., *A Primer on Decision Making: How Decisions Happen,* NY: The Free Press, 1994

Volberda, H., Van den Bosch, F. and K. Heij, *Re-inventing Business: Hoe Bedrijven Hun Business-model Innoveren*, Assen: Van Gorcum, 2013.

[19] In essence, DSM had gone through an experiential learning cycle as described by James March (1994). March also introduced the concepts of exploration and exploitation in the organizational literature. For later developments, see Volberda et al. (2013) and Douma and Schreuder (2013). In Chap. 13, the concept of (strategic) learning cycles as drivers of evolutionary transformation will be elaborated further.

10 Branching Out Beyond Strategy

Propose to us a two-week industrial Marketing program for DSM's Marketing professionals with five to ten years experience!

(Menno de Vries)

Following the successful 1992 launch of the Business Strategy Dialogue (BSD) process, and the establishment of the Strategic Management Course (SMC) program, it was once again the members of the Branch Organization of Marketing (BOM) who took the initiative. Having lost a dedicated Marketing program, the BOM requested from the company a new program that would be singularly focused on the Marketing professional. The person to implement this objective was again Menno de Vries who contacted Jeannet for this task.

The Marketing initiative, undertaken in 1994, expanded into a long series of programs that would at first be focused on DSM's industrial marketing practitioners and result in additional educational programs with special purpose, such as key account management. For almost 20 years, these programs were run under various sponsorships and had undergone different formats. The first section of this chapter will give the narrative on this experience. DSM, however, was to expand further, and additional learning experiences were created that would go beyond mere strategy and Marketing. These initiatives are also detailed in the second half of the chapter.

Launching the Advanced Industrial Marketing Program

It was in 1993 that Menno de Vries broached the idea of BOM having its very own marketing program. Most of the BOM members at that time had been going through the IMPACT seminar courses at IMD and were well aware of the marketing curriculum embedded in the program. In their view, it was not sufficient to only push along the strategy. DSM's most senior marketing professionals had been at

J.-P. Jeannet, H. Schreuder, *From Coal to Biotech*,
DOI 10.1007/978-3-662-46299-7_10

IMPACT but although the level just below them might have be nominated for SMC, nothing existed for the enhancement of their marketing skills.

Since DSM had already been using the Rotterdam School of Management at Erasmus University faculty for a marketing program for young engineering and scientific talent, as well as a second program for recently hired business graduates, the brief for this new program was for experienced marketers with some 5–8 years marketing or sales experience and who also had some marketing planning responsibility. The target became managers with functional titles such as general product managers, senior sales or area managers, business development managers but also purchasing managers or logistics managers.

The BOM was interested in having sufficient focus on the implementation of a marketing plan, not just a design of such a plan. It was expected that participants would be able to deepen their understanding of marketing tools and concepts, and through the program adopt a common language for Marketing across DSM that would also allow for the exchange of ideas and networking. At that time, DSM was very active, through the BOM, in rotating marketing professionals through different businesses and, thus, needed a common approach across its many business units.

The program proposed by Jeannet contained some of the Marketing specific content from IMPACT but also provided more opportunity to reflect on the participants' own marketing plans. The plenary sessions carried the following titles:

- DSM Marketing Issues
- Role of the Marketing Plan ('Islands of Analysis')
- Understanding Your Customer's Business (Industry Analysis)
- Segmenting for Marketing Success (Market Segmentation)
- Meeting Customer Requirements (Customer Activity Cycles)
- Making Product Line Decisions (Depth vs. Breadth)
- Understanding Costs (Cost in Use)
- Setting Price for Specialties (Value Pricing)
- Setting Price for Commodities (Competitive Pricing)
- Directing the Sales Effort (Sales Management)
- Negotiating with Customers (Negotiation exercise)
- Using Logistics Competitively (Down-Stream Logistics)
- Interfacing with other Functions (Marketing versus R&D or Production)
- Anticipating Competitors Reactions (Competitive Analysis)
- Implementing the Marketing Plan (Group Exercise on Real Plans)

The program was set to begin with an interactive group exercise, whereby participants would define key Marketing and sales issues at DSM, discuss them in groups and present them the next day to members of BOM. This interaction allowed both Marketing professionals and BOM members to become more familiar with the current status of issues to be resolved, in order to achieve a higher level of Marketing throughout the company.

Contained within the plenary sessions was an intensive approach of having each participant refine their own marketing plan, one that they were expected to bring to the seminar. At the end of each seminar day, participants were to take notes about how they would apply the concepts of the class sessions to their personal plan. This was to take the form of one or two slides per session. The seminar faculty collected this input and let two or three participants explain their input to the entire class cohort each morning. An additional form of feedback was manifested on a one-to-one basis, whereby participants would exchange their plans and additions resulting from the first week with a self-selected 'buddy.' Finally, at the end of the seminar, the faculty would select four or five plans to be worked on as a team effort for a final round of presentations to some of the BOM members. Faculty also stood ready to counsel and advise individual participants on issues dealing with their plans. This format not only ensured that the program would be focused on practice, but also connected BOM members with the program and gave them a good insight into the level of current marketing practices at DSM.

The Advanced Industrial Marketing (AIM) program was laid out for a cohort of 30 participants. This was less than the 'normal' group of 36 for SMC, but seemed necessary because there would be considerable individual work as well that needed to be supervised by the faculty.

Neither DSM's BOM members nor the Executive Development function represented by Menno de Vries took the initiative in program design. As had been experienced for the IMPACT series and the follow-up program (SMC, described in earlier chapters), DSM requested a proposal against a broad set of specifications and objectives and let the faculty decide how to turn the objectives into a program. In a meeting with the BOM, the program was discussed but invariably DSM accepted the judgment of the teaching faculty.

Given the extensive program agenda, and DSM's experience with the 2-week IMPACT programs, the BOM members accepted that the program would require 10 days of instruction. To reduce the impact on weekends for non-Dutch participants, the program started on Monday late afternoon during the first week, included Saturday morning during the first week, resumed Sunday evening during the second week and ended early afternoon on Friday.

Selecting the Delivery Institution and Team

The decision about who should deliver AIM turned into a more difficult political affair. DSM, based on previous experience, considered AIM to be a new, but on-going, educational and development effort that had to be on par with the expenses of other regular seminars. The cost of attending was charged off to the participants' businesses and had to be in line with the time involvement and charges for SMC. That eliminated the possibility of making this an IMD seminar for the same reasons that the SMC was, after one run, taken out of IMD and turned into an internal company program. However, because the seminar was stretched over 10 days or 2 weeks, Jeannet was hesitant to accept leadership under the same conditions as with SMC—a 5-day seminar that was more easily justified on a private consulting basis with faculty invoicing DSM directly. As a result, he proposed to have the seminar become an institutional program of Babson College's School of Executive Education, which DSM accepted. In making this arrangement, it was easier to recruit Marketing faculty through Babson and, if regular academic classes had to be rescheduled, to have them either substituted or made up in some other way. The result was a 10-day program for which faculty were present for a few days in overlapping assignments. Babson's institutional delivery fees were, at the time, lower than IMD fees, even when five or six faculty members transatlantic airfares were included.[1]

Another issue centered on institutional conflict. Jeannet, also part of IMD's faculty under a 40 % contract, had to get IMD to accept that this program was to be owned by Babson College and that he could teach in the program under their umbrella. This could be ensured through scheduling the AIM program during Babson's regular academic year when it could be argued that he was theoretically not bound by the IMD faculty engagement rules; additionally, a faculty member from IMD was involved in each program.[2]

Material development and selection posed a challenge for a program that was to be as closely aligned as possible to the business environment of DSM's Marketing managers. At that time, it was not typical for business schools to run 10-day programs on Industrial Marketing. To meet DSM's and the BOM's objectives, materials had to be selected from Industrial Marketing situations, and even from chemical industries. Marketing faculty often taught in academic programs on the basis of consumer Marketing (B2C) and first needed to get comfortable with the realities of business-to-business Marketing (B2B). The materials developed for the IMPACT and SMC seminars could not be used because they were too strategic in orientation and participants were often enrolled for both courses.

Over the next few years, under faculty supervision, a number of MBA students from Babson worked as case writers to produce more than a dozen cases on a number of marketing situations that arose in DSM businesses. Initially, those were mostly from the Hydrocarbon and Material Science businesses. Later, materials were also created around the newer Life Sciences business, such as Food Specialties or Nutrition.[3] In addition, new materials were developed on purchasing functions, e-business and logistics. New material creation came from the need to find ways to deal with emerging business processes (internet) or the development of DSM's portfolio. As the company was implementing its portfolio strategies as part of its Corporate Strategy Dialogues (CSD), businesses around the Hydrocarbon cluster

[1] AIM-1 was delivered by Babson faculty Jean-Pierre Jeannet, Robb Kopp, Mort Galper (until AIM-5), David Hennessey and IMD Professor Dominique Turpin. Later programs included Ken Matsuno (as of AIM-6) from Babson.

[2] Professor Dominique Turpin (IMD President 2012 to present) assumed this role and he taught in DSM's Marketing programs delivered under Babson for many years.

[3] See Exhibit X for a list of the cases written for DSM.

Table 10.1 Cases written for DSM marketing programs

DSM UHMW-PE (1995)
DSM Stanyl (1995)
DSM Dyneema (1994)
DSM Polyethylene Segmentation (1996)
DSM Groupe Schneider (1997)
DSM Global Purchasing (Elastomers) (2001)
DSM Elastomers E-Business (A) &(B) & (C) (2002)
DSM RIM-Nylon (2001)
DSM Precious Metal Catalysts (2001)
DSM N.V. (A) (1997)
DSM Nutrition Beta Carotene (2002)
DSM Melamine Logistics (1999)
DSM PeptoPro (2006)
DSM Solutech (2007)

were sold and newer businesses, such as in the area of Life Sciences were acquired. To stay relevant, the cases written around divested business had to be replaced (see Table 10.1 on Cases Written for DSM marketing programs).

The involvement of the AIM program faculty also included support in the creation of various brochures, manuals and even an intranet-based planning tool. The BOM commissioned a group of DSM marketing professionals from among the AIM alumni with the creation of a summary of relevant Marketing concepts and illustrations about how to use them in the DSM context.[4] Behind this effort was the idea that marketing managers would periodically produce marketing plans but when this was required, there was usually no 'central' place to go for support to answer typical questions such as, "Well, what should be in such a marketing plan?" Based upon the AIM teaching sessions, and augmented with other illustrations and concepts, the assigned team created the compendium and asked the faculty to comment on the content. This ensured that AIM's instructional content was closely coordinated with DSM's marketing planning activity. While supporting the creation of a brochure posed no problem, there was a conflict between the designing team expecting the faculty to use the material in their teaching sessions, and the faculty preferring to use their own approach in bringing key marketing concepts to life. When submitting marketing plans prior to joining AIM, participants were expected, by the brochure design team and to some extent by BOM itself, to use the plan as a formatting guide.[5] Program faculty members were not prepared to become the enforcers of the manual and preferred a more free-flowing style. This was accentuated when another group of young marketing professionals devised an intra-net augmented planning tool that included diagnostics, forcing participants to go through a step-by-step process and create pre-set charts. Participants voted with

[4] Team members were: A. Artsen, C. Bruens, F. Crum, B. van Driel, M. Jansen, H. Langen, F. Petit, J. Schueller.

[5] Guide to Marketing Planning, DSM, November 1996: 48

Table 10.2 DSM marketing programs (AIM)

AIM-1	October 31–November 11, 1994 (Vaalsbroek)
AIM-2	October 30–November 10, 1995
AIM-3	March 4–15, 1996
AIM-4	February 17–28, 1997
AIM-5	March 16–27, 1998
AIM-6	February 22–March 5, 1999
AIM-7	February 14–25, 2000
AIM-8	February 12–23, 2001
AIM-9	February 18–March 1, 2002
AIM-10	January 20–January 31, 2003
AIM-11	November 9–18, 2004 (Epen)
AIM-12	November 8–17, 2005 (Genk)
AIM-13	October 31–November 9, 2006 (Genk)
AIM-14	October 30–November 8, 2007 (Genk)
AIM-15	October 7–16, 2008 (Mierlo)

their feet, finding it too difficult to both learn an entirely new approach to creating a marketing plan in combination with just learning the ideas behind the key concepts. The effort, which absorbed quite a number of talented individuals in their own spare time over several months, did not result in the desired use among their own peers.

The AIM Program series was offered until 2008, or for a period of 14 years (see Table 10.2). Overall, the format was left largely intact. The sessions were generally the same with some alterations around the more advanced topics of Marketing. It remained difficult to get into areas such as global marketing, brand building or e-marketing since the participants had little control over these issues. As soon as the faculty strayed into areas such as these, participants were quick to react and suggest changes. As part of the development, the role and format of the personal marketing plan changed. Originally, participants were asked to bring in a plan at the beginning of the program but later it was required that they send the plans in advance, enabling faculty feedback and ensuring that everyone did in fact have a personal plan to work on. The format adopted beyond 2009 is described later in the chapter.

With the AIM program series under way, the BOM soon realized that there was a senior group of Marketing executives not being addressed. These marketing professionals tended to have more than 10 years of marketing or sales experience and were not interested in joining AIM, which they viewed as being for young professionals. It was proposed to the AIM faculty that a 1-week program be developed; one that suited this more senior group who had titles such as Senior Product Manager, Senior Sales or Area Manager, Senior Logistics or Senior Purchasing Manager. The program ended with an exercise around the global purchasing issues of DSM and Schneider Electric.[6] The new program, named

[6] Schneider Electric, case study written by Mark Seitz, Babson MBA Program, under the direction of Professor Jeannet, 1996–1997.

Table 10.3 DSM excellence in Marketing (EM) programs

EM-1 November 17–22, 1996 (Vaalsbroek)
Faculty Babson College & IMD
Organization: Joop Joosen
EM-2 November 2 – 7, 1997 (Vaalsbroek)
Faculty: Babson College and IMD
Organization: Henk-Jan Koenen

Excellence in Marketing (EM), was offered only in 1996 and 1997 at which point it was discontinued.[7] See Table 10.3 **on EM Program Offerings**.

Even though EM was offered twice for a group of about 30 marketing professionals, it became a greater challenge to combine topics for such a diverse group of marketers. As was often the case for such programs, they invariably begin to eat into the target population of the less senior program, not only because participants like to be associated with the 'senior' group but also because some want to avoid the longer 10-day programs.

The work and preparation for the EM program yielded some other interesting results. The development and use of a case around the global purchasing issues with Group Schneider, eventually led to further discussions with Frans van Helmond, one of the initial BOM members who had been part of the IMPACT selection committee, and Jeannet as a regular part AIM, bringing another issue to the forefront.[8] Out of this discussion came the understanding that managing global customers and working through a global key account management system would require new competencies and that the DSM Engineering Plastics organization was not yet ready for this challenge. The Babson AIM faculty team was charged with designing an intervention that would allow DSM account managers to grow into global key account management. Thus, the first Global Account Managers (GAM) program was created, which ran for the first time in Fall 1998 with Frans van Helmond and some 20 managers in attendance.[9]

This first GAM was developed only for DSM Engineering Plastics and dealt with the issues of the global account manager role, the strategic account map, value propositions, as well as implementing target setting and management of accounts. As a final exercise, the participants worked in teams on their own global accounts and presented them to the class.

With the support of the BOM, and particularly Henk-Jan Koenen, the program manager for some Marketing and Strategy programs at that time and a BOM member, the idea of taking the global account program further developed. One of the alumni of the first program became a senior manager for DSM Desotech and two global account management programs were run at Babson for Desotech. Additionally, another program was launched; it was open enrollment and recruited

[7] "Excellence in Marketing," Program Brochure EM-1, DSM, November 1996.

[8] Dinner took place in the evening of Thursday, 26 March 1998.

[9] DSM Program for Global Account Managers, Babson School of Executive Education, Wellesley, MA, US, 28 September 28 to 2 October 1998.

Table 10.4 DSM global account management programs (GAM)

GAM-1 (DSM EP) September 28–October 2, 1998 (Babson College)
Faculty: Babson College
GAM-2 (January 7–12, 2001, at Babson)
KAM-1 for Desotech
Faculty: Babson College
KAM-2 (Key Account Management), January 22–25, 2002, Den Haag NL, for DFS only (Faculty: Babson College)

global account teams from several DSM businesses.[10] Finally, a program was designed for DSM Food Specialties (DFS) and delivered in the Netherlands with material specially designed for that business.[11] While the EP and Desotech programs were considered successful, it was much more difficult to run a mixed businesses program—the DFS didn't lead anywhere because the idea of adopting a global account management system was not supported by the divisional leaders. See Table 10.4 for GAM Program Offerings.

Although there was considerable support for a global account management program from BOM members, and within a short time frame from a succession of program managers on behalf of DSM's executive education arm, the effort had to be ended eventually. One of the main benefits for Jeannet and Hennessey, who worked together in all of these programs, was the publication of a book on global account management in 2003. Without the suggestion of DSM senior managers to look into this issue, much of the intellectual capital that found its way into the book would never have been created (for more on faculty learning cycles, see Chap. 12).

Involvement with the Marketing programs (AIM, EM) also created new opportunities and exposure to new ideas. Over the years, DSM had always made sure that its purchasing community also took advantage of AIM. As a result, Marketers and purchasers were sitting side-by-side in the programs, and the purchasing participants had to submit a 'purchase plan.' DSM's head of Purchasing Services at that time, Willem van Oppen, was also BOM member and was able to convince his colleagues to view Purchasing as "reverse Marketing". Under the sponsorship of the BOM, a team[12] created the *Guide to Purchase Marketing Planning* that promoted a Marketing approach to purchasing.[13] In his letter to the company that accompanied the guide's publication, DSM Chairman of the Managing Board Simon de Bree pointed out that as much as 60 % of DSM's annual sales revenue was spent on purchasing materials and equipment. He also recommended the guide not only for the DSM purchasing community but also to its Marketing

[10] Program was delivered 27 November to 1 December 2000, at Babson College with Christiane Thielens from DSM Management Education & Training as organizers.

[11] Program delivered 22–25 January 2002 in The Hague, NL, organized by Rob van Tilburg (DSM Business Academy).

[12] Team Members were Kees Aartsen, Jan Muller, Willem van Oppen and Walt Sep.

[13] "Guide to Purchase Marketing Planning," DSM Confidential Publication, DSM, 1998: 54.

community since the steps and structures described in the guide were typical of many of DSM's own customers.[14] The involvement of Purchasing with AIM represented certainly enriched the program and served as an additional learning opportunity for the faculty.

Over time, the AIM Marketing programs came increasingly under pressure resulting in slowly declining enrollments. Although the DSM Business Academy (DBA) was vigorously recruiting participants from its businesses, the combination of shifting portfolio through a constant divestiture of the Basic Chemicals cluster reduced the traditional participant base, and many of the newer businesses were slow in coming on board to the DBA programs. In addition, the notion of marketing planning was increasingly replaced by the idea of a business plan for each product/market combination that would include more than just Marketing issues. Under the DBA leadership, it was decided to change the program and split it into two steps.[15] First, the program was restyled as a Business and Marketing Planning (BMP) program while keeping its 10-day format. Just 1 year later, BMP-2 was run as a 1-week program and remained that way for several years. The idea was to lower the cost to the participating businesses and reduce the time needed for the program. This cost and time pressure had become a recurring issue with DSM as the company as a whole was under increasing pressure to improve its financial results.

The challenge remained on what to retain versus what to exclude from the original 10-day AIM program. Given the fact that participants were increasingly coming into the program when they took on their first marketing plan or responsibility, it was decided to focus on the fundamental principles of Marketing: customer insights, customer and market segmentation, product positioning, as well as keep the exercise around a participant-sponsored plan. To maintain sufficient breadth and depth, a shift was made from two to three topics per day by reducing the time for each session.

The first 1-week BMP was offered in 2008 and ran in Rheinfelden, Switzerland, in the vicinity of DNP, one of the major divisions of DSM. Many of the participants, being from DNP who was a recent acquisition, were not familiar with DSM's seminar styles. The level of prior Marketing experience was low and the program disappointed the visitors who joined for the final presentations on the last day. The program faculty, who had included the team from AIM (Jeannet, Hennessey and Turpin) quickly realized that inexperienced participants could not be sent into a presentation to senior managers without a prior dry-run in front of the seminar faculty, something that was promptly implemented in the next running. See Table 10.5 for BMP Program Offerings.

After the second BMP, in 2009, major changes within DSM took effect that greatly impacted all the Marketing-related programs. DSM appointed a Chief

[14] Simon de Bree, Letter to introduce DSM Guide to Purchase Marketing Planning, December 22, 1997.

[15] This evolution from AIM to BMP was under the guidance of Mark Oskam who had at time joined DSM Business Academy from Rotterdam School of Management, Erasmus University. After the retirement of Rob van Tilburg, it was Mark Oskam who took on the management responsibility for both AIM/BMP and also SMC.

Table 10.5 DSM business and Marketing program (BMP)

BMP-1	October 12–16, 2009 (Rheinfelden)
BMP-2	October 11–15, 2010 (Genk)
BMP-3	November 14–18, 2011 (Basel)
BMP-4	May 21–24, 2012 Maastricht
BMP-5	2013 Maastricht (Cancelled)

All Programs under contract to Babson College

Marketing Officer (CMO) who took responsibility for some key Marketing decisions, such as branding the corporate brand. Eventually, this Marketing Office grew with the additions of special teams in Value Pricing, e-Business and the like, focusing on new product launches. The DSM Marketing Office began to offer short interventions and workshops throughout the year, thus making it less attractive to 'wait' for the annual program where a young marketer could learn about the trade. As the BOM was disbanded in response to the creation of the DSM Marketing Office, content responsibility shifted towards the latter. Eventually, the Marketing Office became the primary counterpart for the program faculty and the leader of the Product Launch unit took on a key delivery role in the program.[16] This moved the entire program closer to real Marketing issues but the fact remained that the participants came to the program with progressively less experience.

There was a last major push to launch more BMPs when a new Marketing executive took over at DSM Nutritional Products (DNP)—DSM largest division. Upon visiting a BMP running in Genk, Belgium, it was determined that DNP could benefit from the approach combining conceptual learning with hands on projects that each participant would bring along. Since DNP had a major backlog of Marketing professionals who had never attended AIM, the division contracted Babson and the DSM Marketing Office to deliver four programs for DNP participants only. There were two in Europe, one in North America and one in Asia. All programs followed the same design and were delivered by a combination of Babson faculty and DSM Marketing Office executives. Unfortunately, such a large number of programs to be delivered within a short period of 6 months in 2011 could not be accomplished with the identical staffing and results were mixed. The major effect of this considerable effort was that the pipeline for participants dried out.

A similar impact came from DSM's push into Innovation. The creation of an Innovation Center with its own staff, resources and workshops, as well as the building up of special competencies in such areas as business modeling, had the effect of reducing the willingness of DSM businesses to send participants to programs offered by the Business Academy. Since Innovation was also closely linked to marketing and business planning, the combination of these two Centers was a major contributor to the long-term sustainability of the marketing programs. At the same time, the Centers contributed expertise and its senior members were

[16] Arthur Simonetti was in charge of Product Launch and also became active in delivering the project part of the program.

most generous in attending many final presentations of a number of programs, thus enriching the experience of countless participants.

However, the marketing programs delivered for DSM through Babson's Executive Education arm with faculty teams delivered about 30 marketing programs (AIM, BMP, EM, and GAM) over 20 years, 12 of which were 2 weeks in duration. During this time, DSM did not contract any other educational institution for programs for marketing professionals, although it did maintain a relationship with the Rotterdam School of Management (Erasmus) for a program on Marketing for non-Marketing professionals, such as engineers and scientists.

Learning Dialogue Behavior in a Parallel Stream

While these changes at DSM were taking place concerning the marketing seminars, another event was to substantially affect the educational offerings at the company. Around 2006, some of the DBA program managers were giving thought to offering a combined program for both strategy implementation and leadership development. Up to that point, strategy had been the territory of the SMC program, whereas leadership was developed in separate programs entitled Mobilizing Teams (MT).[17] These programs were launched in the mid-1990s as part of the build-up of the program portfolio. Jeannet made the initial faculty contact, connecting DSM to two former IMD colleagues with extensive experience in this area. After a successful launch, both programs became a staple with several offerings per year under the expert leadership of Chris Parker.[18] However, since the authors did not have direct involvement with these initiatives, some abbreviated comments on these programs will have to suffice.

Explains Parker,[19] "When I first got in touch with DSM in the early 1990s, the company's management culture could best be described as very traditional, very formal, even autocratic and top down. There was a lot of 'surface acting,' i.e. emphasis on what managers or leaders should do."

Parker commented that as the company was shifting towards BSDs in its strategy making processes, there had previously been no dialogue culture in management. According to Parker, DSM managed to have both a strategy and a leadership agenda. He praised the company for having the capacity to also focus on process, not just content, and to recognize that this required righting the behavioral context.

[17] Mobilizing Teams (MT) was offered first as a program with mixed participation from all DSM business groups. In later years the program was offered for specific management teams. In addition, Chris Parker moderated many large DSM-internal conferences. These programs were stopped in 2006/2007 when the MT programs were merged with the SMC programs into the MLP-3 series.

[18] When on the faculty of IMD, Chris Parker was instrumental in building the Managing People program on an open-enrollment basis. Because most of Parker's engagement was later done on a private consulting basis and he was no longer part of the IMD faculty, some elements of the conclusions were not dealt with as part of institutional learning, i.e. IMD or Babson College.

[19] Interview conducted by co-author Jeannet on 5 February 2014.

Commented Parker, "DSM had learned to engage in 'constructive rituals,' i.e., BSDs and CSDs, and to give attention to the sociology and psychology of strategy. The early institution of both challengers and moderators in the BSD process, which happened before I began to engage with the company, was a direct outgrowth of this understanding. There was an appreciation that strategic transformation required a mindset change and they worked diligently to achieve this. In the end, they achieved agility on an industry level."

Two other business school programs were running, partly in parallel, with the Parker programs. When DSM acquired the Vitamins business from Roche, creating DNP, there was a program that IMD had delivered regularly for the Roche Vitamins business. During the early phase of the merger integration, DSM left the Roche-originated IMD program alone. Later, this was transferred to a DSM Leadership Course, largely focused on DNP. Additional MT programs were organized for different DNP sites. Later on, these programs were slowly consolidated into DSM-wide programs.[20]

From the realization that the strategy-making and culture streams needed to be fused for maximum impact, it was but a small step towards the next phase; this one largely driven by DSM's Business Academy.

From Strategy to Leadership

As the DSM Change Agenda emerged as being more central, the DSM Business Academy became interested in creating a single program, combining both SMC and Managing People (MP), each of which were 1 week in length, as well as adding a substantial project that would also deal with the implementation of strategies.

This combined program, under the name of Advanced Management Program (AMP), was articulated by Jan-Peter de Vries for the DBA and intensively discussed with all stakeholders at DSM. The general sentiment was that it might prove a real challenge to combine both topics into one seminar, as the delivery modes of each were so different—experiential for the business team and analytic and case oriented for SMC. DSM's Corporate Planning & Development (CPL) department, as the content owners of the SMC, requested that the new program contain at least as much strategy as the original SMC did. With this in mind, the original proposal for a new AMP also required program leadership that was managerial and experienced in business. The two programs—SMC (Jeannet and team) and MP (Parker)—were essentially terminated and the company started to design from scratch.

Jeannet was asked to provide suggestions for names and institutions that could collaborate on this project. Equally, as a faculty member engaged with his own

[20] The initial IMD program for Roche Vitamins was led by Professor Thomas Malnight and the program continued for a while after the acquisition of the business by DSM. The faculty leader of IMD's DSM/DNP Leadership Course was Robert Hooijberg, who continued to play a lead role in the Executive Leadership Program ELP-1.

home institutions, he was not in a position to take on a 3-week program. The pricing structure of IMD precluded launching the program there and the IMD leadership was unwilling to let its faculty engage individually on this project.[21] After reviewing its options and making several visits to potential providers, DSM decided to go with the University of St. Gallen and obtain one of its adjunct professors to provide the overall leadership, while Jeannet and his SMC team would supply coverage of strategy topics. Detailed planning took place in early 2007 and the program was launched in Vaalsbroek in the fall of that year.

The program represented a complicated design because the third week was to be delivered in China to work on projects on DSM business there. The 1-week modules were given during certain times of the year (October, February, June). One module included the participation of coaches to give the participants feedback on their leadership behavior. The delivery team, although known to each other, had never before delivered a program together. In addition, the cost of bringing everyone to China was considerable, so that in the long run a more cost-effective solution had to be devised. To monitor the program evolution, DSM had created a mirror group consisting of the key area stakeholders, such as CPL and Finance.

There were several challenges regarding the implementation of this 3-week program delivered over 6 months, in three separate 1-week modules. Since previously DSM had offered both a separate strategy program and leadership program (MT), what should be done with participants who had attended one, but not the other? Furthermore, with the complex design, it was expected that one, at the most two, courses could be offered annually, while the company already experienced a backlog of participants. To make matters worse, the pressure of reserving the time for three modules in a row and having to stick to this schedule, meant that there was some attrition over time. As the DBA began to create a whole suite of Management Leadership Programs (MLP-1, MLP-2 and MLP-3), the debate on internal consistency also arose.

In the midst of this, Mark Oskam was appointed program manager after his predecessor at the Business Academy stepped down. His challenge to the delivery team was to reduce the program length to two 1-week modules from the previous three and to see if both modules could be delivered with a smaller faculty. Oskam had a close working relationship with Jeannet and asked him to redesign the program. It was agreed that the restyled program would be housed at Babson and a faculty member from the school's leadership area was recruited—the team of two professors took on the charge of melding the original SMC strategy content and the BT leadership content into a single program delivered over two, separate 1-week modules with a team project in-between. The program was first launched in October 2008, with the second module delivered in February 2009 and was to be called Management and Leadership Program-3 (see Table 10.6 for Program Design MLP-3).

[21] Intensive exchanges between IMD leadership and DSM did not result in a relaxation of the IMD non-compete rules for its faculty. This was despite the fact that DSM's CEO, Feike Sijbesma, was on the IMD Board, and DSM was an active user of IMD programs for other projects, or sponsoring participants for open enrollment seminars.

Table 10.6 DSM management and leadership program level 3 (MLP-3) program block schedule

Program Agenda—Module 1

Monday June 11	Tuesday June 12	Wednesday June 13	Thursday June 14	Friday June 14
08.30–9.00 Opening & Setting the scene Mauricio Adade Pank van de Kooij **09.00–10.45** Role of the General Manager Hayek case Jean-Pierre Jeannet	**08.30–11.15** High performance teams *Experiential learning activity* Karen Ayas	**08.30–13.00** Strategic business environment and systems KSF's & strategic grouping Jean-Pierre Jeannet	**08.30–10.30** Inspiration leadership 2: Personal best Karen Ayas	**08.00–10.00** DFS case study team presentations Jean-Pierre Jeannet **10:15–11.45** Team audit Karen Ayas
11.00–14.45 Panel: Many faces of Leadership Mauricio Adade, Hans Christian Ambjerg, Angelique Paulussen, Kees van der Graaf **(incl. lunch)**	**11.30–13.30** Project Bazar and initialize the project teams Jean-Pierre Jeannet and Karen Ayas **(incl. lunch)**		**10:30–12.00** DFS case study team work Jean-Pierre Jeannet and Karen Ayas	**11:45–12.30** Introduction to Group Projects Jean-Pierre Jeannet
		13:00-14:00 **Lunch**	**12:00-13:00** **Lunch**	**Lunch in project teams**
15.00–18.30 Leadership intro and 360 debrief Karen Ayas	**13.30–17.00** Extracting strategic industry drivers & KSF's Jean-Pierre Jeannet	**14.00–17.30** Inspirational leadership 1 : Influence Karen Ayas	**13.00–16.30** Group work	**12.30–15.30** Project instructions and team preparations Jean-Pierre Jeannet and Karen Ayas **15.30–16.00** Closing Jean-Pierre Jeannet and Karen Ayas **16:00 departure**
		18.00–19.00 Story telling exercise Karen Ayas	**17.00–19.00** Managing Board dialogue Stefan Doboczky (incl. debrief)	
		Dinner and opportunity to watch football	**Dinner and group work**	

Program Agenda—Module 2

Monday October 1	Tuesday October 2	Wednesday October 3	Thursday October 4	Friday October 5
8:30–12:30 Project assignment & debrief Jean-Pierre and Karen Ayas	**8:30–12:00** Creating strategic options and choice Jean-Pierre Jeannet	**8:30–12:00** Deployment of strategy Jean-Pierre Jeannet	**8:30 –12:00** Making your business case Jean-Pierre Jeannet	**8:30–12:30** Team project presentations to DSM Executive Panel Krijn Rietveld Herman Wories Tim Tolhurst

(continued)

Table 10.6 (continued)

Program Agenda—Module 2				
Monday October 1	Tuesday October 2	Wednesday October 3	Thursday October 4	Friday October 5
12:30–13:30 Lunch	**12:00–13:00** Lunch	**12:00–13:00** Lunch	**12:00–13:00** Lunch	**12:30–13:30** Lunch
13:30–18:00 Building Commitment for Accountability for Performance Karen Ayas	**13:00–14:45** Sustaining Accountability for Performance Karen Ayas	**13:00–18:00** Inspiring Action Karen Ayas	**13:00–22:00** Project team work to prepare final presentations Jean-Pierre Jeannet	**13:30–15:30** Peer feedback in learning teams **15:30–16:00** Graduation ceremony Jean-Pierre Jeannet **16.00 The End** (voluntary drinks)
	15:00–17:00 Outside-in view on Business Steering Hans Vossen		**16:00–18:00** The BSD, CSD and Vision 2015 Philip Eykerman	
Individual preparation time (reading, etc) & free time	Individual preparation time (reading, etc) & free time	Team project work	**Between 19:00–21:30** Flexible buffet dinner	
19:30–21:00 Buffet dinner	**19:30–21:00** Buffet dinner	**19:30–21:00** Buffet dinner		

The design of a combined strategy and leadership program posed several challenges. First, both faculty members only had previous experience in single-theme programs. Second, the program design should be an integrated one for participants and help functional managers to make the next step to a general management role. Finally, DSM insisted on a project element—real life experience—that would tie concepts to practice. The real project design aspect was borrowed from the Marketing programs experience (AIM) where each participant brings a project. Because it was also a leadership program, it was decided that these projects would be worked on in teams.

The leadership aspect of the program was delivered through classes, panels, discussions and experiments. Wherever possible, strategy content was mixed or combined with leadership lessons. The opening session on the role of the general managers was both a lesson on how strategy is developed, as well as what roles leaders play.[22] This was followed by an interview and panel session with experienced and recognized leaders from inside and outside DSM. From there, transferring it into a 360-degree exercise feedback was a natural. At other times, the leadership agenda was addressed directly and overtly. The real payoff came when the strategy group exercises themselves were used as feedback opportunities for the participants, something that in a pure strategy course could not be accomplished;

[22] Opening case, *Nickolas Hayek at Swatch*, by Preston Botger, IMD.

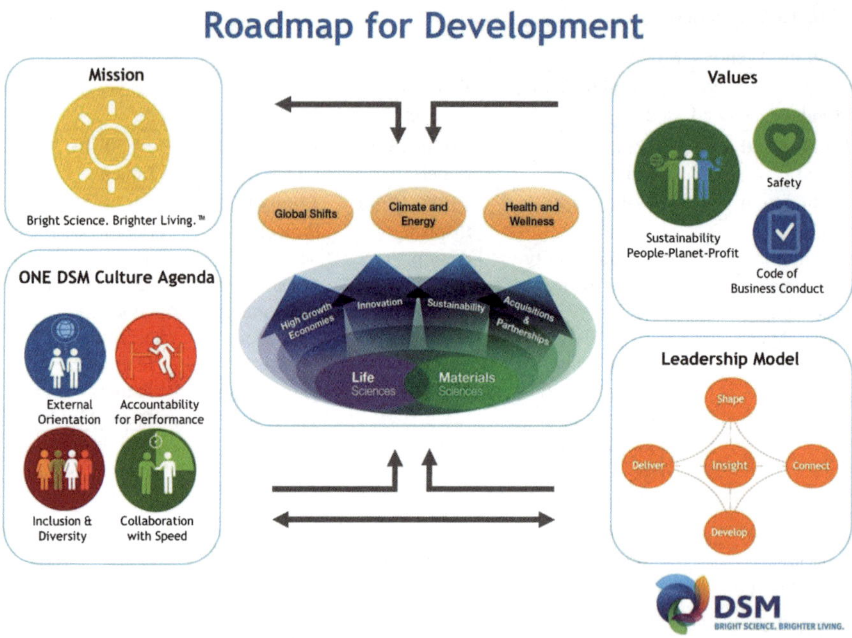

Fig. 10.1 Roadmap for development: DSM cultural change agenda. *Source*: DSM business academy

yet, it was also giving important context to the leadership agenda that did not exist in a typical leadership program.

Particular to DSM was the focus of its top management group on the company culture and the evolution of that culture in line with the requirements of the company and its strategy[23]:

- Mission: Bright Science and Brighter Living
- Values: Sustainability (3 P's); Safety; Code of Business Conduct
- Culture Agenda: External Orientation; Inclusion and Diversity; Accountability for Performance; Collaboration with Speed
- Leadership Model: Insight—Shape, Deliver, Connect and Develop

The MLP-3's program director, Oskam, assumed the role of updating the faculty about the evolution of DSM's culture agenda (See Fig. 10.1 Roadmap for Development). Carefully monitoring developments at the company, the faculty received detailed guidance from him about how they might tweak the program. The learning was much more powerful when leadership lessons were learned via a strategy and

[23] Source: DSM Culture Agenda, DSM internal presentation.

business content or context. Achieving the symbiosis of the two streams—leadership and strategy—required diligent efforts on the part of the program faculty but when carefully connected to the company, the program renewed itself at every turn, adding to the program's longevity.

The projects were offered by participants and for each program a set of four or five were selected. Early in the first week, a 'Bazaar' was held and participants had to select their first, second or third preference. Since the projects offered represented a broad selection from all parts of the company, everyone could be accommodated, at least for their first or second choice. The regular use of these projects also gave the faculty a good sense of current business issues at the company. The projects were launched at the end of module one, worked on in the time in-between, reviewed in a telephone conference before the second module, presented at the beginning of the second module with the work done up to that time and finally presented on the last day of the program. The second to last day was usually largely reserved for working on the final group presentations, which included one or two dry run rounds before facing the panel on the last day.

Contact with senior management was maintained throughout the program modules. Each program was visited by a member of the 'Concern Top' for a private talk on topics of the participants' interest. Panel discussions at the beginning, and for the group presentations on the last day, brought another group of senior executives into the program. Focused presentations and discussions by the heads of strategy and investor relations were part of the format. While these elements were of course highly appreciated by participants, their value was also immense for the teaching faculty. It assured that the faculty was closely briefed on developments at the firm and could quickly adjust their sessions to incorporate any new insights.

By the end of 2013, there had been 12 AMP/MLP-3 programs, of usually 2 weeks in duration, delivered by the Babson MLP-3 faculty team. As DSM expanded its global footprint from Europe to Asia and North America (and locally, more into Switzerland from the Netherlands), the programs also moved; the current rotation included one or two programs for Europe, and one each for Asia and North America. Initially received with great reserve by many inside DSM and by the faculty, the program exceeded the expectations of many and the delivery team came to consider the design superior to separate programs for either topic. See Table 10.7 for MLP Program Offerings.

The economics of the program was driven by the delivery fee charge to DSM by Babson College, as well as by the number of participants admitted to each program cycle (a limit of 30 participants). If the program cohorts were recruited globally, travel costs for many intercontinental flights were added. DSM, similar to many other companies with internal business academies, charges the full delivery cost and the DBA overhead costs to its businesses who must also pay for travel and hotel stays. To save money, there is a tendency to place the programs regionally, the negative being the lack of mixing with many different cultures and regions, something not consistent with the 'One DSM' culture agenda.

But a company such as DSM, with its global businesses subject to global economic turbulence, never stands still. A program such as the MLP-3 can only

Table 10.7 DSM management & leadership programs level 3 (MLP-3) offerings

Advanced Management Program AMP-1/2007/2008 (Jan-Peter de Vries)
Contracted to St. Gallen University,
Module 1: October 22–26, 2007 (Vaalsbroek)
Module 2: February 18–22, 2008 (Vaalsbroek)
Module 3: June 22–26, 2008 (China)
AMP-2 (contracted to Babson College)
October 20–24, 2008
February 16–20, 2009 Vaalsbroek
MLP-1 (Babson College)
June 21–26, 2009
November 22–27, 2009 (Genk Stiemerheide),
MLP-2 (Babson College)
October 4–8, 2010 (Genk)
November 29–December 3, 2010 (Maastricht)
MLP-3 (abridged version, 1 week only for DNP) Babson College
December 6–10, 2010 (Basel, Bad Schauenburg)
MLP-4 (Babson College)
March 28–April 1, 2011 (Genk)
June 6–10, 2011 (Maastricht)
MLP-5 (Babson College)
November 7–11, 2011 (Genk)
February 6–10, 2012 (Maastricht)
MLP-6 (Babson College)
January 9–13, 2012 (Singapore)
March 26–30, 2012 (Shanghai)
MLP-7 (Babson College)
June 11–15, 2012 (Genk)
October 1–5, 2012 (Basel)
MLP-8 (Babson College)
January 28–February 1, 2013 (Genk)
June 3–7, 2013 (Maastricht)
MLP-9 (Babson College)
April 15–19, 2013 (Shanghai)
September 23–27, 2013 (Shanghai)
MLP-10 (Babson College)
June 17–21, 2013 (Genk)
November 11–15, 2013 (Maastricht)

work if the various stakeholders in the different functional and business areas agree to delegate their agenda to the program. With respect to strategy, that is certainly something that needs to be evaluated since all participants are exposed to strategy, although the company may want to maintain some deeper involvement for some of the other executives not attending MLP-3. The cohorts are largely middle and upper middle managers but a newcomer to the company in a senior position will not have been exposed to it. This, over time, could lead to a dilution of strategy and BSD expertise. In a similar vein, a new program was commenced by DSM geared to high potentials, largely emphasizing leadership development in its naked form, and in less combination with strategy issues, as in MLP-3. How does the company assure that all of its executives are exposed to the same messages and, more or less, the same experience and content? When DSM undertook its extensive IMPACT exercise at IMD 25 years earlier, everyone from a certain management level, and upward, was exposed what was happening within the company at that time.

The Big Decision: Exit Petrochemicals? 11

The later developments have proven that Vision 2005 was correct and the exit from Petrochemicals justified. However, that was contingent upon the ability to make further large steps.
—Louk Ligthart, interview

2000–2005: Major Steps in the Transformation of DSM Through 'Vision 2005'

The acquisition of Gist-Brocades had stretched DSM's balance sheet ratios in 1998. However, profit and cash generation in 1998 and 1999 was substantial, allowing DSM to bring its financial ratios in line with its targets already in 1999. This happened despite the execution of a very substantial investment program, fostering organic growth. Of course, the integration of Gist-Brocades consumed a lot of organizational attention and energy during these years but had also been completed within the 300 days of the integration plan. Additionally, DSM had executed some divestments, such as ABS and Curver. With the divestment of the latter, the Plastics Processing cluster had, effectively, been discontinued. It was again time to take stock of the company's development and current status. Moreover, the company had changed its profile so considerably that new strategic priorities were in order.

Thus, DSM kicked off its third Corporate Strategy Dialogue (CSD) in January 2000, called 'Vision 2005: Focus and Value.' Two major external themes played a significant role in this CSD:

- 'Concentration' in many industries was rising fast[1]; this was also happening with industries that DSM was participating in, or supplying to, and, as a result,

[1] In fact, from the mid-1990s to 2001 the fifth merger wave in recorded history was taking place (see Douma and Schreuder 2013: 324–325). After the dot.com bubble burst, a recession set in. A sixth merger wave began to swell in 2005 and reached its peak in 2007.

J.-P. Jeannet, H. Schreuder, *From Coal to Biotech*,
DOI 10.1007/978-3-662-46299-7_11

competition was intensifying to the extent that only the industry leaders would survive and prosper. Could DSM maintain the full breadth of its portfolio or should it 'focus' further? A related question was whether these aspired leadership positions could be attained based on the company's own strength, or whether DSM had to participate in the concentration trend to achieve these?

- Despite its recent growth and successes, DSM remained an undervalued company on the stock exchange. Its Price-earnings ratio was less than half the average of its peer group. This 'undervaluation' could not continue for offensive reasons (the ability of DSM to use shares for acquisitions), but also certainly for defensive reasons (the possibility that DSM could become a takeover target). The market 'value' of the company would have to rise considerably for DSM to remain the master of its own destiny.

These two external themes were seen to reinforce the need for DSM's further evolution to strategic leadership positions with higher value-added products and lower cyclicality (see Fig. 11.1).

Internally, the company's management felt it was on a good track. An update of the portfolio development from 1985 to 1994 (see Fig. 9.1) was made to compare the growth in the recent 6 years of 1995–2000 with that of the 10 years prior, 1985–1994 (see Fig. 11.2). The contrast was now huge—net cumulative growth now amounted to 49 % in 6 years, versus 8 % in the 10 years before. Particularly satisfying was (a) that this net growth had been achieved despite significant divestments and (b) that although DSM had made its largest acquisition ever (Gist-Brocades), most of the growth was 'organic,' coming from increases in existing activities. In effect, the company had almost doubled in size (and any less modest company than DSM would have presented it that way).

The business climate was good in 2000 and, as the CSD was being conducted, the company was heading toward its best financial result ever—a net profit of EUR 580 million.[2] In this climate, and with its financial ratios already restored to satisfactory levels in 1999, the company felt strong enough to contemplate the next large acquisition. After extensive analysis, it was decided to acquire Catalytica, a spin-off from Glaxo Wellcome owned by a private equity firm. In August 2000, the transaction of US$800 million (at the time about EUR 860 million) was announced and in December it was completed. Through this acquisition DSM boosted its sales in Life Science Products (LSP), adding another EUR 450 million to EUR 2.2 billion.[3] As a result, this cluster grew to over 30 % of

[2] The European Euro was introduced in 1999 and has replaced the Dutch Guilder (Dfl) in 2002 at a conversion rate of EUR 1 = Dfl 2.20371.

[3] Catalytica turned out to be a difficult acquisition for DSM. First of all, the company had paid a too high price. Second, it was its first experience with private equity. The Catalytica management had been 'incentivized' by private equity to run the company but all left within a year, after cashing both the private equity incentives as well as the DSM 'stay-on bonus.' Thus, DSM was forced to completely replace top management while the integration was going on. Third, a 'warning letter' from the FDA was received shortly after the acquisition, necessitating an urgent quality

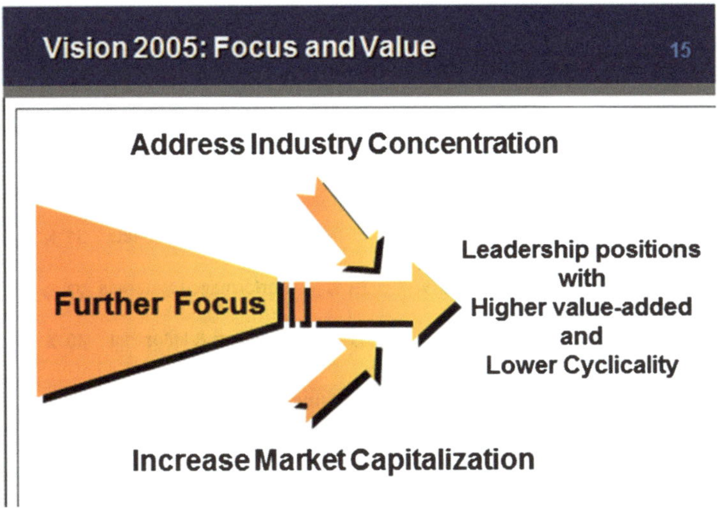

Fig. 11.1 The main themes of 'Vision 2005'. *Source*: DSM company presentations

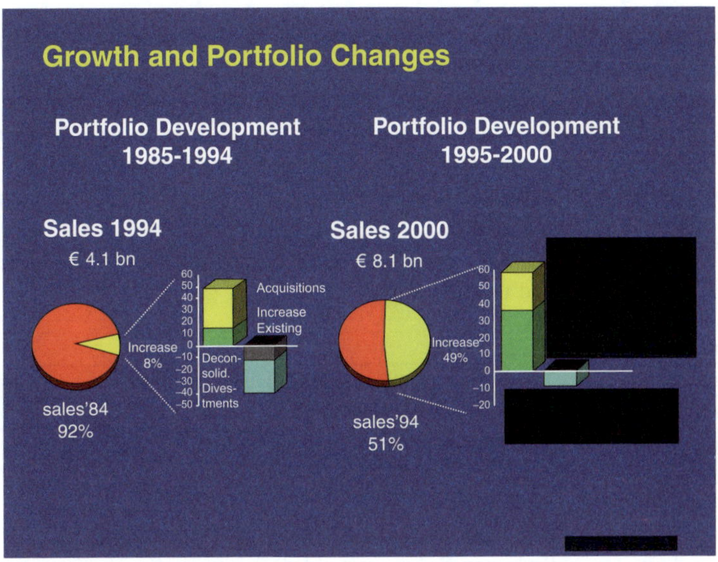

Fig. 11.2 Portfolio development 1995–2000. *Source*: DSM company presentations

improvement program. Finally, it proved more difficult than anticipated to win other business than from Glaxo Wellcome to this site.

Further Focus on Clusters 16

Clusters:	ACS 1994	CSD 1997	1999	CSD 2000	Incl. Catalytica
Fine Chemicals	5 %	11 %	26 %	Life Science Products	31 %
Performance Materials	32 %	26 %	29 %	Performance Materials	27 %
Base Chemicals & Materials	44 %	48 %	43 %	Polymers & Industrial Chemicals	40 %
Processing Plastic Products	16 %	10 %	discontinued		

Fig. 11.3 Development of DSM's clusters. *Source*: *Vision 2005*, internal company presentation, Corporate Strategy & Acquisitions, 2000

DSM sales in 2000 (see Fig. 11.3). Note, however, that the Base Chemicals and Materials cluster still accounted for 40 % of DSM's sales in that same year. Moreover, financial analysis showed that this cluster—despite its cyclicality—had consistently generated the company's highest average return on investment (ROI). Financial projections showed that this could well remain the case in the years to come. Hence, it was by no means clear how DSM's strategic intent to further 'focus' could be realized.

The design of the CSD was again tailor-made to reflect the multitude of issues on the table. This time, it led to no less than ten working groups:

Working group	Assignment
Corporate context	Trends in corporate context, including end markets
Petrochemicals	Trends in industry structure, benchmarking
Performance materials	Evaluation of strategic options
Life science products	Recommendations
External performance	Performance assessment of DSM against peer group
Internal performance	Performance assessment of DSM's businesses
Growth paths	Relative success of DSM's organic growth versus acquisitions
Image/attractiveness	Assessment of corporate strategic options from stakeholder perspective
Innovative growth	Generation of new growth opportunities through 'new business models'
Asia	Evaluation of means to increase DSM's presence in Asia

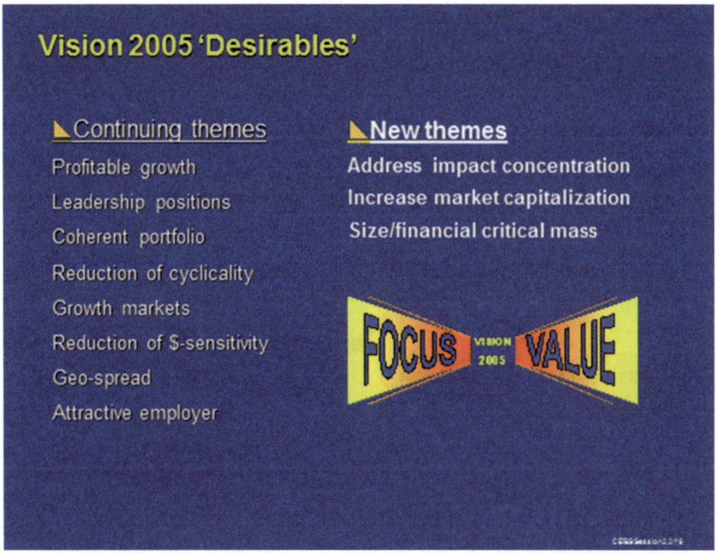

Fig. 11.4 The desirables of 'Vision 2005: Focus and Value'. *Source*: DSM company presentations

These working groups assisted the Managing Board (MB) to work through an agenda from January to August 2000, with results to be communicated internally at an Executive Meeting in late September, to be followed immediately by external communications through press releases and conferences, as well as at an Analyst Meeting. The 'Concern Top' was involved in four 2-day sessions to discuss interim results. It helped enormously in dealing with such a complicated agenda that a deadline was made clear from the outset—at the Analyst Meeting the new corporate strategy would have to be communicated. Having established this expectation in the outside world, there was no way to escape the date. The main risk of such a 'pressure cooker process' was that the decision-making body, the MB, would not come to joint conclusions in time. Therefore, it was determined that during this cycle they would be more closely involved in the supervision of the working groups, while 11 full days of MB discussion had already been planned at the outset of the CSD process. The Supervisory Board would also be involved earlier than usual—before summer 2000, they would be presented with the interim conclusions of the CSD, giving them a chance to influence the final outcomes before they were to be presented for approval. All in all, the circle of people involved in the CSD had widened again, now to over 100 people.

Another mechanism was put in place to reduce the risk of the CSD not yielding shared conclusions and that was to agree to the evaluation criteria for strategic options at the beginning of the process. These so-called 'Desirables' are listed in Fig. 11.4. They reflect the continuing themes of DSM's strategic evolution, as well as the new themes of industry consolidation and market capitalization. It was clear

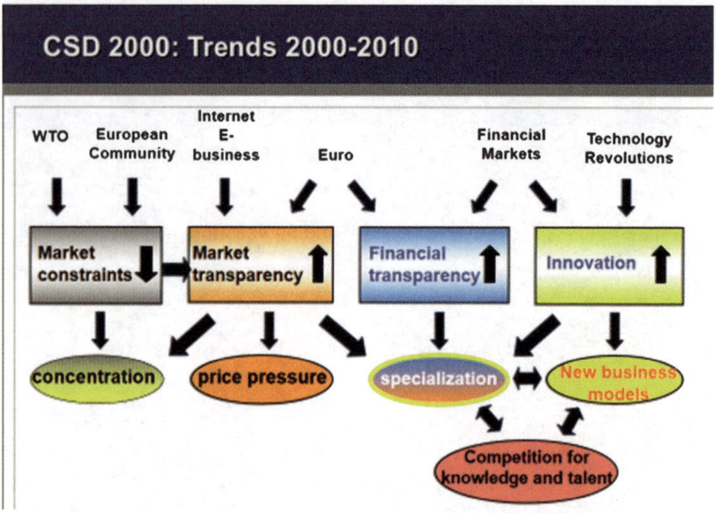

Fig. 11.5 External trends identified in 2000. *Source*: DSM company presentations

that DSM would also have to think through the issue of size—was a certain 'financial critical mass' necessary, for instance to be included in the main European stock indexes? Or, did the valuation of smaller, more specialized competitors, such as Lonza, show that stock markets valued focus more than size? Such questions were particularly relevant at this time because DSM was willing to consider three very different strategic options for its further development:

1. *Current portfolio*: continue the evolution of DSM with roughly the same portfolio of business activities
2. *Further focus*: continue the focusing of DSM toward less clusters of activities (and expanding within these)
3. *Grand design*: making a step change by means of a corporate merger (or a very large acquisition)

The 'Further Focus' option concentrated on continuing with the Life Science Products (LSP) and Performance Materials (PM) clusters. Theoretically, one could also conceive trading in the (valuable) LSP position for a 'big splash' in the remaining clusters, but this was clearly inferior in terms of the 'Desirables.' For the 'Grand Design' option a Corporate Merger and Acquisitions (M&A) list was drawn up. There were seven potential candidates on this list.

An enormous amount of work was performed in this CSD (see the external analyses summarized in Fig. 11.5). Market constraints were shown decreasing and market transparency increasing as a result of various drivers, including the World Trade Organization's (WTO) trade rounds (now with China as a participant), the

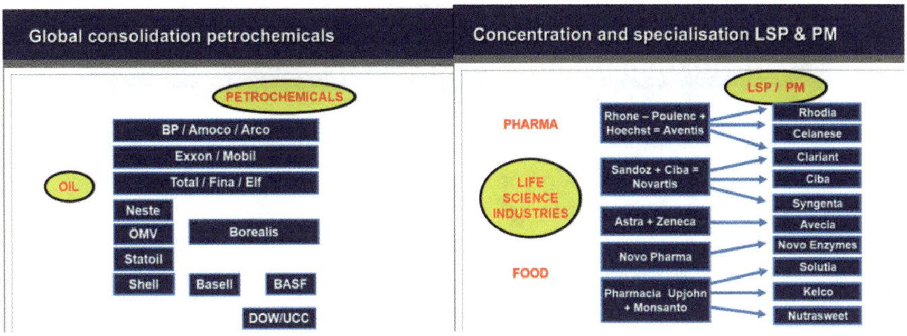

Fig. 11.6 Concentration effects in DSM's industries. *Source*: DSM company presentations

European market integration, the internet and the Euro. This led to increasing concentration in industrial activities and to price pressure on many markets. Similarly, financial market transparency was driving firms to focus on what they could do best, leading to further specialization. Specialization, often combined with new business models, was also necessary to keep up with the innovation waves induced by technological revolutions, such as the internet but also genomics, as well as Nano- and Biotech.[4] This was particularly true in fields where new business forms were emerging and fortunes could be made in a short time. The 'war for talent' was raging and this included the attraction of both the financial sector and private equity for university graduates from many continents.

The trend of concentration played out very differently for DSM in its various industries. The oil industry was concentrating in a rapid pace with mergers like Exxon/Mobil, BP/Amoco/Arco and Total/Fina/Elf (as the left side of Fig. 11.6 shows), causing their petrochemical activities to combine. Moreover, petrochemical assets were also coming together in new joint ventures like Borealis and Basell, while the acquisition of UCC by Dow implied that a significant licensor of technology was now in the hands of a direct competitor. The concentration trend in the petrochemical industry, therefore, implied a threat to DSM because competitors were achieving scale and global reach at an accelerating pace, the oil and naphtha markets were becoming more oligopolistic and new technologies would become less widely available. These factors already made it urgent for DSM to answer the question of whether the company would want to contribute its own petrochemical activities to a larger entity at some point in time. However, with concentration ratios rising, perhaps there was not much time left: at the time, one could anticipate that the Competition Directorate of the European Union would have to become much stricter in allowing new combinations before long.

Within the Life Science Industries, concentration was also rising rapidly (as the right-hand side of Fig. 11.6 shows), however, with diametrically opposed

[4] See, e.g. *The Long Boom* by Peter Schwartz et al. (1999).

Fig. 11.7 Growth opportunities in all clusters. *Source*: *Vision 2005*, internal company presentation, Corporate Strategy & Acquisitions, 2000

consequences for DSM. Here the Pharma mergers of companies such as Hoechst and Rhone Poulenc, or Ciba and Sandoz, led to spin-offs of companies in DSM's fields of activities as the new large Pharma companies focused on their core business. Hence, a whole host of new companies emerged on the scene, for example Rhodia, Celanese, Clariant, Avecia, Solutia and Novozymes. All of these companies contained potentially attractive activities for DSM in the fields of LSP and PM and, as a result, figured on the company's acquisition list. Moreover, DSM was a relatively big fish in this pond, whereas it was a small one in the (oil and) petrochemical pond. As a result, there were many more options for development in the areas of LSP and PM, while the feasibility of executing such options could also be considered relatively high.

In this context, the growth opportunities for all three clusters were analyzed in detail. It turned out that DSM had significant options to further strengthen and expand all its clusters (see Fig. 11.7). In Life Science Products it was felt that the Pharma Intermediates position had now been brought to a leadership position, upon which further expansion could be based. Moreover, this cluster also contained the Food Ingredients business, mainly consisting of the former Gist-Brocades' Food Specialties and Bakery Ingredients divisions, complemented by DSM businesses such as Aspartame; this area also offered an option for further growth, particularly around the Food Specialties core. In PM the CSD analysis had shown that DSM's businesses formed an 'archipelago'—individual islands with some, but limited, (technological and market) synergy. There were opportunities to strengthen the individual businesses but even more significant options to strengthen the whole cluster by acquisitions and these were included in the Grand Design list. Finally, regarding Petrochemicals, an interim conclusion was that further development was necessary given the rapid developments in the petrochemical industry in terms of technologies, scale, concentration and globalization. Leaving DSM's Petrochemical business 'as is' would effectively imply an erosion of its position. Hence, an 'own strength scenario' was elaborated upon, amounting to an investment program of around EUR 900 million. Next to this, alliance options were explored with the conclusion that they were still sufficiently available, but that there would be a threat of 'lock-out' for DSM if the trend for greater concentration in Europe continued. In order for DSM's Petrochemicals to reach their full potential, it was concluded that they would have to participate in the global industry consolidation, effectively implying that it was DSM's preference to seek out a petrochemicals partner.

While the abundance of growth opportunities in all clusters was, of course, good news, it also made clear that a strategic choice was inescapable. For instance, the investment program of EUR 900 million in petrochemicals was seen as absolutely necessary to maintain competitiveness, but the strengthening of LSP and PM was also necessary, preferably including acquisitions from the 'Grand Design' list. Simultaneous execution of all options, however, was impossible, both financially and managerially. A choice had to be made. In making this choice, the MB faced a potential dilemma—the dilemma of 'focus' versus 'size.' It was clear that there would have to be increased focus in order to achieve its Desirables (see Fig. 11.4), particularly in order to reduce cyclicality, achieve a more coherent portfolio and increase the market capitalization. With petrochemicals (and industrial chemicals), DSM would remain a commodity/hybrid type of company. Only by making further choices would it be able to gain a 'specialty' portfolio of products with higher value added and lower cyclicality. The choice for 'further focus' by concentrating on LSP and PM meant that DSM would continue with the 'exploitation' of the pathway that had been found in the previous CSDs. It was only because these clusters had been sufficiently strengthened in previous rounds that it was now possible to consider giving up the (full) ownership of the Petrochemicals division.

Further focus, however, could entail the loss of size. If DSM became a 'small cap' company it would run the risk of dropping out of the relevant stock market indices, which would put pressure on its share price. Moreover, the company would face a significant risk of losing its independence if it just divested Petrochemicals and had a large amount of cash on its balance sheet. Hence, it was decided that both further focus and maintaining critical size were important. Preparations to create a separate Petrochemical entity within DSM would start by making all relations with other DSM units transparent and market-based. This would enable a 'carve-out' of DSM Petrochemicals when an alliance or acquisition partner would present itself. At the same time, LSP and PM would have to accelerate their growth in order to maintain DSM's critical size. The execution of 'Vision 2005' would, therefore, require very careful planning and coordination.

With regard to the growth of LSP and PM, it was decided to first pursue the acquisition of Rhodia, the spin-off from the French company Rhone-Poulenc. Rhodia was attractive to DSM because it contained strong businesses in Food,

Pharma and Performance Materials, most notably Polyamide 6.6 with its precursors (complementing DSM's position in Polyamide 6 with its precursor Caprolactam). Friendly discussions were initiated but did not progress very far without a clear offer on the table. After a thorough preparation, DSM sent an offer letter to the Rhodia board in December 2001 valuing Rhodia shares at more than EUR 15 (a premium of >40 %) and the total share capital of Rhodia at EUR 2.7 billion. The combined company would be called DSM Rhodia, have English as its company language and would be headquartered in, or around, Brussels. Differences of opinion remained about corporate governance (Rhodia preferring a one-tier board and DSM a two-tier board) and about the top positions (DSM claiming the chair position of both boards and offering Rhodia both vice-chair positions). It was these differences that probably led the Rhodia board to summarily reject DSM's offer, although a number of Rhodia shareholders were clearly disappointed. DSM issued a press release in early January 2002 that discussions had ceased. When asked about Rhodia later that year, Peter Elverding remarked, "We shut the door." There seems to have been some confusion among French journalists who had heard him say "Oui, je t'adore." The Rhodia CEO, Jean-Pierre Tirouflet, was forced by shareholders to resign in 2003. One of their grievances was that he had "made a grave error in rejecting a relatively generous takeover bid from DSM."[5]

In the meantime, preparation of the 'carve-out' of Petrochemicals had been progressing well. DSM's announcement that it would seek a partnership for Petrochemicals had attracted the attention of a number of other companies who expressed interest. Among these was Saudi Basic Industries Corporation (SABIC), the Saudi-Arabian petrochemical company that was seeking global expansion. When DSM made its announcement, SABIC was looking at the petrochemical assets of ENI, the Italian oil company. Upon the suggestion of its investment banker, management also took a look at DSM's assets and came to the conclusion that these were of superior quality and would be a better fit for SABIC's strategy. Confronted with such interest, DSM launched a formal auction process inviting bids for part, or all, of its Petrochemicals. In the end, SABIC won the auction process with its bid of EUR 2.25 billion for all of DSM's Petrochemical activities.[6]

In December 2001, DSM had already sold its shares[7] in Energie Beheer Nederland to the Dutch state for EUR 1.2 billion and in 2002 the proceeds from the sale of Petrochemicals came in. DSM now had the problem it had tried to avoid: due to a large acquisition that had not materialized and the large divestments that were successful, the company had shrunk while having a large amount of cash on its balance sheet. The company came up with an innovative solution to safeguard the

[5] *Chemical Week*, 25 Feb 2004. Rhodia was acquired by Solvay in 2011, with Tirouflet's successor, Mr. Clamadieu, becoming the CEO of the combined group.

[6] Thus, DSM had been 'lucky' that SABIC's attention had been attracted just in time by DSM's announcement of the 'Vision 2005' decisions. It was, moreover, lucky because SABIC turned out to be the best bidder in the (thinly populated) auction process, by far.

[7] Technically, these were depositary receipts.

proceeds from the divestments and to protect itself against unfriendly approaches. It established a subsidiary called DSM 'Vision 2005 BV' with the purpose of managing these revenues. The DSM 'Vision 2005 BV' issued one single priority share to a DSM Vision 2005 Priority Foundation. The Board of this Foundation consisted of three members of the DSM's MB and three members of its Supervisory Board. As stated in the *DSM Annual Report 2002* (p. 80), "The only criterion to be used by the Priority Foundation in assessing the proposed decisions (of the 'Vision 2005 BV') is whether they are compatible with the 'Vision 2005: Focus and Value' strategy." The authors are not aware of any other example where such a mechanism has been used to safeguard the implementation of a company strategy.

Fortunately, this unusual situation did not have to last long. The Swiss Pharma company Hoffmann-La Roche approached DSM in 2002 about whether it would possibly be interested in acquiring its Vitamins, Carotenoids and Fine Chemicals (VCFC) activities. Again, this is an example where DSM's pro-active communication about its strategic ambitions and intent triggered other companies to approach them. Roche's VCFC business had not figured on DSM's Grand Design list because management had no idea that Roche would be willing to sell these divisions. Roche was the inventor of many synthetic vitamin production processes and, as such, these activities were the 'roots' of the company. It had been hit, however, by an investigation and had been heavily fined as an "instigator" in the operation of eight specific cartels for separate vitamins.[8] Moreover, in its own strategic reorientation, Roche had decided to fully concentrate on its Pharma and Diagnostics businesses. The company's management was therefore willing to explore the divestment of the VCFC business but was hesitant to do so in a fully open process, which would once again expose the business and its cartel history to public scrutiny.[9] Also with the private sale to DSM the cartel case came back to haunt Roche; in the US, foreign companies tried to claim their commercial damages due to the price fixing, since the awarded amounts are much higher in the US than elsewhere. The District Court had refused these foreign claims stating that the law was only applicable for American companies. However, during the negotiation process with DSM, the Court of Appeals overturned this decision and allowed foreign companies to file their claims in the US; the consequences of this decision were enormous in terms of the potential amounts involved. There was no way DSM could ever run the risk of potentially being confronted with these amounts as the buyer of the VCFC business. Initially, Roche downplayed these risks and stated that the US Supreme Court would overrule the Court of Appeals.[10] At the time, Schreuder still vividly recalls after having heard this news during the negotiations calling Peter Elverding that under

[8] See: http://europa.eu/rapid/press-release_IP-01-1625_en.htm and http://www.justice.gov/atr/public/press_releases/1999/2450.htm (Both accessed on 2 Dec 2014)

[9] Internally, the company followed a two-track process by (1) preparing for an IPO and (2) exploring a private sale. Chris Goppelsroeder, who later joined DSM, was in charge of the IPO-track and was very unpleasantly surprised to find out that Franz Humer, the CEO, preferred the private sale.

[10] The US Supreme Court eventually indeed overturned the decision of the Court of Appeals in 2004. See: http://www.law.cornell.edu/supct/html/03-724.ZS.html

these circumstances the deal would have to be terminated—it would have been 'betting the farm.' Fortunately, soon afterward Roche came to the conclusion that DSM indeed needed full protection against these risks and a lengthy document to that effect was negotiated and agreed upon.

The acquisition of the Roche VCFC was a very protracted process for a number of reasons. First of all, this would be by far the largest acquisition DSM had ever made. Second, Vitamins and Carotenoids were quite unknown territory for the company and it would be necessary for management to quickly familiarize itself with the competitive landscape and health of the Roche business.[11] Third, the business was suffering in the aftermath of the cartel break-up; performance was going down month-by-month. Analysts were commenting that DSM was attempting to 'catch a falling knife.' And finally, the competition authorities (both in the US and in Europe) were, of course, very alert and performed a lengthy and detailed scrutiny of the case. While the companies had basically reached an agreement in early February 2003, it took until late September 2003 to obtain the necessary antitrust approvals. DSM acquired the business then for about EUR 1.75 billion[12] and immediately started an intensive integration program, managing to restore the competitiveness of the business quite rapidly. Feike Sijbesma, who had supervised the transaction at the Board level, and Henk van Dalen, the CFO, were in charge of this successful integration, which at the operational level was conducted by Emmo Meijer and Jos Schneiders from DSM with Chris Goppelsroeder and Matthias Waehren from the (formerly) Roche side. Roche management let it be known that it was surprised at what DSM had been able to achieve in turning around the business. With the sale of Petrochemicals and acquisition of the VCFC business, DSM had achieved the portfolio shift it had aimed for in 'Vision 2005: Focus and Value.' Only the Industrial Chemicals activities remained as 'commodity cluster' with its portfolio share at less than 20 % (see Fig. 11.8)

[11] A very large DSM team was involved in this acquisition. Key people on the business evaluation side were Emmo Meijer and Jan Wolters, who led the due diligence. The negotiation team was led by Hein Schreuder and included Arnold Gratama van Andel and Pieter de Haan (with Maarten Muller of Allen & Overy as external legal counsel). Feike Sijbesma should be credited with the overall coordination at the Board level and for the perseverance to orchestrate several breakthroughs when progress of the transaction was seemingly stuck. The success of the Roche deal probably secured Feike's subsequent appointment as CEO of DSM.

[12] Because the financial results of the business were deteriorating month-by-month, the delay in the acquisition process cost Roche a substantial sum, since the contract provided for price adjustment in such circumstances.

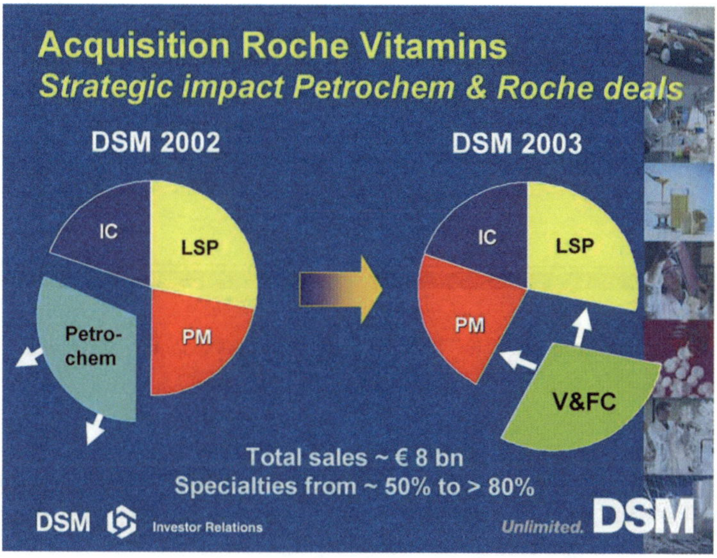

Fig. 11.8 Portfolio impact of petrochemicals and Roche vitamins deals. *Source*: DSM presentation, *Vision 2005: Focus on Profitability*, Peter Elverding, Chemical Analysts Conference, 1 October 2003

Reflection 1: DSM as a Learning Company

One of the CSD Working Groups for 'Vision 2005' was called 'Growth paths,' led by Jos Wassen and Loek Radix. Its task was to examine the various ways in which DSM had grown and the company's relative success. Overall, the question was whether organic growth was more successful than growth by acquisitions. However, the working group came up with many more insights, particularly regarding DSM's track record in M&A and has had a substantial impact on the way DSM subsequently (re) organized its M&A approach and activities. Therefore, it will be used here as an example of DSM as a 'learning company.'

The working group examined 20 years of DSM's growth, from 1980 to 2000. It made the distinction between Investments and Acquisitions. Investments included organic growth in existing businesses as well as new business development: DSM invested an amount of Dfl 8.5 billion over this period. Investments alone did not contribute significantly to DSM's growth within this timeframe (see the left-hand side of Fig. 11.9 where the line is virtually flat). This is due, in part, to the fact that DSM divested Dfl 2.6 billion of existing business during these years.[13] However, if these divestments are disregarded, the autonomous growth of existing business was

[13] Dfl 600 million was invested in New Business Development in this time period, which generated only Dfl 300 million of revenue at the time (Stanyl, Aspartame, Dyneema, SMA).

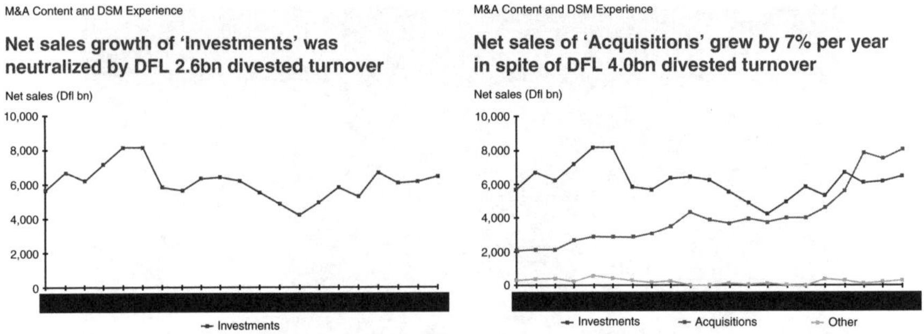

Fig. 11.9 Acquisitions needed for DSM growth 1980–2000. *Source*: CSD working-group 'Growth Paths,' 2000

still only 3 %, roughly in line with the gross domestic product (GDP). One can see that acquisitions 'saved the day' for DSM by contributing 7 % growth per year, despite the very significant divestments of this category to the tune of Dfl 4.0 billion[14] (see the right-hand side of Fig. 11.9). DSM invested Dfl 6.3 billion in acquisitions and a further Dfl 5.4 billion on follow-up investments in these businesses. The conclusion for this time period was rather clear—for topline growth and portfolio rejuvenation, acquisitions had been vital.

What type of acquisitions did DSM make? Here the working group adopted the standard classification of acquisitions into the following categories:

- *Horizontal*: one company acquires another in the same industry
- *Vertical*: the acquired company is either a supplier or a customer of the acquiring company, for example upstream (backward integration) or downstream (forward integration) in the value chain
- *Concentric*: acquirer and target company are related through basic technologies, production processes or markets
- *Unrelated*: no such relationships between acquirer and target

The classification of 57 acquisition deals made by DSM between 1980 and 2000 can be seen in Fig. 11.10. In the 1980s, during the 'hurry up' phase of diversification, the category of unrelated acquisitions was the largest and included, for instance, the assembly of the Construction division. In line with the experiences of many other firms, DSM learned the hard way that unrelated diversification is usually not a path to success. Such acquisitions were therefore abandoned in the early 1990s, when the largest category became the vertical acquisitions. DSM management was particularly interested in forward integration with the belief that

[14] Acquisitions that were subsequently divested included the Construction division, Fardem, Curver, MacIntosh, EPP-sheet and parts of Resins.

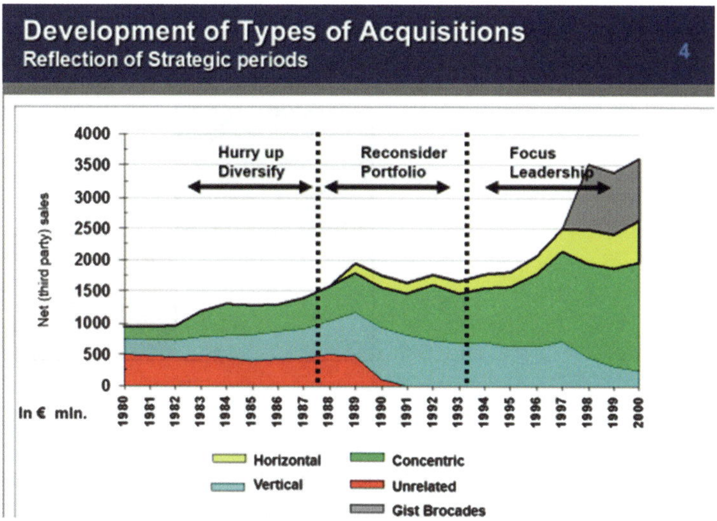

Fig. 11.10 Development of types of acquisitions over time (1980–2000). *Source*: CSD working-group 'Growth Paths,' 2000

it made sense to move closer toward the end markets of products (this category would include acquisitions such as Engineering Plastic Products, Curver and the packaging company Fardem). Since the mid-1990s, when DSM started focusing and building leadership positions, the category of concentric acquisitions became dominant, while horizontal acquisitions in the selected industries were also on the rise. As such, Fig. 11.10 shows the learning DSM management went through in finding its way in terms of making acquisitions. All unrelated acquisitions and forward integration moves were divested later. The company paid some heavy dues for this learning experience as the following statistics show:

1980–2000		
Acquisitions	57 deals	Dfl 6.3 billion costs for Dfl 7.3 billion sales
Divestments	84 deals	Dfl 2.8 billion proceeds for Dfl 6.6 billion sales

The statistics above already indicate that DSM's track record in M&A was not impressive during this time period, to say the least. Indeed, the working group estimated that 50 % of the 'number' of acquisitions made had resulted in financial failure, while this percentage rose to 61 % based on deal 'value.' This is in line with the percentages found in the literature.[15] There was some good news in the finding

[15] See Douma and Schreuder, *Economic Approaches to Organizations*. Harlow: Pearson, 5th edition, 2013, Chap. 13.

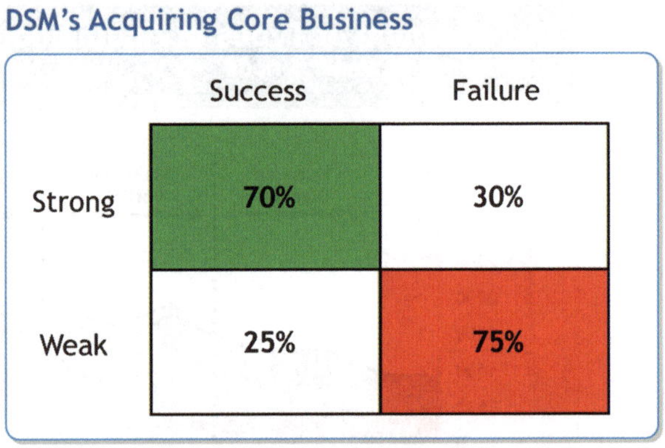

Fig. 11.11 Success rate of acquisitions heavily dependent on strength of acquiring business. *Source*: CSD working-group 'Growth Paths,' 2000

that the failure rate had decreased significantly since the mid-1990s[16] but overall the picture was, of course, not one to be proud of. Therefore, the working group proceeded to examine the reasons for the failures and found many interesting results. One of the most prominent findings is captured in Fig. 11.11: 55 % of DSM's acquisitions were executed by a relatively weak DSM business, while in 45 % of the cases the acquiring DSM business was strong. As the Figure shows, the success rates were dramatically different: if DSM's acquiring business was strong, the success rate was 70 %; if the acquiring business was weak, it was only 25 %. Jos Wassen summarized this finding in the saying, "Two lame ducks don't make a flying eagle." This saying became a standard observation whenever a relatively weak DSM business proposed an acquisition that would 'solve its problems.'

This study served as a wake-up call for DSM to professionalize its approach to M&A. The Corporate Planning and Development (CPL) department was entrusted with this task and became the Corporate Strategy and Acquisitions department (CS&A). A clear process was designed for acquisitions, as well as for divestments, with manuals detailing the various steps. This M&A process would take the approved BSDs and CSD as a starting-point by making 'acquisition shortlists' upon which attention would be focused. Thus, a clear link was made between strategy and M&A. Contacts with investment banks were centralized at CS&A. Whenever a strategically desirable acquisition opportunity was identified, a clear mandate letter had to be agreed upon between CS&A and the business(es) involved, which had to be Board approved. This mandate letter specified the business case (the 'what' for which the business was responsible), as well as the transaction rationale (the 'how,' which was the responsibility of CS&A). It also specified the delineation of tasks to ensure that the assumed business case was fully tested in the due diligence phase. For large transactions, 'challenge teams' were fielded to counter any wishful thinking that might come from within the acquisition teams. Finally, it recommended that the integration manager be part of the acquisition

[16] For 1994–1998 the working group estimated 29 % of the number of acquisitions to be a failure, but 6 % when based on deal value.

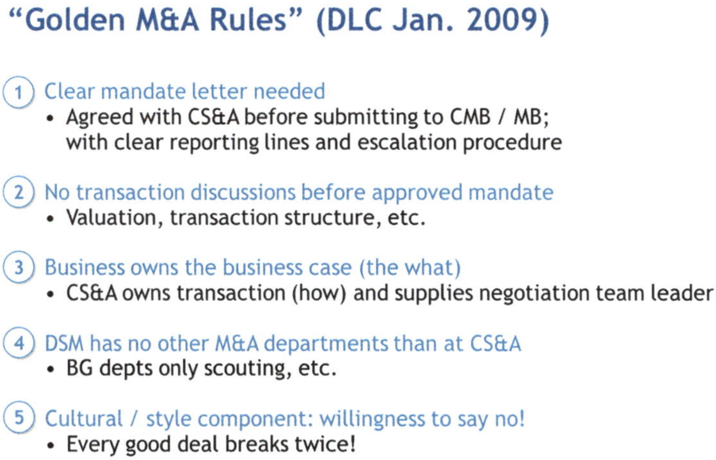

Fig. 11.12 Golden M&A rules. *Source*: Presentation Feike Sijbesma to DSM Leadership Council, January 2009

team and 'signed off' on the transaction before hand-over. Initially, CS&A was staffed with DSM executives with significant M&A experience, like Jos Wassen and Chris Slavenburg. When these retired, investment bankers were recruited from outside, thus further professionalizing the M&A discipline within DSM. The new set-up allowed DSM to build cumulative acquisition (and divestment) experience. Time and again, the 'golden M&A rules' were reinforced by discussion in the DSM Leadership Council (DLC, the former 'ConcernTop'), as Fig. 11.12 illustrates. Arguably, this professionalization of M&A contributed to the relative success of DSM's acquisitions and divestments after 2000.

The M&A example shows how DSM has been willing to examine in-depth the 'existential questions' of its strategy and how it subsequently implemented the lessons learned. This has not been restricted to noting these lessons in a strategic document only. Following a BSD or CSD an implementation program was formulated with clear deliverables, targets and milestones and the CSD implementation program was regularly monitored by the MB; when organizational adaptations were necessary to reach the strategic objectives, they were instituted. This sometimes led to structural changes, while in other cases projects and programs were set up. As a result, the 'managerial systems' (the ways of working) often changed as well, as the M&A approach exemplifies. In this way, DSM was able to work its way through various learning cycles of Strategy > Organization > Systems, as will be further illustrated in Chap. 13. Such learning cycles are the essence of evolutionary change.

Reflection 2: From 'Exploration to Exploitation' and the Path-Dependency of Strategy

The story of how DSM, since 1994, was basically trying to 'find its way' in terms of corporate strategic process, mindset/intent and direction was told in Chap. 9. The CSD of 1994 can be seen in hindsight as an experiment, which allowed DSM to 'learn' whether the new approach could work. When this experiment succeeded, the CSD was repeated in 1997, albeit with a different set-up. The success of this second CSD, with the subsequent acquisition of Gist-Brocades, confirmed the chosen exploratory pathway in several ways:

- In terms of a 'process' for investigating, discussing and formulating corporate strategy, the CSD had established its legitimacy within DSM. People had now come to expect that the main corporate strategic issues would be addressed every few years in the dialogue format. Moreover, they had come to expect that the CSD outcomes would be leading for the further development of the company in the next few years. This gave the CSD process considerable power and momentum (as long as it could live up to these expectations). For instance, in 2000 it was widely known in the company that choices would have to be made regarding the commodity chemicals. When the CSD decision about Petrochemicals was announced, this was accepted as a legitimate outcome and the implementation followed smoothly.
- With regard to 'strategic mindset and intent,' the first two CSDs had established the validity of focusing on the clusters with higher value-added products and lower cyclicality. DSM had maneuvered itself out of the dilemma of the early 1990s when only a swap or a merger were identified as ways out of the predicament as perceived by the 'ConcernTop' (see end of Chap. 1). The fact that a focus on Life Science Products and Performance Materials had proven to be a viable route enabled DSM to switch 'from exploration to exploitation' of this pathway. Thus, it had set the scene for the decisions of the CSD 2000 and 2005 to complete DSM's transformation by completely divesting the commodity chemicals (which still constituted 40 % of the company in 2000 [see Fig. 11.3]).
- While the above points already illustrate that specific next steps in a certain direction can only be taken if previous steps in that 'strategic direction' have been sufficiently successful, the 'path-dependency' of the strategic development of a company can be illustrated further by recounting how DSM became a large player in Nutritional Products. In the CSD of 1997 the business area of Food and Feed had been investigated, since at the time DSM had a few products that it supplied to these industries (like Aspartame and Benzoic acid). The conclusion was that supply positions toward these industries were 'nice to have,' but not essential. At the time, the Pharma industry was the main target market for DSM's fine chemicals. Also in evaluating Gist-Brocades the Pharma-related Antibiotics position was of most interest (and concern), while the Food Specialties division was again seen as 'nice to have' and a potential new growth

area.[17] Only 5 years later, the fact that DSM had become a player in the Food market and that Feike Sijbesma (who was the divisional president of Food Specialties at Gist-Brocades) had joined the DSM Managing Board proved to be very important factors in the acquisition of the Roche Vitamins, Carotenoids and Fine Chemicals (VCFC) business. Since 2003, DSM has further built this platform to a position in 2013, which accounts for almost one-half of the total sales and two-thirds of the EBITDA.[18] In the quote at the start of this chapter, Louk Ligthart correctly observed that the success of the decision to exit Petrochemicals was contingent upon the ability to make further large steps. With hindsight, we can add that the specific further large step taken (Roche VCFC) was contingent upon an earlier step (Gist-Brocades), just as later acquisitions (Martek, etc.) were dependent on the earlier steps of building a nutritional platform.

References

Douma, S. and H. Schreuder, *Economic Approaches to Organizations*, Harlow: Pearson, 5th edition, 2013

Schwartz, P., P. Leyden and J. Hyatt, *The Long Boom: A vision for the coming age of prosperity*, NY: Perseus, 1999

[17] The third division, Bakery Ingredients, was seen as uninteresting and would be 'actively maintained' by DSM. See: Minutes of the extra meeting between the Supervisory Board and the Managing Board DSM NV, held on 7 February 1998, at Rabobank Headquarters (Utrecht).

[18] *Royal DSM Integrated Annual Report 2013*: 5.

Leveraging Faculty Learning Cycles 12

How could several faculty teams maintain effective relationships with DSM when the company was undergoing such major changes through mergers, acquisitions, divestments and reorganizations? The substantial transformation of DSM moving from a largely European-based, regional player into a global player—and in a number of different sectors—surely required different sets of competencies. How then could the faculty rejuvenate its own competencies and remain of value to DSM over all of these years?

Sustaining this 25-year relationship did not stem from the close collaboration with DSM alone. Over this entire period, there had to be enough in it for faculty to remain engaged; financial rewards alone would not suffice. Content and learning was continuously enhanced through other experiences that made the faculty valuable contributors. Some of those internal DSM-based learning cycles were most valuable to the faculty, and the external learning circles very important to DSM. Eventually, both served to enrich participants on the academic side as well as at DSM.

Engagements as Learning Laboratories

Those experiences that occurred outside of DSM became learning laboratories and through faculty engagement with other companies, sources of new insights. Two principle sources arose: First, there were a series of other, similarly structured programs that allowed DSM faculty teams to learn and bring back important improvements to their DSM programs and second, there were certain IMD programs, such as Managing People (MP). Important company programs within this context were delivered for Sulzer, ICI, Serono, Novartis and Medtronic. In some significant ways, these companies became important learning laboratories that provided stimulations to generate insights and create intellectual capital for the benefit of DSM and its own programs. Equally important was the fact that these

J.-P. Jeannet, H. Schreuder, *From Coal to Biotech*,
DOI 10.1007/978-3-662-46299-7_12

other company engagements forced the faculty to become familiar with other industry contexts, often before DSM itself was expanding into those new areas.

Learning from IMEDE/IMD Sulzer Programs

The Sulzer programs were held at IMD from 1985 to 1990 (see Chap. 2). They were the precursor programs that created the basis for the DSM IMPACT programs and the Strategic Management Course (SMC) series for DSM that lasted until 2007. In the 2-week long Sulzer programs, the IMD faculty teams learned to combine strategy and industrial marketing materials into a challenging, homogenous program. It exposed a number of marketing faculty members to the art of industrial analysis as the basis for company strategy. Several members of the Sulzer faculty team became core team members for the DSM IMPACT program at IMD and, from that core team, members for DSM's SMC teams were recruited.[1]

The Sulzer programs, and the subsequent ties to the company produced a number of teaching materials that were later used in other DSM programs as well. The cases on Sulzer Metco, the company's materials coatings business, saw use in several DSM SMC programs, as did the Sulzer Refrigeration case.[2] Those cases, written originally with Sulzer's assistance and cooperation, were intended for free use and were also adopted in the academic MBA programs of other business schools. Both cases were written by Strategic Management Course (SMC) faculty team members and, coming to a strategy program with proprietary materials substantially enhanced credibility and, thus, the learning effectiveness.

The Learning from the ICI Market Focus Initiative

In the Spring 1989, the UK chemical company ICI undertook a major effort to become more market focused.[3] As one part of this initiative, a series of management development seminars were planned and a special organizational unit was established, Market Focus Bureau, reporting to the head of Human Resources. It

[1] Among the faculty, John Murray and Joe D'Cruz mostly taught Marketing sessions at IMD and then made a transition to increasingly teaching Strategy based upon industry analysis. Both of them were major contributors to the SMC programs for many years.

[2] *Sulzer Metco Strategy in Thermal Spray Industry*, case, (IMD 1996); *Sulzer Merger Integration*, case, (IMD 1996), both co-authored by Robert Collins and Jean-Pierre Jeannet; *Sulzer Metco Post-Merger Integration*, case, (2000) and *Sulzer Metco Global Strategy for the 21st Century*, case, (2000), Babson College Glavin Center, Jean-Pierre Jeannet and Martha Lanning; *Sulzer Refrigeration*, case, (1993) IMD, Jean-Pierre Jeannet.

[3] ICI was once a leading UK firm that was subject to strong shareholder pressure when underperforming. Through divestitures, spin-offs and restructuring, the company ended up selling all of its operating businesses over time with the remaining one (ICI Paints) acquired by AkzoNobel in 2008.

was the desire of the Market Focus Bureau and ICI to run these programs in-house in its own Warren House retreat in the Richmond area of London. For the 2-week programs, external faculty from several different business schools was recruited. Faculty and program leadership was entrusted to Professor Joe d'Cruz, a member of the University of Toronto business school and also of the IMEDE/IMD IMPACT program team for DSM when he was on a leave from his home institution. Since it was more difficult for ICI to hire regular full-time faculty from IMD, the company actively pursued past and current visiting faculty with IMD teaching experience. Effectively, several members of the IMPACT team were recruited into the effort, including Jeannet and Murray.

The ICI programs were also a combination of strategy (based on the industry analysis framework) and industrial marketing. Similar to DSM's IMPACT, participants were recruited and mixed from all businesses and functions. The ICI business portfolio was also heavily into basic chemicals but with little overlap to DSM. Paints was a major ICI business unit and, at that time, the global leader in the Paints and Coatings sector. Additionally, ICI also owned important global Agrochemicals and Pharmaceutical businesses. The ICI faculty team delivered a large number of programs, which meant that the faculty team strengthened its ability to collaborate. This is important when faculty have to take turns, so called 'passing the baton,' where it is not always possible for the entire team to be on site at the same time, and where faculty need to pick up from colleagues with the knowledge 'where they were and what they said before.'

The ICI connection led to some important pieces regarding teaching materials that have been used to the present time in DSM programs. Early on, cases were written on ICI Paints and its globalization challenges.[4] As a result of these contacts, the 'World Paints Industry Note' was created with intent to use in strategy programs.[5] In the early 2000, a newer version of this note was written and used mainly in DSM's SMC and later the Management Leadership Programs (in the MLP-3 version). Countless DSM participants learned from, and were trained, using the ICI materials. These materials saw extended use because they were specifically designed for the kind of teaching roles envisioned at DSM. The ability to bring teaching materials from the same industry into DSM programs was a great asset to maintain relevance and credibility.

A further learning opportunity was offered for the faculty team by the ICI connection because it required connecting to the life sciences—Agrochemicals and Pharmaceuticals were different industries than traditional Petrochemicals and posed different strategic challenges. Although ICI Pharmaceuticals, eventually to merge into Zeneca, did not participate extensively in the ICI Market Focus

[4] *ICI Paints (A), (B)*, cases, (IMD 1990, 1992, 1995), by Jean-Pierre Jeannet.

[5] *World Paint Industry Note*, case, (1990 GM 451) and *World Paint Industry Note 1992*, case, (IMD GM556, 1993), by Robert Howard and Jean-Pierre Jeannet. *Global Paints and Coatings Industry Overview*, case, by Caleb McCann and Jean-Pierre Jeannet, Babson College Glavin Center, (2003); *Global Paints and Coatings Industry Competitors*, case, (2003), by Caleb McCann and Jean-Pierre Jeannet, Babson College Glavin Center.

initiative, the Agrochemicals business was a frequent user of the processes. This created learning opportunities later on and some ICI business executives requested business-specific initiatives, of which the ICI Agrochemicals division was a major user. For the purpose of those programs, internal company materials were created, eventually leading to an interesting use of industry analysis and value chain models in combination with Marketing. The result was a concept later termed 'Value Chain Marketing' that originated in the ICI Agrochemical business request (which by that time had merged into Zeneca Agrochemicals and was later to be combined into Syngenta).[6] ICI's Market Focus Bureau was spun off into an independent consultancy and remains active to this day.

Serono Experience as Introduction to Biotechnology

Initially, when the faculty team engaged with DSM, the company had only a minor foothold in Biotechnology processes or businesses. It could not be foreseen that a company based in traditional Petrochemicals would become a major player in Life Sciences and rely, to an increasing extent, on Biotechnology for its production. An early opportunity for some faculty team members to experience this very different production model came through a Babson Executive Education contract with Ares-Serono, a Geneva-based Biotech company active in the field of healthcare. Serono, whose management had been assumed by a Babson alum, turned to the school for what they called a mini-MBA course geared to its upper-middle management.[7] The programs, taught over several years, in length of initially 3- and later 2-week intervals, covered a full range of management topics. What made them valuable learning experiences was the requirement to run the sessions, as much as possible, in the Serono industry context—niche Pharmaceuticals and Biotechnology.

The Serono faculty team was initially to include Jeannet and Hennessey, and later also Henderson, all faculty members who were to play major roles in the SMC (Strategy) and AIM (Marketing) programs for DSM.[8] To bring the Babson faculty team into the world of Biotechnology, Serono organized, among other events, plant tours of Biotech facilities, providing the first contact for the faculty with these types of processes. Serono was also very interested in creating program-specific materials with Pharmaceutical and Biotech industry content. Several cases were written on

[6] ICI demerged its Agrochemicals and Pharmaceuticals businesses into Zeneca in 1993. In 1999, Zeneca merged with Astra to form AstraZeneca. In 2000, the Agrochemicals business was spun off and combined with the Novartis Agrochemicals business into Syngenta.

[7] Ernesto Bertarelli, Babson BSBA and Harvard MBA, took over the role of COO in 1992 and became CEO upon the death of his father Fabio Bertarelli soon after.

[8] H. David Hennessey from Babson College first connected with DSM through the AIM Marketing programs in 1994. James Henderson, at that time also on the Babson faculty, taught in SMC-11–19, from 2000 to 2007, until he joined IMD on a full-time basis.

the company itself and its strategy.[9] Cases were later developed for Serono seminars that dealt with the Biotech industry and major industry competitors.[10] Later on, the same faculty team led several workshops for franchise strategies at Serono, further intensifying their exposure to this industry sector.[11]

Developing Healthcare Industry Expertise

Several companies also served as learning laboratories for the faculty teams in the broader healthcare industry. Although Serono could be added to that group, the healthcare learning was broader when dealing with firms that were less defined by technology and whose management had more exposure to healthcare policies and strategies, which were central to their businesses. Most of this learning came through educational programs or case research but sometimes it included project consulting provided by members of the faculty team.

Through working with Johnson & Johnson (J&J) in Europe, Jeannet made initial contact with medical equipment and supplies, experiencing the role material science played in the strategy of those segments. A next major learning opportunity occurred when Nestlé contacted IMD for a possible interest in writing a case about its Alcon Laboratories subsidiary and focused on the ophthalmic industry. The business' future strategy was the cornerstone of the case and course materials were divided into an industry note and a separate company case about Alcon placing students, or executive participants, into the role of Alcon management plotting a global strategy for the coming 10 years.[12] In the research for this case study, long-time Alcon CEO, Ed Schollmaier, was a collaborator and an outstanding model as a general manager.[13] The Alcon case series and industry note became a teaching material widely utilized in other programs and continued to be used in the later

[9] *Ares-Serono*, case, by Michael Yoshino (HBS), Jean-Pierre Jeannet and Carin Knoop, Harvard Business School Publishing, 1995; *Ares-Serono: Creating the World Leading Biotech Company*, case, by Jean-Pierre Jeannet and Sam Perkins, Babson College, 1999; and *Serono: Global Strategy for Reproductive Health*, case, by Jean-Pierre Jeannet and Sam Perkins, 2001, Babson College. Some cases are unpublished.

[10] *Note on the Biotech and Pharmaceuticals Industry*, case, (2000), *Note on the Worldwide Pharmaceuticals Industry*, case, (2000) and a case series on *Global Biotechnology Winners* (Amgen, Biogen, Chiron, Genentech, Glaxo Wellcome, Novartis, Upjohn and Schering), 2002, Babson College Glavin Center, Jean-Pierre Jeannet and Glavin Center research staff and associates.

[11] John Murray, Professor at Trinity Dublin and a frequent Visiting Professor at IMD, was a longstanding colleague of Jeannet's and played major roles in Sulzer, DSM IMPACT and SMC seminars.

[12] *The Ophthalmology Industry Note*, case, (1988) and *Alcon Laboratories (A)*, case, (1988), IMD Institute, Jean-Pierre Jeannet and Sam Perkins (Babson College).

[13] Ed Schollmaier joined Alcon in 1962 and took over as CEO in 1972, developing Alcon from USD 36 million to USD 2 billion in global sales until his retirement in 1998.

SMC and MLP-3 strategy sessions. Sam Perkins, who was to write many cases as a Babson College case writer, also worked on this case.

A different experience was provided by an assignment carried out for IMD creating a special program for Medtronic. The medical equipment company in the field of cardiac care and heart pacemakers, requested a program with global Marketing content for its European managers. The program was delivered in 1999 by two IMD faculty members (Jeannet and Turpin) and generated an opportunity to write company-specific cases (unpublished), intensifying the clinical understanding of the medical equipment business.[14] A further healthcare engagement occurred when Roche Diagnostics commissioned a marketing program for some of its European managers. Similar to earlier programs in the same industry, the company wanted key marketing materials connected to its industry environment. To learn the industry, the faculty began visiting hospital-based diagnostics laboratories.

Finally, Novartis also provided an important experience for faculty to explore the healthcare industry on an even broader scale. Prior to the creation of Novartis in 1996, the Babson Marketing faculty had exposure to Ciba-Geigy's over-the-counter (OTC) business through a series of seminars and the creation of related learning materials.[15] Cases written about the OTC business were widely used in Babson's global Marketing courses and the Babson Marketing faculty had taught several programs for Ciba-Geigy OTC.[16] In around 2004, Novartis contacted Babson Executive Education to launch what turned out to be a long series of programs intensifying the faculty understanding of healthcare. The exposure to veterinary medicine through Novartis was a contributor to understanding animal health more broadly, and connected directly to DSM's major business in animal feed.[17] When DSM began to expand into the Pharmaceuticals Intermediates sector, and into materials for use through other healthcare equipment companies, the faculty had already been exposed to the realities of those sectors.

Many of the executive development programs delivered for DSM included important project work. Participants brought their own strategic or marketing issues to the seminars and the faculty was constantly challenged to guide participants into industries that were forever changing. Without the constant renewal process, being engaged in different industry contexts, the faculty guidance would not have been as effective and the relevance of the programs would have invariably suffered.

[14] *Medtronic: Conducting Global Marketing*, case, IMD, by Jean-Pierre Jeannet, 1999 (unpublished).

[15] Novartis was created in 1996 through a merger of Ciba-Geigy and Sandoz, two Swiss-based Pharmaceuticals and chemicals companies.

[16] With a Babson MBA-team and under the supervision of Jean-Pierre Jeannet, four cases were written: *The World OTC Industry Note*, case, (1996), *Note on the Competitors in the OTC Industry*, case, (1996), *Note on OTC Brands*, case, (1996), and *Ciba Selfmedication*, case, (1996), published through ECCH/Case Center UK.

[17] *Novartis Animal Health*, case, by Jean-Pierre Jeannet and Martha Lanning, Babson College Glavin Center, 2010 (unpublished).

Conceptual Learning Brought to DSM

No company can sustain its success without continuously absorbing new ideas. This is not a matter of industrial technology but an issue of management understanding. For continual renewal, a company needs to have processes that allow for open exchanges, active scanning of the world for new insights and deliberately searching out knowledge holders. DSM's case was no different. This deliberate exposure to new ideas and, in particular, the channels, which existed through executive development and business school contacts, were all important in the evolution of DSM's engagement with many different academic institutions, on several fronts. Here, the recounted incidents reflect only the authors' limited knowledge and exposure and do not represent the entire activity across all engagements and institutions of higher learning. The stories behind the concepts cited are of interest because they are not part of any initial program content. Instead, these ideas were added later to programs, eventually finding their way into the company's basic behavior.

Invariably, as part of the faculty exposure to the business realities, there are opportunities to bring ideas, or new concepts, to the client's attention. In this case, it is the faculty who will take the initiative. A number of such situations arose in DSM programs. The idea of global business strategies and the requirements of global mindsets, as part of the research, were often introduced into DSM programs. When commencing the relationship, there was little interest at DSM because executives did not see themselves as dealing with deliberate global strategies. Not until the company management made it explicit that it wanted to pursue global leadership positions in its business lines did the interest for these strategic ideas really take off. Like anything else, the timing had to be right—an idea that comes too early often finds a great deal of resistance.

As the Babson and IMD faculty teams dealt with a number of Marketing programs, the concept of a market orientation and the notion of franchise building were introduced during different programs. Once the programs moved from 2 weeks to 1 week in length, and participants were increasingly recruited from junior positions, more advanced topics became much harder to insert. Market orientation as an overall philosophy was eventually absorbed by DSM's change agenda as the company's external orientation. But, this did not occur until after some 10 or more years of exposure. The topic of customer franchise building as the central concern of a Marketing effort was even more difficult to establish, due, primarily, to the lack of support by Marketing leadership. This clearly showed the limits of the role of unsolicited outside influence when directed at lower levels of the organization. In contrast, as many of DSM's businesses were moving in the direction of branding materials, or products being absorbed by downstream customers, the idea of engaging in ingredient branding became attractive and receptivity to the idea increased.

With more interest in real projects and action learning as part of the regular DSM programs, the business school ideas regarding entrepreneurship or business development were easier to place. The fact that projects needed to be presented, and that many of these projects evolved around new technologies, new products, or new

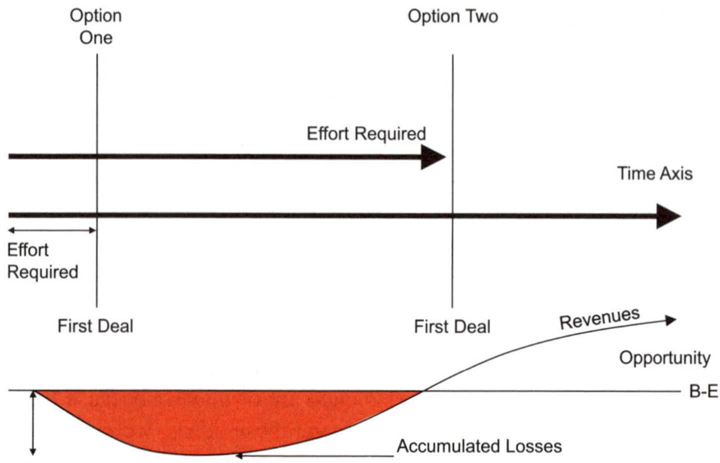

Fig. 12.1 Business development chart. *Source*: J.-P. Jeannet

business lines, made it a natural to bring tested ideas and concepts from Babson's long-established entrepreneurship teaching practice into the DSM class rooms. Most recently, the MLP-3 provided room for delineating managerial versus entrepreneurial thinking. Along those lines were concepts on business developments that centered on a chart showing the cumulative use of funds over a project's lifetime.[18] This chart was used a number of times in several DSM programs and the faculty knew instinctively that it was a big success. See Fig. 12.1 for a sample of this chart.

There was a real need to differentiate for DSM participants that the concept of a business case is quite distinct from a more detailed business plan or an intensive financial evaluation of investments. It was always a struggle to work with technically- or scientifically-oriented managers on a business case based on the question of 'is this worth pursuing;' that it could be staged with limited resources and prior to a full-scale technical development. The evolution of DSM's MLP-3 seminars containing the presentation of a business case as the final presentation delivery made the introduction of the business case concept possible.

A second opportunity to bring a new idea to the attention to DSM managers arose when the discussion around business models and innovation came up internally. There were different school of thoughts about how to conceptualize business modeling and how to make it relate to the DSM Business Strategy Dialogues (BSD) strategy process. Earlier, at IMD, faculty created, several cases about European football clubs with the intent of teasing out the business model idea and how to link it to strategy discussions by defining the business model as a sub-issue of, but not a

[18] The ideas behind this chart are owed to Professor Les Charm from the Entrepreneurship Division of Babson College.

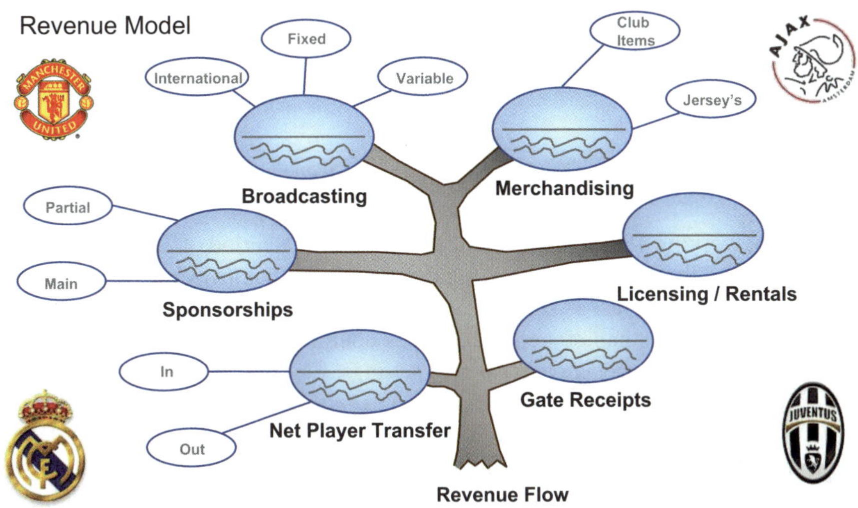

Fig. 12.2 Charting business models based upon professional football clubs. *Source*: J.-P. Jeannet

replacement for, strategy. Again, having visuals that captured the idea was helpful and the input could be made to the bi-annual facilitators workshops organized by DSM's Corporate Strategy and Acquisitions office.[19] See Fig. 12.2.

When DSM commenced its internal innovation drive with the creation of the DSM Innovation Center, there was a desire to incorporate the innovation issues into the BSDs. Again, as part of the regular facilitators workshops, Schreuder and his corporate strategy team asked Jeannet to bring a conceptual overview of innovation to the meeting—innovation as it was viewed by other businesses at the time. It was not possible for a single faculty member to be completely knowledgeable about all of these new domains, including innovation. The excellent internal faculty contacts at Babson or IMD allowed immediate access to the relevant expertise; the information had to be summarized succinctly and could then be brought to the workshops as state-of-the-art. It was then up to the DSM's facilitators to decide how and when to bring this up in the strategy sessions in order to serve DSM's interest in reaching higher levels of innovation.

Part of these facilitator workshops organized by DSM Corporate Strategy and Acquisitions included an intensive exchange of best practice and sample outputs from past BSDs. It was during these sessions that Jeannet, representing the faculty, was provided with a close look of the current status of strategic planning and BSD practice. In turn, this experience was included in the teaching and commentary provided in the strategy workshops, be it for SMC or MLP-3 programs.

[19] The four cases developed were *Football Club Ajax*, *Juventus Football Club*, *Manchester United PLC* and *Real Madrid Club de Footbol*, IMD, 2003, written by Robert Collins, Jean-Pierre Jeannet and Lisa Schuepbach, ECCH/Case Clearing House.

Conceptually, this learning was not only restricted to DSM engagements; the issues discussed had relevance for other teaching engagements by the faculty.

DSM as a Learning Laboratory for Faculty

Invariably, working with a single client company over a period of 25 years leaves a big imprint on the faculty working regularly with the company's executives and program participants. Just as DSM underwent an enormous change and transformation in its businesses and strategy, there was continual learning by the faculty in terms of being constantly engaged in new settings. Certainly, a complete rendering would be impossible but by mentioning a few areas where the learning was particularly lasting, and led to the accumulation of new intellectual capital, the hope is to provide insight into a highly valuable collaboration. Two bundles of topics stand out. The first bundle includes a number of experiences resulting in highly relevant learning for the teaching practice at business schools and other executive programs. The second is comprised of some specific topics, encountered through these experiences, which led to new conceptual knowledge for the faculty and, in many situations, led to publications.

Teaching in the field of strategy, or about business unit strategy in particular, stands out as the first topic where constant engagement with DSM offered a number of new faculty insights. When the first contact with DSM was made at IMEDE in 1988, it was standard practice to teach a single session on industry analysis in executive programs, as well as some company level business strategy. With the DSM engagement, the faculty had to learn to use multiple steps (in various sessions, for example) through industry analysis; in the process, they became much more skilled at dividing the entire body of knowledge into a number of elements covering business value chains, key success factors and competitive analysis. The requirement to do all of this in the context of the Chemicals or Process industry created a body of expertise that was easily transferable to other, similar industry settings. To make the teaching material relevant to participants, a number of cases had to be developed; there were also some new ones inspired by the DSM teaching experience. All of this experience could be used when members of the faculty team engaged other client companies for their home institutions, or could use it in their business school degree programs. At Babson, the materials were continuously used in the Global Strategy and Global Marketing courses by a number of the faculty and some of the case material was also published in textbooks.[20] To the extent to which the cases were released for listing through the

[20] *Global Marketing Strategies*, Jean-Pierre Jeannet and H. David Hennessey, Babson College, Houghton Mifflin, Boston (6th ed. 2004: 613); from the 2nd edition of this text (1st ed. published in 1988), cases have been used that were related to DSM programs.

European Case Clearing House (ECCH), the material could be accessed for teaching by any academic institution.[21]

Different from the classroom teaching experience was the contact with the BSD process. Initially brought to the attention of DSM by the IMPACT faculty, albeit at the request of DSM, the value of defining the strategy finding process as a dialogue on the basis of deep industry understanding left a lasting impression on the members of the faculty. This process could be applied in many other settings and the faculty was often invited to render this as a consulting service. Despite the fact that DSM preferred to run its own BSDs with internal moderators, thus excluding external consultants such as faculty, the contact with the process as embedded in the SMC programs was sufficient to allow faculty to become familiar with the process.[22]

The engagements with DSM senior staff from the Corporate Strategy and M&A office also led to many conceptual discussions. For the strategy concepts, the discussions around key success factors (KSFs) and their relevance, as well as on the strategic groups were most enlightening. Initially, faculty generally treated KSFs across an entire industry sector. After frequent exchanges about this, and on DSM's own views of KSFs, the faculty adopted the DSM practice of treating KSFs as specific to a given strategic group in an industry. Later, the faculty also taught KSFs as relevant to different levels—industry, strategic group and segment level KSFs were discussed. Closely connected were the exchanges about strategic groups. Again, the initial faculty teaching was approaching this more from a generic strategy perspective, whereas DSM, under Schreuder's leadership, brought the faculty around to help participants see the value of strategic groups and that companies had the opportunity to select membership in their preferred strategic group. These exchanges were valuable to faculty and were also debated within the team; some of the teaching materials were later created to allow for the teaching of these subjects and specific in-class exercises treating these issues of importance to DSM were eventually created.

An important aspect in both strategy and marketing programs (SMC, MLP and AIM) was the element of projects being used as ending presentations. Each program saw the use of four to six such project presentations, demanding of the faculty increasing skills of guiding, moderating and debriefing the presentations. For the SMC, where an internal company case was used, the program, over time, developed different presentation and de-brief formats, veering from the standard up-front group presentations by the distribution of some of the slides to all the other groups and going straight into discussions. In the end, the understanding of how to select the presentation sequence to achieve better learning in the plenary room, and how to use both participants or faculty to bring out deeper learning, could be refined

[21] The European Case Clearing House based at Cranfield (UK) changed its name in 2013 to Case Center. Many of the cases mentioned in this chapter and referenced in the footnotes can be accessed and ordered from there.

[22] Among the IMPACT and SMC faculty team members most often engaged in this form were Professors Murray and Jeannet.

because the faculty had to do this several times each year. Moderating presenting teams and debriefing through questioning are essential faculty skills that come to bear in almost any teaching environment. DSM offered an excellent stage on which to learn this well.

With the steady globalization of DSM over the period under review, the company accumulated an increasing number of staff in North America and Asia, particularly in China, as well as in Switzerland. The relative importance of the main locations in South Limburg declined resulting in increased calls for programs delivered overseas and away from its traditional base in The Netherlands.[23] As had been mentioned already in Chap. 10, the Strategy program (SMC) was the first management development program to go 'on tour' with deliveries in Shanghai (2005), Boston (2006) and Basel (2007). The Marketing programs went 'international,' for example in Switzerland in 2009 and global in 2011 with deliveries in North America, Europe and Asia. To run programs on a consistent basis in different locations and geographies is quite different from running them on the home campus of a business school. DSM, when expanding its global footprint, was very early in the trend towards global delivery and was helpful in letting business schools and faculty gain experience with this. From today's perspective this is, of course, commonplace.

The encouragement that came from the DSM audience for visualizing classroom discussions was a critical learning experience for the faculty—it was the first signal from DSM participants during the IMPACT seminar held at IMEDE/IMD regarding the interest in the visualization of discussions. Jeannet had gotten a call from Menno de Vries informing him that he wished to send a photographer to IMEDE to take pictures for use in DSM's internal company magazine. When the photographer arrived, he spent quite some time taking pictures of the black board notes as depicted in Fig. 12.3. The Bignami Wing had just been inaugurated and had those wide blackboards, three per room, that were a faculty member's dream. When those pictures showed up in the DSM magazine, the faculty realized that there was much more value in this presentation than previously realized—that was just the beginning in terms of illustrating, visualizing and graphing discussions to great effect.[24]

When teaching at DSM sites, particularly the venerable Kasteel Vaalsbroek with its lack of business school-type blackboards, finding ways to condense discussions on the much smaller, mobile whiteboards developed into something like a passion for charting. The skills to chart and visualize became central for keeping tabs on BSD discussions. As an extension, this skill was applied to many other programs and became a central feature to most of the faculty's classes.[25]

---

[23] Employee geographic distribution, 1990–2013.

[24] "IMPACT: To the Top," DSM Magazine, internal publication, 1991.

[25] The author remembers one instance when he was traveling on the way from the US to the SMC seminar site. He was able to visit a special Mondrian exhibition in Rotterdam on the way and arrived just in time to teach the Sulzer Refrigeration case. When charting the discussion, using geometric squares and lines, it suddenly occurred to him that this was very similar to Mondrian and his various styles, moving from no delineation in earlier works to stark, black, even double black lines later on, just to have them disappear in his last paintings. Since this was a largely Dutch

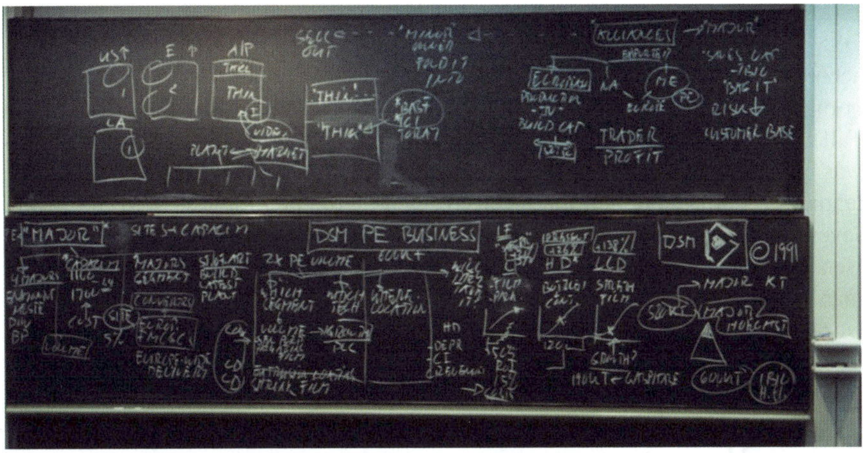

Fig. 12.3 IMD board plan IMPACT program. *Source*: DSM (1991)

Conceptual Learning from DSM

While the previous section dealt with learning about the teaching processes, it is also necessary to point out the faculty teams engaged with DSM also learned more about content matter. This list is extensive and cannot be fully addressed here, a sample of what was learned from engaging with DSM can be discussed. Such learning usually came from DSM initiatives and required responses from the academic teams. When building programs in order to respond, the learning could be applied later on to other companies or academic programs. The conceptual learning around strategy has been covered in the earlier sections of this chapter. Now, the learning that went beyond the original course program mandates and led to new fields will be expanded upon.

In Spring 1998, Frans van Helmond, one of the original BOM members and IMPACT initiators, had a dinner meeting with Jeannet and talked about a recent issue confronting him: "We have a large French client in the Engineering Plastics business who is moving aggressively into global markets. We are serving this client in the regions through our local organizations. Suddenly they request from us a global deal and we are not prepared to handle this."[26]

group, to make the connection between classroom charts and an artist like Mondrian intensified the learning experience. Later on in his teaching career, he has often used artists as inspiration for charting. Without DSM and the need to do this on small surfaces, he might never have reached this level in visualization.

[26] Dinner conversation between Frans van Helmond (DSM) and Jean-Pierre Jeannet, 26 March 1998.

In a subsequent meeting, the two sketched out a program that would help local DSM sales managers with key account responsibility to turn them into global key account managers. Thus, the Global Account Management (GAM) program was born and the first version of this program was delivered on the Babson campus in Fall 1998 (See Chap. 10). Initially, delivering GAM into several DSM businesses was undertaken using readily available teaching materials and cases. As the learning accumulated, and the faculty became more comfortable with the issues, several cases[27] were written and, eventually, a book was authored under Hennessey's leadership.[28] The faculty practice gained regarding global account management issues was later leveraged into a program for WWL, a Swedish-Norwegian car shipping company dealing with many of the largest automotive firms. Both Jeannet and Hennessey teamed up on delivering these programs for IMD in Europe and the US. Some of the exercise assignments for the WWL program had originally been developed for DSM programs.

The GAM programs were, to a large extent, built on leveraging the understanding of industry requirements for the benefit of the global account. Thus, conceptually it was closely related to DSM's SMC industry analysis teaching and offered a way to enhance customer understanding based upon the customer's industry. The learning not only originated from the company who had initiated the idea for the program, it also came from leveraging earlier concepts developed for a different purpose, such as strategy finding, or for a new purpose, such as account strategies.

On a recurring basis, the faculty was exposed to different industries through working with DSM businesses. DSM itself was active in many different sectors of the Chemicals and Materials Science industries and later in the Biotechnology sector as well. What became of great value was the learning about industries that DSM was selling into. The concept of 'customer's customer' was widely used and exposed faculty to the many user industries. Of particular interest were a number of materials processing industries—the food and animal feed processing industries, as well as the automotive sectors. In all three of these cases, it was possible for participating faculty to obtain an in-depth learning about how these industries worked, the value chain and their KSFs. What was acquired in the 'DSM Learning Laboratory' could be put to good use for other companies without running afoul of insider or confidential knowledge. As happened on a number of occasions, familiarity gained with various industry sectors through working with DSM could be turned into credibility elsewhere, leading to many other programs and engagements. The fact that DSM was undergoing transformation, and changing its own business portfolio as described earlier, meant that the learning opportunities

[27] *Groupe Schneider (DSM)*, case, Jean-Pierre Jeannet, Babson College Glavin Center, 1996 and DSM Groupe Schneider (1997), and *DSM EPDM Purchasing*, case, Jean-Pierre Jeannet, 1997; *DSM Catalytic Materials Purchasing*, case, Jean-Pierre Jeannet, 2001.

[28] H. David Hennessey and Jean-Pierre Jeannet. *Global Account Management: Creating Value* . London: Wiley, 2003: 260.

were ever-changing and new sectors had to be explored. It was not a one-time learning but instead a continuous flow of the exploration of new and different sectors.

DSM also served as a great learning platform to the exposure of current business issues and learning how these issues were, or might be, tackled. Because DSM was very advanced in sustainability issues, how to deal with the '3 Ps' (people, planet, profit) became a constant concern, which participants brought to programs. With the many programs featuring current and real business projects, more and more of these projects began to include sustainability. Although one could of course read about sustainability in the business press and other related media, that coverage went only so far. When dealing with real business projects, balancing the '3 Ps', not only one or two of them, could be experienced. With sustainability as one of the company's core values, it became a constant request to include this in programs. This also enhanced the learning, as it was now not just a matter of 'what is it?' but became a matter of 'how do we deal with it?' That DSM held sustainability up as a top concern was illustrated by the recognition the company received from many international agencies, including the United Nations.[29]

Faculty Take-Away from DSM Involvement

Reflecting on DSM as a learning laboratory for faculty invariably raises the question, 'What did faculty learn from this engagement?' As was pointed out, learning differed for the two main course streams described. What can be said is that the three groups of faculty—Strategy, Marketing and Leadership—were able to experience new elements in their fields, could bring some of that back to their other programs and class rooms and had an opportunity to create new intellectual capital for teaching and for publications. The longer the engagement with DSM continued the longer lasting the impact was for faculty.

Because the same faculty teams were also part of other long-lasting initiatives, comparisons were invariably made. The initial IMPACT team from IMD was part of the Sulzer programs at IMD, was heavily engaged with ICI on a consulting basis and, to some extent, also participated in several Serono programs. From a faculty perspective, the question is why a company such as ICI disappeared from the scene entirely, Serono was acquired and Sulzer continued to exist on a much smaller scale. And there alone is DSM still standing, growing and prospering! What would account for the difference in these outcomes?

Most closely involved with the company over the past 20 years or more, Parker and Jeannet both believe that DSM was most effective in combining a well thought-

[29] As per DSM Royal N.V. website information, accessed 5 February 2014. DSM has been listed in the Dow Jones Sustainability Index since 2004, four times ranked among the very top leaders, and six times held the worldwide sustainability leader position in the materials industry group (previously named Chemicals sector). Equally, DSM has been a signatory to the United Nations Global Compact since 2007.

out strategic agenda with a carefully developed change agenda. DSM did not just engage in a conceptual development of the minds but also invested in the behaviors of its managers. This behavior agenda was closely tied to the required strategic moves. Both agendas, strategic and behavioral, were anchored in long-lasting development programs.

Looking at this from an internal point of view, Schreuder observed that over these 25 years top management succession always came from within, thus avoiding the 'sudden breaks' typical of other companies. The '3 P' philosophy adopted by DSM led to a tempering of other companies' dominant maximizing shareholder value approach. An inherently conservative approach to business and finance avoided undue risk-taking. And finally, as Schreuder believes, the evolutionary mindset of DSM and its top management leads to an attitude of 'transformation is in our genes' (See Chap. 15).

This demonstrated diligence, persistence and steadfastness as applied to strategy is truly rare in today's quick-moving corporate world. This sustained effort was never derailed by outside events, such as business cycles, energy or financial crises, changes in top leadership, or even going public—all events that in many companies often lead to a complete abandoning of well-meaning initiatives.

As this chapter demonstrates, both business school faculty and DSM profited enormously from the mutual enrichment that resulted from the intensive and long-term collaboration. From DSM's perspective it was important that the business school faculty engaged had contacts and experience from other engagement with companies in related industries. If the faculty engaged with DSM had not had this opportunity to learn about industries that became future areas of activities for DSM, their value at the moment of changes in DSM's business portfolio might have been reduced. If no other exposure to such industries had taken place, the faculty would have to learn about the new industries along the way at considerable investment in time. Through this close collaboration, DSM turned into a huge "learning laboratory" for business school faculty engaged over the years. At the same time, faculty could tap into the experiences gained from other companies to turn them into "learning laboratories" for the benefit of DSM.

Completing the Transformation of DSM 13

By the mid-2000s, Mr. Sijbesma was chief executive and the company had divested itself of all its petrochemical plants. It was no coincidence that Mr. Sijbesma, a trained biologist, drove the company's shift towards nutrition. Coming from its biotechnology side, he was 'seen as one of the new boys,' he says. And he credits his biology training with not only helping to form his views on how DSM should evolve but also his determination to force it to happen. 'I always found it astonishing how cells adapt to changed environments, and DSM is obviously an example of a company that has adapted quite a bit,' he says.

—Feike Sijbesma, interview ("Feike Sijbesma, Chief of DSM," interview in the *Financial Times* on 18 August 2013.)

Introduction

In 2005, DSM was clearly in a 'winning' mood. The transformative but risky steps of divesting Petrochemicals and acquiring the Roche Vitamins business (now renamed DSM Nutritional Products) had been executed well. Additionally, it had sold off the low-performing Bakery Ingredients business and had acquired Avecia NeoResins to strengthen its Performance Materials (PM) cluster. Despite adverse economic conditions in 2001–2003, operating profits had held up well and were now approaching a historic high of EUR 808 million. The new businesses were contributing to this achievement, as well as a very successful Operational Excellence program across all of DSM. Moreover, the external world started to recognize the company's accomplishments and significantly changed profile. For 2 years in a row, DSM was the global number one in the Chemical sector of the Dow Jones Sustainability Index. Even the financial markets started to value its performance—the share price had indeed more than doubled in the period of 'Vision 2005.' A shareholder who had invested in DSM in September 2000, and had reinvested dividends, had enjoyed a Total Shareholder Return (TSR) of 217 % in September

J.-P. Jeannet, H. Schreuder, *From Coal to Biotech*,
DOI 10.1007/978-3-662-46299-7_13

2005, compared with a decrease of the Amsterdam Stock Exchange (AEX) with about 40 % and a decrease of about 2 % for similar European chemical companies.

The Corporate Strategy Dialogue 2005: 'Vision 2010'

In such circumstances, it is often difficult to conduct a critical analysis of the company's strategic situation. Yet, this is what DSM set out to do in 2005 in a Corporate Strategy Dialogue (CSD) that was to be named 'Vision 2010: Building on Strengths.' The groundwork for this CSD had already begun in 2004 (see Fig. 13.1). A number of pre-studies were conducted by Corporate Strategy & Acquisitions (CS&A) and were discussed by the Managing Board (MB) and the Supervisory Board to determine the CSD themes. These themes and the pre-study results were subsequently handed over to the working groups in the four focus areas of Nutrition, Health, Performance Materials and Industrial Chemicals. For instance, the external world and competitive environment were scrutinized. The rise of the 'emerging economies' was thought through thoroughly and the consequences for DSM's products were charted. On the one hand, the economic growth of countries like China, India and Brazil offered opportunities for geographic growth and expansion. On the other hand, there would be increasing competitive pressure on a number of DSM's products by exports from these 'low cost' countries. All in all, the estimate was that for 35 % of DSM's portfolio the opportunities prevailed, while for 25 % the threats were predominant. Included in the latter category were products like antibiotics and some vitamins. It became clear from such analyses that DSM had to accelerate its adjustment to these geographical shifts. For some products the main challenge would be to capture a larger share of the growth in these rapidly developing markets. For some other products it became obvious that increased sourcing from, and production in, these low cost environments was essential. While DSM wanted to generally improve its geographical spread, a very specific target was eventually set for China: the company aimed to double its sales in China to a level of USD 1 billion between 2005 and 2010.

Another critical analysis was conducted on the 'specialty' nature of DSM's portfolio. In 'Vision 2005' a generic definition had been used, classifying Petrochemicals and Industrial Chemicals as 'commodities' and, by contrast, Life Science Products (LSP) and Performance Materials (PM) as 'specialties.' At the time, this was an expedient approach but after the portfolio shift the question arose, 'How special are our specialties?' To answer that question, sharper criteria were needed. Moreover, it had always been DSM's ambition to achieve leadership positions with its products. For how many products had such 'specialty leadership positions' been achieved? The answer was sobering. While the share of 'specialty leadership positions' had increased from 21 to 40 % in 2000–2005, a full 60 % of DSM's sales still depended on cost leadership. However, in terms of profit contribution, specialties (40 % of the company) generated 70 % of DSM's profits. This strongly supported DSM's drive for a larger share of high value-added products, a drive that would also have to be accelerated in forthcoming years. An ambition to

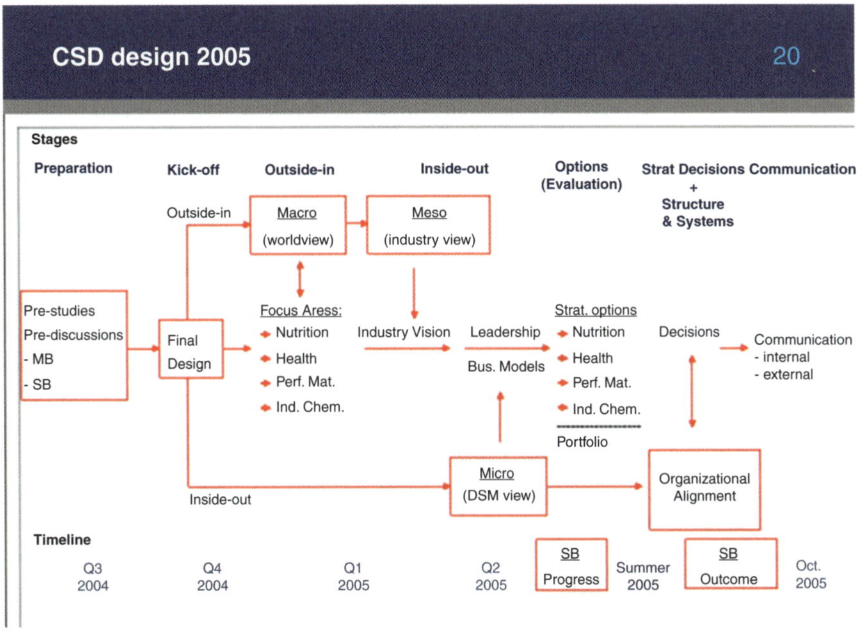

Fig. 13.1 The design of the corporate strategy dialogue 2005 ('Vision 2010'). *Source*: Internal company presentation, 'Corporate Strategy and Acquisitions'

grow and strengthen the 'specialty leadership businesses' from 40 % to the range of 50–60 % of sales was formulated. At the same time, the competitiveness of DSM's cost leadership positions would have to be safeguarded by the continuation of its Operational Excellence programs.

A very prominent topic in the CSD 'Vision 2010' was Innovation. While the 'old DSM' had always boasted strong Research and Development (R&D) and had produced a number of exciting process- and product innovations, the 'new DSM' would need many more of these and at a higher speed of market introduction and success. The company had shifted from relatively mature 'commodity-type' activities to products with shorter life cycles, higher rates of technological progress, more complicated 'customer value propositions' and much higher market dynamics. Moreover, it wanted to further accelerate this shift. This was recognized as a major challenge. It required, first of all, a clear view where the company should place its 'innovation bets'—where to play? But even more important were changes in mindset, organization and people that would determine whether DSM could become a truly innovative company. To illustrate the required change of mindset the company adopted a working definition of 'innovation' in the CSD being: the commercial and financial success of something new. This definition highlighted that innovation was not always dependent on R&D; a change of business model could, for instance, lead to very successful innovation. Furthermore, the ultimate success of innovation needed to be established on the market; technological 'inventions,' as such, were not (yet) innovations. With this approach, the company attempted to counterbalance the strong historical 'technology push' R&D culture within DSM with a stronger 'market pull' innovation orientation. A second change of mindset pertained to the adoption of an 'open innovation' approach seeking collaborations and partnerships with others.[1] The required change of perspective was characterized by the motto: "We have to change from 'the lab is our world' to 'the world is our lab'."

But where should DSM place its innovation bets, in both the shorter- and longer-term? Various approaches were employed to answer this question. First, all of the innovation programs that were running at the time were scrutinized regarding their potential to contribute to growth and profitability. The first conclusion was that more focus and dedication were necessary; DSM's innovation pipeline had been scattered over too many individual projects. Eleven programs were evaluated as the most promising and were, therefore, selected to receive a boost of dedicated attention and resources in order to accelerate their progress. The second conclusion was that a separate approach was needed for truly longer-term, radical innovation. Relying only upon the criterion of 'expected market success' would potentially lead to short-term myopia and endanger the future of a company reliant on innovation. Longer-term innovation potential was identified at the crossroads of where societal needs and trends meet with potential new solutions driven by technology developments. Applying this perspective four 'key innovation pockets' were identified (see Fig. 13.2). In three of those, DSM's knowledge and competences gave it a 'right to play.' But, the question then arose: which specific innovation programs should be targeted in these areas? To answer that, the company launched an internal contest to come up with ideas. All DSM employees were encouraged to offer suggestions, based on a number of guidelines. One of these guidelines was that the suggested area could, over the longer-term, become a true business for DSM with a minimum size of EUR 500 million. In the CSD, 13 of these ideas were examined carefully to evaluate DSM's chances of success. Eventually, four Emerging Business Areas (EBAs) were selected: Biomedical Materials, Specialty Packaging, Personalized Nutrition and White Biotech.[2]

It was recognized that such EBAs should not simply be combined with the running business of the existing Business Groups because they required a different steering than the day-to-day business. This was one of the reasons why DSM set up a new unit—the DSM Innovation Center. A second reason was that DSM

[1] See: Sanderijn Cels, *Rigor by Design: DSM's Approach to Open Innovation*, Amersfoort, Institute for Sustainable Process Technology (2014), as well as Robert Kirschbaum (VP Open Innovation), 'Open Innovation applied by DSM,' presentation 6 May 2011.

[2] White Biotech is Industrial Biotechnology: the application of nature's toolbox (for example, micro-organisms, enzymes) to the production of chemicals, materials and fuels from renewable resources. In the CSD of 2010, it was decided to continue with Biomedical Materials and White Biotech (renamed Bio-based Products and Services) and to add Advanced Surfaces as an EBA. Also, see **Reflection 1** at the end of this chapter.

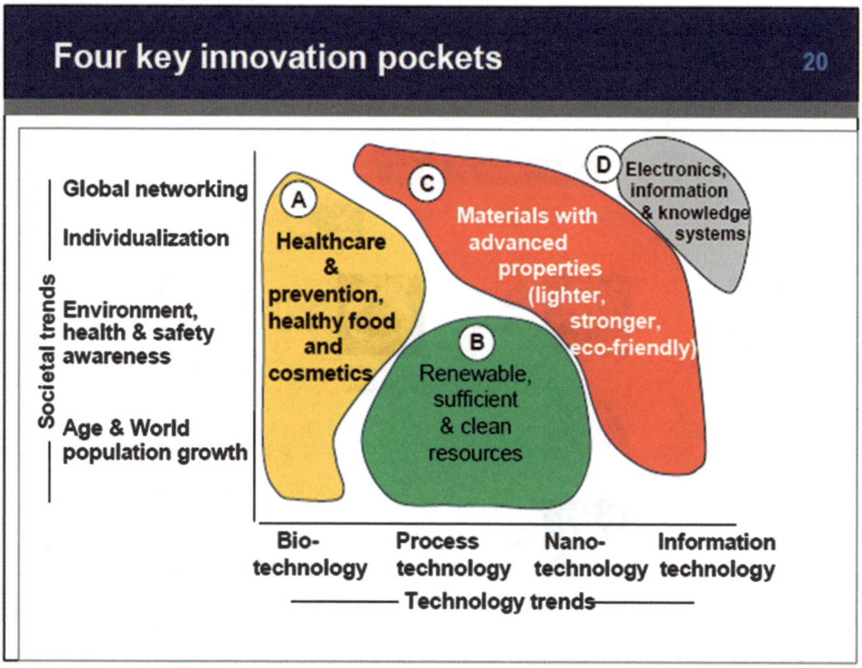

Fig. 13.2 Four key innovation pockets identified in 'Vision 2010'. *Source*: Company presentations, see also: Peter Elverding, 'Vision 2010: Building on Strengths,' presentation to Chemical Analyst Conference, 6 October 2005

formulated a very ambitious innovation target in 'Vision 2010'—the company aimed to increase its sales from innovation with an additional EUR 1 billion in 5 years; 20 % of this amount should come from the EBAs and the remaining 80 % from increased innovation in DSM's existing businesses. Such an increase would not materialize without additional efforts and support. The DSM Innovation Center, therefore, had a twofold task: (1) to support DSM's existing businesses with the acceleration of their innovation and (2) to manage the Emerging Business Areas. Through its 'Excellence in Innovation' program, the DSM Innovation Center has indeed supported the businesses to such an extent that they could contribute the lion's share of achieving the overall goal of EUR 1 billion in additional sales from innovation in 2010, thereby doubling the speed of their innovation. At the end of this chapter, we offer a further reflection on the successful implementation of DSM's innovation drive resulting from 'Vision 2010.'

The design of DSM's Corporate Strategy Dialogues was different every time (as has been discussed in previous chapters). The reason being that each CSD had to be tailor-made in order to address the particular issues and themes at that point in time. Looking back at the CSD design in 2005 (see Fig. 13.1), it can be noted that this most closely resembles the outline of the Business Strategy Dialogue (BSD) process. As in the BSD process, the prescription was to first look outside

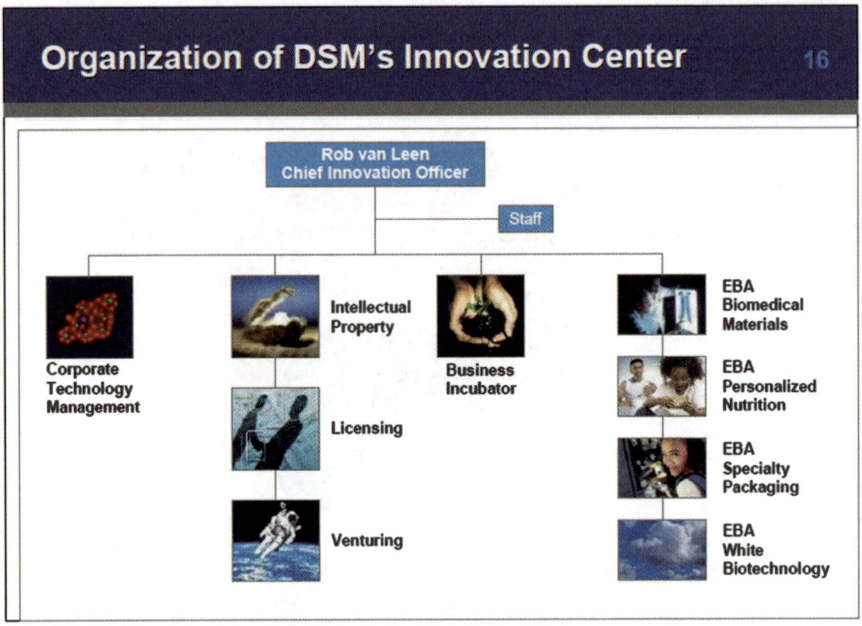

Fig. 13.3 The DSM innovation center. *Source*: Company presentations

(worldview and industry view) in order to develop a vision of the relevant future environment (industry vision). One could then look 'outside-in' to DSM's business to determine how best to achieve leadership within this industry context. At that point, the results of an 'inside-out' analysis are important, in order to show the strengths and capabilities of the businesses which could be incorporated in a particular business model to achieve the leadership position. The prescription that the CSD 'working groups' should produce strategic options and not a 'one way to Rome'-type of strategic recommendation was also similar to the BSD process. The strategic options per business area became the ingredients of corporate evaluation and decision-making. It is important to note that the CSD design had already incorporated the concept that any strategic decisions should be thought through regarding the consequences of organizational alignment in terms of both structure and systems.

The results of the CSD 2005 were published under the title 'Vision 2010: Building on Strengths.' The chosen subtitle indicated the confidence that DSM had built over time. The CSD results included corporate targets under the following headings:

Quality: increasing the % of Specialty leadership and the presence in emerging economies

Growth: sales growth and the innovation target of EUR 1 billion additional sales in 2010
Profitability: increased margins, operational excellence and value creation
Sustainability: top rankings on Safety, Health and Environment (SHE) and sustainability,[3] leader in Industrial Biotech

The cluster results were specified with respect to (1) market-driven growth and innovation, (2) emerging economies and (3) operational excellence, as well as in terms of the EBITDA margins to be achieved. The strategic missions of the clusters were defined as follows:

Nutrition: Grow and Strengthen
Pharma: Improve and Strengthen
Performance materials: Grow and Strengthen
Industrial chemicals: Actively Maintain

These strategic missions indicated that the Nutrition and Performance Materials clusters were the focus areas for growth, while the Pharma cluster had to improve its performance. For the Industrial Chemicals cluster the decision was to 'actively maintain' it, meaning that (only) the necessary investments would be made to allow it to maintain its competitive position. In hindsight, this decision constituted a 'delay of execution' as subsequent events would show.

Accelerating 'Vision 2010'

Already at the time of publication of the 'Vision 2010' strategy, in 2005, it was announced that the strategy would be reviewed by 2008 in order to amend priorities if required. This was a rather unusual statement and reflected the anticipation that significant changes at the top of the company might occur between 2005 and 2008, as indeed turned out to be the case. In 2006, Nico Gerardu joined the Managing Board (MB) while a new CFO, Rolf-Dieter Schwalb, came from outside the company, replacing Henk van Dalen, who had left for TNT (an international express and mail delivery company headquartered in the Netherlands). In May 2007, Feike Sijbesma succeeded Peter Elverding as Chairman (Sijbesma had joined DSM in 1998 when Gist-Brocades was acquired and had become a member of the DSM's MB in 2000). Stephan Tanda also joined the MB from the outside, succeeding Sijbesma in his previous role (also in 2007). It was, therefore, under a very different MB composition that 'Vision 2010' underwent a mid-term review in 2007. While the new board fully endorsed the main elements and the strategic direction of 'Vision 2010,' it

[3] Over the years, DSM had broadened its focus on Safety to Sustainability. The ranking on Sustainability was the Dow Jones Sustainability Index, where DSM regularly scored the top position in the Chemical industry.

concluded that its implementation could and should be accelerated. This led to some significant changes in growth and profitability targets—to an increase of the China sales target from USD 1 billion to USD 1.5 billion to be reached in 2010, and to the announcement of the divestment of businesses that did not fit the 'specialty leadership' profile. This latter decision, in particular, represented a true acceleration of the strategy implementation. The list of divestment candidates featured seven businesses in all clusters. Additionally, two businesses were to be 'carved out' and made ready for partnerships. Combined with acquisitions in the focus areas, it was thought that this would enable DSM to grow in 2010 towards a 60 % specialty profile. Most significant, however, was the decision to divest all businesses in the remaining Base Chemicals and Materials cluster, except for the Fibre Intermediates (caprolactam and acrylonitrile). Reflecting on such decisions, Feike Sijbesma remarked in 2013: "The easiest way [to make the decision] is to wait too long, until the business has lost its value. When it is still contributing a large part of today's profit it is very difficult to take it out. [But] that is the right moment, because then it still has a value that you can harvest and reinvest."[4]

Execution of the Strategy

The years of 2007–2010 were, needless to say, not the easiest for the execution of a strategy that entailed significant divestments, as well as ambitions for performance improvement. The financial crisis that engulfed the world after the fall of Lehmann Brothers made most assumptions questionable and all players uncertain. Nevertheless, DSM succeeded in divesting Stamicarbon (urea licensing to Maire Technimont) and DSM Energy (to TAQA) in 2009 and Fertilizers/Melamine (to OCI), Elastomers (to Lanxess), Citric Acid (to Adcuram) and Special Products (to Emerald) in 2010. At the same time, the company stepped up its acquisition pace making an average of four deals per year. In 2008, for instance, DSM acquired the Polymer Technology Group in the US to strengthen and expand its Emerging Business Area (EBA) of Biomedical Materials, to be followed by a joint venture (JV) in surgical materials (Actamax) with DuPont in 2010. This illustrated the desired pathway to success of the EBAs: learning about the business first in a period of organic growth and subsequently building a successful platform by targeted acquisitions (and/or JVs).[5] In its focus areas for growth, the company strengthened its engineering plastics and resins businesses with several transactions, while Nutritional Products.

[4] '*Feike Sijbesma, Chief of DSM*, *Financial Times*, 18 August 2013. It is fair to say that DSM has learned this lesson the hard way, since it has missed several opportunities to sell, for example, the Energy business at the various peaks in oil prices. The natural tendency is then to 'enjoy the ride' for a little while longer but, inevitably, the cycle will turn in cyclical activities. A similar observation can be made about the Caprolactam business, which could have been (partially) sold in 2010/2011 before the peak prices plummeted again.

[5] The next acquisition for Biomedical Materials was Kensey Nash in 2012.

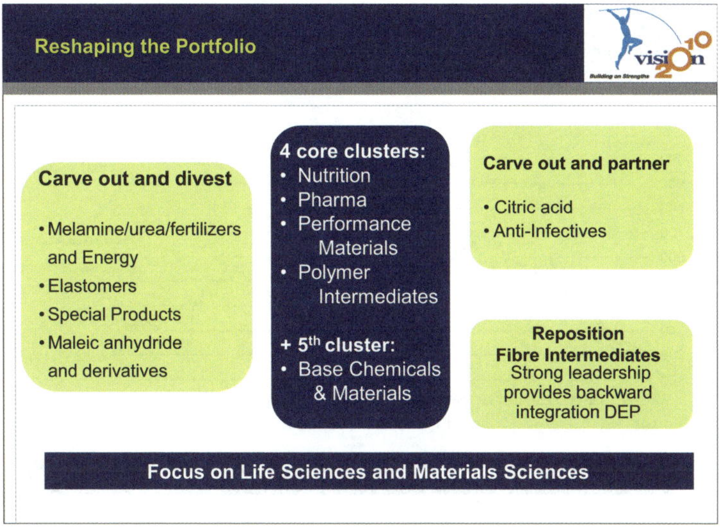

Fig. 13.4 Reshaping the portfolio in 'Acceleration Vision 2010'. *Source*: Company presentations, see also: Feike Sijbesma, 'Accelerating Vision 2010,' presentation to DSM Analysts Conference, 27 September 2007

DSM was working on the relatively large acquisition of Martek Biosciences (for over USD 1 billion) that would be announced in December 2010. This acquisition was the result of the approved strategy of the 'Vision 2010' working group in Nutrition to build a new growth platform for nutritional lipids (better known as Omega-3 and Omega-6).[6] Finally, DSM announced in December 2010 the global joint venture with Sinochem in Antibiotics, the area for which the company had long sought an Asian partner. All in all, despite the difficult economic conditions, it must be concluded that the portfolio restructuring envisioned in 'Acceleration Vision 2010' was completed according to plan (Fig. 13.4).

Perhaps even more remarkable was that the company also achieved its ambitious targets of EUR 1 billion in additional sales from innovation and USD 1.5 billion of sales in China. In order to achieve the China strategy, it was very important that the company appoint its first Chinese president, Weiming Jiang, of DSM China in 2007; formerly the company had relied on 'expats' to lead the country's organization. The leadership of Weiming made a world of difference in China and heralded the further strengthening of DSM's regional organizations in 2010. DSM management also realized its growth and profitability targets in four of the 5 years included within the 'Vision 2010' timeframe, despite the adverse economic conditions. Only its EBITDA margin targets for clusters were not achieved with the exception of its new Nutrition cluster. Nevertheless, DSM shareholders had little to complain about

[6] The next step in this strategy was to acquire Ocean Nutrition in 2012.

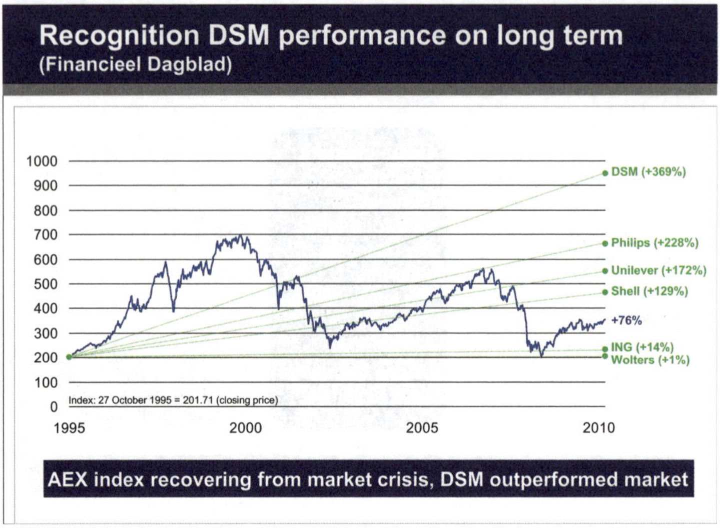

Fig. 13.5 DSM's shareholder value creation versus AEX, 1995–2010. *Source*: DSM Investor Relations, based on: Dertien jaar later zijn de weduwen en de wezen de absolute winnaars op de beurs," *Het Financieele Dagblad*, 5 March 2009

(see Fig. 13.5): the company had easily outperformed all other companies listed on the AEX over the period of its transformation.[7] All in all, the Managing Board felt justified to issue the press release with the proposed heading (see Chap. 1): 'DSM finalizes portfolio transformation and enters era of focused growth.'

Reflection 1: The Learning Cycles of Evolutionary Transformation

DSM as a learning company was reflected upon in Chap. 11. Using the example of M&A in 2000, it was shown how DSM was willing to address the 'existential questions' of its strategy, trying to learn from its track record of acquisition successes and failures. Based on the 'lessons learned,' the company adjusted its strategy (types of acquisitions), organization (setting up the M&A department within CS&A) and managerial systems (the 'ways of working,' see Fig. 11.12). When these adjustments were perceived as successful, the company reinforced this M&A strategy and approach, building on its success. In this last section this theme

[7] Shareholder value creation includes share price growth and distributed dividends. For an external reference, see: "Dertien jaar later zijn de weduwen en de wezen de absolute winnaars op de beurs," *Het Financieele Dagblad*, 5 March 2009. This article tracks the development of the share price (excluding dividend) of all companies listed in the AEX in the period 1995–2009. It concluded that the DSM had shown the best performance (+93 %), while the AEX index itself grew only 5 % over this period of time.

will be expanded. Reflecting on the various CSDs more generally, one can consider them to be 'strategic learning cycles.' At the start of each such learning cycle, the company determined clear strategic objectives with corresponding targets and milestones. And at the end of such a learning cycle, the company took stock of its successes and failures in reaching these objectives. Thus, the 'lessons learned' are the starting point of the next cycle and help shape the strategic objectives of this new cycle (together with anticipated changes in the external context). While this may sound abstract so far, several specific lessons learned by DSM in the various CSD cycles will be illustrated below. But first, it is important to further specify what is meant by a 'strategic learning cycle' and to do so, 'innovation' serves as an excellent example.

In 2005, DSM management set out to achieve EUR 1 billion of additional sales in 2010 through innovation. The driver of this strategic objective was the awareness that the company's portfolio had changed significantly over the past decade, away from the 'commodity' type of activities where low-cost competition prevailed and, therefore, operational excellence was paramount for achieving competitive success. Instead, the portfolio had migrated toward activities with generally shorter lifecycles, higher rates of technological progress, more complicated 'customer value propositions' and much higher market dynamics. Leadership positions could lead to higher margins, but these could only be sustained by delivering continuous innovation and rejuvenation. As a result, it was essential that DSM would learn to excel in this game as well. DSM management realized that it would not be sufficient to exhort the existing businesses to realize this ambitious target. The organization had to be fundamentally adapted for this purpose. Changing the organization means changing the organizational structure but it means much more than that. In this case it involved change regarding:

Structure: The creation of the Innovation Center (see Fig. 13.3). The function of Chief Innovation Officer (CIO). The decision that the reporting line would be to the CEO.

Processes: From technology-push and R&D-led to more market-driven and customer-focused. The drive toward Open Innovation processes.

Culture: Perhaps the most difficult part—how to become a truly innovative company? This was explicitly managed for innovation, just like DSM was explicitly managing an overall 'cultural change' agenda.[8]

Human Resources: The appointment of the right people is key, starting with the CIO. Rob van Leen turned out to be the right person for this challenging new function. The people responsible for innovation within the businesses and the Innovation Center together formed 'the Billion Bunch.'

[8] DSM's overall 'culture change' agenda emphasized: (1) external orientation, (2) accountability for performance and (3) inspirational leadership.

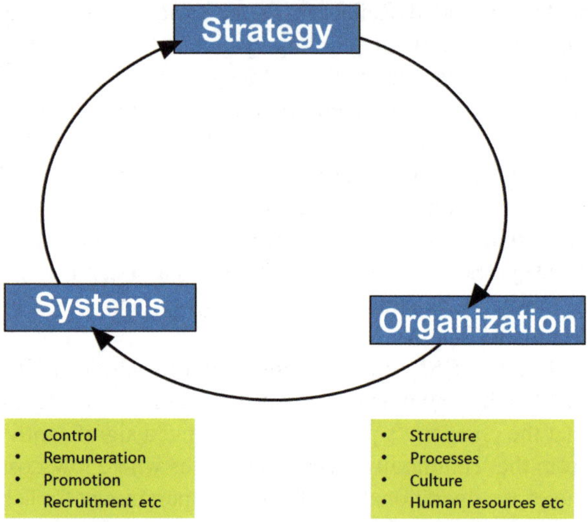

Fig. 13.6 The strategic learning cycle. *Source* Hein Schreuder, 'Evolutie en Transformatie (van bedrijfstakken en ondernemingen),' FOCUS-lezing, Utrecht, 7 Nov 2000

Many companies realize that 'structure follows strategy,' but they don't appreciate the full scale of the organizational adaptation needed. Strategy implementation often fails because the necessary organizational adjustments are not (sufficiently) made. However, even if a company makes the required organizational changes, there is yet another step that needs to be taken to facilitate strategy implementation. That step is the necessary change in the company's 'Systems' (see Fig. 13.6). The word Systems is used broadly to denote all management systems in an organization. It includes the control systems, reward systems, recruitment and promotion systems, as well as the reporting systems. All of these systems send signals into the organization telling people what is important. If a company significantly changes its strategy and adjusts its organization, but leaves its management systems unchanged, people will continuously receive signals that 'nothing much has changed.' Meetings will be conducted the same (old) way, reports still need to be filled out in the same (old) format, rewards are still handed out on the same (old) basis, the same types of people are recruited and promoted—there are no signals in daily organizational life that reinforce the message that the company is serious about achieving its strategic goal(s), other than perhaps the occasional speech from the CEO or article in the company magazine. How could a change in people's behavior be expected, or the strategy taken seriously? Implementing an ambitious strategy, like achieving EUR 1 billion extra revenue from innovation within 5 years, requires that the management systems are changed to continuously signal the importance of the goal.

So, what are some of the measures that DSM management took to adapt its management systems? The following are some examples. First of all, reporting systems had to be adapted. Regular management reporting at DSM did not enable the monitoring of innovation. The aggregate goal of EUR 1 billion in extra revenue was broken down to the project level and assigned to the DSM businesses (80 %), as well as to the Innovation Center (20 %). A separate stream of 'innovation reporting'

Fig. 13.7 The strategic learning cycle for DSM innovation (2005 to 2010). *Source*: Hein Schreuder, 'DSM Transformation: The Learning Cycle of Innovation,' CEEMAN keynote address, 2013. See: http://www.ceeman.org/docs/default-source/exed-presentations/hein-schreuder-the-learning-cycle-of-innovation.pdf?sfvrsn=0

was created allowing the company to track progress. Innovation became a prominent topic of business review meetings and the innovation report was discussed at such meetings. The Innovation Center developed, together with McKinsey, an Innovation Diagnostic, which allowed benchmarking of DSM's innovation practices. The diagnostic was first applied in 2006, showing that DSM was scoring below the average of 27 of its peers in the chemical industry. Although perhaps understandable given DSM's long history with Operational Excellence and limited focus on innovation, the results came as a shock. It led to improvement programs being executed across all DSM businesses. In 2008 the diagnostic was applied again showing that DSM had made substantial progress, having moved ahead of the industry average, although still not ranked at the top end. Again, a program was formulated and implemented to reach the very top. As noted above, the appointment of the right people was key. After some time, many of the Innovation officers who had been initially appointed at the business level had to be replaced. Increasingly, replacements were recruited from the outside: an intense familiarity with innovation at the customer level proved to be essential. Finally, remuneration systems were changed to appropriately reward the people responsible for making innovation happen for reaching the target. Rob van Leen commented with a smile: "In 2006 and 2007 innovation in the Business Groups was lagging, compared with our targets. I, therefore, convinced the Managing Board to incorporate Innovation as a determinant of the bonus incentive of Business Group Directors. How important this was I cannot really say, of course, but in 2008, 2009 and 2010 we achieved our targets." See Fig. 13.7, which captures the full strategic learning cycle for boosting innovation at DSM in the period 2005–2010.

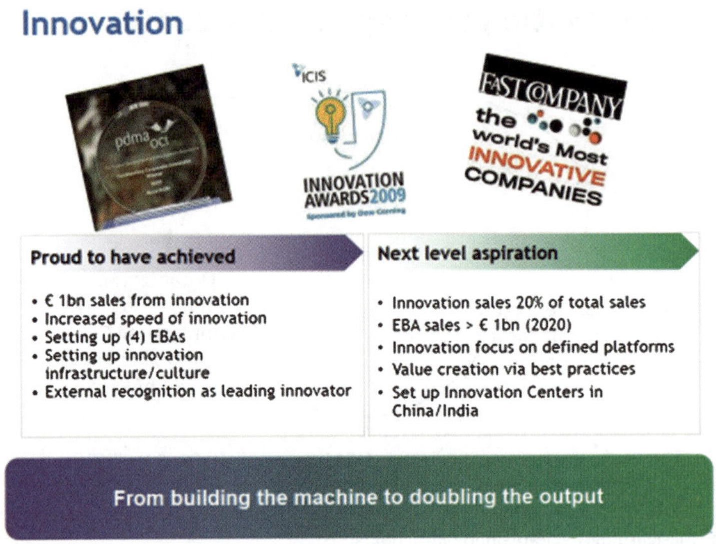

Fig. 13.8 From building the innovation machine to doubling the output. *Source*: Feike Sijbesma, 'DSM in motion: Driving Focused Growth,' presentation at DSM Capital Markets Days, 23 September 2010

So, a complete strategic learning cycle consists of following through on Strategy > Organization > Systems, allowing yourself the experience of whether the strategic objective is achievable, yes or no, when all the conditions for successful implementation have been met. Lots of learning occurs along the way, as the examples of the innovation diagnostic and the changed recruitment policies illustrate. At the end of the cycle, the organization can take stock of its successes and failures. Regarding DSM Innovation, there was a mixture of both. Overall, it was a success since in 2010 DSM could announce that it had not only reached, but even surpassed, its overall target of EUR 1 billion. Moreover, company management was itself convinced that it had become much better at innovation and the outside world recognized DSM as a leading innovator. This allowed the company to build on this success and reinforce it. After its CSD 2010, DSM announced that it was proud to have built the innovation machine but would now move to the next level of its aspirations—doubling the innovation output (see Fig. 13.8). Using the terminology introduced earlier (see Chap. 11), the company 'switched from exploration to exploitation' of this successful pathway. There were also lessons to be learned from failures along the way. The company had started four new Emerging Business Areas (EBAs) in 2005. Two of these were developed successfully (Biomedical Materials and Industrial Biotechnology, now called Bio-based Products and Services) and could be taken further. The two others (Personalized Nutrition and Specialty Packaging) had proven to be less promising for DSM than originally thought. Although there were different reasons for both, the common denominator was that the business model required to develop these fields was not a good fit for DSM. In the CSD 2010, DSM created a special working group called Business Models to draw further lessons on this topic. With regard to the EBAs, it was concluded that two failed areas would be replaced by one new one—Advanced Surfaces. Thus, while DSM switched to 'exploitation' for two EBAs, it started 'exploration' of a new EBA at the same time. Although difficult to realize in practice, such new explorations are necessary for evolutionary transformation.[9] Success is never permanent; at some point it will begin to erode. Therefore, for longer-term success, a company will always need a mix of exploitation (of current successes) and exploration (of new pathways to future success). In the next and final section, this perspective will be applied to DSM's overall strategic development during the time period covered in this book.

Reflection 2: DSM's Evolutionary Transformation

In Chap. 11, the example of M&A was used to illustrate the concept of a 'strategic learning cycle,' where DSM attempted to learn the lessons of its past and then move toward an adaptation of its Strategy > Organization > Systems to incorporate the lessons learned and to explore a new M&A approach. In this chapter, the example of Innovation elaborated on the concept of a strategic learning cycle, particularly the multi-faceted nature of the Organization and Systems adaptations that are often required. Both examples also illustrate how the company could move to the 'exploitation' of a new pathway after successful 'exploration.' In this final section, let's look at DSM's development more generally from the perspective of evolutionary transformation, driven by the completion of various strategic learning cycles. The following CSDs will be our overall frame of reference:

Year	Name CSD	Horizon
1994	'Clarifying the Corporate Strategy'	1994–1997
1997	'Priorities for Profitable Growth'	1997–2000
2000	'Vision 2005: Focus and Value'	2000–2005
2005	'Vision 2010: Building on Strengths'	2005–2010

Before the CSD of 1994 is addressed, it should also be emphasized that this year is, of course, only one point in the evolutionary development of DSM. In order to reach that point, the company already had needed to successfully complete the transformation of a Mining company to a Chemical company (see Chap. 1). Thus, the company culture was already imbued with the notion that transformational change is sometimes required for long-term survival and success. As the saying went, "At DSM, transformation is in our genes." After this first transformation, the company embarked on a period of diversification and expansion, exploring various strategic routes to broaden the base of the company beyond the Gas-based and

[9] This is comparable with the evolutionary principle of variation > selection > retention. New variations are necessary to keep the evolutionary process going. Some will be selected and retained (exploitation). Others will be rejected ('selected out'). New variations (explorations) are then necessary for optimal adaptation to the changing environment.

Petrochemical cores. In hindsight, it is fair to say that the company had a hard time finding its way. This period can be characterized as one of 'strategic drift,' leading to the 1993 memo expressing that "none of the directors believes in hanging on." However, let's note that important developments did take place in the 1980s, upon which the company could build its later evolution. These included the privatization of the company, which was managed very successfully by Hans van Liemt and his team, and the continued effort to explore the Fine Chemicals field, despite various setbacks. Additionally, the company had learned the hard way that several strategic routes that it had explored (like forward integration and unrelated diversification) were not leading to success. Thus, the company could also learn from its failures.

Also, in the late 1980s DSM had set up its collaboration with IMD to invest in the Industrial Marketing competencies of its executives through the IMPACT program (see Chap. 3). Thus, an essential building block of the later strategy dialogues had already been put in place. Moreover, as another example of 'path dependency' (see Chap. 11), this had set up the conditions for DSM and IMD to broaden their collaboration when the need arose to invest in DSM's business strategies. The success of the early BSDs in turn led Simon de Bree to ask his question, "If strategy dialogues are successful at the business level, can we also conduct them at the corporate level?" It was this question that led to the CSD of 1994.

In hindsight, the CSD of 1994, diplomatically titled 'Clarifying the Corporate Strategy' was, in many ways, an experiment (see Chap. 9):

1. First of all, DSM explored whether a strategic 'process' could be conducted in a dialogue format at the corporate level
2. In terms of the 'strategic mindset and intent,' the perspective was changed from a diversification drive to an exploration of the ability to focus
3. Finally, in terms of 'strategic direction,' the outcomes of this CSD triggered the exploration of 'growth pathways' in Performance Materials and Fine Chemicals

As recounted in Chap. 9, DSM managed to execute the strategy of tripling its presence in Fine Chemicals and Polypropylene (Performance Materials) within 3 years, to such an extent that the company gained confidence in this new approach to its corporate strategy. A momentum had been built up which naturally led to Simon de Bree's follow-up question, "Now that we have been successful with the previous CSD, can we do one again?" In the new CSD of 1997, 'Priorities for Profitable Growth,' the new growth pathways would be further explored and the intent was, again, to focus by setting clear priorities.

In each CSD cycle, more detailed strategic learning was experienced as well. For instance, in 1994 DSM started to apply the 'cluster' concept. Clusters were defined as strategic groupings of activities with broadly similar characteristics and Key Success Factors (KSFs), thus providing a strong link to the outcomes of the BSDs. Applying the cluster concept helped in the drive to focus; in 1994 it revealed that DSM had only three 'real' clusters: Base Chemicals and Materials (44 % in 1993), Performance Materials (32 %) and Fine Chemicals (4 %). The hope that there might be a fourth cluster (Plastic Processing, 16 %) was proven to be false, since there was substantial heterogeneity in the characteristics and KSFs of companies like Curver, Fardem, Reko and Engineering Plastic Products. They were subsequently sold off one-by-one. The cluster concept, a perspective that has been retained until today, also proved to be useful in determining which type of acquisitions might fit and strengthen DSM's activities in certain areas. The acquisitions of Chemie Linz, Deretil and Vestolen were early test cases of this approach.

The CSD 1997, 'Priorities for Profitable Growth,' was designed very differently than its predecessor. Now, DSM's three core clusters had been defined and the growth pathways to be explored further were reasonably clear—the main purpose was to 'test' these choices to determine whether they offered sufficiently robust strategic options to allow DSM to continue building its future on them. Hence, the design to examine the overall portfolio from four angles: Competitive Analysis, Performance, Scenarios and Competences. As detailed in Chap. 9, the top priority was the desire to expand the Fine Chemicals cluster, possibly along the established growth paths of 'product trees' and 'custom manufacturing,' but preferably by adding Biotechnology (fermentation, enzymatic processes). This latter option implied the broadening of the Fine Chemicals cluster into Life Science Products. This was essentially a very risky choice since there were so few options to execute this main priority well. Fortunately, 'luck favored the prepared mind' when Gist-Brocades was willing to open discussions about a potential combination. Of course, the successful acquisition and integration of Gist-Brocades strongly reinforced the choices made in 1994 and 1997. DSM had basically found its new strategic repertoire. It was building the two clusters of Performance Materials and Life Science Products to sufficient strength to one day be able to face the question about whether further focus (on two clusters) was possible, necessary and/or desirable. Hence, DSM subsequently shifted from exploration to 'exploitation' of its new strategic repertoire. With regard to the strategic 'process' used to formulate corporate strategy, the Corporate Strategy Dialogue had established its legitimacy.

Let's examine two more detailed learnings emanating from the 1997 CSD and its implementation. The CSD working group Performance produced an overview of DSM's businesses in the categories of 'Performing' and 'Non-Performing.' Furthermore, it indicated whether it evaluated the future performance, as projected by the businesses, as 'Attainable' or 'Hard to Attain.' This performance classification clearly reinforced the message, announced in 1994, that performance would, thereafter, be a major element of the focusing process. In later years, this message would again be strengthened by application of Value Based Business Steering (with the so-called 'C-curve'), indicating that a non-performing business should first address its performance problem before applying for further corporate funds.[10]

[10] See: *Value Based Business Steering at DSM: An Introduction*, company brochure, 2000. The 'C-curve' was meant to convey the message that for any business not recovering its cost-of-capital, the prescription was to reduce its Gross Asset Base by shedding structurally weak, low-return positions. Only after improving profitability would the business be allowed to grow again by investment. Applied to making acquisitions, please refer to Chap. 11 and the genesis of the saying "two lame ducks don't make a flying eagle."

Along this learning route, strategic and financial evaluations of the businesses became intertwined, whereas they had been treated rather separately in the past.[11]

A second example of more detailed learning occurred in the process of acquiring and integrating Gist-Brocades. In order to project the acquisition as a 'friendly transaction,' DSM and Gist-Brocades agreed to use the word 'merger' instead of 'acquisition or takeover.'[12] Right from the start this created some tension and confusion. The Dutch financial daily *Het Financieele Dagblad* reported the following quotes from the joint press conference in February 1998 under the headline "The takeover that may not be called a takeover:"

> Quickly it becomes clear that De Bree and not Scheffer claims the main role: 'I shall answer first and then I shall pass the floor to Mr. Scheffer who may be able to add something.' The transaction with Gist-Brocades is a takeover that may not be called a takeover. 'We call it a merger. I shall repeat that every time I hear the word takeover,' says Scheffer. But when De Bree points toward the sales diagrams of both companies (depicted in pie charts), he delicately remarks: 'As you see, the pie chart of DSM is somewhat larger.'[13]

This approach was chosen not only for appearances, but also to try to preserve 'the best of both worlds' from the two companies. In some areas this was totally appropriate. For instance, it would have been disastrous if DSM had applied its 'commodity chemicals mindset' to running the Biotech-based businesses of Gist-Brocades. However, in most other respects (reporting, IT, HR, pensions, etc.) choices had to be made and these choices were severely complicated and delayed by upholding the appearance of a merger. DSM learned from this integration process how important it is to clearly specify what should be preserved in an acquisition and what should simply be integrated 'the DSM way.'[14]

During the CSD 2000, 'Vision 2005: Focus and Value,' DSM was finally ready to face the existential question of the future of its Commodity Chemicals and Materials. In the meantime, it was without question that this difficult issue would be addressed by means of a Corporate Strategic Dialogue. In the CSD, it was established that the clusters of Performance Materials and Life Science Products had grown to sufficient size and strength to enable an option of 'further focus' by considering the partnering or divestment of Petrochemicals. As such, the company could continue its strategic pathway. What was new was the sheer size and complexity of the decision to be taken. Although DSM had significant experience with divestments, partnering or divesting Petrochemicals was of another order of magnitude. It had, for instance, numerous repercussions for the remaining DSM businesses, often customers of the company's petrochemical products. All these relationships would have to be made 'arm's length' if DSM Petrochemicals was to

[11] See, for example: Fig. 1.12 for a typical strategic evaluation in the early 1990s.

[12] See: http://www3.dsm.com/newsarchive/1998/~nl/230298_nl.htm (accessed 2 Dec 2014)

[13] "De overname die geen overname heet," *Het Financieele Dagblad*, 24 February 1998. Translated by the authors.

[14] This part of the DSM M&A manual was to be based on P. C. Haspeslagh and D. B. Jemison, *Managing Acquisitions: Creating Value Through Corporate Renewal*, NY: The Free Press, 1991.

be shared or sold. Furthermore, it could be anticipated that any new partner or buyer would want to have a substantial say in the operation of the DSM site in Geleen, where the largest part of the Petrochemical plants were located. Hence, the governance of the site, traditionally the 'home base' of DSM, would have to be changed to accommodate a new owner. Finally, there was the issue of the overall size of DSM—the company could not risk 'shrinking itself to insignificance.' It had to be confident that it could grow fast enough to compensate quickly for such a loss of revenue and profit. For all of these reasons, the decision that Peter Elverding and his team took required a lot of confidence and courage.

The strategic learning cycle of 'Vision 2005' allowed DSM to experience that it could handle such a large and complex process as the divestment of Petrochemicals. A dedicated team, led by Just Fransen van de Putte, managed the process for about 1 year and a half. During this process the DSM site in Geleen was basically transformed into an industrial park, called Chemelot, which could accommodate multiple users. Having elaborated the concept of an industrial park, DSM could more easily transfer the ownership of other plants located in Geleen in later years. Moreover, the site was significantly strengthened because it could now independently attract new activities. At the end of 2012, 113 companies were located on Chemelot—77 on the industrial park and 46 on the Chemelot Campus, which was added later.[15]

As discussed in Chap. 11, another lesson learned by DSM in 'Vision 2005' was that the pro-active announcement of its strategic intent helped significantly in the implementation of its plans. Saudi Basic Industries Corporation (SABIC) would perhaps already have bought ENI's petrochemical operations if DSM in 2000 had kept quiet about its intent to partner or sell. Similarly, Roche would perhaps not have contacted DSM about its Vitamins, Carotenoids and Fine Chemicals division, if DSM had not made its intent to expand in the Life Science Products space so clear. By pro-actively communicating its strategic priorities and ambitions, DSM could not only go out into the world to realize its plans but sometimes the world also came to DSM.

Finally, the CSD 2005, 'Vision 2010: Building on Strengths,' and more specifically the interim review in 2007, 'Accelerating Vision 2010,' allowed DSM to complete its transformation. The experience gained with divesting the Petrochemicals could be utilized in the divestment of businesses from the Industrial Chemicals cluster, where again a large 'carve-out program' was required. Good growth in its remaining businesses (after the slump in 2008/2009), as well as a strong acquisition and partnering drive compensated for the loss of revenue from divested business: the company managed to grow between 2005 and 2010. In this strategic learning cycle, the company explored whether it could boost its innovation. As discussed in this chapter, it went through the full cycle of Strategy > Organization > Systems adaptations to see whether it could generate an additional EUR 1 billion of sales from innovation. When, in 2010, DSM could legitimately claim that it had successfully built its 'innovation machine,' it could

[15] See: http://www.dsm.com/countrysites/dsmnl/nl_NL/over-dsm/innovatie/chemelot-campus.html

switch to 'exploitation' by striving to double the output of this machine. Similarly, it could announce that it now expected more than EUR 1 billion of sales from Emerging Business Areas in 2020. Another point worth noting is that by 2010 DSM had sufficiently explored the implications of the rise of emerging economies that it announced significant adjustments of its organization, like the relocation of businesses, the creation of regional innovation centers and the creation of 'dual desks' for some members of the Managing Board.[16] Finally, the company took leadership in setting very ambitious Sustainability targets, for example that 80 % of its innovation pipeline and 50 % of its running business should be ECO+ in 2015, meaning that the DSM products offer clear environmental benefits over their mainstream alternatives. Thus, the company was exploring whether it could take Sustainability from a 'corporate responsibility' perspective to a true business driver.

In conclusion, it is hoped that a perspective on DSM's evolutionary transformation has been provided in this section. Taking four successive CSD rounds as our frame of reference, the company can be seen as an excellent example of a 'learning organization.' Viewed through this lens, one can look at organizations and see multiple learning cycles going on at any point in time. Some of these may be consciously planned, while others may be spontaneous (such as when organizations learn to cope with unexpected developments). Some may be exploratory, aimed at new learning, while others may be more aimed at further testing and exploiting already accumulated learning. Organizations probably differ in the amounts of learning cycles they conduct and how many of these are consciously planned and evaluated. Such learning cycles may take place in all parts of the organization. They may pertain to very diverse business and functional fields, like technological learning, commercial learning and learning to conduct business in new regions. In this section, DSM's various rounds of Corporate Strategic Dialogues have been looked at as consciously planned 'strategic learning cycles.' In each CSD the issues and themes to be addressed were based on a rather explicit evaluation of the company's recent experiences and on an anticipation of further changes in the relevant environment(s). It was also important that these issues and themes were collected and discussed by involving a large (and, over time, growing) number of people. Business Strategy Dialogues and Corporate Strategy Dialogues are clear examples of 'participative strategy formulation.' Thus, the strategic priorities emanating from the dialogue process have widespread support, which greatly enhances the ease and speed of implementation. It has been the intention to show that each CSD could be considered a portfolio of prioritized strategic initiatives and targets, with a mix of exploitation (reinforcing current successes) and exploration (of possible pathways to future success). Since all success is transient, a company should enjoy its current successes while they last, but should also regularly prepare for a future that will be different than today.

[16] See: *DSM in Motion: Driving Focused Growth*, DSM Capital Markets Days, Bergisch Gladbach, 2010. The 'dual desk'-policy, whereby one MB member is also based in Asia and another also in the US is most probably an intermediate step toward further internationalization.

References

Cels, S., *Rigor by Design: DSM's Approach to Open Innovation*, Amersfoort: Institute for Sustainable Process Technology, 2014.

Haspeslagh P.C. and D.B. Jemison, *Managing Acquisitions: Creating Value Through Corporate Renewal*, NY: The Free Press, 1991.

14 Lessons for Academia and Business

The development of DSM and its academic partners over 25 years has been documented in this book, highlighting the various interactions along the way. It is remarkable that this kind of cooperation has been sustained, and even broadened, over such a long period of time. In this last chapter, the authors want to jointly draw some conclusions from this case and present suggestions, all of which we believe may have a wider significance for companies and academic institutions in general.

In the previous chapters, the focus has been on the interactions between DSM and its academic partners that the authors are most familiar with. Here, the first discussion will be on the wider impact of this long-term collaboration. When a corporation, such as DSM, and academic institutions, such as IMD or Babson, are linked in a close cooperation over 25 years, both are likely to experience lasting impacts. What were these impacts and how did they transform the participating institutions? How DSM's strategic transformation process created an entirely new company, over time, was illustrated by the strategic learning cycles that DSM went through (see Chaps. 9, 11 and 13). The way in which this close cooperation influenced other parts of DSM will be examined here, followed by a look into how the relationship influenced the two business schools most closely involved.

Having broadened the perspective, the book will conclude with some recommendations for companies and academic institutions, particularly business schools that wish to achieve such long-term collaborations. While one should not 'generalize from one case' both authors have been sufficiently involved with other companies and business schools to apply a wider perspective.[1] Moreover, the recommendations offered have been discussed with many interviewees at DSM and at both academic institutions, whose views are included. In the end, however, the authors offer their own conclusions and suggestions.

[1] See the biographies in About the Authors.

J.-P. Jeannet, H. Schreuder, *From Coal to Biotech*,
DOI 10.1007/978-3-662-46299-7_14

Impact on DSM as an Organization

As observed by Jeannet and other members of the faculty team, an important role in all of DSM's strategic changes was assumed by Corporate Planning (CPL), later expanded and renamed Corporate Strategy and Acquisitions (CS&A). If the company's transformation can be seen as rebuilding a house, CS&A acted in the role of architect. An architect works on behalf of principals who have their own desires about what their future house should look like. An architect does not actually (re-)build the house but relies on many others to do so. It is, however, the architect's role to translate the many desires and preferences of the principals into a design that can actually be built. Similarly, it was CS&A's role to produce a coherent and consistent strategy that could be executed by DSM management. In addition, CS&A became responsible over time for Mergers and Acquisitions (M&A) strategy and execution at the corporate level, thus playing an important role when particular parts of the house had to be removed or added.

CS&A was staffed with experienced DSM executives who had come from various businesses. They were all experts at the use of the strategic tools and processes, in particular the Business Strategy Dialogue (BSD) process. Many CS&A staff members were frequently utilized as either challengers or facilitators for BSDs in major business units (BUs). And, of course, CS&A played an important role in the CSD discussions that led to the portfolio shifts. CS&A staff contributed to many DSM executive seminars creating a close collaboration between the academic institutions' faculty and the CS&A staff. Faculty could use the regular guest lectures of CS&A staff as a constant update about DSM strategy, thus calibrating their programs accordingly. CS&A in 2012 was not the same group as Corporate Planning and Development (CPL) in 1990! Their role, function and contribution to strategy had changed substantially. As a result, the collaboration with business schools also changed over time. At the outset of the collaboration on Industrial Marketing (IMPACT), the faculty served more in the role of initiator, coming to DSM with new concepts unfamiliar to many senior executives; they could drive the agenda with their material and teaching approaches. Once the company began to absorb the concepts such as BSDs, marketing planning and modern team work, the faculty was increasingly moved into the role of teaching those who were new to the company, younger in experience and not yet exposed to the senior executives who were already working on the next strategy phase. The faculty teams were needed to bring newcomers into the concept world of DSM but not necessarily shape the frameworks as they had at the outset, which was increasingly done by DSM itself.

Reflecting on the collaboration between academic institutions and DSM over time, Schreuder commented that at the beginning, and during, the IMPACT program cycles, DSM primarily looked to the academic team led by Jeannet for input and concepts. Then, DSM changed the collaboration during the BSD development and pilot projects more in the direction of co-creation and collaboration as equal partners. Subsequently, it continued to develop the BSD on its own, sharing new issues and themes like innovation and soliciting input from its academic partners. In the field of corporate strategy and the CSD processes (see Chaps. 9, 11 and 13), DSM has always set up and executed its own strategic learning cycles.

In combination with a significant shift in portfolio, sales, employment and asset footprint, came a substantial change in DSM's management culture. Where in 1988 still two-thirds of DSM employees were based in the Netherlands and only 15 % were outside of Europe, by 2004 this had reversed to less than 30 % in the Netherlands and almost 45 % located outside Europe (Americas and Asia)[2]; a shift that was actively promoted by DSM's top leadership (see Chap. 10). As new businesses and companies were welcomed into the DSM family, the tone of management behavior became distinctly more international, more inclusionary, and also friendlier towards women. Where in the earlier DSM programs hardly any women managers were represented, there were substantially more 20 years later. Earlier programs were largely dominated by the Dutch, while later programs had half or more non-Dutch participants; if the programs run outside of Europe were included in the total, Dutch participants accounted for no more than 25 % of total. Of course, the driver was business needs but there was also aggressive support lent to DSM's cultural change program coordinated out of a dedicated office with a small staff.

Finally, and no less importantly, was the impact of all these changes on DSM's Business Academy (DBA); the organizational unit coordinated and organized most of the management development programs out of DSM's Head Office in Heerlen, the Netherlands. At first, programs were organized on a one-time basis in China, Switzerland and the US, each time accompanied by a DBA staff member from the Netherlands. As the regional clusters in China and North America grew in importance, some of the DBA responsibility was transferred overseas. Today, DBA is as globalized as the rest of the DSM footprint, resulting in a substantial change in its organization and staffing. Today, the DSM DBA maintained a hub each in Europe, North America and Asia, coordinated through a Chief Learning Officer (CLO).

Over time, DBA expanded its network of academic partners beyond the initial group of IMD, Babson and Rotterdam School of Management, Erasmus University (RSM). Among the suite of three Management and Leadership Programs (MLP), DSM assigned each to a dedicated academic partner. MLP-1 was assigned to a UK consulting group and designed as a 5-day program for young graduates or professionals who recently joined DSM from university with little prior professional experience. MLP-2, also a 5-day program, was delivered by RSM-Rotterdam and focused on younger managers who had been with DSM for a few years. The MLP-3, a 10-day program delivered in two separate modules of 5 days each, was entrusted to Babson College and targeted senior managers.

DSM also offered an Executive Leadership Program (ELP) suite. ELP-1 was delivered in conjunction with IMD over 10 days in two separate weeks with executives as the target audience. For senior executives, DSM used Wharton School

[2] Source: DSM *Annual Report 1988* and DSM *Annual Report 2005*: 9.

for a program that lasted 8 days in several modules. Finally, there was a program 'Bright Talent' Program taught by the Center for Creative Leadership.[3]

The interesting question to ponder is the relative contribution of the collaboration between DSM and its main academic partners—IMD and Babson College. Clearly, the academic partners did not drive the strategic transformation of DSM. The role of the academic institutions was to offer some of the tools and to instruct a large cadre of DSM managers in the use of those tools. They covered both strategic and behavioral aspects. By laying the groundwork, the later moves considered necessary by a subsequent group of senior managers were most certainly supported, if not enabled.

DSM's culture of underpinning a required strategic move with an educational thrust was already evident while mounting the IMPACT seminar series with IMEDE/IMD. It continued with the experimentation and implementation of the BSD process, strengthening the marketing acumen and changing the managerial behavior into the adoption of a new culture. On one hand, the strong reliance on educational programs to support the changes inevitably led to the foundation of DSM's DBA with its permanent staff, own programs and outreach towards academic partners to staff and deliver the content.

On the other hand, the emerging and growing DSM DBA also led to the in-house management of most of DSM's programs, as opposed to populating external programs for individual participants. This concentration on its own Business Academy assured that the programs were tailored to the targeted 'change,' becoming part of an institutional learning, as opposed to a multitude of individual learning experiences, which are different for each participant due to being delivered at various institutions with different philosophies.

Since the DBA was very well networked into the top levels of DSM management, it was the DBA with its program managers who ensured that any academic programs were in line with the current strategic and cultural orientation of the company. DBA program managers took the initiative in bringing senior managers into programs and briefed those managers beforehand, acting as a critical link. Participating faculty were always amazed how DBA program managers were able to get easy access to DSM's top leadership. There was often a close personal link that went beyond the regular hierarchical rank. As a result, they strengthened the programs by constantly making faculty input more relevant to participants.

DSM Initiatives Seen as a Series of Waves

In order to fully appreciate the collaboration model adopted by DSM over the 25 years, it helps to see the various initiatives at DSM as a series of 'waves' coming in different ways at the business school community. Each of these waves could be

[3] Source: Pank van de Kooij, DSM Business Academy and Program Manager, exchange dated 26 March 2014.

seen as concentrated on a particular theme that was of crucial importance to DSM's development at a particular period of time. While the waves were initially pre-occupying the company for a limited period of time, work and efforts around those themes continued unabated, albeit at a different pace and required, most importantly, different approaches on the part of the business school community. The ability to keep up with DSM, and to adjust their input accordingly, was probably decisive in maintaining the contact with the company over the long haul. The following is a look, in some detail, at the four waves and an explanation of the difference in collaborations.

The **first wave** can be identified as DSM's search for a higher level of industrial marketing capability. In this phase of the company's development, DSM relied primarily on its academic partners, largely IMD, in formulating and shaping the content of what leading edge industrial marketing was and how a market orientation could be achieved. The IMD faculty team in charge of IMPACT was driving content, curriculum and emphasis based upon its own experience gained from other firms. DSM's contribution was the realization that the firm needed a higher level of marketing professionalism but DSM did not come to the table with a clear idea about how this was to be achieved. This type of collaboration, where the business school community can contribute its full expertise and be fully accepted by the company, is the most comfortable for faculty. The faculty was seen as the fountain of knowledge and the company accepted that their participants had much to learn.

This first wave was the most intensive during the first 3 years of collaboration. Once it was superseded by the attention of the second wave, the effort to enhance marketing capabilities continued but was relegated to lower staff levels and no longer involved the senior executive ranks. Eventually, DSM created the position of the Chief Marketing Officer (CMO) who, with his own organization, incorporated best practice around the company and assumed much of the role previously assigned to business school faculty. When marketing programs were taught, rarely did business school faculty act alone and the programs moved quickly into action learning mode with DSM specialists working in the role of best practice disseminators and even in a consulting mode as problem solvers.

The **second wave** was the BSD process that came out of the IMD IMPACT seminar, the core of the first wave. In the strategy wave, business school concepts were teamed up with a desire to co-create a DSM-specific strategy finding process at the business unit (BU) level. Since many of these processes had to be created for DSM, the role of the business schools was to collaborate on an equal footing with DSM and the organizational units entrusted with the strategy processes, such as DSM's CPL unit. There was collaboration and co-creation in pilot programs for the BSDs. Faculty were engaged in helping obtain the endorsement of top management and support for these new ideas and, finally, were entrusted with teaching large numbers of executives tools and concepts required for the roll-out—the focus of the Strategic Management Course (SMC) seminars.

In this second wave, business school faculty members were still expected to contribute heavily to build challenging programs and courses. But DSM drove the agenda and the faculty had to find the most effective ways to bring the required concepts to life. It would not have been useful or productive if the faculty had continued to teach its own view of DSM strategy. Instead, the faculty had to enhance the strategic mindsets of many company executives so that they could effectively participate in this demanding way of creating and communicating DSM business strategies. It was expected of the faculty to find challenging and engaging ways to teach the concepts, to teach the program in the context of DSM realities and to create teaching materials based upon DSM's business realities. Clearly, the faculty role in the second wave differed from the role in the first wave.

As the BSD process gained acceptance within the company, and as more and more of these elements were becoming part of DSM's DNA, efforts to continue to expose new hires to this particular way of creating strategy were required. The seminar participants included increasingly younger executives, or executives who joined DSM either as outside hires or through acquisitions. It is actually surprising that none of the new acquisitions, however large and important, succeeded in ever supplanting the DSM strategy processes and that the newly joined companies quickly absorbed the DSM strategy way. Teaching successive strategy programs by the same faculty team engaged in the co-creation of the process was certainly an important element in keeping the faith. The faculty role moved from teaching senior executives on strategy to teaching younger executives in acquiring a strategic mindset, allowing them follow the design and vision of DSM leaders. Efforts in this direction continue to this day, despite the fact that new initiatives were created afterwards.

The **third wave** can be seen as the effort to change the behavior and attitudes of DSM executives and staff first identified under 'Mobilizing Teams' and later summarized as DSM's 'Change Agenda,' described earlier. DSM aspired to change its leadership and management style and the behavior of senior executives from a rather top-down style to a more participative, open, inclusive style of leadership that was also responsive to society's emerging themes regarding the roles women play in management, and sustainability. This wave, gaining strength from the late 1990s onwards, was first nurtured in a seminar series named Mobilizing Teams (MT). When there was sufficient support, and agreement among DSM's leaders to fully support these new leadership styles, DSM took steps to actually shape and create a particular DSM response. Once this response became clearer when Feike Sijbesma took the helm in 2007, specific programs were used to introduce large numbers of junior and senior executives to the changed vision, entitled 'DSM Change Agenda.' While initially the teaching faculty was allowed to follow their own, generally accepted, ideas as to what a 'ideal' leadership style might be, DSM eventually asserted itself; the company managed this style conversation internally until ideas emerged and were clarified and again enlisted business school faculty to build programs that assisted individual managers to migrate to this new style.

Initially, large numbers of management and supervisory staff were exposed in various workshops and seminars to these new ideas. Over time, as the concepts of leadership became better defined, DSM decided to combine this third wave with the second wave into its own form of management and leadership teaching programs. Some faculty members believed that the third wave reinforced the dialogue requirements of the BSD process and that the new emerging management style also contributed to the lasting success of the second wave, the BSD strategy process.

At the time this manuscript was being completed, significant efforts were under way to expose future managerial talent worldwide to these ideas that saw their expression in many seminars. The faculty leading these seminars was challenged to create learning experiences that would allow participants to explore the new leadership style in conjunction with learning about the DSM way of looking at the strategy-making process as a whole. DSM and its senior managers who also participated regularly in these programs drove the agenda. The faculty was challenged to find engaging approaches and exercises to make participants understand what these concepts and ideas were. Faculty interaction with the change agenda was focused on exchanges with senior managers. Faculty members were constantly challenged to find new, and more effective ways, to make participants 'see it.' This collaboration was experienced as highly creative and led to the constant rejuvenation of materials and teaching methods.

Could there still be anything new and different in the **fourth wave**, devoted largely to innovation? The initiators of this push for innovation were senior DSM executives who saw the need to become more effective at innovating. As we have seen in previous chapters, an entirely new process of innovation management was created that was again home grown at DSM. The company surveyed many other efforts at innovation management. In around 2005, DSM articulated some very aggressive goals for its innovation drive. The organizational structures, and the governance system, for this drive were created internally and were based upon a thorough understanding of what worked elsewhere. The business school community was taking the role of the disseminator and teacher of cutting edge processes, such that more executives at all levels within DSM could understand the innovation drive and that a larger number of executives could actively participate and contribute. The campus and infrastructure of collaborating business schools, such as IMD's, were the places where DSM's innovation community would meet regularly and where new ideas were discussed further. With many of the sessions led by DSM executives, one might say that DSM borrowed the infrastructure and the pedagogy of business schools and applied them directly to its innovation process. Thus, the business school community's role in this fourth wave was smaller than it had been in the earlier waves. This could only happen because DSM had learned the 'teaching of ideas' and began to use the business schools community's tools independently and ever more effectively on its own.

There was a particular sequencing pattern of the waves that was unique and different from what faculty have experienced at other companies. DSM did not follow the pattern of a singular initiative and then stop. Nor was it more than an occasional wave. The waves included a continued effort after the initial shock delivery. The continuation and maintenance of the initial shock wave meant that DSM avoided practicing what at so many other companies can be observed as "flavor of the month" activity where one initiative follows another, then is easily and quickly forgotten. DSM also avoided the close sequencing of initiatives thereby endangering the completion of old ones through a premature launch of the next wave. DSM practiced what can be described as launching cumulative waves whereby each earlier wave was maintained over a long period of time and beyond the launch of sequential waves, who again where maintained and institutionalized. This cumulative wave effect led to an amplification of the forward momentum helping strategic transformation and change.

It struck observers as amazing to see how, over a period of 25 years, DSM had collaborated with and enlisted the business school community, built an ability to absorb many of the core skills of business schools and increasingly make them part of the next waves. Not only as an organization had DSM been able to learn from this collaboration, it had, to a large extent, learned to teach itself. Maybe there was not only a 'learning organization' emerging but also a 'learning and teaching' organization developing. In addition to the four phases described above, DSM had assumed an ever larger portion of the 'wave content' and 'wave delivery,' while at the same time carefully managing and enlisting the business schools to focus on their ultimate territory of teaching pedagogy for emerging executive talent; so that the top management's agenda and strategic vision could be understood and that skills to execute the agenda and vision were spread widely across the organization, both in terms of management hierarchy and levels, as well as in emerging geographies where DSM moved. Were DSM to engage some day into the next, fifth wave, for whatever its mission and agenda, the company is more likely to continue on the path begun by the fourth wave, rather than return to the mode of the first wave.

Maintaining long institutional relationships on the part of the participating business schools required either fielding successive faculty members able to pick up the ball, not only for the successive waves, but also to shift gears during those waves as each was continued over the long haul. When a company, such as DSM, preferred to work with the same delivery faculty team for an extensive period, it challenged the teaching teams to be adept at shifting gears, moving the contribution from design and driving ideas towards an emphasis on pedagogy and teaching. The benefit of engaging over longer periods did not only come from getting to know the company well. Rather, and more importantly, it came from understanding the context of the client's business. When a company such as DSM changed its business portfolio in substantial ways, the academic institution partners were constantly challenged to deal with increasing complexities stemming from learning new businesses, segments, nationalities and geographies, as well as industry realities so that underlying core teaching concepts and materials illustrated and reflected the changed strategic realities. As one faculty member observed, it seemed that with the announcement of each new CSD, a good part of the teaching material became obsolete as some businesses were spun off.

The rewards for collaborating with DSM for participating faculty and business schools were substantial because it exposed faculty talent to ever-changing circumstances, enriching their skill set and giving access to multiple learning laboratories that could have enormous potential beyond one single client company. Engagements for DSM became great training grounds for many faculty members who acquired skills that could be applied to other executive programs.

Managing successive waves conjures up comparisons to standing on a beach and running in and out with the incoming waves, always trying not to be swamped. When you stand at the beach and keep an eye on the incoming waves, only focusing on the most immediate wave, it is surely going to be a surprise when the second or third wave arrives. One has to watch out for the successive and emerging waves and demonstrate that one can master them, time and time again. That will enhance business schools and their valuable partnerships to companies over time.

Impact of DSM 'Waves' on Participating Academic Institutions

The close cooperation with DSM has also left its imprint on the academic institutions. Both IMD, and its forerunner IMEDE, as well as Babson College have benefited from the collaboration. In this section, the focus will be on those two business schools, leaving out others with whom DSM has had close contact over the years.[4] First, the common impact will be explored, before reviewing the differences.

Both IMEME/IMD and Babson had, through participating faculty, gained experience in delivering strategic programs with transformational impact. Both schools, to the extent that these were institutional programs, had also gained financially from the association with DSM. Both of their faculty have also benefited from the partnership through direct contact with executives and teaching at DSM. What was different, however, was the extent to which these two business schools got involved. The difference is largely a result of the various institutional policies governing faculty involvement in outside programs, for example those done on a private consulting basis.

The creation of the DSM DBA was an important event that had consequences for the collaborating business schools. Organizationally, the DBA was part of the Human Resources (HR) function and included a CLO and several program managers. Once DBA became established, it was another step in the direction of organizing course and programs internally, although with substantial recourse and support from outside faculty and collaborating business schools, such as Babson and IMD. Commented Menno de Vries, then Manager for Corporate Development and Training, who had retired prior to the creation of DBA:

> DSM was not interested in standardized turn-key courses developed by outside suppliers or business schools. Instead, we wanted to have tailor-made programs and co-development. Most universities or business schools, we contacted were not interested in this. IMD and Babson were exceptions to this prevailing attitude. We at DSM preferred to work with groups of professors, not business schools, and faculty hand-picked by us. But in order for us to do this, we had to be working in the field with business schools for a period of time to learn about and locate talented faculty. We could not have started this effort from scratch.[5]

[4] Erasmus School of Management in Rotterdam also had long-term programs with DSM.

[5] Interview with Menno de Vries, Manager Corporate Development and Training (retired 1995), DSM, and responsible for the administration of the IMPACT seminar series, held by Hein Schreuder and Jean-Pierre Jeannet, in Genk on 30 January 2013.

The creation of DSM's DBA in 2003, although helpful as a single organizing point for faculty and program development, still caused regular friction with established policies of collaborating business schools.[6] In the sections below those will be described, with a subsequent comment about business academies, a commonly found phenomenon in the world of executive development. Business schools want to provide programs and sell turnkey delivery, something business academies often shy away from.

Impact on IMD

When IMPACT was delivered at IMEDE, and later IMD, the faculty team involved consisted of IMD-based faculty, either permanent faculty such as Collins, or visiting faculty, such as Jeannet and D'Cruz. Any learning on the part of the faculty members became part of IMD institutional learning and could be leveraged into other programs. However, when DSM decided to bring the IMPACT program in-house, and to style it into a separate SMC and Advanced Industrial Marketing program (AIM), as well as a third program on Managing Teams (MT), it became more difficult for IMD to harness the learning for its own internal purposes.

A break occurred after the first six IMPACT programs and was played out through a series of communications between DSM (the HR Department) and IMD. Much of the reason for the break had to do with finances and IMD's faculty engagement rules in existence at the time. After DSM had completed its first six programs, of 2 weeks each, the continuation of the project lay in the hands of the Corporate Management Training function at DSM, with Menno de Vries in the lead. De Vries had managed the DSM side of the IMPACT program administration. The financing for those programs originated from a separate budget as it was considered a 'Special Project.'[7] In anticipation of bringing the IMPACT/SMC program in-house, de Vries had negotiated with IMD that, (a) DSM could do so, and (b) could continue to use Jeannet as faculty director, but DSM would "not invite too many other IMD faculty members for this course."[8] Consequently, from that time on SMC programs were staffed without permanent full-time faculty members,

[6] DSM's Business Academy (DBA) came into existence on 1 July 2003 through the combination of the Corporate Training Department in Heerlen with the Dutch Training Department (MO&T) and was initially headed by Harm Bakker, who succeeded Christiane Thielens. Up to that point, the faculty teams from IMD and Babson primarily had contact with the Corporate Training Department whose first head was Menno de Vries. Source: email exchange with Pank van de Kooij, dated 19 February 2014.

[7] At the time, IMEDE/IMD charged CHF 125,000 per week, or CHF 250,000 for each program.

[8] Agreement made between DSM (Menno de Vries) and IMD (President Juan Rada) in Rotterdam on 10 April 1991.

for example faculty who had previously been at IMD on leave and had since returned to their home institution, or were from other schools.[9]

The specific formulation of the IMD faculty engagement policy was intended to protect the emerging IMD in-company program business from being poached by its own faculty. For several years, the policy was articulated as 'a program of more than 3 days and involving two or more IMD faculty is considered an institutional program.' At the same time, programs for up to 3 days and involving no more than two IMD faculty members would be delivered as private consulting by the faculty. The policy originated from different market prices for institutional programs versus faculty consulting rates that essentially made company's in-house programs about half the cost of programs run at IMD.[10] Since DSM had begun to offer other programs in-house, this new SMC program was compared internally and had to fit into the existing price structure of other DSM internal programs.

The internal debate at IMD on what to do with DSM programs was to continue for years. Initially, the policy was applied with more flexibility and IMD allowed, on a grandfather clause basis, for faculty to continue their relationship with DSM. When the IMD Presidency changed (to Peter Lorange) in the early 1990s, the policy was more stringently applied. Again, old programs were continuing on previous arrangements (AIM); but, when in 2007 both Strategy and Leadership programs were merged into the MLP-3, the debate arose anew as the grandfather clause could not be applied. As Jeannet was uncomfortable delivering 2-week programs on a consulting basis and the IMD pricing level was beyond what DSM was prepared to pay, the MLP-3 program was moved first to University of St. Gallen and then to Babson College, where different price levels existed due to the then existing competition in the US. So, it happened that since 2007 the MLP-3 program became a Babson College institutional program delivered with Babson faculty.[11]

[9] John Murray (Trinity Dublin) and Joe D'Cruz (Toronto University) were teaching as visitors at IMD during the IMPACT program and thus, were not covered by the IMD policy. Later on, James Henderson (Babson) and Dan Muzyka (INSEAD, previously from Babson) were not part of the IMD policy. When Henderson later joined IMD on a full-time basis, he was no longer able to participate; but, when SMC was terminated and continued under MLP-3 Jeannet was allowed to teach all of the strategy sessions.

[10] IMD was charging about CHF 30,000 per delivery day at its Campus in Lausanne-Ouchy. Faculty consulting rates at that time averaged about CHF 5,000 per day, or CHF 10,000 for two faculty members which was the common staffing model for executive programs. Additional costs had to be considered as well. IMD offered an all-inclusive price for a day-package, including venue, classroom, group meeting rooms, lunch and coffee breaks (but did not include hotel charges). For in-house programs, DSM had to cover all of the inclusive items that were part of the IMD package and the extras, such as hotel charges. Hotel stays in Holland, however, were cheaper than in Switzerland and with mostly Dutch participants, travel costs were minimized. Only faculty travel costs had to be covered.

[11] When DSM assigned the program to the University of St. Gallen (Switzerland), Jeannet was the only faculty member held over from previous programs to participate.

A similar development occurred when the marketing program (AIM) commenced in 1994. Again, DSM was eager to work with proven faculty members with IMPACT program background. But for the 2-week program, DSM refused to pay IMD-level prices and the program moved to Babson College. Although Jeannet was also part of the IMD faculty on a reduced load basis, the program was held once a year during the Babson semester when he was teaching there anyway. However, due to the connection with IMD, one faculty member from the institution was selected to teach first on an institutional basis and later on a private consulting basis. This continued until the end of the AIM Marketing program series when moving to BMP-type shorter programs.[12]

Despite the many discussions about the role of IMD faculty for private DSM programs, there continued to be excellent relationships on many levels. Between 1989 and 2013, some 780 DSM participants participated in IMD programs. Of those, about 200, or more than 25 %, attended public programs. This showed that despite the move towards internal programs run by DSM's own Business Academy, there remained a substantial activity in terms of attending IMD programs.[13]

The numerous contacts with faculty were taken care of by members of the DBA who frequently visited the IMD campus. Whenever DSM had a new initiative, IMD was among the schools invited to contribute or compete for programs. This opened new possibilities for cooperation, such as in the innovation area.[14] Furthermore, Feike Sijbesma, DSM CEO, joined the IMD Foundation Board and other senior executives visited IMD as part of various programs. Stefan Dobowski, member of DSM Executive Board, is a graduate of IMD's Executive MBA program.

Impact on Babson College

Babson became institutionally involved with DSM in 1994 with the start of the Advanced Industrial Marketing (AIM) program. Prior to that time, there had been individual faculty contacts. Since Jeannet was both a member of the IMD and the Babson faculty, most of his earlier association with DSM tended to be perceived as IMD-originated. The marketing related programs, of which Babson delivered about 30 during the period 1994–2013, were held at DSM sites or locations outside the US or at Babson. Of this seminar activity, totaling about 45 weeks, only a few, such as the Global Account Management programs (GAM), were held on the Babson Campus. By 2014, Marketing-type programs had ceased to be offered through

[12] From 1994 to 2009, Professor Dominique Turpin from IMD participated in the Marketing programs under the Babson umbrella. At first, transfers were made from Babson to IMD for the relevant time. Later on, IMD agreed that Turpin could do this on a private consulting basis. When Turpin himself assumed the presidency of IMD, his involvement was discontinued.

[13] IMD internal statistics on DSM participants, IMD sources, for the period of 1989–2013.

[14] Innovation programs delivered by IMD faculty for DSM were led by Professor Bill Fisher.

Babson; due mostly to DSM-internal issues since, increasingly, marketing was taught by the DSM Marketing Office.

Since 2007, Babson had the institutional lead for the SMC sequels, such as the Advanced Management Program (AMP) and Management and Leadership (MLP-3). After DSM turned to Babson for delivery of these 2-week programs (see Chap. 10)—some 11 programs had been held and the frequency was three to four cycles of 2 weeks each. By end of 2013, through its School of Executive Education, Babson had delivered 22 weeks of MLP-3 programming, mostly in Europe and Asia. More recently, due to DSM's increasing business footprint in the US as the result of a number of acquisitions, MLP-3 program cycles have also been offered on the Babson campus.[15] In total, Babson Executive Education had delivered almost 70 program weeks of education, over the 20 years, representing the institution's longest lasting executive education client relationship.

Babson Executive Education profited from these institutional programs on several levels. First, there was the business impact of the programs, representing a steady business for the organization.[16] Important was the exposure of its faculty to many of the DSM programs, as well as new ideas and concepts. For a long period of time, the rules of engagement for Babson faculty differed from those at IMD and, although more prescribed now than previously, still differ in some key aspects.

For many years, Babson had no formal policy against in-house competition of faculty with its own programs. Potentially, however, the same issues existed at Babson as at IMD, with faculty who could become cheaper providers and compete for business that otherwise would flow into the school. More recently, the policies have changed, and faculty members engaged in programs were requested to sign an agreement that they would not privately engage in any business that had been brought to them by the school. Whereas IMD basically made much of the business associations (such as institutional corporate supporters), automatically off-limits and subject to approval, initially Babson only restricted competition regarding existing programs. More recently, the direction has moved into blanket prohibition for work with client companies, which are customers of the school. Since the DSM program opportunities were always brought to Babson, institutional business conflicts have been rare in this relationship.

Comparing the institutional impact at IMD versus Babson, one cannot avoid pointing out that in the earlier part of this long-term relationship, such as the first

[15] Babson College had its own Center for Executive Education located on the Babson College Campus in Wellesley, Mass., some ten miles outside Boston. It was an integrated facility combining classrooms, meeting rooms, dining facilities and bedrooms under one roof.

[16] At Babson, the Babson School of Executive Education (BSEE) was a separate unit under its own Dean. The focus of the school was on custom programs for companies, rather than open-enrollment programs. BSEE was located within the Babson Center for Executive Education (BCEE). BSEE rented space as needed from BCEE but other clients could also rent space there and run their own programs. About one-third of the capacity used at BCEE was originated from Babson's BSEE. As was the case for DSM, Babson also runs many programs off-campus or overseas.

10 years, the impact felt at IMD was greater—there were both institutional programs and a large cadre of faculty who had been involved with DSM. As the executive development program for both public and custom programs grew at IMD to a size ten times the volume at Babson, the relative impact in the second half of the relationship was much heftier for Babson.

Lessons for Academic and Business Institutions Alike

Having explored the impact that both DSM and business schools experienced, here is an opportunity to review and pass on some lessons learned. Many companies would like to access the long-term support from premier academic institutions that DSM has achieved. Conversely, many academic institutions, and particularly business schools, vie for long-term relationships with interesting clients such as DSM. What does it take to shape such a relationship? This is an important question, which is addressed in the next two sections. First, the business perspective will be covered and second, the academic perspective. Again, these are only the conclusions of the authors, albeit supported by interviews held with the various stakeholders and participants alike. For both types of institutions, this theme has been approached from the point of view, 'What would you have to undertake to make such a relationship work?'

Lessons for Businesses Interested in Long Lasting Relationships with Business Schools

The case of the long-term collaboration between DSM and its academic partners offers some suggestions for other companies that may want to build up such relationships. The authors believe it is necessary to put the following key ingredients in place:

- Clear articulation of dissatisfaction with existing management practices
- An indication of the desired direction of change
- Creating the necessary conditions for successful implementation
- Partner selection
- Using the learning opportunity
- Continuity and consistency

The following is a review of these factors, one-by-one, drawing upon the DSM case to make the general point more specific.

Clear Articulation of Dissatisfaction with Existing Management Practices

Collaboration with academic institutions can, of course, be sought for its own sake; for example, to keep up with available knowledge or to 'outsource' continuous education. However, the chances of a fruitful cooperation are greatly enhanced if the company is able to 'clearly articulate' its reasons for seeking the cooperation. Moreover, the more these reasons are rooted in dissatisfaction with existing management practices within the company, the better the cooperation can be tailored toward a learning cycle of improvement. Each company faces its own situation and is confronted with different challenges. As a result, each company will need to make its 'case' differently. DSM experience suggests, however, that there is a preferred sequence of questions to ask when addressing the need for change. As Feike Sijbesma explains: "You ask four questions: Why? What? Who? and, eventually, How?; in that sequence. Some companies think this through in a number of 'away sessions.' With us, it takes about 9 months because you want to keep a large organization keenly aware in which direction they are heading."[17]

Originally, DSM approached IMD because of a clear dissatisfaction with the state of industrial marketing knowledge within the company (see Chaps. 3 and 4):

WHY? The company recognized that it had, at the time, a predominant 'technology and production orientation.' Due to both the shifting industry context (for example, the dissolution of joint sales offices) and its own shift in product portfolio, DSM became aware that this was an insufficient basis from which to compete in the future—it would have to move from Selling to Marketing its products.

WHAT? Originally, DSM framed its dissatisfaction as the need to increase marketing capabilities in the company. In the discussions with IMD's Jeannet, it became clear that this perspective was too narrow. The 'what' question was reframed to 'achieving a market-orientation throughout the company.'

WHO? The who question pertained to partner choice (IMD) but at least as important was who should be involved from DSM side, in the effort to achieve market orientation. Originally, the DSM intent was to focus on the marketing professionals (only). Concomitant with the broadened perspective to 'market orientation,' the target group was enlarged to include the whole group of DSM executives.

HOW? The IMPACT program was the ultimate answer to the 'how' question.

Please note the profound effect that the shift in the answers to the first three questions had on the program's design philosophy. Without such clear answers, the program would probably have taken the shape of a 'run-of-the-mill' Industrial Marketing course. As Feike Sijbesma elucidates: "You have to pause after the first three questions. If you go too fast to the 'how,' you lose track. That is a real

---

[17] "Feike Sijbesma: Dilemma's verzoenen is niet altijd eerlijk," *MT Management Team*, 9 September 2011, see: http://www.mt.nl/157/44895/magazine/feike-sijbesma-dilemma-s-verzoenen-is-niet-altijd-eerlijk.html. While the last part of the quote refers to the CSD process, this approach to change has been adopted quite generally at DSM. See also: Joseph Jaworski. *Synchronicity*. San Francisco: Berrett Koehler, 1996.

pitfall. You have to recognize how far you have come without yet answering the 'how exactly' question."

Let us further illustrate the latter point with the example of the development of Business Strategy Dialogues (BSDs). This also started with a clearly articulated dissatisfaction. In this case, the perspective shifted profoundly as the company went through the four questions (see Chap. 5):

WHY? Originally, McKinsey pointed toward the need for 'measuring performance and contracting.' However, in the subsequent discussions it was recognized that performance should be the outcome of strategy and that DSM lacked thorough strategy processes. The Strategic Multi-year Planning (SMP) process had, over time, become a routinized 'numbers exercise.' It no longer provided sharp business or corporate strategies.

WHAT? From the original emphasis on performance measurement, the focus shifted to the development of sound business strategies. DSM wanted the issues and dilemmas in its business strategies to be explicitly addressed in a wider discussion than with only top management. Finally, based on clear business strategies, it wanted a link between strategy and performance.

WHO? From the answers to the first two questions, it is clear that the initial focus would have to be on the businesses. Corporate strategy could only be constructed when the building blocks of business strategies were sufficiently solid. Within the businesses a wider participation than with only the top management team was encouraged.

HOW? The Business Strategy Dialogue (BSD) process was the eventual result. Instead of 'shareholder value,' as propagated by McKinsey, DSM adopted Key Performance Indicators (KPIs) based on the Key Success Factors (KSFs) of the business strategy as the tools for performance measurement.

Note that again the explicit reflection on the first three questions led to a profoundly different outcome than originally proposed by McKinsey. If DSM had unquestioningly adopted the McKinsey proposal for performance measurement, it would have implemented a 'shareholder value' approach. This illustrates Feike Sijbesma's point above—that it is a real pitfall to go to the how question too quickly. Taking your time to explicitly address the why, what and who of a perceived need to change, often leads to a change of perspective that has a large impact on the quality of the outcome (the how). While 'shareholder value' may have been an appropriate prescription for other companies, for DSM with its long-term view and stakeholder orientation it would almost certainly have failed as a tool for performance measurement. DSM needed to formulate its own answers to the why, what and who questions in order to be able to articulate its dissatisfaction with existing management practices in its own terms. On the basis of this formulation, it could work together with Jeannet at IMD to co-develop the BSD process upon which performance measurement was based.

An Indication of the Desired Direction of Change

As the discussion above demonstrated, quite a lot of 'learning' can already take place during the phase of a company's articulation of its dissatisfaction with existing management practices. In the course of this process the original formulation of its dissatisfaction can become reframed. It is important that the company takes the time to specify its dissatisfaction as clearly as possible, answering the why, what and who questions before arriving at the how. This often requires an intense dialogue within the company, perhaps complemented by external parties acting as sparring partners (like IMD did for DSM's Marketing initiative). This process also allows the company to outline the contribution it seeks from its academic partner more clearly. The second element that the company needs to clearly convey to its academic partner is an indication of the desired direction of change.

Now, it may sound rather vague to only give 'an indication of the desired direction of change' to your academic partner. Why not give a detailed and complete description of the required outcome? Our answer would be twofold. First, it is often just impossible to make a blueprint of the required outcome at the outset of the change process. Usually, there will still be differences of opinion within the company about what that outcome should look like. Moreover, it may take a process of 'trial and error' to arrive at a solution that is optimal. The blueprint approach may lead the company to jump to a premature conclusion. A second, and even more important reason, to avoid the blueprint approach is that it deprives the partners of a learning opportunity. It is preferable to see the articulated dissatisfaction with existing management practices as the starting point of a learning cycle of improvement. By agreeing to a direction of change the company and its academic partner can shape their relationship as a 'co-creation' process. In a co-creation process both partners bring their perspectives and expertise to bear in order to jointly shape the outcome. Hence, it presents a further opportunity to 'learn,' as well as to do so from each other. When DSM set out to replace its dysfunctional SMP process by BSDs, it was unable at the outset to completely specify what the BSDs would look like. The company was, however, able to formulate a number of 'desirables:' characteristics of preferable outcomes. These include the following:

- *Line management activity*. The SMP process, over time, had become primarily a staff activity. Ownership of the business strategy process should return to where it belongs—business top management.
- *Dialogue*. DSM wanted to encourage wider participation in the process than only top management. A dialogue approach was deemed very suitable for this purpose.
- *Focus on issues and dilemmas*. The SMP process tended to produce polished stories with a hockey-stick type of performance projections. The BSD should focus on the real strategic issues and dilemmas that every business faces.
- *Strategic options*. In order to counter the tendency of management to produce only its own preferred strategic recommendation as the 'one way to Rome,' the BSD process should encourage thinking in strategic options.

- *Performance measurement*. In the end, the BSD should enable DSM to construct a system of performance measurement and management.

A list of desirable outcome characteristics, like the above, gives guidance to the design process without overly constraining it. Moreover, it allows both the company and its academic partner to contribute their own specific expertise and capabilities to achieving the optimal end result. The specific design of the BSD has indeed been a process of co-creation between partners, each with their own specific contributions (see Chaps. 5 and 6). Hence, the end result not only incorporated the best available academic knowledge but was also tailor-made to DSM's specific needs.

Creating the Necessary Conditions for Successful Implementation

In the previous chapter, the concept of a 'strategic learning cycle' was introduced. It was argued that any company aiming to make a significant strategic change should think through the organizational adaptations and system changes needed to enable effective implementation. It has to identify the potential blockages along the Strategy > Organization > Systems cycle and attempt to address these pro-actively. However, since perfect foresight is usually not obtainable, it should also be prepared to deal with unexpected blockages as they arise in execution. Lots of learning therefore takes place along the way. Following through on a strategic learning cycle of Strategy > Organization > Systems allows the company to experience whether a strategic objective is achievable, yes or no, when all conditions for successful implementation are met.

It's important to look at the setting up of a long-term relationship between a company and its academic partner(s) in the perspective of an important strategic objective to be achieved. What are some of the *necessary conditions for implementation* that the company can anticipate? First of all, it will be paramount to obtain the backing of top management for the process. After sufficient discussion the entire Board should feel the need to make the new relationship work and should actively promote this objective. All too often, such projects are delegated to one Board member with the result that the company comes to view it as the 'pet project' of that particular member. This is a very effective way to undermine company-wide adoption. Schreuder acted as an advisor to a company wishing to install more rigorous strategic processes as a starting point for better business plans and projections. It had invested a significant amount of resources to get a new approach going with outside help. Responsibility was given to one particular Board member to supervise the rollout across the whole company. While this process was unfolding, his colleague, the CFO, sent out the usual letter requesting operational plans and budgets to the business units. No reference whatsoever was made in this letter to the ongoing project to improve the strategic process leading to such operational plans and budgets. The consequence was predictable: the organization came to see the project as part of the agenda of one Board member, not the entire Board. The seeds for failure of the project had been sown. It took a significant 'reset' by the whole Board (after retirement of the CFO) to get it started again.

One particular aspect of the required top management backing that is often overlooked is the required training of the top management itself. Let's take the example of the introduction of BSDs in DSM. With this approach, a lot of new concepts were introduced into the business strategy process. Concepts like strategic groups, KSFs and corresponding KPIs were hitherto unfamiliar within DSM and, hence, also at the top management level. Business teams and facilitators had been trained to understand these concepts and apply them in their own situations. When the first BSD pilots were scheduled for presentation to the Board there was a clear risk that the business teams and the Board would fail to 'connect' on these new concepts. It would have been devastating for the new BSD approach if a Board member would have said something like, "Well, that's all fine with these KSFs and KPIs but now just focus on your projected EBIT, please." As so often in the introduction of new approaches, the bottleneck would then have been at the top of the bottle. Fortunately, the Board recognized this danger and addressed it in two ways:

1. Inviting Jeannet and Schreuder to give a 'pressure cooker' introduction to the BSD before the first pilot project of ABS was presented.
2. Adopting the routine of a two-stage discussion of BSDs. One week before the presentation the Managing Board would discuss the BSD amongst themselves and come up with a joint list of most important questions. These would be sent to the business in order to prepare well and focus the discussion on the most salient issues.[18]

A second very important question to ask at the outset is how the company will manage the relationship with the academic partner. What part of the organization will be responsible? What will be the role of the Board itself? As documented in this book, the cooperation with IMD arose out of a 'Marketing initiative' within DSM. There was a functional group within DSM, the Branche Overleg Marketing (BOM), that felt responsible for the co-creation of the content of the IMPACT program with IMD. In addition, the Management Development department provided an important link to the business school community:

- Initially, the link with the business school partners was maintained by the Department of Corporate Management and Training. Its first head, Menno de Vries, played an instrumental role in the organization of the IMPACT seminar series with IMEDE/IMD. Since IMEDE was used to provide a complete turnkey service for seminar organization and supervision, there was no need for DSM to provide an on-site supervision for those programs. Once SMC, the follow-up program to IMPACT, was commenced, and in combination with the decision to bring it in-house, the organizational umbrella for an academic partner, such as

[18] In both meetings a staff member of Corporate Strategy & Acquisitions, as well as one from Corporate Finance & Economics, would usually be present.

IMD, did not exist anymore. DSM's Department of Corporate Management and Training assumed this role and provided for on-site administrative coverage throughout the programs. As the portfolio of programs expanded to include the marketing area (AIM) and team building, the numbers of programs to be supervised and organized, as well as accompanied on-site, expanded such that the staff had to be expanded as well. The initial organizational anchor point, the Branch Organization of Marketing (BOM), with its ever-changing membership, was only capable of providing content oversight but had no organizational staffing capabilities. Eventually, the expanded staff was transitioned into the DSM Business Academy where the contracting, participant recruiting, maintenance of relationship with academic partners and faculty teams, as well as further program development were combined. Within DBA the company accumulated a valuable store of knowledge and expertise that made its members and staff officers capable of engaging leading business schools on a partnership level.

- DSM's DBA was staffed with a number of senior program managers who had the credibility to engage DSM's top management in programs, provide access to the top for business school faculty and, due to their long-standing within DSM, who served as important links in this process. The fact that DSM's CEO, Feike Sijbesma, eventually joined the IMD Foundation Board was but one of the outcomes of this close relationship which elevated DSM activities to the top of the agenda of business school leaders. IMD's President, Dominique Turpin, and his predecessor, Peter Lorange, made it a point to meet at least once a year at the DSM head office, exchanging views and further deepening the relationships to a deep awareness of DSM's business issues. It contributed to the sense at DSM that the company was truly valued as a customer and that the customer was also listening and acting on what was exchanged. In this way, the DBA did not become a bottleneck to the relationship with business schools but, instead, a porous conduit or membrane that provided for a maximal two-way exchange.

As a third, and final, step of thinking through the Strategy > Organization > Systems cycle, the company should ask itself how the collaboration with its academic partner(s) will impact the existing management systems within the company? Such an impact is the primary purpose of the collaboration if dissatisfaction with existing management practices is driving the company to this partnership. By itself, however, this will not ensure that the desired change comes about. Too often, educational programs are experienced as 'one off events' with no impact on 'what to do on Monday morning.' Such an impact has to be designed into the programs and 'into the management practices of the company.' Even then, success is not guaranteed. The example of the original IMPACT course is a good one. Undoubtedly, the course had increased marketing capabilities and market orientation among DSM's executive ranks. The company had also required that marketing plans should incorporate the IMPACT approach and concepts going forward. Nevertheless, after some time (and considerable investments) DSM came to the conclusion that 'marketing planning had become a rain dance: filling out forms' (see Chap. 5). Something more was apparently needed than only requiring the new approach to be incorporated into the DSM marketing management systems. That 'something more,' was to ensure that the new system is a 'living system:' a system that is intensively used for *significant purposes* and produces *consequential outcomes*. The BSD process did become such a 'living system.' BSDs were not only adopted as the main vehicle for setting business strategies, incorporating the functional strategies but, more importantly, it became the vehicle for which to obtain Board approval of the most consequential decisions the business wanted to propose. No wonder there was intensive participation and interaction in the BSD process. While not all management systems in a company can aspire to such high levels of energy, the authors maintain that far too many fail to produce any enthusiasm at all. Too many management systems in companies are of a 'box ticking' nature, not serving significant purposes and/or not producing consequential outcomes. Such management systems drain energy. A 'living system' generates energy. In its collaboration with its academic partner(s), a company should strive to develop living systems of management practices.

Partner Selection

When it comes to *partnership strategy and partner selection*, a company will need to take a multi-year perspective. The selection of the academic partner to support the initiative will be critical. In particular, the focus should be on the institution's faculty. The faculty will need to be able to bridge academia and practice. That means, the faculty can be conceptually oriented but not theoretical—a big difference. There are quite large differences between academic institutions in this respect. At some universities there is a very strong emphasis on publications in academic journals for the whole faculty. Where this is the case, the faculty tends to become theoretically focused and rather specialized. At other institutions, differences between types of faculty are recognized or even encouraged. At such places particular faculty members may be stimulated to pursue a career that involves a substantial amount of executive education. And finally, there are institutions where executive education is such a large part of the 'raison d'être' that all faculty are expected to perform well in the interaction with practitioners. Such institutions, which include some of the premier business schools, also have a much larger customer focus, driving them toward the generation of knowledge that is not only academically interesting but also practically relevant. They want to have *impact* on their business customers. As Feike Sijbesma observed, "I have been affiliated with a number of academic institutions and I see clear differences. For instance, IMD has a pronounced customer orientation: its Dean visits DSM every now and then. This allows us to compare notes on developments in practice and in academia. It is no coincidence that IMD, compared with some other academic institutions that I know, has a more practice-driven research agenda."

As a first filter, companies seeking academic partners for long-term collaboration could ask themselves which type of institution fits their partnership needs best. It makes quite a difference whether well-defined functional expertise is sought, or the ability to work together across a wider range of topics. A second filter would apply to the faculty itself. The faculty of the chosen academic institution needs to be able to connect the company reality to the outside context, or industry conditions. This will require a thorough understanding of the industry context of the company and the emerging competitive challenges. Is the faculty familiar with leading-edge examples and also from outside the company's industry? Have they personally worked with such examples or not? Do faculty members have experience with co-creation of programs, or is their preference to teach 'off the shelf?' Are they oriented to 'hard knowledge,' 'soft skills,' or both? Finally, can the faculty bring to the table breadths across several business disciplines, such as Finance, Technology, Marketing or Organizational Behavior that will allow for cross-functional integration? As a well-known saying puts it, 'The world is not organized like universities are.' Significant business problems usually cannot be 'pigeon-holed' into one academic discipline. If long-term collaboration is the objective, it cannot be predicted which business problems will need to be addressed over time. This requires from the faculty that it can work together in novel, unfamiliar ways not required in their standard programs.

Increasingly, large companies need to look for academic partners with a multi-regional delivery capability, or even a global one if the company operates worldwide. Attention should be paid to the commitment of the faculty and administration to avoid situations that operate more like 'transit halls,' rather than destinations resulting from frequent faculty changes. On the other side, companies have to pay attention to particular needs of academic institutions. Companies need to accept the fact that academic institutions have longer term planning needs of 12–18 months. Once programs are set and planned, academic institutions have less flexibility than businesses and thus, need predictability in terms of keeping dates. And finally, it is advisable that firms allow the wider use of learning outside the specific partnership relationship, such as through the use of cases, presentations and other materials by academic partners in other programs or academic courses. Unless such material is very confidential, it is of mutual benefit to the business community that learning is allowed to spread. Companies are often too restrictive. At DSM, the initial position was that all material related to BSDs was 'company confidential.' Over time, the company came to realize that the ability to conduct BSDs well required many more skills than could be described in a case or a booklet. As Schreuder came to say, "the BSD brochure describes a bike. Reading it is not enough to enable you to ride a bike."

Finally, the third filter should be at the individual level. Whatever the type of institution and whatever the qualities of the faculty in general, there needs to be a specific 'click' between particular faculty members and those responsible for the collaboration at the business side. It is similar to long-term business collaborations with consultancies, law firms or investment banks. Whatever the general qualities of the partners are, at the heart of such collaborations you nearly always find a few people who 'make it work.' Therefore, it is important in the partner selection phase that these people are identified. Make the effort to really get to know one another well, thereby investing in the foundation of a relationship that can stand the test of time. When it came to selecting and working with IMD at first, and Babson later,

DSM adopted a number of these recommendations. Both IMD and Babson employ a large number of faculty members with business understanding and an ability to adapt to different industry settings. Their orientation is more conceptual than theoretical and fit well with the practical orientation of DSM managers. Both schools were able to deliver globally although at the outset of the relationships this was less important, but it grew in importance as DSM itself expanded its global footprint. The long-term nature of the relationship was underlined by the fact that both institutions collaborated over a period of 25 years. Although there were some changes among executives, such as several changes of CEO at DSM, different Presidents at IMD or at Babson, and several changes in the responsibility within DBA, there were also constants, such as in the persons of Jeannet and Schreuder, as well as a number of long-term involvements of particular faculty members and business representatives.

Using the Learning Opportunity

Collaboration with an academic institution provides learning opportunities for a company. As argued previously, 'learning cycles' are viewed as the motor of evolutionary change of companies (see Chaps. 11 and 13). Such learning cycles can be consciously planned and evaluated, while some may also occur spontaneously. A 'learning company' attempts to conduct as many consciously planned learning cycles as is feasible (and also stimulates spontaneous learning). Moreover, it consciously evaluates the outcomes of these learning cycles, distilling lessons from successes and failures alike. Incorporating these lessons in subsequent actions and new learning cycles drives 'purposeful evolution.' It is the organizational equivalent of DNA mutations in the natural world. From this perspective, when speaking of 'organizational DNA' it refers to the accumulated learning of an organization over time.

Setting up the collaboration with the academic institution as a co-creation process allows both partners to learn. The relationship is then not a one-way street on which 'knowledge' is transported from the academic institution to the company. Rather, it is a bridge that is constructed to connect two countries by two groups of engineers working together from both sides in a joint endeavor. It is important that the company states this intention clearly and follows up with the nomination of selected people that will commit themselves to shaping this learning opportunity and distilling the lessons from the joint learning cycles. It is our experience that it is useful to engage people from both the content aspect of the collaboration (such as, Marketing or Strategy) and from the relationship angle (usually HR or a more specialized function like a DBA officer). The former should concentrate on the content lessons to be learned, while the latter accumulate knowledge about fruitful ways to interact with the partner. DSM applied this approach from the very outset. Menno de Vries, the DSM Manager for Corporate Development and Training who was the relationship manager in the early stages of working with IMD, commented earlier in this chapter: "DSM was not interested in standardized turn-key courses developed by outside suppliers or business schools. Instead, we wanted to have tailor-made programs and co-development." More than other companies, DSM was always pushing to take programs a step further, based on the evaluations of previous program versions and on the newly emerging needs of the company as it developed over time.

There are three more points to be made. The first point refers to the attitude of a learning company like DSM: it has a clear preference to 'learn in its own way.' It does not want to take a 'ready-made piece of knowledge' for granted and apply it unquestioningly in its own context. Rather, it wants to examine it, experiment with it and modify it to make it fit better with the requirements of its own context and culture. There is a close parallel in this respect with the engineering mentality that DSM has always had—this has been described as a 'tinkering' culture, always aiming to improve existing processes. When DSM acquired technology from other companies, the continuous tinkering with it over time led to processes that were unrecognizable to the original licensors. Similarly, DSM has always shown a preference to modify concepts taken 'from outside' and adapt these to its own requirements and liking. In this way, a company develops its own shared language and approaches. The BSD language and approach is a clear case in point. It is company-specific and newcomers have to be educated to understand and apply it. Therefore, the academic partners supplying this education have to 'grow with the company' as it continues to develop its approach.

The second point is that by developing its own shared language and approach, like the BSD for business strategy, the company managed to significantly decrease the reliance on outside consultants for such purposes. During the 1980s there were various consultancies, which were heavily employed by DSM; each of which had their own concepts and methodologies. As a result, there was ample room for confusion and misunderstanding between managers 'educated' in different ways. In later years, DSM would still use consultants but only for very specific (content) questions, not for the supervision of a strategy development process. By educating the DSM managers to do this themselves, the company offered them an opportunity to grow and learn which would otherwise have been relegated to outside consultancies.

The third, and final, point is that this combination of attitudes of a learning company (learning in its own way, modifying knowledge to better fit its own context, educating people in a shared language and approach) leads to an outcome where the management systems of a company 'fit together' rather than being a patchwork of imported approaches. Once it was clear that the BSD had been adopted as the core process for strategy development at DSM, the other functions developed related tools and services to link in with the BSD process (see Chap. 7). In this way, much better functional integration was achieved than previously existed. Time and again, DSM adopted such an approach, whether it was to 'operational excellence,' its 'culture agenda,' or innovation. In all such cases, DSM has sought to develop an approach that would be consistent with its own identity.

Continuity and Consistency

One of the greatest enemies of any new approach, or process in corporate life, is the lack of *continuity and consistency*. At the individual level, job rotations reduce tenure in a single position. While job rotation has many benefits, one of the drawbacks can be that individuals do not last in their position long enough to experience a full learning cycle. As a consequence, learning at the individual level is hampered, while organizationally it is more difficult to distill the lessons learned and apply them in a next learning cycle. At the institutional level, there are marked differences between companies with respect to the effects of personnel changes. At some companies, the culture and the expectation is that the 'new broom sweeps clean.' As a result, significant policy changes result from new appointments. While this may be necessary at times, companies where this is the prevailing culture can be perceived as inconsistent and their behavior as zigzagging. At other companies, of which DSM is one, the approach is more evolutionary than revolutionary (see Chap. 15). Top leadership sees itself as 'stewards' of a company that is leading a life of its own. Their task is to make the necessary adaptations to company policies (in order to leave the company in better shape for their successors), but not to make radical changes per se. They realize that truly transformational changes may take more than one generation of leadership to achieve. As a result, there is more continuity and consistency in the company policies of such companies.

For academic institutions, companies with an evolutionary approach offer better opportunities to build truly long-term partnerships. Just like for the companies themselves, for the academic partner there also needs to be sufficient time to complete a full learning cycle and apply the lessons learned in new versions of the programs, if these run for a longer period of time. The experience of DSM shows that a company that wants to go down a path of transformation cannot only delegate participants to an executive development program and leave it at that. Rather, the company needs to bring the entire organization around the new approaches and coordinate the organizational change with the educational effort for best results and to stick with that over a long time. It is no coincidence that DSM adopted the motto 'Staying the Course' when adversity struck due to the financial crisis and economic downturn beginning in 2007. As explained in DSM's 2008 Annual Report: "These more difficult conditions are no reason for us to change the course we have charted for the coming years. Instead, we will tighten the rig to continue our journey against the wind. We are staying the course." The comparison with other firms having undertaken similar initiatives comes to mind. As a member of the faculty team of several other company's projects, Jeannet experienced major development efforts for firms such as ICI, Sulzer, Ares-Serono and Siemens. These firms engaged some of the same faculty teams and assigned similar teaching mandates. Early on, it was clear to the faculty that DSM had a rather unique approach to these educational initiatives. By deliberately pulling the learning through the organization, by incorporating the concepts quickly into internal processes and by constantly, deliberately, consistently and persistently applying them and mandating them at all levels, DSM reached a state where learning was not for 'them,' but for 'everyone.' In too many companies, learning gets assigned only to lower levels and upper levels of the organization exclude themselves from it. Under such circumstances, a company will not adopt any new concepts and incorporate them into its own organizational DNA.

Lessons for Academic Institutions Interested in Building Long-Term Relationships with Business

Parallel to our previous section on learning for business organizations, the same question should be posed to business schools and academic institutions: 'So you also would like to engage in such a long-term partnership with a company?' It is understood that the benefits can be substantial. First, there is the prestige that comes from landing such long-term contracts with prominent companies. Second, there are significant benefits for faculty development. And finally, there are substantial financial benefits for participating business schools. All of these reasons make it desirable to engage in such relationships. Reflecting on the necessary conditions for a business school is thus a relevant process.

The lessons described in this section are meant for business schools, or similar academic institutions, desiring to be selected for long-term relationships with major corporations. For an institution with a sole focus of academically accepted research, what is said here will not apply. The authors do not consider these recommendations relevant for all business schools except for those who aspire to have such long-term collaborations. The lessons for business schools have impact on stated missions and the partnership criteria, as well as organization and governance. The focus of this section is on institutions; the individual faculty issues will be dealt with later.

Most academic institutions, and even most business schools, have an 'academic' mission. The problem lies in the specificity of what is understood as 'academic.' Engaging in longer-term collaborations, such as the one described with DSM, challenges business schools to have a natural inclination to appreciate the applicability of business school concepts to the *practical side of business* (plus a natural curiosity to obtain inspiration and input from developments in practice; it is a two-way street.). This emphasis on practical impact for business is of particular importance for issue-oriented in-company programs. When it comes to business school programs chosen for personal growth, there is greater tolerance for delivery that is academic or degree-oriented.

There are a number of indicators to look at if a school has, in fact, this understanding for practical business. The types of publications, research undertaken and teaching material development can give a hint about the orientation of a business school. While one can always find individual faculty members developing away from narrowly stated missions on research, a significant faculty pool that can participate in such programs and thus attract company contacts will hardly occur if the mission of the school is not officially stated to recognize and desire the direct business impact.

For business schools, there are also organizational implications. A dedicated group of professionals, both faculty and administrators, focused on executive education is a prerequisite for success with long-term relationships. This leadership group needs to engage in deliberate faculty recruiting with executive education skills. To make this work, an effort has to be made to decouple rewards and compensation for executive education from promotion tracks for regular academic programs.

Compensation for executive education teaching is a perennial issue. Of course, at institutions such as IMD, where faculty are paid a salary with executive education part of the load, discussion is easier. In other schools, and Babson is one of these, executive education compensation is extra. Despite that, there are many faculty members who would like to exchange an executive education load for regular academic teaching, causing conflicts with the staffing for regular academic programs. No matter what regime is followed, the corporate clients expect a high degree of flexibility and availability and are not always willing to have programs slotted in the off-degree program period of the year. Running programs during the year for 1 or 2 weeks at a time, often in overseas locations, is a real challenge for academic institutions that are not used to freeing up faculty for such roles. Frequently it is said that faculty can earn more when engaging directly with companies on a consulting basis. However, when an engagement is of a longer duration, absences from the home institution are not always easy to manage. When an entire faculty team is required, arranged payments through the executive education arm is often competitive; it also excuses absences since the benefit is clearly not only personal but also institutional. Regardless, without a flexible compensation and staffing policies, a business school will find it difficult to attract the needed faculty and provide the rewards to make them commit to programs and clients on a long-term basis.

On the support side, access to a dedicated facility designed for executive education learning will be needed. It can often be used to attract company clients. As part of such a dedicated facility, there are ample auditoria with horseshoe seating arrangements, full technology in the rooms and a large number of smaller discussion rooms available on a flexible basis. However, as has been observed at many leading institutions, clients often want programs delivered on their locations, raising the specter of underutilized facilities. A shift to distance-learning approaches is only noticeable for lower level courses. And finally, excellent administrative support staff ranging from program and teaching support to logistics are an absolute must to maintain long-term client relationships.

Just as companies need to carefully select their academic institutions, so must business schools be selective about their *partnership choices* to enhance a long-term program relationship. What then are indicators that a long-term relationship might evolve? Companies facing complex issues that are also relevant to other firms make for great learning laboratories of value to academic institutions and faculty alike. From the company management, it is important to see evidence of a long-term commitment to its strategy. Indications should be strong for active involvement in training and development, particularly on the part of senior management. It is even better if training and development is seen as playing a well-articulated role in the company strategy. The company management should be well informed about management development issues and willing to give the faculty access to discussions. When management has a conceptual and analytic orientation (but not theoretical), conversations with business schools are usually helped. And then there is the long-term orientation: there should be a clear culture of continuity, independent of the business cycle and changes of management. In the case of DSM, all of these criteria were not only present but extremely highly developed.

Lessons for Business School Faculty

Again, it is important to begin with the question, 'So you would like to become management development faculty?' and look at what it takes to grow into that role. First, there are the reasons, or motivations, to embark on such a course. As described in detail in earlier chapters, close cooperation with companies over the longer term can provide invaluable experiences and companies can turn into great learning laboratories that enrich teaching and research over an extended period of time. Regardless of the interest, an intrinsic motivation for engaging with business and its executives must be present. Beyond that, faculty should bring to this career step an executive education personality with the desire of not only 'teaching' content but also engaging actively in 'performing' it.

Mastering the client company's industry or business environment in strategic terms is often more important than just knowing the company and its activities. It is also a precondition to engage senior management and CEO's, not just middle managers or Human Resource managers. Companies highly value faculty members as partners who can think creatively beyond standard solutions, such as 'out of the box thinking' and yet remain grounded in the industry realities. Since most of the major management development programs involve faculty teams, the ability to play as part of a team is also highly regarded. Faculty members, often solitary in their work, do not always or easily make the transition to being a team member. Additionally, not all faculty members have a sense for the 'practical' details of business. Regardless of the practical aspects that will always be present, faculty need to work on developing intellectual capital that is their own and is of generalized interest to companies and managers in multiple industry settings.

How one develops an executive education competence is of interest to prospective faculty, as well as academic institutions that need to nurture their talent. Teaching in executive programs where the participants usually already have some experience in the topic under discussion differs from regular academic programs where the professor can assume to be the only one who knows. This requires a skill to move the teaching interaction to an interactive dialogue that can connect with the participants at their readiness level. Faculty need to get used to, and develop, an ability to listen to business issues before jumping at proposing 'solutions,' based on their favorite concepts or theories. This puts a premium on diagnosing business situations, which then can develop into executive program design competence. Due to the obvious financial rewards, many faculty members are eager to jump into the fray, few are willing to take the time to learn the trade. The role of the academic institution is to make sure that the talent pool is deep and that the conditions are right to develop younger faculty into this activity.

Once embarked upon, executive education faculty often need to invest the time to create company specific learning materials. Whether this takes the form of exercises or cases, the challenge is to make it count as sufficiently worthwhile academically. Faculty members build credibility with client firms through the creation of specific learning materials rather than employing off the shelf materials accessible to everyone. Of course, academic institutions play a role in this as well. Again, they must create the necessary pre-conditions, such as negotiating with client firms for sufficient resources to compensate faculty for their time involvement, in addition to helping them get clearance for the material to be used in regular academic programs and for faculty to obtain research credits. The creating of customized teaching materials is a skill that needs to be nurtured. It is important for faculty and academic institutions alike.

Life as an executive education faculty member has its own challenges that are quite different from those traditional academic challenges that arise when working in regular degree programs. The requirement to be responsive to client companies is of the utmost importance. The expected reliability on responding to inquiries, or the dependability of getting deliveries in on time, is often a hurdle for faculty members to make the transition. This does sound rather obvious but the response cycle of communications with client firms is very demanding. While the emergence of readily available electronic communication has been of great assistance, it should not be assumed that this has done away with the requirement to create and maintain a culture of response at the highest levels.

Why Could the DSM Relationship Endure for More than 25 Years?

In our fast-paced and ever-changing business world, it is hard to find relationships between businesses and academic institutions that endure 25 years or longer. Although the actions at both DSM, and IMD and Babson, have been described in detail, one still wonders what was the key ingredient that led to such an enduring relationship. Asking the effort's insiders to reflect on this might render a biased result. Nevertheless, it is worth a try.

On the surface, the reader might be tempted to write it all off to unusual personal circumstances, or chemistry, between a few individuals who have been involved throughout these years. But one needs to consider that around both Schreuder at DSM and Jeannet at IMD and Babson, key positions changed repeatedly. Two individuals, however strong and purposeful, could not have maintained these relationships against the will of their own internal organizations.

The wave-like character of the DSM initiatives, and how at all times DSM was in the driver's seat, was described earlier in this chapter. Clearly, keeping up the momentum with DSM required the participating schools to carefully interpret and act on the signals from the company. Those signals suggested different roles for schools for different initiatives, as well as shifting responsibilities within a given initiative over time.

The impetus for all of these DSM initiatives did not always come from the same office or department. In the beginning it was the BOM; then it was the corporate planning unit. Another time it was the Managing Board; later it was the Business Academy and the Innovation Center. Contacts with the academic partners were broadly based across the entire DSM organization, signaling a strong preference to support required changes with an educational or development initiative. This pervasive style of working most likely contributed to the sustained effort to rely, over and over again, on academic institutions to support something the company thought was important to accomplish.

This should not be interpreted that the academic partners were simply following orders and doing as they were told. DSM specified its requirements, articulated what it had to achieve, and led the academic partners; the company did not make its academic partners mouthpieces of its strategy or processes but instead used them to enlighten the underlying concepts so that its own cadres of executives could more easily find their way through the DSM concept tool boxes. There is also ample evidence to demonstrate that the faculty did influence the DSM projects or transformation approaches, and if there were reasons for criticism, the academic partners faculty were able to bring those to the attention of senior management. The ability to be a fully independent partner in the DSM transformation led to a higher level of interest and satisfaction, as well as contributing to the notion that the faculty would learn something in return that had application in other situations, for other programs, or in academic degree courses.

Elaine Eisenmann, Dean of Babson School for Executive Education, commented on the longevity of the Babson/DSM relationship which happens to be the longest-lasting client relationship for the school[19]:

> You need to ensure that there is a strong fit between the faculty delivery team and the client. The faculty need to be interested in the client and bring to this a consultative bend with good listening ability. When faculty teams get to really know a client they also know when to refresh the offering and not constantly get surprises. The faculty program leader needs to be able to shift gears as you cannot go there with the same material or role on a constant basis. Bench strength and access to a network of people will be needed to follow up as clients needs do change over time.

In the same vein, DSM did change gears on numerous occasions. The strong relationships with the main academic institutions meant that DSM tended to go back there first, even for new initiatives. In the case of IMD, the faculty pool was large enough that DSM, or the Business Academy, could connect with different talent directly. In the case of Babson, DSM primarily utilized Jeannet as a conduit to lead them to other faculty or to enlarge the team.

[19] Elaine Eisenmann, telephone interview with Jean-Pierre Jeannet at Babson, 29 October 2012.

A string of 25 years is already a remarkable enough collaboration to write this book. Will this relationship and collaboration between DSM and its key academic providers, IMD and Babson, continue? As the finishing touches are being made to this manuscript in 2014, there have been substantial changes in key positions at DSM, in the Managing Board, in Corporate Strategy and Acquisitions, in the Business Academy and through the changing portfolio in many businesses. On the academic side, the leadership in the core programs of the Business Academy has changed due to retirements. It can only be speculation as to what will happen next. However, as long as DSM maintains the penchant for supporting its strategic objectives and changes with educational initiatives, as well as investing in its people, it is likely that the relationships will endure beyond changes in key personnel. Over the long run, that will be the real test of this collaboration. Many of the key ingredients for success, as discussed in this chapter, remain in place.

The Seven Traits of a Successful Company 15

Introduction

We have often been asked: "Why has DSM been successful in transforming itself, where so many others have failed? What is the secret of its success?" Let's be clear: there is no one answer to this question. First of all, because there is no single factor, let alone a 'secret,' that would explain the developments covered in this book. A whole host of various factors come into play during each time period. And as we have made clear, 'luck' has played a part in it as well. Second, different observers would point to different factors. As the saying goes: "Where you stand depends on where you sit."[1] We see things and form judgments based on our own background, interactions and experiences. Others may come to different conclusions. Finally, one should not generalize from just one case. Whatever we may perceive to be important factors contributing to DSM's successful transformation may just as well have been present at ICI or Hoechst, to mention only two of the large chemical companies that have disappeared. Other factors may have escaped our notice. Only a systematic comparison of a large set of both successful and failed companies might reveal to what extent certain factors can be regarded as valid explanations for DSM's success.[2]

Nevertheless, the question is too intriguing to let rest completely. We do want to offer some observations based on our own personal perspectives. We will focus on some *company traits* that we believe have contributed to DSM's successful transformation. Seven traits are discussed below. These are based on our personal observations, but have also been discussed with 'company insiders' over the period

[1] Sometimes referred to as Miles Law, after Rufus E. Miles, Jr. (1910–1996), an assistant secretary under three US Presidents, who wrote *Miles' Law and Six Other Maxims of Management*.

[2] Schreuder conducted such a study in the 1980s to determine success factors for firms in 'bear markets': See H. Schreuder et al., "Successful Bear-fighting Strategies," *Strategic Management Journal*, Vol 12, No. 7, 1991, as well as De Nationale Investeringsbank, *Overwinnen bij brancheproblemen*, Den Haag, 1989.

J.-P. Jeannet, H. Schreuder, *From Coal to Biotech*,
DOI 10.1007/978-3-662-46299-7_15

of DSM's second transformation and again in the interviews that we held for this book (See **List of Interviewees**). At the end of this chapter, we compare our observations with the relevant literature to examine whether they may have any wider validity. But let's start first with an anecdote to give some color to the discussions below. Each year, on the occasion of the publication of DSM's annual results, a 'Directors' Dinner' is organized by the Board of Management. Before this dinner, the CEO/Chairman of the Board of Management elucidates the annual results to former (retired) members of the Board of Management, as well as former (retired) most senior business and staff directors, the so-called 'ConcernTop.' In 2013, the audience for Feike Sijbesma consisted, among others, of his predecessors Hans van Liemt, Simon de Bree and Peter Elverding. The eldest person present was Leo Kretzers, member of the Board of Management from 1967 to 1986. Before starting his talk, Feike looked into the audience and said: "I realize more and more that whatever we are accomplishing today has been made possible because we are standing on the shoulders of you giants." The fact that DSM organizes these dinners with retired top managers and, thus, keeps in close touch, as well as the introduction articulated by the current chairman, says a lot about the company, specifically about the traits 2, 4 and 5.

We identify the following seven company traits as potential contributors to the successful (second) transformation of DSM, as described in this book:

1. Long-term orientation
2. Evolutionary perspective
3. Stakeholder orientation
4. Sense of community and identity
5. Stewardship
6. Learning organization
7. Conservative financing

The Seven Traits

Let's examine these traits one-by one:

1. Long-Term Orientation

Already in its first transformation, from coal mining to chemicals, DSM displayed its long-term orientation. It was the company's management, which determined that there was no future in coal mining in The Netherlands. It then proceeded to convince the company's shareholder (at that time the Dutch state) of this conclusion. It's clear that the conclusion was correct, when one compares the early closure of the mines in The Netherlands with the drawn-out process in Belgium and Germany, which has cost enormous amounts of subsidies.[3] DSM's long-term orientation probably also derives from the characteristics of the industries in which it has operated—mining and chemicals. Both industries are characterized by capital intensity and long cycle times, meaning that it usually takes a long time before a strategic change can be implemented and its impact evaluated. Building a mine or a chemical plant requires a lengthy period of planning and construction. Thereafter, it may also take many years before it can be assessed as to whether the results justify the large investments. In such an industry environment companies will therefore have to base their strategic decisions on their perceptions of the long-term (structural) factors determining competitive success.

Through its Corporate Strategy Dialogues (CSDs) the company continued to look many years ahead in order to identify such structural factors. For instance, thinking through the consequences of the rise of the emerging economies, or the identification of Sustainability as a business driver, came relatively early. Today, the company's strategy is built on the three structural societal trends: (1) global shifts, (2) climate and energy, (3) and health and wellness.[4] DSM aims to contribute to the unmet needs resulting from these societal trends with innovative and sustainable solutions. As Rob van Leen, DSM's Chief Innovation Officer (CIO), remarked: "This was the largest difference I noticed between DSM and Gist-Brocades, where I worked before. At DSM there was a profound long-term orientation to the strategy and to the approach of business decisions. At Gist-Brocades we were probably more flexible and entrepreneurial, and perhaps a bit more opportunistic. If your job is to realize significant innovations, the long-term orientation is a blessing." Reflecting on the decision to set up the DSM Innovation Center in 2005 and its evaluation in the CSD 2010 as successful he adds: "This success has encouraged our Managing Board to continue the experiment of the whole Innovation Center until 2015, giving us the time to build new business groups for DSM. When we do a review in 2015, we will have reached the point of having a well-oiled machine that is delivering new businesses. Now this is quite rare, and I think the reason that we are successful is that our Managing Board has been able to control the usual management impatience, where similar experiments in other companies have died because after 3, 4, 5 years people say, 'Yeah, you have spent now so much money on these new initiatives and nothing has come out.' Whereas most statistics show that only after 10–15 years we'll get to see the benefits of these long-term investments."[5]

---

[3] See: http://www.l1.nl/nieuws/237074-sluiting-mijnen-soepeler-dan-bij-buren, based on J. D. P. Kasper and A. Knotter, "Na de mijnsluiting in Zuid-Limburg," see: http://www.etil.nl/wp-content/uploads/2013/12/Na-de-mijnsluiting-in-Zuid-Limburg-Etil.pdf (accessed on 2 Dec 2014).

[4] See: "DSM in Motion: Driving Focused Growth," Capital Markets Days 2013 (publication of DSM Investor Relations).

[5] See: http://www.dsm.com/content/dam/dsm/cworld/en_US/documents/conversations-on-the-cutting-edge.pdf (Accessed November 2013).

Peter Elverding, the former chairman of the Managing Board, reflects on this DSM trait as follows: "Yes, the company has a clear long-term orientation. We take the time to develop our strategy, encouraging the constructive confrontation of diverse views. When we have determined our strategy, we take the time to execute it, usually 3–5 years. We anticipate that not everything will go 'first time right.' You need to be tolerant for that and take the time to correct along the way. We stay the course when we encounter headwinds. When an organization is confronted with the challenge to transform itself, you need such long time periods. And you need consistency."

2. Evolutionary Perspective

After its first transformation the company had adopted the saying that 'transformation is in our genes.' What this meant was made explicit in a document titled 'Strategic Beliefs' in the CSD 1997[6]:

> A look at the few other companies that have survived for a hundred years, shows that it is the rule rather than the exception that they have been completely transformed during their history. And this is, of course, no coincidence. Over such a long time period circumstances change so dramatically that it would be remarkable if companies could survive with basically the same set of activities or the same structure... What we have learned from our past, then, is that we should anticipate such a complete transformation of the company if we take a really long-term perspective. In practice, this means that our strategy will emphasize two main tasks:
> a. being excellent competitors in our current major activities, as well as
> b. developing new businesses which may provide a basis for transformation in the future, if and when our current strong activities should decline.

The evolutionary perspective has been reinforced by Feike Sijbesma who regularly refers to his training as a biologist and his fascination with Darwin's evolutionary theory. He often quotes Darwin's famous phrase "To my own surprise: it is not the biggest, nor the strongest, nor the fastest, but the fittest who will survive." He then explains that 'fitness' does not refer to being well-trained but instead refers to 'adaptability.' "Adaptability, that is the core concept. Those who cannot adapt when environmental requirements change, will disappear... It is one of the main strategic responsibilities of company management to adapt to changing circumstances."[7] Within his perspective, there is also a direct link to the content of DSM's present Sustainability strategy as one of its main drivers: "Charles Darwin wrote 150 years ago: You need to adapt in order to survive. It is my belief that business... needs to address how they serve society, rather than the other way

[6] "Strategic beliefs," document 176 CPL-HS/97, 16 December 1997. See also *DSM Magazine*, No. 144, May 1998, reporting on the Corporate Strategy Dialogue 1997.

[7] Voorwoord Feike Sijbesma in: Henk Volberda et al., *Re-inventing Business*, Assen: Van Gorcum, 2013. Translated by the authors.

around. Especially since: 'You cannot be successful, nor even call yourself successful, in a society that fails.' What this basically means is that business needs to take a long-term view and focus on sustainability in the broad sense of the word. At DSM we distinguish three stages of sustainability, and as a company we are now at the third level. In the 1970s and 1980s sustainability was about compliance, in the 1990s and 2000s about Corporate Social Responsibility. Now however, we are talking about sustainability as a business driver, and are fully integrating it into all our activities."[8]

3. Stakeholder Orientation

The 'Strategic Beliefs' of DSM (CSD 1997) stated clearly: "DSM's purpose is to serve the interests of its stakeholders. Our most basic goal is the continuous growth of DSM's business value, for the benefit of its stakeholders." Feike Sijbesma identifies four main stakeholder groups: "Shareholders (who put their money in our company), Employees (who partly put their life in our company), Customers (who are providing our company with the right to exist) and Society-at-large (which is partly dependent and is confronted, positively and negatively, with the activities of the company)."

The stakeholder orientation of DSM goes a long way back. Already as a mining company, the company was asked by the Dutch state to be 'an example for private firms' with respect to its social policies: "The Dutch State Mines had to secure a gradual and orderly transition from an agrarian to an industrial society by only employing Dutch workers and aligning the expansion of the company with the supply of local workers. Furthermore, the State instructed the company board to avoid social conflicts as much as possible. The assumption was that good social policies and an awareness of the coal miners' interests eventually would also result in financial returns." Also in periods when the private mines showed better financial results than the State Mines, the company maintained these social policies: "The aim of the State Mines board to avoid conflicts with the workers as much as possible is an important explanation for the relatively harmonious development of the mining area in comparison with foreign coal basins."[9] The company was a frontrunner in the creation of mechanisms for workers' participation and co-determination, having worked with 'workers' committees' since 1906. In 1945

[8] "On the evolution of business," Blog Feike Sijbesma, World Economic Forum, 1 September 2012. See: http://forumblog.org/2012/09/on-the-evolution-of-business/#disqus_thread (Accessed 2 Dec 2014). The various stages of corporate approaches to Sustainability can, of course, also be seen as learning cycles. For Schreuder who wrote his Ph.D. on "Corporate Social Responsibility and Corporate Social Reporting" (1981), it has been particularly gratifying to have been affiliated with a company that has pushed the frontiers of this approach.

[9] Loek Kreukels, Mijnarbeid: Volgzaamheid en Strijdbaarheid. *Geschiedenis van de arbeidsverhoudingen in de Nederlandse steenkolenmijnen, 1900–1940*. Assen/Maastricht: Van Gorcum, 1986. Translated by the authors.

the Mining Charter (*Mijnstatuut*) established the Mining Industry Council (*Mijnindustrieraad*), where representatives of employers and employees determined the general rules for wages, labor conditions and social policies.[10] This was an early example of what the Dutch call 'polderen,' referring to institutionalized and consensus-oriented consultation between employers and employees (and the government) about economic and social policies. It is a feature of the Dutch version of Rhineland Capitalism.[11]

The company is a clear example of the Rhineland model. In contrast to the Anglo-Saxon company model, in a Rhineland company the shareholders are not seen as the owners of the company. Rather, the company is seen as a more independent entity, serving the interests of various stakeholder groups. In the 1990s the Anglo-Saxon perspective was, however, on the rise in Northwest Europe. The concept of 'maximizing shareholder value' was propagated. DSM had difficulty with such notions. As recounted in Chap. 5, it rejected a proposal by McKinsey in 1991 to install a system of performance management based on the shareholder value approach. In 2007, a few months after stepping down as chairman of the Managing Board of DSM, Peter Elverding was invited to give a public lecture.[12] He reflected on 30 years of socio-economic development in The Netherlands and, in particular, the rise of Anglo-Saxon notions at the time, including the predominance of the 'shareholder value' orientation. He makes it rather clear that the Rhineland model remains his clear preference: "In the Anglo-Saxon perspective, the market has the power and rules are always lagging because the market, as such, is normless. In The Netherlands and in Europe, however, we also want matters to be organized in a fair way. That means that norms and values are the starting-point. In other words: there is tension between the market and values. In the Rhineland model cooperation, stability and trust are important. At the other side of the spectrum the individual, efficiency and profitability are important, as well as rules to prevent excesses. A kind of 'organized distrust,' therefore... In all the turbulence of today I remain convinced that the dominance of capital tends to go too far... capital as such does not give meaning or purpose to our existence... In the end, life is not about money... capital, land and labor—nowadays called people, planet and profit—are the three classical elements of an economy and should be

[10] G. Heerma van Voss, *50 jaar Ondernemingsraad bij DSM*: *van meepraten naar meebepalen. Een formule voor mensen*, DSM Limburg B.V., Geleen, 1996 and W. Buitelaar (ed.) *DSM*: *Portret van een Maaslandse Reus*. Amsterdam: Mets en Schilt, 2002. In private correspondence with Schreuder, Wout Buitelaar also pointed toward other forms of workers' participation, which were adopted by DSM in 1945, like workers' councils (ondernemingsraden), job consultation (werkoverleg) and 'trusted employee representatives' (eenheidsvertrouwensmannen).

[11] The term 'Rhineland' capitalism (versus 'Anglo-Saxon' capitalism) was introduced by Michel Albert in his book *Capitalism Against Capitalism* (London: Whurr, 1993). See also: http://en.wikipedia.org/wiki/Polder_model

[12] Frank Sweenslezing 2007 with the title "Everything has Changed, the Rest Stayed the Same." Translated by the authors. See: http://www.rijnland-weblog.nl/2007/05/20/alles-is-veranderd-de-rest-bleef-hetzelfde/ (Accessed 2 Dec 2014).

seen as interrelated. We need a balance between the three or, in other words, a 'triple bottom line.'"

Since the financial crisis in the first decade of this century, there is again a more widespread appreciation of the dangers of an excessive focus on 'shareholder value' by companies. There is nothing wrong with tracking this indicator as an ex-post measurement of the financial value created for shareholders. But using it ex-ante as a steering mechanism for the firm leads to short-termism, over-reliance on financial projections and it uproots the balance that is required between the interests of various stakeholders. As such, it undermines the 'social fabric' of the organization. Short-term value can be created by tweaking financial parameters but long-term (financial and non-monetary) value derives from serving customers and society well and having an engaged workforce. It is worthy to note that DSM has never wavered in its belief that the company should create value for all its constituents. The company states in its *Integrated Annual Report 2012*: "DSM sees the creation of shared value for all stakeholders, now and in the future, as basis for the continuation of its success... DSM creates for all stakeholders—customers, shareholders, employees, but also society at large—value in three areas: People, Planet and Profit." In this context, it is noteworthy that DSM created the largest (ex-post) shareholder value of all firms listed on the Amsterdam Stock Exchange (AEX) in the period covered in this book, as Fig. 13.5 testifies. At the same time, it consistently scored very high on the Dow Jones Sustainability Index, demonstrating that the creation of shareholder value can go hand-in-hand with a sustainability focus.

4. Sense of Community and Identity

From the 1930s to the 1950s, co-author Schreuder's father was an expatriate for a Dutch Company named Internatio and located in Asia. During that era, Dutch expatriates met at various occasions and in many countries there was a 'Dutch Club.' Of course, there was a lot of rotation in the membership of such clubs, due to the limited period of expatriate assignments to a particular country. However, in some sense there was a lot of stability as well. The largest groups of members were inevitably the 'Shell men,' 'Philips men' and 'Unilever men.'[13] Schreuder's father could recognize the members of these various clans with great precision. Apparently, company culture—with corresponding (self) selection and socialization processes—was so strong that a particular type of 'company man' resulted.[14]

[13] Yes, they were all men back then. The spouses were involved in social, cultural and charity functions, as well as being homemakers. In his influential book *The Organization Man* (New York: Doubleday, 1956), William H. Whyte analyzed this phenomenon incisively, pointing toward the 'collectivist pressures toward conformity,' which were at odds with the individualistic ideals of American society.

[14] Schreuder studied such processes by comparing Dutch accounting firms with their 'Big eight' international counterparts with a strong US-orientation. See: J. Soeters and H. Schreuder, "The

Today, we are acutely aware of the negative effects of such processes—the lack of diversity and the pressures toward conformity. However, there were also significant positive effects—a sense of inclusion and belonging and the values of commitment and loyalty. Today's large companies often struggle to maintain these positive outcomes under the pressure of a growing, more international and diverse workforce.

In the 1980s the annual meetings of the top-100 or so DSM executives were still called the 'Family meetings.' When Schreuder joined his first such meeting in the early 1990s, he recalls Chairman Hans van Liemt observing: "You know, it's strange, I used to know everyone at these meetings and now I only recognize half." The 'Family meetings' have evolved into yearly Executive meetings. Since 2010, when the CSD 2010 ('DSM in motion: driving focused growth') was presented in Shanghai, the meetings also have been held outside of Europe. At the 2012 DSM Executive meeting in Washington, D.C., 403 participants attended with 15 different nationalities. Yet, DSM has been able to maintain a sense of community and identity (so far). For the generation of executives who led the strategy execution covered in this book, values like 'loyalty' and 'commitment' were strong. Farewell speeches often alluded to these values, as well as to the context of personal/family where sacrifices were often made. In recent years, DSM has strongly stimulated 'employee engagement' and leaders have been assessed based on the feedback from their employees.

It is no coincidence that DSM has adopted Strategy Dialogues as the process of strategy formulation. The company has always had a strong participative and consensus-seeking culture. While consensus-seeking may be a Dutch trait in general, some companies exhibit more of this behavior than others. Historically, DSM has also had a strong 'informal culture,' in which important decisions are pre-discussed before any formal meetings are held. In this sense, it has often compared itself with the Japanese 'nemawashi' culture.[15] While such a participative, consensus-seeking culture may have its drawbacks, such as long lead times for decisions and pressure toward 'common denominator' outcomes, the greater advantage is the cohesion and inclusion felt by organizational members. Moreover, DSM can be characterized as relatively free of organizational politics. In this organizational context, Strategy Dialogues can be used as fora in which diversity of opinion is encouraged while everyone is aware that, ultimately, conclusions will have to be drawn which are widely supported.

Finally, DSM has always nurtured a strong Management Development system, again of a rather participative nature. In the past, managers were assessed on their performance and potential for promotion by a rather wide group of higher-ranking colleagues. Today, this is done in a '360° evaluation' involving those who report to the manager, as well as their peers. Also, the Managing Board has always discussed

interaction between national and organizational cultures in accounting firms," *Accounting, Organizations and Society*, Vol. 13, No. 1, 1988: 75–85. In that study it was found that (self) selection forces appeared to be the most explanatory for the observed differences.

[15] See: http://en.wikipedia.org/wiki/Nemawashi

all high-level appointments with the group of 'corporate high potentials.' Peter Elverding observes: "The DSM Management Development systems allowed us to come to joint evaluations of people, based on diverse inputs. The wide participation in these evaluations created a robust, collegiate group of people who knew each other's strong and weak points. This is important because I have always been convinced that there is a strong link between the particular person you appoint to a certain position and the type of results you will get. Yes, appointments need to be in line with the strategy, but the strategy will also be partly determined by the type of person you appoint." Against this background, there was a certain preference to promote home grown talent rather than make appointments from outside, although there were periods when it was felt that more of these should be made. For the top appointment, CEO/Chairman of the Managing Board, the company has, for decades, been able to reach inside.[16] This is in marked contrast with, for example, AKZO Nobel, where the last three appointments for its CEO/Chairman position came from outside.

For all the reasons discussed in this section, there is a definite sense of community and identity within DSM. The concept of 'identity,' although difficult to define precisely,[17] has always played an important role in discussions whether DSM should merge or allow itself to be acquired. At DSM, most people in top management have felt that something important would be given up if DSM would disappear as a separate entity.

5. Stewardship

If one sees DSM in an evolutionary perspective as a company with a long-term perspective and a strong sense of identity, then it is indeed a separate entity. It is not 'owned' by the current shareholders. Rather, it serves wider purposes toward its stakeholders, including society as a whole. In this sense, it is a 'living company' (de Geus, 1997). It develops over time as it learns the lessons of its past and adapts to changing circumstances. It tries to anticipate the requirements of the future and it 'places its bets' on how to deal with these. In this longer-term perspective, the 'living company' is indeed leading a life of its own. If it is successful, it may outlive several generations of management, as indeed DSM has done with its current life span of 113 years.

It is interesting to note how, in this perspective, DSM top management sees its roles and responsibilities. On the occasion of his retirement, Peter Elverding participated in a television interview together with his predecessors Hans van

[16] Both Peter Elverding and Feike Sijbesma had careers prior to joining DSM. However, they had been at DSM for 14 and 9 years, respectively, before becoming CEO/Chairman.

[17] Arie de Geus (1997: 104) refers to "the set of institutional values that rest at the core of the company's persona," which allow members to identify with "what this company stands for" or "what this company is about."

Liemt and Simon de Bree. He reflected as follows: "Together, we cover a period of 24 years. You realize that as chairman you are a 'passer by,' who tries to advance the company in line with its development."[18] The 'passer by,' however, has a task that Elverding likes to summarize as *rentmeesterschap* in Dutch, a biblical term that we can translate as 'stewardship': "As a steward, you try to leave the company in better shape for your successor than it was handed over to you by your predecessor.[19] In this perspective the 'living company,' the entity with a life of its own, is entrusted for a while to top management. Top management's task is to guide the company through a particular phase of its existence, to make the necessary adaptations to the changing times, and to leave a better 'architecture' of the company in view of future requirements. This resonates well with one of the main findings of the study 'Built to Last,' that sought to establish the habits of 'visionary companies' that attain extraordinary long-term performance: "A charismatic visionary leader is absolutely 'not required' for a visionary company and, in fact, can be detrimental to a company's long-term prospects. Some of the most significant CEOs in the history of visionary companies did not fit the model of the high-profile, charismatic leader—indeed, some explicitly shied away from that model... they concentrated more on architecting an enduring institution than on being a great individual leader"(Collins and Porras, 1996: 7–8).

In line with his predecessor, Feike Sijbesma recently observed: "Darwin is about adaptability in order to remain successful. I strongly believe in that. The world changes, you have to adapt. Stewardship denotes how I think we should be part of the world. That is also the way I see being CEO here. I operate in a line of earlier CEOs, who have also implemented far-reaching changes. One should put one's own role in perspective. I know that 'stewardship' is a Christian concept but for me it is more than that. It also connotes responsibility and respect."[20] In line with that latter remark, it can be noted that the stewardship perspective not only determines how DSM's top management sees its role but also permeates the company more widely. DSM has been one of the early companies to adopt Sustainability as one of the drivers of its strategy. Taking unmet societal needs as the starting points of your strategy and defining Sustainability as one of the main drivers of that strategy, of course, corresponds very well with the stewardship perspective. The company has consistently felt responsible for people, planet and profit.

---

[18] "Elverding voelde zich passant in dienst van DSM," *Het Financieele Dagblad*, 8 May 2007.

[19] We have translated the Dutch term 'rentmeesterschap' as stewardship. See: http://managementscope.nl/magazine/artikel/400-peter-elverding-rijnlands-model. For a similar perspective, see the interview with Sam Palmisano, former CEO of IBM, in the *Harvard Business Review*, June 2014: "You're a proprietor at a point in time: you're a steward. You're not the founder. You're there to protect the entity for long-term returns. We made it to a century; we want to make it to 200 years, not just to 105 years because we did something stupid when I was the CEO" (p. 84).

[20] "Feike Sijbesma: Dilemma's verzoenen is niet altijd eerlijk", *MT Management Team*, 9 September 2011, See: http://www.mt.nl/157/44895/magazine/feike-sijbesma-dilemma-s-verzoenen-is-niet-altijd-eerlijk.html (Accessed 2 Dec 2014). Translated by the authors.

6. Learning Organization

While the evolutionary perspective on the development of organizations is very instructive, it should not be equated with a purely Darwinian process in the natural world. The evolutionary mechanism, however, is the same: variation—selection—retention. In the natural world, the variations are thought to come about in a random, 'blind' process.[21] Subsequently, these random variations are subjected to the process of 'natural selection,' an entirely unconscious process in which the environment selects the variations that enhance adaptation of the organism. In our human world, organizations can make 'conscious choices' and try out variations, by way of experiment. Subsequently, they can consciously evaluate these experiments and choose to select which to pursue further and which to abandon. Next to these conscious choices, spontaneous, unplanned actions take place as well. These can also be evaluated after some time to determine whether they are worth continuing. All in all, the development of human organizations can be better characterized as a process of 'purposeful evolution.'[22]

In Chap. 11 we have used the Mergers and Acquisitions (M&A) example to illustrate how DSM has consciously evaluated its track record of success and failures with acquisitions and how, subsequently, it has implemented the lessons learned, adapting its approach, organization and management systems. In this chapter, the example of Innovation served to illustrate the wide range of conscious adaptations necessary to fully run through a learning cycle of Strategy > Organization > Systems. Only by consciously setting the conditions for successful implementation could the company conclude, after 5 years, that this particular 'experiment' (of accelerating Innovation) was a success and decide to further build on it. We believe that DSM is a pronounced example of a 'learning company' with respect to the amounts of learning cycles it conducts within the company and how many of these are consciously planned and evaluated. Moreover, we have argued more generally that, at the overall company level, the various CSDs can be seen as 'strategic learning cycles'. Each CSD can be viewed as a corporate portfolio of prioritized strategic initiatives and targets, with a mix of exploitation (reinforcing current successes) and exploration (of possible pathways to future success).

We have argued that the completion of such learning cycles is the motor of evolutionary change. In that sense: the more learning cycles, the better. This is the position that Collins and Porras take in *Built to Last* (1996, Chap. 7): "Try a lot of stuff and keep what works." However, we believe there is a limit to this statement. In organizational life, it is seldom the case that 'letting a thousand flowers bloom' is

[21] R. Dawkins, *The Blind Watchmaker*, NY: Norton, 1987.

[22] This is a term coined by Collins and Porras, *Built to Last*. London: Random House, 1996: 149. In the organizational literature it is a matter of debate to which extent organizations can purposefully influence environmental selection. See: Sytse Douma and Hein Schreuder, *Economic Approaches to Organizations*. Harlow: Pearson, 2013, in particular Chap. 11 on 'Evolutionary approaches to organizations.'

a recipe for success. Companies can be overburdened by an overload of initiatives. Organization is about the aligned, coordinated action toward common goals and such alignment and coordination should be enabled by management. This can be done in various ways but a clear understanding of the main organizational priorities should result. It has been DSM's experience that the consistency of focus on the CSD priorities over a period of time[23] has enabled the firm's step-by-step, evolutionary transformation.

7. Conservative Financing

In countless meetings during the 1990s and early 2000s, investment bankers exhorted DSM to move toward 'a more efficient capital structure.' What they meant was, use more debt (increase your leverage) and, thereby, increase the returns to shareholders. While this recommendation has validity when times are good and overall returns are above the cost of capital, it turns against you when times are bad. When overall returns decrease and the debt still has to be serviced first, returns to shareholders decrease and can easily become negative. Moreover, in such circumstances the company can lose some or all of its autonomy to make its own decisions, for example when the company breaches the 'covenants' of its bank loans. This is a lesson that history has taught longer-lived companies over and over again; a lesson that used to be incorporated in Finance 101.[24] Yet, when times turn good again, the lesson appears to be lost on many companies. A popular way of decreasing equity financing (and thereby increasing debt financing) in the recent decades was to have 'share buybacks.' It is only recently that the insight that share buybacks can undermine the company's necessary long-term investments and, therefore, its future growth and profitability—gains ground again.[25]

DSM has always emphasized that it wants to remain solidly and, therefore 'conservatively,' financed. Again, this goes back to the company's history as a mining and commodity chemicals company. In its last loss year (1993) the CFO at the time, Ad Timmermans, declared: "A strong balance sheet is required in our cyclical sector. If you cannot or don't want to accept that, you should not play this game."[26] DSM has adhered to its conservative financing policy over the years. In 2009, Peter Elverding reflected on this trait as follows: "Some American

[23] That period of time should correspond with the 'cycle time' — sometimes called 'clockspeed' (Fine, 1998) — of the company, as discussed in the section on 'long-term orientation.'

[24] It was one of the lessons Schreuder taught when he was student-lecturer of Finance 101 at the Erasmus University Rotterdam in the early 1970s.

[25] See: Arnoud Boot & Kees Cools, "Bedrijf moet stoppen met inkopen eigen aandelen," *Het Financieele Dagblad*, 4 June 2013. Similarly, one of the largest worldwide investors, BlackRock, has warned companies not to emphasize dividends or share buybacks if they come at the expense of future growth. See: http://www.reuters.com/article/2014/03/26/us-blackrock-dividends-idUSBREA2P09U20140326

[26] "DSM wil balans schoonhouden in zwaar weer," *Het Financieele Dagblad*, 30 July 1993.

shareholders said to DSM: 'We own your company.' Then I always said, 'not in The Netherlands.' We have gone too far in our appreciation of the importance of the stock exchange... As a company you cannot deviate too far from the crowd but you can deliberately walk at the back. You have to know how to play the game a bit: every quarter you make the required speech but, in the meantime, you follow your own long-term plan. It requires some acting talent. At DSM we had to deal, for example, with a call to buy back shares because of our conservative balance sheet. We have resisted that call as much as possible. Sometimes we bought back a small amount, if the pressure became too high." In 2014, the CFO Rolf-Dieter Schwalb was still proud to proclaim that DSM had a 'conservative financial policy driving a robust balance sheet.'[27] By that time, conservative financing had become more fashionable again as the world had witnessed the pernicious effects of debt financing once again during a financial crisis.

Conclusion and Comparison with the Relevant Literature

So far, we have discussed the seven company traits one-by-one, which we believe have contributed to DSM's successful transformation. In conclusion, we first want to make it clear that we see the traits as being interconnected. For instance, for a company with an evolutionary perspective it 'comes naturally' to have a long-term orientation. In such a company, top management is probably more inclined to define its role in terms of 'stewardship'—passing the company on in better shape to their successors. A long-term orientation may also foster the historical awareness that conservative financing is a desirable feature over the booms and particularly the busts of the financial-economic cycle. A stakeholder/people orientation is likely to contribute to a sense of community and identity. And as a final example, an evolutionary perspective is conducive to the 'experimental mindset' that is characteristic of the learning organization. In many such ways the individual traits are interconnected: they have co-evolved and they form a constellation. We would even go a step further to say that together they form a 'Gestalt.' With this term German psychologists denoted that the human personality is more than the sum of its individual characteristics or traits. Similarly, a corporate 'persona' (de Geus, 1997), or identity, cannot be fully captured by the enumeration of its individual traits. The whole is more than the sum of its parts. In more modern terms, we can conceive of the corporate 'persona' as a 'complex, adaptive system,' as defined by complexity theory. Due to the numerous interactions of their constituent elements such complex, adaptive systems have emergent properties that cannot be deduced by only examining these elements one-by-one (see Douma and Schreuder, 2013, Chap. 12).

[27] See: https://www.dsm.com/content/dam/dsm/cworld/en_US/documents/2014-02-27-rolf-dieter-schwalb-credit-bond-investor-presentation.pdf (Accessed 2 Dec 2014).

As stated in the introduction, we cannot be sure that our description of DSM's 'Gestalt' of company traits that have contributed to its successful transformation is accurate or complete. The description depends on our own personal observations, albeit that they have been tested in discussions with company insiders over many years and again specifically for this book. As the many quotes in the sections above also testify, we are sure that many top managers of DSM in the 1990s and 2000s will identify with these traits, although each might have discussed them slightly differently. In that sense, the list is not subjective; it is what philosophers of science call 'intersubjective'—a shared construction. If we accept, on this basis, that the list may be valid for DSM, a final question arises which we will address in conclusion. It is the question whether these traits may have any wider validity as contributing to the health and success of companies over the longer-term, which usually implies some extent of transformation? To address this question, one would like to survey a vast literature of systematic studies comparing long-term successful companies with less successful or failed companies. However, if we define the long term as decades (at least), the literature is not vast; it is sporadic.

Three studies stand out with which we will compare our findings. We have already used two of them occasionally in the discussions thus far. The first is summarized by Arie de Geus in *The Living Company* (1997). Based on a study conducted by Shell, together with a business school, De Geus identifies four key factors explaining the survival and success of long-lived companies[28]:

1. *Sensitivity to the environment*, representing a company's ability to learn and adapt
2. *Cohesion and identity*: aspects of a company's innate ability to build a community and a persona for itself
3. *Tolerance and decentralization*: both symptoms of a company's awareness of ecology; its ability to build constructive relationships with other entities, within and outside itself
4. *Conservative financing*: the ability to govern its own growth and evolution effectively

It will be clear that these four factors are, to a large extent, embedded in our list of seven traits. Particularly, if one interprets 'tolerance' like De Geus explains elsewhere: "These companies were particularly tolerant of activities at the margin—outliers, experiments and eccentricities within the boundaries of the cohesive firm, which kept stretching their understanding of possibilities" (1997: 7). This interpretation reinforces the overall emphasis of De Geus on learning and adaptability as key features of successful 'living companies.' Thus, the Shell study is very well in tune with our findings regarding DSM. Please note that while the study

[28] The original question was to study companies that were older than Shell, of similar significance in their industries and with their corporate identity still intact. The researchers found only 40 such companies, of which they studied 27 in depth (De Geus 1997: 4–5).

was conducted by Shell, another Dutch company, its conclusions were based on a worldwide search for companies that approached or succeeded centenarian age with lasting success.

In contrast, the study by James Collins and Jerry Porras ('Built to Last,' 1996) pertained only to US companies and they used a minimum age of 50 years. The study's authors looked for 'visionary companies' as indicated by:

- Premier institutions in their industry
- Widely admired by knowledgeable businesspeople
- Made an indelible imprint on the world in which we live
- Had multiple generations of chief executives
- Been through multiple product (or service) life cycles
- Founded before 1950

These visionary companies were compared with 'comparison companies' from the same industries (a 'matched pairs design'). They found that the visionary companies attain extraordinary long-term performance with their cumulative stock returns outperforming the comparison companies by a factor of six and the general US stock market by a factor of 15.

Again, there are many overlaps between our list of DSM's traits and the 'habits of visionary companies' as described by Collins and Porras' findings. While not always exactly defined the same way, we attempt to compare the findings below:

Visionary companies (Collins and Porras)	DSM case
Clock building, not time telling	Stewardship: top management focus on leaving 'a better company than they inherited'
More than profits	Stakeholder orientation: People—Planet—Profit
Preserve the core (ideology)/ stimulate progress	Evolutionary perspective (with preservation of corporate 'persona')
Try a lot of stuff and keep what works	Learning organization (with priorities)
Home-grown management	Home-grown management
Good enough never is	Transformation is in our genes: today's successes are not good enough
The end of the beginning: the power of alignment	Alignment, focus and consistency through CSDs

To be sure, there are also 'habits of visionary companies' that we did not recognize in the DSM case (three, in fact: (1) No 'tyranny of the OR,'[29] (2) Big Hairy Audacious Goals,[30] and (3) Cult-like cultures). Nevertheless, it is again striking how much overlap exists between the 'habits of visionary companies,' as found by Collins and Porras, and our list of DSM company traits.

Finally, we wish to point toward an interesting Dutch study, performed by Henk Volberda et al. (2013).[31] In the study 'Re-inventing Business' the focus is on 'business model innovation' at the company level. In the quantitative part of the study, a large set of Dutch firms were examined to establish whether they had achieved such business model innovation and if so, how? In the qualitative part of the study, a number of company cases were investigated in more detail. One of these was DSM. The authors use the terminology of 'exploration' (business model innovation) and 'exploitation' (business model replication) to illustrate the choices companies have to make. One of the interesting findings is that the few companies that are able to apply a 'dual focus,' in effect combining business model innovation (exploring new avenues to success) and business model replication (exploiting existing successes further) show the highest financial performance. This is consistent with the results of Collins and Porras and with the DSM case.

All in all, the (scarce) relevant literature about the survival and success of long-lived companies suggests that the 'Gestalt' of DSM's company traits that we have discussed in this final section may, more generally, be rather typical of the characteristics of 'visionary,' 'living' companies. Furthermore, it seems to be the case that such companies, whilst they do not focus on profits or shareholder value alone, succeed in generating the highest financial performance over time. If so, we hope that the DSM case, as documented in this book, will contribute to further reflection on the conditions for long-term corporate success and, ultimately, to more such companies being part of our economies and societies.

References

Albert, M., *Capitalism Against Capitalism*, London: Whurr, 1993.

Buitelaar, W. (ed.), *DSM: Portret van een Maaslandse Reus*. Amsterdam: Mets en Schilt, 2002.

Collins J.C. and J.I.Porras, *Built to Last*: *Successful habits of visionary companies*, London: Random House, 1996

Dawkins, R., *The Blind Watchmaker*, NY: Norton, 1987

[29] Although Feike Sijbesma likes to speak of the "reconciliation of dilemmas" to avoid suboptimal 'compromises' and one could indeed maintain that the stakeholder orientation, executed well, indeed involves such reconciliation.

[30] Although DSM has, of course, pursued a number of very ambitious goals over time. Collins and Porras argue, however, that visionary companies set such Big Hairy Audacious Goals (BHAGs, a phrase coined by Jim Collins) as a habit. We would say that DSM is, in principle, a more cautious company that only sets such very ambitious goals if it has convinced itself that it is the right way forward.

[31] Henk Volberda et al. (*Re-inventing Business*, Assen: Van Gorcum, 2013).

De Geus, A., *The Living Company: Habits for survival in a turbulent business environment*, Boston, Mass.: Harvard Business School Press, 1997

Douma, S. and H. Schreuder, Economic Approaches to Organizations, Harlow: Pearson, 5th edition, 2013

Fine, C.A., Clockspeed: winning industry control in the age of temporary advantage. Reading. Mass: Perseus, 1998

Heerma van Voss, G., *50 jaar Ondernemingsraad bij DSM: van meepraten naar meebepalen. Een formule voor mensen*, DSM Limburg B.V., Geleen, 1996

Kasper J.D.P. and A. Knotter, *Na de mijnsluiting: herstructurering en reconversie in internationaal perspectief,* Roermond: Stichting Behoud Mijnhistorie,2013.

Kreukels, L., *Mijnarbeid: Volgzaamheid en Strijdbaarheid. Geschiedenis van de arbeidsverhoudingen in de Nederlandse steenkolenmijnen, 1900-1940*. Assen/Maastricht: Van Gorcum, 1986.

Nationale Investeringsbank, *Overwinnen bij brancheproblemen*, Den Haag, 1989

Schreuder H. et al, "Successful Bear-fighting Strategies," *Strategic Management Journal*, Vol 12, No. 7, 1991.

Soeters, J. and H. Schreuder, "The interaction between national and organizational cultures in accounting firms," *Accounting, Organizations and Society,* Vol. 13, No. 1, 1988: 75-85.

Volberda, H., Van den Bosch, F. and K. Heij, *Re-inventing Business: Hoe Bedrijven Hun Business-model Innoveren*, Assen: Van Gorcum, 2013.

Whyte, W.H., *The Organization Man*, NY: Doubleday, 1956.

About the Authors

Professor Jean-Pierre Jeannet served on the faculty of Babson College (1974–2013) where he last held the F.W. Olin Distinguished Professorship, while serving simultaneously on a joint-appointment at IMD Institute (1981–2010). His teaching and research focused on marketing, strategy, and globalization. At IMD, he was responsible for the DSM IMPACT seminars leading to many further strategy engagements. At Babson, he headed the seminars for DSM in the marketing area and the leadership and strategy seminars. He is a native of Switzerland and earned his MBA and PhD from the University of Massachusetts at Amherst. He holds the rank of Professor Emeritus from both Babson College and IMD. He is the author of *Managing with a Global Mindset* as well as co-author of *Global Marketing Strategies* and *Global Account Management*. He currently is the Qiushi Chair at Zhejiang University School of Management in China. He shares his residency between Lausanne, Switzerland and Vienna, Austria.

Hein Schreuder was Executive Vice President Corporate Strategy and Acquisitions at Royal DSM N.V. until 2012. He has a MBA from the Erasmus University Rotterdam and a PhD from the Free University of Amsterdam. He joined DSM in 1991 in the management team of the Polymers Division. In 1994 he became Deputy Director of Corporate Planning and Development DSM. In 1996 he assumed full executive responsibility for all DSM's corporate strategic and M&A activities.

In his early career, he has been Director of a research institute in the field of economics and business, Professor of Strategy and Organization at the University of Maastricht and Fellow of the European Institute for Advanced Studies in Management at Brussels, Belgium. He was a Visiting Professor at the University of Washington, Harvard Business School and the China Europe International

J.-P. Jeannet, H. Schreuder, *From Coal to Biotech*,
DOI 10.1007/978-3-662-46299-7

Business School in Shanghai. He has written numerous articles and seven books, including (with Sytse Douma) *Economic Approaches to Organizations* (5th edition, 2013), which has been published in six languages (Chinese, English, Japanese, Korean, Portuguese and Spanish).

Currently, he is a Board Advisor, Executive Coach, and Non-Executive Director on several boards. He is also Board member and Adjunct Professor at Vlerick Business School in Belgium. He lives in Maastricht, is married and has four children.

Belmont-sur-Lausanne, Switzerland — Jean-Pierre Jeannet
Maastricht, The Netherlands — Hein Schreuder

List of Interviewees

DSM
(All of the interviewees have fulfilled several roles at DSM. We have only listed the main role(s) relevant in the context of this book)

Martin Aertsen	Corporate Controller, WG Performance Measurement
Simon de Bree	Chairman of the Managing Board (1993–1999)
Wim Donners	Business Unit Director ASP
Gerard Duyfjes	Business Unit Director Structural Resins
Peter Elverding	Chairman of the Managing Board (1999–2007)
Just Fransen van de Putte	Marketing Director PP, President Polymers Division
Paul van der Grinten	Director Corporate Planning and Development
Frans van Helmond	Marketing Director EP
Willem Klaassen	Director CSV, Director Concern 2000, Director BG Agro
Rob van Leen	Chief Innovation Officer
Hans van Liemt	Chairman of the Managing Board (1984–1993)
Louk Ligthart	Managing Board member (1988–2000)
Feike Sijbesma	CEO and Chairman of the Managing Board (2007–)
Theo Vermeegen	Chairman WG Performance Measurement
Menno de Vries	Officer Executive Development and Corp Man Training
Jos Wassen	Director BG EP, Dep. Dir. Corporate Strategy and Acquisitions
Jan Wolters	Director Corporate Planning and Development

IMD

Derek Abell	Professor and Dean IMEDE (1981–1989)
Robert Collins	Professor (Emeritus), Director In-Company Programs
Jean-Philippe Deschamps	Professor (Emeritus)
Bill Fischer	Professor

J.-P. Jeannet, H. Schreuder, *From Coal to Biotech*,
DOI 10.1007/978-3-662-46299-7

Xavier Gilbert	Professor (Emeritus) and former President
Robert Hooijberg	Professor
Kamran Kashani	Professor (Emeritus)
Dominique Turpin	President and Professor

Babson College

Elaine Eisenmann	Dean School of Executive Education

Further Input was Obtained from

Hans Dijkman	Chairman BOM, Director BG Melamine DSM
Gina Domanig	Former Sulzer Head of Corporate Planning
Pieter de Haan	General Counsel and Director Legal Affairs DSM
Marthijn Jansen	Corporate Planning and Development manager DSM
Pank van de Kooij	DSM Business Academy
Leo Kretzers	Managing Board member DSM (1967–1986)
Jan-Hessel Kruit	Director BG Hydrocarbons DSM
Mark Oskam	DSM Business Academy
Chris Parker	Consultant and former IMD Professor
Harry Strijkers	Archivist of DSM
Marc Silvertand	Investor Relations manager DSM
(+ from the Archive of DSM)	

Glossary

3 Ps	People, Planet, Profit
4 Cs	Customers, Competitors, Costs and Company
4 Ps	Price, Product, Promotion and Place
5 Cs	Customer, Competition, Costs, Company and Context of a business
ABS	Terpolymer of Acrylonitrile, Butadiene and Styrene
ACS	*Aanscherping Concern Strategie*, Clarifying the Corporate Strategy the CSD (1994)
ADNOC	Abu Dhabi National Oil Company
AEX	Amsterdam Stock Exchange
AIM	Advanced Industrial Marketing Program
AMP	Advanced Management Program
AP	Annual Program at IMEDE
AKU	Algemene Kunstzijde Unie, a Dutch company
AKZO	Dutch company, merger of AKU and KZO
ARG	Aethylen Rohrleitungs Gesellschaft mbH & Co. KG, a pipeline company
ASP	A DSM Business Group which consisted of three products: ABS, SMA and PC
ASR	Annual Strategic Review
BCEE	Babson Center for Executive Education
BASF	Badische Anilin- & Soda-Fabrik, a German chemical company
BG	Business Group
BHAG	Big Hairy Audacious Goal
BMP	Business and Marketing Planning Program
BOM	DSM Branch Organization of Marketing (*Branche Overleg Marketing*)
BRIZE	Code name for merger discussions DSM—AKU
BSD	Business Strategy Dialogue
BSEE	Babson School of Executive Education
BTA	Business Technology Analysis
BU	Business Unit
BV	Private Limited Company (*Besloten Vennootschap*)

J.-P. Jeannet, H. Schreuder, *From Coal to Biotech*,
DOI 10.1007/978-3-662-46299-7

CEI	Centre d'Etudes Industrielles, Geneva
CEIBS	China Europe International Business School
CEO	Chief Executive Officer
CFO	Chief Financial Officer
CFROI	Cash-Flow Return on Investment
CHF	Swiss franc, currency
CIA	Convention de l'Industrie de l'Azote
CIO	Chief Innovation Officer
CLO	Chief Learning Officer
CMO	Chief Marketing Officer
ConcernTop	The Managing Board with its top business and staff directors
CPL	Corporate Planning and Development (later renamed: CS&A)
CS&A	Corporate Strategy & Acquisitions
CSD	Corporate Strategy Dialogue
CSO	Chief Strategy Officer
CSV	Centraal Stikstof Verkoopbureau, a joint fertilizer sales office
DAF	Dutch car and truck producer
DBA	DSM Business Academy
DCF	Discounted Cash Flow
Dfl	Dutch florin, currency
DFS	DSM Food Specialties
DNP	DSM Nutritional Products
DSM	Royal DSM NV (originally: *Dutch State Mines*)
E.C.S.C	European Coal and Steel Community
EBA	Emerging Business Area
EBITDA	Earnings Before Interest, Taxes, Depreciation and Amortization
EBN	Energie Beheer Nederland
EC	European Community
ECCH	European Case Clearing House
ELP	Executive Leadership Program
EM	Excellence in Marketing
ENI	An Italian oil & gas company
EP	Engineering Plastics business
EPDM	Ethylene Propylene Diene Monomer, a synthetic rubber
EPFL	École Polytechnique Fédéral de Lausanne
EU	European Union
EUR	Euro, the currency
FSD	Functional Strategy Dialogue
GAM	Global Account Management programs
GDP	Gross Domestic Product
GE	General Electric, a company
HBS	Harvard Business School
HDPE	High Density Polyethylene, a polymer

HPO	A production technology for Caprolactam, the precursor to PA6
HR	Human Resources
ICI	Imperial Chemical Industries, an English chemical company
IMD	International Institute for Management Development, a business school
IMEDE	Institute pour L'Etude des Methodes de Direction de L'Entreprise, a business school in Lausanne
IMI	International Management Institute, a business school
IMP	International Management Program, taught by Harvard Business School
IMPACT	Industrial Marketing Power as a Competitive Tool, a marketing program
INSEAD	Institut Européen d'Administration des Affaires, a business school
JPE	Program for Junior Executives
JSR	Japan Synthetic Rubber, a Japanese chemical company
KPI	Key Performance Indicator
KSF	Key Success Factor
KZK	Koninklijke Zout-Ketjen N.V., a Dutch company
KZO	Koninklijke Zout—Organon N.V., a Dutch company
LDPE	Low Density Polyethylene, a polymer
LLDPE	Linear Low Density Polyethylene, a polymer
LSP	Life Science Products
M&A	Mergers and Acquisitions
MB	Managing Board
MBA	Master of Business Administration
MCR	Managing Corporate Resources
MLP	Management and Leadership Program
MLP-1/MLP-2/MLP-3	Management Leadership Program series
MO&T	DSM Training Department (*Management Opleidingen & Training*)
MP	Managing People
MT	Mobilizing Teams
NAK-1 to 4	DSM naphtha crackers
NAM	Nederlandse Aardolie Maatschappij, a company
N.V.	Public limited company (*Naamloze Vennootschap*)
N.V.C.P.	Nederlandsch Verkoopkantoor voor Chemische Producten N. V., joint sales office for chemical products
ÖMV	Austrian state-owned oil company (*Österreichische Mineralöl Verarbeitung*)
OTC	Order to Cash
PA6	Polyamide 6, a nylon

PC	Polycarbonate, a polymer
PE	Polyethylene, a polymer
PED	Program for Executive Development
PM	Performance Materials
PP	Polypropylene, a polymer
PPF	Polypropylene plants: PPF 3, PPF 4, PPF 5, for example, refer to plants built for the DSM Polypropylene business
R&D	Research and Development
R&T	Research & Technology
ROCE	Return on Capital Employed
ROI	Return on Investment
RSM	Rotterdam School of Management, Erasmus University
RWKS	Rheinisch-Westfälische Kohlen-Syndikat, a German coal cartel
S.H.V.	Steenkolen-Handelsvereeniging, a Dutch company
SABIC	Saudi Basic Industries Corporation, a company
SHE	Safety, Health and Environment
SMA	Styrene Maleic Anhydride, a polymer
SMC	Strategic Management Course
SMP	Strategic Multiyear Plan
SSE	Seminar for Senior Executives
SVC	Strategic Value Contract
Triple P	People, Planet, Profit
TSR	Total Shareholder Return
UHMWPE	Ultra High Molecular Weight PolyEthylene, a polymer
UP	Unsaturated Polyester
USD	US dollar, currency
VCFC	Vitamins, Carotenoids and Fine Chemicals, a division of Roche (acquired by DSM)
VPV	Verenigd Plastic Verkoopkantoor, a joint plastics for sales office
WG	Working Group
WTO	World Trade Organization

Index

J.-P. Jeannet, H. Schreuder, *From Coal to Biotech*,
DOI 10.1007/978-3-662-46299-7

Printing: Ten Brink, Meppel, The Netherlands
Binding: Ten Brink, Meppel, The Netherlands